THE BIBLICAL ARCHAEOLOGIST READER

THE
BIBLICAL ARCHAEOLOGIST
READER

edited by

G. ERNEST WRIGHT and

DAVID NOEL FREEDMAN

Anchor Books
Doubleday & Company, Inc.
Garden City, New York

Cover design by Robin Jacques

The articles in this volume are reprinted from

THE BIBLICAL ARCHAEOLOGIST

a quarterly journal, published by the American School sof Oriental Research, and edited by G. Ernest Wright and Frank M. Cross, Jr., as a service to those who wish a reliable but non-technical survey of current research and discovery in the field of biblical archaeology.

"New Radiocarbon Method for Dating the Past" by Donald Collier is reprinted by permission from the *Chicago Natural History Museum Bulletin*, XXII:1 (Jan. 1951).

The Anchor Books edition is the first publication of *The Biblical Archaeologist Reader*, edited by G. Ernest Wright and David Noel Freedman.

Anchor Books edition: 1961

CONTENTS

PREFACE

For more than one hundred years, the lands of the Fertile Crescent have been the object of archaeological investigation. Excavations at many important sites have produced vast quantities of relevant data, thus enabling scholars to recover the most ancient civilizations of mankind. While these have importance in their own right as fields of study, public interest in this area and its history has always been especially strong because of its close association with the Bible. The recent discovery of the Dead Sea Scrolls has confirmed this truth in a sensational way.

Despite extensive scholarly work in decipherment and analysis, and brilliant efforts at synthesis,[1] much of the newly available material remains inaccessible to the general reader. On one hand, competent archaeologists and linguists have not been sufficiently concerned to communicate their findings beyond their own circles or have been unable to interpret their significance in non-technical terms. On the other hand, books deliberately aimed at the public too often fail to meet even minimum standards of scientific accuracy. Between the extremes of the scholar's scholar who is trapped in his own specialized jargon, and the professional popularizer who can-

---

[1] E.g., W. F. Albright, *From the Stone Age to Christianity* (Anchor Edition, 1957); H. Frankfort, *The Birth of Civilization in the Near East* (Anchor Edition, 1957).

not control the sources of information, or distinguish fantasy from fact, there is, happily, an occasional unclassified individual whose work is both scholarly and readable.

Since its inception in 1938, *The Biblical Archaeologist* has achieved remarkable success in discovering such individuals and publishing popularly written articles based upon sound scholarship in its field. Under the guidance of its distinguished editor, Professor G. Ernest Wright, himself a frequent contributor and a skillful practitioner of the art of "readable scholarship,"[2] and his associates, Frank M. Cross, Jr., and Floyd V. Filson, *The Biblical Archaeologist* has provided accurate information about the latest archaeological discoveries in biblical lands, and their significance for the understanding of the Scriptures. There is scarcely a page of the Bible which has not been illuminated by such discoveries, and the sampling of articles from the *BA* which follows, extends from the first chapters of Genesis to the last chapters of Revelation.

Two principal considerations have influenced the choice of articles in the present anthology. First was the concern to present a wide variety of subjects, thus indicating the range of archaeological research: from the unorthodox Jewish community at Elephantine, in Southern Egypt, to the third-century synagogue at Dura-Europos; from the ruins of Sodom and Gomorrah buried under the Dead Sea, to St. Catherine's Monastery on Mt. Sinai. Second was the decision not to include any articles on the Dead Sea Scrolls, although the *BA* pioneered in this area with the first report to appear in an American periodical: "A Phenomenal Discovery," *BA*, XI.2 (May, 1948). Since then, numerous articles have been published on the progress of Scroll studies, including a recent survey by the team of scholars working with the manuscripts ("Editing the Manuscript Fragments from Qumran," *BA*, XIX.4 [Dec., 1956]). There is, however, a sizable literature on the Scrolls already available to the public; and properly to do justice to this vast subject would require several articles, if not an entire volume.

A central theme of modern research is the relationship between biblical and pagan religion of the ancient world. The chief monumental evidence for ancient religion is the sanctu-

[2] His recent work, *Biblical Archaeology* (Philadelphia: Westminster Press, 1957) is a splendid example.

ary, the house of deity. The results of separate studies of the temple in Egypt (H. H. Nelson), Mesopotamia (A. L. Oppenheim), Syria-Palestine (G. E. Wright), are described in No. 12, alongside detailed investigation of the biblical center of worship from the early days of the Tabernacle (F. M. Cross, Jr., No. 13), through the period of the Temple (No. 12), down to the Synagogue (H. G. May, No. 14), and Church (F. V. Filson, No. 12). Before and after this *pièce de résistance,* the articles follow roughly the order of the books of the Bible. The Old Testament section begins with J. Philip Hyatt's discussion of book-writing in Old Testament times (No. 2). Different stories in Genesis are dealt with by John Bright (the Flood, No. 3), and J. Penrose Harland (Sodom and Gomorrah, No. 4). One of the strange phenomena of the Wanderings in the Wilderness is the subject of F. S. Bodenheimer's paper on "Manna" (No. 5). No. 6 ("Musical Instruments of Israel," O. R. Sellers) and No. 7 (on the Cherubim, W. F. Albright) are not easily datable, but belong to the period after Israel's settlement in Canaan. Numbers 8 ("A New Letter in Aramaic," J. Bright), 9 ("King Joiachin in Exile," Albright), and 10 ("The Babylonian Chronicle," D. N. Freedman) all center on the last years of the kingdom of Judah, concerning which much new information has recently come to light. Number 11 (E. G. Kraeling) brings us down to the fifth century B.C., and the strange colony of heterodox Jews at Elephantine.

A parallel to Hyatt's paper is C. C. McCown's treatment of New Testament book-making (No. 15). Kenneth W. Clark carries this further with a description of the great libraries of manuscripts at Sinai and Jerusalem and the microfilming project undertaken in co-operation with the Library of Congress (No. 16).

William R. Farmer's paper on Ezekiel's geography is a by-product of the Dead Sea discoveries (No. 17); Howard Wallace's discussion of the "beast" in Revelation is based upon investigation of mythological motifs in recently unearthed Canaanite epics (No. 18). "The Gnostic Library of Chenoboskion" (V. R. Gold, No. 19) describes a hoard of third- fourth-century (A.D.) manuscripts which turned up in 1946, just before the discovery of the Dead Sea Scrolls. While they constitute the earliest known literature of the Gnostics, and are

extremely important for understanding the nature and recon-
structing the history of Gnosticism *vis à vis* Christianity, little publicity has attached to their discovery and decipherment
(perhaps because no one has branded them a medieval
forgery).

The final section (D. Collier, No. 20) deals with the abstruse
subject of radiocarbon dating—a process which gives hope of
establishing an absolute chronology of the Near East. Its chief
value is in connection with the earlier archaeological periods,
for which no written records are available, though it can also
be used for dating the linen wrappings of the Dead Sea Scrolls.

We are grateful to the American Schools of Oriental Research, publisher of *The Biblical Archaeologist,* for permission
to use the articles printed in this book, as well as to the authors
of the several papers, for their willing co-operation in this project. Thanks are due also to Anchor Books, for encouraging the
editors in the preparation of this volume, and arranging for its
publication.

David Noel Freedman, *Editor*
THE BIBLICAL COLLOQUIUM

ABBREVIATIONS

LIST OF ILLUSTRATIONS

PLATES

FIGURES

THE BIBLICAL ARCHAEOLOGIST READER

1

EXPLORING
SOUTHERN PALESTINE
(THE NEGEV)

NELSON GLUECK

Follow almost any well trodden Bedouin trail in the Negev
and it will lead you from one ancient site to another, datable
by fragments of pottery among their foundation ruins, razed
often to the very ground by time or tragedy or both. Unchanging topography has conditioned the locations and directions of
the cross country pathways or roads, whose lines have varied
but little throughout the long story of man's coming and going
along them. Look for springs, however few they may be, and
wells and cisterns too, and they will indicate the presence of
settlements of centuries in their vicinity. Gaze at the slopes of
hills, however rocky and barren, for the telltale grooves cut
into them for considerable distances to lead the rare rainwater
to reservoirs or cisterns or to terraced fields in or alongside the
dry stream beds below. Check every shrub-fringed, frequently
stone-lined channel leading across any slightly sloping wilderness plain, even if blanketed with a shattered cover of dark-
ened sandstone pebbles and glaringly black flint fragments.
You will find almost invariably that at its end is a cistern or a
stretch of good soil, held firmly in place by a series of strong
cross walls to withstand the scouring freshets of the occasional
winter and spring rains. Acquaint yourself with the needs and
fears, the moods and manners, of the broken array of peoples
and civilizations that appeared at intervals along the horizon
of time and, in a general way, you will know in advance where

to look for the clues they left behind in the course of their passage. Isolated hilltops overlooking cultivable stretches and strategic roads were preferred in the Judaean period of Iron II; fertile slopes open to the breezes were the predilection of their predecessors of Middle Bronze I during the Age of Abraham. And above all, read the Bible, morning, noon and night, with a positive attitude, ready to accept its historical references in whatever context they occur as arising from fact, until or unless other factors suggest other procedures.

And then go forth into the wilderness of the Negev and discover, trite as it may sound, that everything you touch turns into the gold of history, and that it is almost impossible not to stumble across the treasures of a robust past, whose existence becomes as real and as full of content and color and sound and fury and the thrill of progress and the pity of failure as the transient present, which is always ticking away so furiously to join the throng of those that need no longer hurry.

For several months each summer during more than a Sabbath of years commencing in 1951, the Louis M. Rabinowitz and David W. Klau archaeological expeditions, under the auspices of the Hebrew Union College—Jewish Institute of Religion, and with the assistance of a grant-in-aid from the American Department of State, under the Special Cultural Program for Israel, have been venturing forth into the Negev, learning that it was inhabited by civilized peoples from at least the Late Chalcolithic period (the second half of the fourth millennium B.C.) on. Its tattered history was conditioned by its enduring geopolitical importance, which it obtained as a birthright through the providence of creation. As a key part of the immensely strategic strip of land along the eastern end of the Mediterranean, binding Asia and Africa together, it has suffered frequently and frightfully from their mutually antagonistic forces. The ambitions and anxieties of the rulers and populations of both have been like regularly recurring plagues of locusts bringing devastation to the land. The objective of Egypt has always been the fertile Tigris-Euphrates basin and that of Mesopotamia the rich Nile valley. The failure of either to vanquish the other for long has never deterred their successors from repeating their folly and seeking or securing dominion over Palestine and the Negev and Sinai, to pave the way for their volatile victories.

The existence of Late Chalcolithic settlements in the Negev is now a matter of record. To be sure, only a few have been found[1] and they were threadbare poor in comparison with the Tell Abu Matar of that period, on the outskirts of Beersheba, which has been so brilliantly excavated by Jean Perrot. But then, in general, the ancient settlements in the Negev, with some Iron II and fairly many Nabataean and Byzantine exceptions, differ from their contemporaries in the more favored areas to the north of it, as do stands of wheat, planted on soils and under conditions ranging from unfavorable to excellent.

Our assumption that Chalcolithic sites of the same vintage as those previously discovered in the northern Negev might well be found also in the central Negev[2] was borne out during our archaeological explorations in the summer of 1959. The production of sophisticated copper articles at Chalcolithic Tell Abu Matar, which, as Jean Perrot has shown, included smelting and manufacturing processes based upon selected ores of high mineral content obtained from the Wadi Aravah,[3] emphasized in part its high cultural achievements and its connections with a widespread Chalcolithic civilization. Basalt bowls and pottery vessels and other objects also underscored the relationship, which thus involves trade routes serving as lines of communication and acculturation.[4]

Our discovery this summer of an extensive Late Chalcolithic to Early Bronze I site overlooking from the south the Wadi Murrah (Nahal Zin) and of another farther southeast along the Darb es-Sultani, which passes in part above and alongside it before bending away to follow the line of the Wadi Merzebah down to the Wadi Aravah, reveals the existence of such early settlements in the central Negev, in addition to those in

[1] *Bulletin* 152, p. 19; 145, pp. 13–15; *Rivers in the Desert*, pp. 54–59.

[2] *Bulletin* 152, p. 19; *Rivers in the Desert*, pp. 86–87.

[3] *Israel Exploration Journal* V:1, 1955, pp. 79, 80, 84; *Rivers in the Desert*, p. 44.

[4] *Israel Exploration Journal* V, 1955, pp. 17–40, 73–84, 167–89; VI:3, pp. 163–79; *Bulletin* 145, pp. 13–15; *Rivers in the Desert*, pp. 49, 56–59.

the northern Negev.[5] It is likely, furthermore, that similar sites, datable by clear pottery fragments, will yet be found also in the southern Negev and in the Wadi Aravah (Arabah), particularly along important travel routes. The boundaries of civilized settlement in the Negev are thus being pushed farther back with these new discoveries. We found another Late Chalcolithic site at the western approach to the Wadi Hathirah (Machtesh Gadol).

It may be said in connection with the mention of the Darb es-Sultani, that as a result of our very careful examination of it in the summer of 1959, along its entire length from Sede Boqer on the border between the northern and central Negev[6] and continuing ESE and SE down to 'Ain el-Weibeh (Ain Yahav) in the Wadi Aravah, which it crosses ultimately to join under a different name the north-south King's Highway in Transjordan, we found that it was one of the most important travel routes in the entire Negev. It connected at its western end with others that led north to Beersheba and southwest to Kadesh-barnea in Sinai. Experience should have taught us that when a name such as Darb es-Sultani, the Road of the Sultan, which is the Arabic equivalent of the biblical name of King's Highway, is attached to a travel route, it means exactly what it says both for ancient as well as modern times. We found a whole series of stone built villages or caravanserais alongside of it, belonging to the Late Chalcolithic-Early Bronze I (ca. 3500–2900 B.C.), Middle Bronze I of the twenty-first to nineteenth centuries B.C., Iron II of the tenth to sixth centuries B.C., Nabataean-Roman and Byzantine periods, with the last coming to an end in the seventh century A.D. The gaps in between these periods of history correspond exactly to those of the broken pattern of the history of civilized, permanently or semipermanently occupied settlements in the Negev that has manifested itself during all the previous years of our archaeological investigations there.

Most of the settlements along the Wadi Murrah (Nahal Zin) and the Wadi Merzebah were occupied in nearly every one of the above mentioned periods, with the exception of the Late Chalcolithic, and the explanation may be that we suc-

[5] Rivers in the Desert, pp. 56–59.
[6] Rivers in the Desert, pp. 86–87.

ceeded in finding the confirmatory potsherds of only two sites there of that particular period. The direction of the Darb es-Sultani was fixed during all these periods by the compulsions of unchanging topography. The possible places for villages or caravanserais along the way were so limited in number, that each wave of occupants in widely separated centuries had to establish itself again on the same spots its predecessors had chosen. The discontinuity as well as the nature of the various occupations precluded, however, the development of *tells* at these places, such as can be found in the Negev only in the Beersheba basin.[7]

Some of the largest Middle Bronze I sites we have ever come across in the Negev were among the sites we found along the banks of the Wadi Murrah (Nahal Zin) and the Wadi Merzebah this summer, each spread over many acres of area. The stone foundations of houses with attached courtyards, with many of the houses belonging apparently more or less to the "beehive" type,[8] which seem to be characteristic of the age at least in the treeless Negev, and fragments of pottery strewn among them absolutely similar in large measure to those of the same period commonly found in the entire range of Middle Bronze I sites from southern Syria to the borders of Egypt,[9] gave abundant evidence of their particular centuries in the calendar of history.

Our expedition came across other Middle Bronze I sites elsewhere in the Negev this summer, including one overlooking the Wadi Khureisheh. Our belief, expressed in this journal some years ago, that numerous Middle Bronze I sites would be found in the Negev beyond those we had already discovered then, and the existence of which confirmed the general validity of the historical memories of the Age of Abraham surviving in chapters 12, 13 and 14 of the Book of Genesis, has been fleshed out into firm knowledge by discoveries of Middle Bronze I sites made every time we have gone forth into the Negev during the successive years since then.[10]

It may be remarked parenthetically with regard to the Mid-

[7] *Rivers in the Desert,* pp. 6–7, 50.
[8] *Rivers in the Desert,* pp. 76–77; *Bulletin* 149, p. 15.
[9] *Rivers in the Desert,* pp. 60–61.
[10] *Biblical Archaeologist* XVIII:1, 1955, p. 6.

dle Bronze I sites of the Age of Abraham in the Negev that one of the ways to find them is to look for cup-holes or cup-marks. We have come to the conclusion, fortified by modern examples, that they were generally used as rock-bound mortars in which kernels of grain, for instance, were placed to be pounded into flour with a stone pestle. Grain is still ground in exactly this fashion in some primitive villages in Basutoland in South Africa.[11] We found these cup-holes again at almost every Middle Bronze I site that we came across this summer. Wherever we found the ruins of conical or oval houses we would look first of all for Middle Bronze I potsherds and then for cup-holes on flattish rock-surfaces close by or among the ruins of the site. Sometimes, we would come across the cup-holes first, which served almost as a signboard of the existence in the immediate vicinity of a Middle Bronze I site.

The next period of civilized settlement in the Negev is that of Iron II, extending from the tenth to the sixth centuries B.C. The land was dotted then with fortresses on strategic hilltops, and with agricultural villages usually on the slopes below them. Their inhabitants tilled strongly terraced fields generally in or alongside wadis or dry stream beds, dug cisterns, many of them still in use by modern Bedouins,[12] and engaged also in extensive pastoral, commercial and industrial activities. These included tending their flocks and herds of domestic animals, trading with Egypt and Arabia, mining and smelting mainly copper found in and alongside the Wadi Aravah, and refining it and manufacturing it into finished copper articles at Ezion-geber: Elath, as established by our excavations there. The amazing correctness of historical memory in the Bible was emphasized years ago, in one of many instances which might be cited, by our discovering, and dating through pottery finds, copper mining and smelting sites in and alongside the Wadi Aravah. This was in full accord with the hitherto enigmatic statement in Deuteronomy 8:9: "You shall inherit . . . a land

---

[11] *Bulletin* 149, pp. 10, 15–16; *Rivers in the Desert*, pp. 77, 83–84; *Illustrated London News*, Sept. 7, 1957, p. 375.

[12] Cross and Milik, *Bulletin* 142, pp. 5–16; Glueck, *Bulletin* 152, pp. 23, 30, 32–34; no. 155, pp. 3, 4, 7, and notes 2, 3, 12; *Rivers in the Desert*, pp. 172, 174, 222; II Chronicles 26:10.

whose stones are iron and out of whose hills you can dig copper."[13]

It was only from the time of David, who beat back the Amalekites and the other Bedouins of the Negev to the perimeters of the desert whence they came and from which, to be sure, they emerged again during every period of weakness of the authority of the throne in Jerusalem, that it was possible for the people of Judah to exploit the potential of the Negev. This occurred particularly under kings like Solomon and Uzziah. One of the results which can now be proven archaeologically was that the southwesternmost part of the territory of Judah extended through the Negev to the natural boundary line formed by the Brook of Egypt, the Wadi el-Arish, which bisects north–south the center of the length of Sinai (I Kings 4:24). We have discovered, for instance, a whole line of Judaean, Iron II fortresses, guarding the ancient route leading directly through the Wadi Khureisheh to and from Sinai. An Iron II Judaean fortress was discovered at 'Ain Qudeirat (Kadesh-barnea) years ago by T. E. Lawrence, and others have been discovered in Sinai, as well as numerous Middle Bronze I sites since then.[14]

It is understandable, therefore, why we have found no Iron I (twelfth to beginning of the tenth century B.C.) Israelite sites or pottery in the Negev during the years of our archaeological explorations there. The power of Israel before the reign of David was not great enough to create and maintain by force of arms and effective governmental authority the conditions of political and economic security and peace which are prerequisite for the rooting and blossoming of civilized settlement, with its appurtenances of agriculture, animal husbandry, industry and commerce. The Iron II or Judaean occupation of the Negev is evidenced by an impressive number of the nearly 500 ancient sites we have thus far discovered there. The remains of fortresses and villages, some of whose walls with corners of characteristic header and stretcher construction are, in

---

[13] *Biblical Archaeologist* I:2 (1938), p. 8; I:3 (1938), pp. 15–16; II:4 (1939), p. 40; III:4 (1940), p. 54.

[14] *Bulletin* 145, pp. 15–16, 21–25; 152, pp. 30–38; *Rivers in the Desert*, pp. 170–72; Rothenberg, *Tagliyot Sinai*, pp. 120, 133–52; Aharoni in *Antiquity and Survival*, II:2/3, 1957, pp. 295–96.

places, amazingly well preserved, and of cisterns and terrace
walls, some of which are still practically intact and serve their
original purpose to this very day, and the datable pottery fragments found among them, tell the story of the Judaean occupation of the Negev in Iron II in considerably more detail
than is found in the pages of the Bible. It was, however, the
testimony of the Bible, which convinced us, before we ever
commenced the archaeological exploration of the Negev, that
it was not in ancient times almost completely an uninhabited
and uninhabitable land, as prior to that time it had generally
been conceived to be.

There are two kinds of Iron II pottery found in the Negev:
the smaller proportion is generally the same as types commonly
found in Judah and Israel of the same period, while the other
is a more common kind which prior to our excavations of
Ezion-geber: Elath was totally unknown and which appears
to be much earlier to the uninitiated. It is coarse and crude
and almost always handmade, frequently employing horn or
ledge or knob handles and often with spirally grooved bases
reflecting the coiled straw mats on which the pottery clay was
placed before being fashioned by hand into the desired shape.
This type of pottery was, we believe, largely the handiwork
of the Kenite, Rechabite, Calebite, Yerahmeelite and related
inhabitants of the Negev,[15] who adopted a sedentary or semi-
sedentary civilization in Iron II, but who had lived an almost
completely nomadic life in the Negev and the Wadi Aravah
and Sinai and probably in the areas of Midian in Arabia during and perhaps even before Iron I.[16] There can be no question but that the Kenites were at home in Sinai and the Negev
and the Wadi Aravah also during and before the time of Moses
and the migratory movements of the Israelites through these
latter territories en route to the Promised Land.[17] That the
particular journey of the Israelites, described in the Bible,
through Sinai, the Negev, part of the Wadi Aravah and east

[15] *Bulletin* 155, pp. 10–12; 152, p. 34; 145, p. 23; *Smithsonian Report for 1941,* p. 478. This type of crude Iron II pottery has also been
found by others in the Negev during the last couple of years; cf.
Israel Exploration Journal VIII:4, 1958, p. 241 and pl. 49–52.

[16] *Smithsonian Report for 1941,* p. 478.

[17] Exodus 2:15–22; Numbers 21:8–10; 33:43; Judges 1:16; I
Samuel 15:5–7; *Rivers in the Desert*, pp. 45, 86, 111–12, 132–34.

around Edom and Moab before turning west to cross the Jordan and enter the Promised Land at Gilgal could not have taken place before the thirteenth century B.C. was demonstrated by our archaeological explorations, which showed, in harmony with biblical accounts, that these kingdoms were strongly entrenched at the beginning of Iron I, with sufficient power to deny the Israelites permission to utilize the King's Highway through their territories.[18]

Following the Babylonian conquest of Judah in the sixth century B.C., the works of civilization in the Negev came to an end, with the elements and the Bedouins breaking down what had been reared in painful labor. The land remained waste and empty with the exception of the northernmost part which touched the territory of the Idumaeans. In time, however, the void was filled, the Bedouins repelled, the desert reclaimed, the terraces and cisterns of the Judaeans included in vastly larger and more intricate systems of water and soil conservation, and villages and towns and temples by the scores were established completely anew, when the Nabataeans incorporated the Negev and Sinai into their swiftly developed kingdom. Its heyday extended between the second century B.C. and the second century A.D. With the base of their kingdom in the former territories of the kingdoms of Edom and Moab, their capital at Petra, where the biblical Selaʿ had been located, their domain including also northern Arabia and southern Syria, as well as the Negev and Sinai, the Nabataeans fashioned with furious creativity a magnificent civilization, whose meteor-like brilliance was extinguished all too soon by Roman conquest.

The Negev was of great importance to the Nabataeans. The incense and spices and other precious products of the East were transported in large measure across it for reshipment to Palestine and Egypt and to other lands bordering the Mediterranean Sea. Great emporia sprang up in connection with this commerce, with one of them, known as Abda today, named probably after one of the Nabataean kings called Obodas. A small sculpture discovered there recently resembles some of those from our excavations of the Nabataean temple of Khirbet

[18] *The Other Side of the Jordan*, pp. 128, 140–47.

Tannur in Transjordan. Every available inch of soil was put under cultivation, every possible drop of water channeled into terrace-corseted fields or into many hundreds of reservoirs and cisterns. Whole hillsides were used as catchment basins and barren slopes were dotted often with intricately designed rows of piles of small stones (wrongly called *teleilat el-'anab*, "grapevine mounds"), or with whole rows of such stones. These patterns served to help catch and lead some of the rare rainwater (as has correctly been explained, we believe, by Hebrew University scholars) to terraced fields or into cisterns below.[19] Fragments of the inimitable Nabataean pottery of sophisticated beauty and delicacy litter the surfaces of hundreds of Nabataean ruins in the Negev, with Nabataean inscriptions and rock-drawings frequently visible at various places to attest further to the fleeting presence of Nabataeans in the land.

After a comparatively brief period of decline following the Roman conquest of the Nabataean kingdom, the Negev experienced an efflorescence of civilization which equalled and in some ways surpassed the Nabataean one. Every skill employed by the Nabataeans to wring sustenance from a marginal land of extremely limited rain was exercised by the Byzantines, who were by and large the Christianized descendants of the Nabataeans. Retaining their identity, however, were communities of Jews, whose synagogues were contemporaneous with the vastly larger number of resplendent Byzantine churches that sprang up in the Negev to replace every vestige of the preceding Nabataean, pagan temples. The history of early Christian art and architecture and particularly of Byzantine churches can no longer be studied without considering such previously known sites as Abda and Isbeita, now being partly restored and being made accessible by the Government of Israel, and without considering the hundreds of Byzantine ruins discovered during the course of the last eight years by our expeditions of archaeological exploration. The Byzantine period in the Negev came to an end early in the

---

[19] *Bulletin* 155, pp. 4–6, n. 8–9. [Cf., however, the views of Myerson in *Bulletin* 153, pp. 19–31, who has made a fine case for an interpretation of these mounds as places where vines were planted. It is difficult to see how such little mounds could efficiently distribute the run off of water. Editor.]

seventh century A.D. as a result of the Mohammedan conquest.
Darkness and disintegration and reversion to desert have characterized its history since then, with the dawn of a promising
new day breaking over it once more since the return of modern
Israel to the Southland of the ancient kingdom of Judah.[20]

THE ACHIEVEMENT OF
NELSON GLUECK

G. ERNEST WRIGHT

During the summer and early fall of 1959 President Nelson
Glueck of Hebrew Union College–Jewish Institute of Religion,
brought to completion his great archaeological survey of
Transjordan, the Jordan Valley, and the Negeb (Southern
Palestine). Having learned how to identify and to use ancient
pottery fragments in surface surveys from W. F. Albright, he
began his Transjordanian survey in 1932 and continued it year
by year until halted by political disturbances in 1947. During
the late 1930s he conducted small excavations at Khirbet et-
Tannur on the border of ancient Edom where a Nabataean
temple was uncovered, and at Tell el-Kheleifeh, ancient Ezion-
geber, on the shore of the Gulf of Aqabah, where the stratified levels of an originally Israelite copper refinery were unearthed. After conditions had sufficiently quieted following the
Israeli-Arab war in 1948, he began in 1951 detailed work in
the Negeb, with results which are described briefly in the preceding article.

The technical reports of the Transjordanian survey are published in a series of volumes entitled, *Explorations in Eastern
Palestine I–IV*. These are found in *Annual of the American*

[20] For the history of the Nabataean and Byzantine occupation of
the Negev, cf. *Rivers in the Desert*, pp. 191–284.

Schools of Oriental Research, Vols. XIV (1934), XV (1935), XVIII–XIX (1939) and XXV–XXVIII (1951). The less technical and less detailed reports appear in two books, *The Other Side of the Jordan* (New Haven, 1940) and *The River Jordan* (Philadelphia, 1946). In January 1959 the New York publisher, Farrar, Straus and Cudahy, published the third of Dr. Glueck's popular books, this one being a survey of his post-War exploration: *Rivers in the Desert: A History of the Negeb* (pp. xv + 302, three maps and fifty-five photographs; $6.50). Clear and frequently colorful writing, a good map on the end papers, and lavish biblical illustration make the book easy and interesting reading.

It may be stated without hesitation that Glueck's work is to be rated as one of the two most important individual contributions to the field of Palestinian archaeology in our generation. First, of course, is the work of Albright at *Tell Beit Mirsim* (Debir), the reports of which constitute the primary critical source in the interpretation of Palestinian digging, including especially the first definitive treatment of the chronological basis on which the discipline rests. In Glueck's work great stretches of semi-desert region on the eastern and southern fringes of the country are now made to render an account for the historian of ancient man. Areas which have appeared almost lifeless to the modern traveler have now yielded a story of life. Hundreds of sites, for the most part unknown hitherto, have been found, described and made a dot with a name or a number on a map.

Patterns of settlement have been observed, and though the historical conclusions Glueck has drawn from these patterns have sometimes been challenged, and though subsequent discoveries will surely modify details, the over-all picture which he has presented will probably stand the test of time. The results of the excavations at Dhiban (biblical Dibon) have so far been in complete harmony with his conclusions. The history of the northern Jordan Valley and of parts of northern Transjordan follows closely the pattern of fairly continuous occupation in western Palestine throughout historical times. In the southern part of the Valley, in the Negeb and in southern Transjordan, on the other hand, the history of settlement is spotty with long periods when nomadism returned. Looking at

Glueck's results beside a map of the country's rainfall, one would judge that density and continuity of village settlement need a minimum of twelve inches of rain each year, and preferably more for intensive habitation. True tells, made up of successive strata of occupation, become increasingly rare in areas below that figure, though occasional examples are to be found in areas with as little as *ca.* 8 inches (e.g., the mounds of ancient Jericho and Beersheba). Khirbet Qumran, the community center of the Dead Sea Scroll people, and Kadesh-barnea in Sinai, on the other hand, are in areas with little more than some four inches of rainfall. In other words, people have lived in the Palestinian areas with between four and eight inches of rain per year, but they have tended to do so in certain periods and not others, when political and cultural factors, not always recoverable by us today, made it advisable.

Why, for example, did a flourishing series of villages spring up during the Chalcolithic period of the mid-fourth millennium along the eight inch rain line in the Beersheba and Jordan Valley districts? We do not know, nor do we know why the settlements became much fewer in number there during the third millennium. During Middle Bronze I (*ca.* 2100–1900 B.C.), on the other hand, southern Transjordan and the areas with between four and eight inches of rain were suddenly dotted with settlements. Settlements again appear between the thirteenth–twelfth centuries and the sixth century B.C., only to disappear in the period between the sixth–fifth centuries and the second century, B.C. The most intensive occupation of all extended from the time of the marvelous Nabataeans of the early Roman Age to and through the Byzantine period, with only a brief period of decline between them.

For Glueck, Middle Bronze I is "The Age of Abraham." He argues that the biblical associations of Abraham with the "cities of the plain" (Gen. 14) and with inhabited areas in the Negeb are only meaningful in Middle Bronze I. Indeed, we may say that this is the only concrete bit of archaeological information bearing directly, rather than indirectly, on the dates of the Patriarch. Glueck has argued further that the Israelites under Moses could not have traversed Transjordan before the thirteenth century. Some have countered this by saying that Israel could have encountered nomads, but such a position scarcely does justice to the biblical tradition which definitely includes towns as well as national groups of people. The discovery of Middle Bronze Age tombs and a Late Bronze Age temple (unpublished) with rich imports of Greek pottery at Amman have also been cited as evidence for the necessity of revising Glueck's views.[1] Yet nomads also buried their dead and may well have had temples as centers of common worship (cf. Kadesh-barnea and Shiloh in early Israelite tradition). In a surface survey, one's analysis of individual sites needs correction by excavation, but the over-all results from an examination of hundreds of sites are probably not far wrong, especially in areas where true tells are few.

It is a pleasure, therefore, to write these lines in tribute to a great and significant work, completed by one whose patience and persistence are objects of admiration and highest praise.

IS GLUECK'S AIM TO PROVE THAT THE BIBLE IS TRUE?

G. ERNEST WRIGHT

In the magazine *Commentary* for April, 1959 (Vol. 27, No. 4, pages 341-50), Professor J. J. Finkelstein of the University of California presents a lengthy review of Glueck's new volume, *Rivers in the Desert*. In actuality, however, the article is not so much a review of Glueck's discoveries as a critical essay on the question as to whether archaeology proves the historicity of the Bible. Through the medium of Glueck's book, the author takes the occasion to administer a sound "spanking" to all of us concerned with biblical archaeology for making claims that the facts do not really support. He expects such claims

[1] Cf. G. L. Harding, *Four Tomb Groups from Jordan* (London, 1953).

from popularizers and from those with some particular axe to grind, but he does not think it right for those of us who are supposed to be scholars, who are able to handle the original data with critical understanding, to say the same things in just the same way. Thus, as a text for his remarks he takes the following sentence from page 31 of Glueck's book which he believes to be the real theme of the volume: "It may be stated categorically that no archaeological discovery has ever controverted a biblical reference." There is also Glueck's repeated assertion of "the almost incredibly accurate historical memory of the Bible, and particularly so when it is fortified by archaeological fact" (page 68).

As his chief illustration of "many instances where archaeologically provided fact or near certainty has contradicted a biblical statement," Finkelstein, like Martin Noth in Germany, cites, of course, the problem concerning the fall of Jericho. To make his point, he first quotes my remarks in the first edition of the *Westminster Historical Atlas to the Bible,* where, as a result of Garstang's work, I stated the conclusion that the final fall and abandonment of Jericho was in the fourteenth century, one hundred years before the time of Joshua. In the 1956 edition of the same book, however, I pointed to the Kenyon excavations which began in 1952 (see *BA* XVI.3 and XVII.4), and asserted that we now know little about the date of Jericho's capture by Joshua. But, says Finkelstein, it is in my larger work, *Biblical Archaeology* (1957), that my remarks on the subject are most revealing. There I say: "The most surprising and discouraging result of the work so far has been the discovery that virtually nothing remains at the site between 1500 and 1200 B.C." Finkelstein asserts that the word "virtually" is simply a scholarly hedge for "nothing," and that what I am actually saying is that the site was unoccupied in the Late Bronze Age. Furthermore, says Finkelstein, my word "discouraging" in this connection "speaks volumes on the subject of scholarly detachment in the area of biblical studies." He continues: "The dictates of the new trend, which requires that every contradiction between archaeological evidence and the biblical text be harmonized to uphold the veracity of Scripture, has apparently driven Dr. Wright—in this case at least—beyond the reach of common sense."

Putting aside for a moment the question as to whether Professor Finkelstein has really been fair to Glueck, or whether he has really read the Jericho source material and knows what the real issues are at the site, I think it should be said immediately that he has indeed raised an important issue, the significance of which is far broader than the particular examples he quotes from Glueck or me. Furthermore, I personally would wish to be the first to say that in my judgment we have indeed been guilty of overstatement in particular contexts and that the time has come for a more cautious and judicious qualification of the positive assertions in question, so that it may be quite clear what the evidence really is. On the other hand, a word is in order about the background and origin of the manner of speaking which Professor Finkelstein here challenges.

There are many people both here and abroad who honestly think and frequently assert that Palestinian and biblical archaeology was conceived and reared by conservative Christians who wished to find support for their faith in the accuracy of the Bible. As a matter of actual fact, however, that is not the case at all. In the great fundamentalist-modernist controversy that reached its height before the First World War, archaeology was not a real factor in the discussion.[1] Indeed, the discoveries relating to the antiquity of man and the Babylonian creation and flood stories were usually cited against the fundamentalist position. As for the excavations in Palestine, one need only call the roll of the leading American sponsors and contributors to indicate what the true situation has been: Harvard University (Samaria), University of Pennsylvania (Beth-shan), University of Chicago (Megiddo), Yale University (Jerash), the American Schools of Oriental Research, etc. Palestinian archaeology has been dominated by a general cultural interest, and one can say that "fundamentalist" money has never been a very important factor. Archaeological research *by and large* has been backed by the humanist opinion that anything hav-

---

[1] Among the first tentative steps at introducing it, Prof. L. J. Trinterud has pointed out to me Chaps. I and II by G. F. Wright and M. G. Kyle in *The Fundamentals: A Testimony to the Truth* (Chicago, 1910).

ing to do with historical research, with the investigation of our past, is an obvious "good" which needs no justification.

The introduction of the theme, "archaeology confirms biblical history," into the discussion of *scientific* archaeological matters is a comparatively recent phenomenon. And it is to be credited to the pen of William Foxwell Albright more than to any other one person. Since the 1920s, Albright has towered over the field of biblical archaeology as the greatest giant it has produced, and more than any other single person he has influenced younger scholars, Protestant, Catholic, and Jewish, to take the subject seriously as a primary tool of historical research. At the same time, he has been a most important encouragement to young conservative scholars. Through his writings, they have come to realize that if they but master the tools of research there is indeed a positive contribution that they can make to biblical research, and that the radical views which they could not accept do not necessarily find support in recent research.

Yet Albright has often been misunderstood at this point. He has never been a "fundamentalist"[2] and the encouragement of that movement could scarcely be farther from his center of interest. He came to maturity after the First War at a time when England and America in their critical Old Testament scholarship were dominated by a fairly uncritical acceptance of the Vatke-Graf-Wellhausenist developmental reconstruction of Old Testament history—and this at a time when in Europe the whole direction of scholarship had shifted, particularly through Hermann Gunkel's introduction of new perspectives and methods of research. The latter were producing a fresh and original scholarly product of great significance in such men as Albrecht Alt, Johannes Pedersen, Sigmund Mowinckel and their pupils. At the same time Albright's deep interest in ancient history and his mastery of several disciplines within it brought him to the conviction that a whole new environment for biblical study was emerging of which the nineteenth century knew nothing. Consequently, at first in his popular writings and finally in his scholarly synthesis of the evidence (*From the Stone Age to*

---

[2] Note, for example, the robust attack on him as an old-fashioned liberal at heart by Oswald T. Allis, "Albright's Thrust for the Bible View," *Christianity Today*, May 25, 1959 (Vol. III.17), pp. 7–9.

Christianity, 1st edition, 1940), he led the attack in the English-speaking world on the unexamined presuppositions of "Wellhausenism" from the standpoint of ancient history and particularly archaeology. The early historical traditions of Israel cannot be easily dismissed as data for history when such a variety of archaeological facts and hints make a different view far more reasonable, at least as a working hypothesis, namely, that the traditions derive from an orally transmitted epic which has preserved historical memories in a remarkable way, that "pious fraud" was not a real factor in the production or refraction of the traditions, and that in Israel aetiology was a secondary, never a primary, factor in the creation of the epic.

Nelson Glueck in archaeology has been a student of Albright and in matters of biblical history was educated in the same skeptical atmosphere toward biblical traditions prevailing both in this country and in Germany where he took his doctorate. In many ways his own archaeological achievements have kept him in constant contact with the Bible and in every case he has been led to the view that the biblical traditions derive from a real history and they can be fitted within the framework which archaeological, historical, and topographical research provides. It is in this sense and with this background that his sentence quoted by Finkelstein is to be understood. It is an extreme statement, to be sure, but one must note the qualifications Glueck places around it. For one thing, Glueck affirms that no one can "prove" the Bible, for it is primarily a theological document. "Saga and song, legend and myth, fact and folklore were woven into the text to illustrate and emphasize this central theme. Those people are essentially of little faith who seek through archaeological corroboration of historical source materials in the Bible to validate its religious teachings and spiritual insights." Glueck says this very clearly and at some length. Consequently, I do not find his total context as extreme as Finkelstein claims that it is. As for Glueck's reference on page 68, about "the almost incredibly accurate historical memory of the Bible," he is there speaking of the date of Abraham, or "of the period with which the biblical writers associate him." For many this is a moot question, he says, "but not for those of us who rely heavily" on the Bible's historical memory. For the latter, the question is quite simple:

either Abraham is to be associated with the Middle Bronze I occupation of the Negeb, or else the entire saga is to be dismissed from scientific consideration. What is wrong with this statement? It seems fair enough. Indeed, Finkelstein's charge that proving the Bible's historicity is Glueck's real theme I do not find sustained on reading the book myself. Glueck in a popular and colorful manner is simply narrating his discoveries on Palestine's desert fringe, and, in doing so, relating its patterns and periods of settlement to the biblical narratives which he tells at length. Furthermore, those who know Glueck understand him to be a warmly emotional person who is deeply attached to the things that really matter to him. He is one who really loves and respects his Bible, not simply as a cultural treasure, but as a religious testimony to faith. In his scientific writings this side of him is restrained, but in his lectures and popular books his personal involvement with his work can be seen. (He can make an archaeological lecture a moving experience!) In this type of writing, what he really believes may be given explicit expression without the qualifications necessary in a more reflective and scholarly context. Is this totally wrong? In the general thrust of their scholarly work are not Albright and Glueck correct in pointing to the great foundation of archaeological research that now forms the basis of biblical history?

It is still a debated point, but the lines are being more sharply drawn and the factors of disagreement more closely defined today than in former years. What type of *historical* inference is legitimately made from internal literary critical, form-critical, and history-of-tradition research? Since the reconstruction of ancient *history* is an abstracting from the facts by means of hypothesis, in what way is that reconstruction to use the data and hypotheses drawn from archaeology? The differences of opinion at this point are to be observed in the two basic histories of Israel now available. One is Martin Noth's *The History of Israel* (published in English in 1958), an important work by a pupil of Albrecht Alt in Germany. The other is John Bright's, *A History of Israel*, just published by Westminster Press in this country, an equally important work by a pupil of W. F. Albright.

Meanwhile, however, it may still be charged that the time

when "Wellhausenism" needed continuous attack is rapidly receding, and that from now on more must be done to evaluate the new evidence in precise terms. If Professor Finkelstein's review is read in this light (and not simply as a way of attacking a work for one rather extreme, though qualified, statement within it), then I could not agree more heartily. But this work will have to be done by those who have a precise knowledge of the archaeological data. For example, the Jericho issue is not a simple one, as might too easily be inferred. The statement that there was "virtually" no Late Bronze Age occupation recovered means this: in the Early and Middle Bronze Ages Jericho was a fortified city of considerable significance. About 1550 B.C. the Egyptians destroyed it violently along with most other major Palestinian cities, and it was never again a significant city. As far as the evidence goes, it was not even fortified. However, there was indeed subsequent occupation. During the fourteenth century, at least three Middle Bronze Age tombs were opened and new burials inserted, and some very fragmentary remains of buildings and floors of the same general age were found above the spring. An unfortified Israelite village with what appears to have been a government granary also existed there, beginning about the tenth century. The evidence suggests that the Late Bronze Age occupation was slight, but most of what there was of it was eroded away in the unoccupied centuries which followed, just as happened there much earlier to the villages at the end of the Neolithic period (Kenyon's Neolithic Pottery A) and in the early Chalcolithic period (Kenyon's Neolithic B and Garstang's Jericho VIII), both of which were followed by long periods when the mound was unoccupied.

This information from Jericho was said to be "disappointing," and the reason is this: not only is it now difficult to interpret the biblical narrative of the fall of Jericho, but it is impossible to trace the history of the tradition. For my part, I do not believe that it can any longer be thought "scientific" simply to consider stories such as this one either as pure fabrications or as "aetiologies." They have had a long history of transmission, oral before written, and they derive from something real in history, no matter how far removed they may now be. In a number of instances, both the origin and history of a given tradition can be made out by historical, form-critical, and other methods of study. But the problem of Jericho is more of a problem than ever, precisely because the history of the tradition about it seems impossible to penetrate.

2

THE WRITING OF
AN OLD TESTAMENT BOOK

J. PHILIP HYATT

When a modern author begins to write a book, he sits down at his desk and writes on paper with pencil, or pen and ink, or typewriter. He may be affluent enough to have a secretary; if so, he dictates directly to her or him, or uses a dictaphone. Later the secretary transcribes the dictation on a typewriter. Ultimately, the work is printed on a press, bound, and issued as a book.

Did you ever wonder how the author of an Old Testament book did his work? We do not mean to inquire concerning the mental and spiritual processes involved, but the physical process of writing and the materials employed. Thanks to archaeological discoveries and a few hints here and there in the Bible itself, we can give a fairly complete answer to the above question. The answer will show that an ancient author's procedure was not as different from that of a modern author as you may have imagined.

The First Edition of Jeremiah's Book

The thirty-sixth chapter of Jeremiah gives us an account of the way in which that prophet composed the first edition of his work. There we read that Jeremiah was commanded of God to take a "book-roll" and write upon it all the words which God had spoken to him up to that time, 605 B.C. Thereupon the prophet summoned Baruch, his secretary, and dictated to him the messages he had received, and "Baruch wrote from the mouth of Jeremiah all the words of Jehovah which He had spoken unto him, on a book-roll" (vs. 4). Baruch was sent to read this roll in the temple, and subsequently it was read to an assembly of Judaean princes. When asked by them how the book was written, Baruch said, "With his mouth he [Jeremiah] recited unto me all these words, and I wrote them on a book with ink" (vs. 18). Still later it was read to the king by a man named Yehudi, but the monarch was displeased with its contents and had it destroyed. In vss. 22–23 we read: "The king was sitting in the winter quarters in the ninth month, and the fire of a brazier was burning before him. And it came to pass, as Yehudi would read three or four columns, he would cut it [the roll] with a penknife and throw it into the fire which was on the brazier, until the whole roll was consumed." After the destruction of this first edition, the prophet dictated a second edition to Baruch, making a number of additions.

This is the clearest and most complete biblical account of the procedure followed in writing an Old Testament book, and we may assume that it was generally used in the writing of other books. Of course, we cannot be certain that all were written in the same manner, but the method would not have varied greatly.

Writing Was a Learned Profession

Perhaps the most striking feature of this account is that the prophet did not actually write down his own book, but dictated it to Baruch. Perhaps, then, Jeremiah himself was unable to read and write. This need not surprise us, for in the ancient Orient in general the knowledge of writing was not widespread, but was confined to a small class. The rate of literacy was undoubtedly very low. Even kings apparently could not usually read and write, for the Assyrian monarch, Ashurbanipal, boasts in his annals that he had learned "all the art of writing." The knowledge of writing was generally a prerogative of the priesthood. This may have been the case in Israel, but there is no indication that Baruch was a priest; it is likely that there was a professional class of scribes outside the ranks of the priesthood. Certainly the great majority of people could neither read nor write. Those who had occasion to "sign" their names frequently to legal and commercial documents owned seals with which they made impressions on such documents. Many probably only made an X mark like the modern illiterate; the Hebrew word for "signature" is *taw*, the letter T which in ancient script looked like our X (see Job 31:35; cf. Ezekiel 9).

Several Hebrew words may be translated "scribe" or "secretary," but the most common one is *sōfēr*. There are many indications in the Old Testament that the *sōfĕrîm* (plural of *sōfēr*) did a great deal more than serve as stenographers or amanuenses, and occupied positions of authority and power. The Royal Scribe (*sōfēr ham-melek*) was more than private secretary to the king, and served virtually as Secretary of State. In post-Exilic times the *sōfĕrîm* acquired more and more authority and power, and subsequently developed into the "scribes" (scholars and interpreters of the Law) of the New Testament.

The education of a Hebrew scribe probably involved a long period of study, especially in those countries which employed cuneiform, a complicated and difficult system of writing. Palestinian scribes wrote the easier Hebrew, but some of them doubtless also were able to employ cuneiform and had to know Aramaic as well as Hebrew. In Babylonia and Syria, scribal schools were frequently attached to temples, and this may have been true also in Palestine. At Ras Shamrah in Syria, excavators uncovered near the temple the remains of a large building which was both library and scribal school.

Materials on Which Scribes Wrote

Papyrus was probably the material on which Baruch wrote the words dictated by Jeremiah. This is not stated, but certainly the material was perishable and could be burned in a brazier. It was not clay, and probably not leather nor vellum. The latter materials, made of animal skins, would have been somewhat difficult to cut with a penknife and to burn, and the odor produced would have been well-nigh intolerable.

Many inscriptions of Old Testament times have been found,

but no biblical manuscripts. There are many reasons for thinking, however, that most of the Old Testament books were written on papyrus, and that this was the commonest form of
writing material employed in Palestine from the time of the
Hebrew Conquest down to the end of the composition of the
Old Testament. While some papyrus manuscripts of Christian
times have been uncovered in southern Palestine, the climate
of the country is generally so damp that most of the papyri
long ago perished. However, the earliest fragment of the Old
Testament known, containing the Ten Commandments and
the Shema (Deut. 6:4–5), is of papyrus. It was found in
Egypt, and may be dated about 100 B.C.[1] An indication of
the early use of papyrus is the discovery at Lachish of a clay
seal impression of the sixth century B.C. which still had on its
back the marks of the fiber of the papyrus document to which
it had once been affixed.

Egypt is the land in which writing on papyrus was first
practiced, and in that country, with its favorable climate, tons
of papyrus have been discovered in modern times, wrapped in
mummies of men and crocodiles, deposited in tombs, and especially thrown out in waste heaps. In the land of the Nile
this writing material was used as early as the third millennium
B.C., and we may presume that it was introduced into Syria
and Palestine during the course of the second millennium B.C.

Papyrus is made from the stalks of a reed, *cyperus papyrus,*
which in ancient times grew in the Nile delta, in Italy, and in
India. It may also have grown in Palestine; the present writer
has seen papyrus plants around Lake Huleh in northern Palestine. The manner in which writing material was made from
this plant is not exactly known, and the description given by
Pliny (*Nat. Hist.* xiii. 12) not only contains some obscurities
but its correctness has been doubted by some modern scholars.
The method may, however, have been about as follows: After
removal of the rind, the stem of the plant was cut longitudi-
nally into thin strips with a knife. (It was the stem rather than
the pith which was used, in all likelihood.) Some of the strips
were then laid vertically upon a board, and across these another layer was placed at right angles. The upper surface then

[1] See W. F. Albright, *JBL,* LVI (1937), 145–76.

became the "right side" (*recto*) on which writing was done, and the lower surface the "back side" (*verso*) which was generally not written upon. The papyrus was then moistened with water. Whether glue was used or not is a debated subject; some scholars believe that glutinous matter in the strips was dissolved by water, while others (with much less probability) have advanced the view that Nile water itself contained a glutinous substance. At any rate, the sheets were finally hammered out and dried in the sun. Rough places were rubbed down with ivory, pumice-stone, or the like.

When finished the papyrus could be used either as single sheets or as rolls, which were made by pasting single sheets together. The length of the roll naturally depended upon the length of the writing, but rolls were usually not longer than thirty feet; in Egypt, however, a few rolls longer than a hundred feet have been found. Isaiah 8:1 tells of the prophet's writing upon a great *gillāyôn;* this may be the Hebrew word for a single sheet of papyrus. Sheets were used for many everyday purposes, but a book or long document was written on a roll, the name for which was *mĕgillāh* or *mĕgillat-sēfer.* The latter is the technical name for a book-roll and is used in Jeremiah 36. Each roll was divided into columns, for which the Hebrew is *delet.* This word properly means "door"; it has been suggested that it was derived from the name for a single wooden tablet. Several rolls could be stored together in a large pot, the "earthen vessel" of Jer. 32:14 (which refers, it may be remarked, to a deed of sale written on papyrus rather than on clay, as many scholars still think).

Egyptian reliefs show how a scribe wrote on papyrus. Ordinarily he stood or sat with an unsupported papyrus sheet or roll in his left hand, and wrote with the pen in his right hand. In some cases, he sat at a desk, on which might be piled numerous papyrus-rolls that looked like modern college diplomas.

Other writing materials were used in ancient Palestine. Animal skins were doubtless used as they were in many other lands of the ancient East. Leather was employed at an early time. For example, an Egyptian tomb inscription of the Eighteenth Dynasty (fifteenth–fourteenth centuries B.C.) states that laws were written on rolls of leather, and documents of this material of the fifth century B.C. written in Aramaic by Persian officials in Egypt have recently been found. Parchment or vellum was apparently not manufactured until about 200 B.C. Leather is made of tanned animal hides, while parchment or vellum is treated with limewater and refined much more than leather (vellum, properly speaking, is made only of calfskin).

Wooden tablets also were employed. Ezekiel 37:16 speaks of writing on wood, but whether this means on wooden tablets or sticks is not clear. The tablet (*lûăh*) on which Isaiah was instructed to write (30:8) may have been of wood. Assyrian and Syrian reliefs picture scribes who seem to be holding wooden tablets. It is likely that in Old Testament days only double leaves (diptychoi) were used, not a number of wooden tablets bound together which eventually gave rise to the codex, the familiar modern book form.[2] Wax-covered wooden tablets seem not to have been used before Graeco-Roman times.

Potsherds (that is, pieces of broken pottery) were used in ancient Palestine as a writing material. Many of these have been found in archaeological excavations. The largest number comes from Samaria. Here were uncovered more than sixty inscribed potsherds which were receipts for taxes of oil and wine paid to the king in the eighth century B.C. Twenty-one ostraca were found at Lachish (Tell ed-Duweir), most of them being letters written to the commandant of that city shortly before its fall in the early sixth century B.C. One was found at Ophel, the southeastern hill of Jerusalem, and a few at other places.

Ostraca were not suitable for the writing of biblical books, but they may well have been used for the writing down of prophetic sayings, proverbs, and the like, which eventually became incorporated into books. It would not be wholly surprising if archaeologists should some day uncover small portions of prophetic books, or even other Old Testament works, written down (or dictated) by the prophets, their disciples, ancient wise men, or others.

Ostraca were doubtless cheaper than papyrus, and might be compared with modern notebook paper. They were em-

[2] See C. C. McCown, *BA*, VI (1943), 23–24, and fig. 5 for illustrations of wooden tablets (nos. 4–6).

ployed mainly for letters, brief memoranda, receipts, and other documents requiring only small space. Fortunately they are of imperishable material and have survived even in the Palestinian climate. The type of script used on them is usually a flowing script of the kind which would have been developed from frequent writing on papyrus and leather.

Clay tablets have been found in the Holy Land. They are the kind of writing material widely used, and first developed, in Mesopotamia. Many of the Amarna Letters of *ca.* 1400 B.C., found in Egypt, were written in Palestine, as their contents clearly indicate. At Eglon and Taanach in Palestine were found letters on clay tablets from the period. The language usually written on such tablets was the Accadian cuneiform, but at Beth-shemesh was discovered a tablet inscribed in the alphabetic language of Ugarit (Ras Shamrah).

Clay tablets were written on by impressing a stylus upon the soft clay and then drying the tablet in the sun or baking it in an oven. A few tablets were found in Mesopotamia which contain both cuneiform characters and Aramaic written with pen and ink. It is not probable, however, that clay was widely used by the Hebrews, for it was not well adapted to their language and script. Only a few tablets of the time after the Hebrew Conquest have been found in Palestine. A good description of the way in which clay tablets were made may be found by the reader in Chiera, *They Wrote on Clay*, Chapter 2.

Moses is reported to have written the Ten Commandments on tablets of stone, and there are a few other references to writing on stone in the Old Testament (e.g., Deut. 27:2; Josh. 8:30–32; Job 19:24). Inscriptions have been found in the Holy Land made upon stone and upon various kinds of metal. Many inscribed seals made of various hard stones are known. None of these materials would have been used, however, for writing works of literature.

Ancient Pens and Ink

The pen (*'ēt*) used by the Hebrew scribe was usually made of reed. No examples have been discovered in Palestine, but Egyptian and Assyrian reliefs contain representations of them, and a few examples have been preserved in Egypt.

Writing on papyrus was done with a reed-pen which was made almost into a brush, perhaps by chewing the end of the pen until the fibers were softened and loosened. With this brush-like tip the scribe almost painted the letters or signs. It was only when parchment offered a hard writing surface that the sharp-pointed split pen, resembling our modern pen, came into use.

For writing on clay tablets, on which the signs were impressed, the stylus was made from a reed and given a square or three-cornered tip. The individual wedges were made by impressing the clay with one corner of the tip at an oblique angle. The upper end of the stylus was sometimes round, with which circles could be made if necessary. Archaeologists have not uncovered objects which can, with certainty, be identified with the ancient stylus, although some objects of stone or metal may have been such. However, the modern scholar can make a stylus and produce a cuneiform inscription which looks almost exactly like the ancient one.

Writing upon stone and other hard surfaces must have been done with a chisel, of the kind referred to in Job 19:24 as "an iron pen" (cf. Jer. 17:1). Archaeologists have not found any objects in Palestine which can be definitely identified as such.

The ink (děyô) used by the ancient Hebrew scribe was usually black. The scribe made his ink by mixing soot or lampblack with an aqueous solution of gum. The chief ingredient was apparently carbon. Chemical tests made upon the letters of Lachish showed the possible presence also of iron.[3] It is thought that oak-galls (which would furnish iron and tannin) and copperas may have also been used in making the ink of these letters. In Egypt red ink was frequently employed for the introductory words of a paragraph (a custom from which came ultimately our word "rubric"), and the Egyptian scribe is often shown with two pens behind his ear. The red ink was made by using a red iron oxide instead of carbon.

The Scribe's Kit

In Ezekiel 9:2, 3, 11 occur the Hebrew words qeset hassōfēr, usually translated "writer's inkhorn," the object which

[3] A. Lewis in Lachish I (Oxford, 1938), pp. 188–95.

was on the loins of the man clothed in linen who was commanded to go through Jerusalem and make an X-mark upon the foreheads of certain people. This word is equivalent to the Egyptian word *gsty,* the name of the scribe's kit or outfit which is well known from reliefs and surviving examples. According to Breasted, the Hebrew word was borrowed from Egypt,[4] and so it is likely that the object used by the Israelite scribe was very much like those found in Egypt. The earliest reliefs (from the Old Kingdom) show the scribe carrying over his shoulder or in one hand the kit composed of a jar of water, his reed pens in a protecting case, and a little wooden palette for mixing ink. A picture of this scribal outfit became the hieroglyphic sign for "writing, to write, scribe." In later times this outfit was simplified and streamlined. The small palette block, with two circular recesses for mixing red and black ink, was lengthened to furnish room for the reed pens, and the water jar was disconnected from the palette. In all probability we should translate the phrase *qeset has-sōfēr* in Ezekiel not as "inkhorn," but as "scribal kit."

A scribe needed other utensils in his work, but he did not usually carry them around with him. A "scribe's knife" or penknife (*ta'ar has-sōfēr* in Jer. 36:23) was necessary for cutting the papyrus sheets or rolls as occasion might require, and for sharpening the reed pen after the split-point type came into vogue. Erasing was probably not done with a knife but with a sponge. In Palestine many examples of knives have been found; it may be that some of the smallest ones were used as scribes' knives. The ancient writer sometimes needed a ruler (probably of wood) for scoring lines on papyrus or animal skins, and also a pumice-stone or similar object for smoothing papyrus. The ancient scribe doubtless kept these objects and others in his "office," and carried with him only his *qeset,* the ancient equivalent of a modern fountain pen, and the necessary "paper."

Although we do not possess any of the original manuscripts of the Old Testament, and it is very unlikely that any will ever come to light, we are able to look at and study the many

[4] *AJSL,* XXXII (1915–16), 246–47.

inscriptions found in Palestine which show us what the finished work of an ancient Hebrew scribe looked like. The illustrations to this book include a photograph of an ostracon of Lachish written in the early sixth century B.C., near the end of Jeremiah's lifetime. Baruch's writing must have looked very much like the writing of this ostracon. Hebrew scribes before the Exile employed a script generally known as "Old Canaanite." This is apparently a lineal descendant of the alphabetic script in which were written the Serabit inscriptions of *ca.* 1500 B.C. found near the traditional site of Mt. Sinai. The so-called square Hebrew characters came into use after the Exile, and from them developed the letters used in printing modern Hebrew books.

The discoveries made in the region northwest of the Dead Sea in the Wadi Qumran and Wadi Murabba'at, including what are usually called the Dead Sea Scrolls, have added immeasurably to our resources for the study of ancient manuscripts. These discoveries date mostly from the second century B.C. to the second century A.D. Most of the scrolls and fragments are made of animal skins, but some are of papyrus. One papyrus found at Murabba'at may have been written before the Babylonian Exile. Various kinds of script are represented in these manuscripts, and they are very valuable for the study of ancient Hebrew and Aramaic writings.

3

HAS ARCHAEOLOGY FOUND EVIDENCE OF THE FLOOD?

JOHN BRIGHT

There is surely no one down to the smallest tot in the Sunday School who has not heard the story of Noah and the Great Flood. It is a story, simply yet boldly delineated, such as lays hold on the fancy, a story such as children delight to hear. Most of us heard it first as little children. But as we have grown older and have ceased in all things to be little children, few of us rest content with the mere telling of so matchless a tale or the reading of it for what it seeks to tell us. Our minds have become far too critical for that. Instead, we must ask our questions: Did such a flood actually occur? And if so, what physical causes could possibly account for it? Are there relics to be found which would prove irrefutably to the skeptical the truth of Genesis 6–9, and so of the Bible?

Archaeology, which has in so many ways supported and illustrated the Bible narrative, has naturally been asked its testimony on the question. Does archaeology in any way prove or illustrate the Flood story of Genesis? Inasmuch as some very extravagant claims have been made in recent years, not only by zealous but imaginative defenders of the Scriptures, but by men closely connected with scientific archaeology as well, some evaluation of the evidence is in order.

As a preliminary consideration we should remind ourselves that the Hebrews were by no means the only ancient people who preserved a tradition of a great Deluge. Indeed, such a story is to be found in a hundred varying forms in countries as far separated as Greece, Mesopotamia, India, Malaya, Polynesia, and the Western Hemisphere—where it is diffused from Tierra del Fuego (islands off the southern tip of South America) to the Arctic Circle. (A useful compilation of these stories is in Frazer's *Folklore in the Old Testament* [1923], pp. 46–143.) No two of these accounts are alike in detail, and most of them bear but the faintest resemblance to Genesis 6–9. Yet common to most of them is the recollection of a great flood which in the ancient past covered all, or a great part of, the earth, and in which all but a select few were drowned. These few, it may be added, usually escaped in a boat or by taking refuge on a high mountain or in a tree. While some of the stories are no doubt exaggerations of local catastrophes such as pluvial inundations, tidal waves and the like, and others perhaps false inferences from such phenomena as marine fossils found far from the sea, it is difficult to believe that so remarkable a coincidence of outline as exists among so many of these widely separated accounts can be accounted for in this way. It is difficult to escape the conclusion that many of them are recollections of a common event, or at least are diffused from a common tradition.

Has Archaeology Found Traces of the Flood?

Of late there has been a tendency on the part of certain archaeologists to answer the question in the affirmative. Further, this tendency has unfortunately been heightened into a dogmatic and positive statement of fact: archaeology *has* proved the Flood story (so for example, Marston, *The Bible Is True* [1935], pp. 67 ff.). We shall pause at this point, therefore, to marshal the evidence. Have the excavations in ancient cities uncovered evidences of the Flood?

For the excavations in Palestine and Syria the answer is an unqualified "No." In these two countries some of the oldest towns in the world have been excavated. We now know that Jericho was founded near the beginning of the Late Stone Age. While we cannot be certain of exact dates in such an early period, we can be sure that the town was first settled between about 5000 and 4500 B.C. This city and others in Palestine established after it show no evidence whatever of a flood. In North Syria the mound of Tell ej-Judeideh (we do not know the ancient name of the city there) was first settled about 4500 B.C. in all probability. Yet its ruins and those of other towns in the same area show no evidence of a flood during the course of the subsequent five thousand years.

In Mesopotamia, however, the situation is different.

1. The evidence from Ur. Between 1922 and 1934 Sir C. Leonard Woolley directed some twelve campaigns of excavation at the site of the ancient Ur of the Chaldees in southern Mesopotamia. In 1929, in order to establish the true sequence of the levels of occupation in the mound, a section was cleared down to virgin soil. In order to understand his discoveries we must pause for a few words about the early civilizations of the country. The historical period dawns with the Early Dynastic Age which began some time after 3000 B.C. The people responsible for this cultural epoch were the Sumerians, who produced the first great literary works and through them exerted a tremendous influence on the subsequent cultural history of Western Asia. Before this period a series of distinct civilizations existed which have been named after the site where they were first identified. The Jemdet Nasr Period is the one which immediately preceded the Early Dynastic, and is to be dated just before and after 3000 B.C. Still earlier is the Uruk Period, during which writing was first invented—second half of the fourth millennium. Before that is the Obeid Period of painted pottery—probably first half to middle of the fourth millennium. In northern Syria and Mesopotamia a still earlier painted pottery culture existed (the Halaf Period) which was probably in existence about 4000 B.C. Before this time is the period known as the Neolithic or Late Stone Age when pottery was invented and when the first settled communities were established.

At Ur Woolley found a continuous occupation from the Early Dynastic back through the Obeid Period. In the middle of the Obeid level he found a stratum of river mud or deposit some ten feet thick—conclusive proof that a deluge had interrupted the occupation of the place, at least temporarily, during the fourth millennium. Woolley is confident that he has here the evidence of Noah's flood (see, for example, his *Ur of the Chaldees* [1929], p. 29) and his assurance is enthusiastically shared by most of the popular handbooks which deal with the subject.[1]

2. The evidence from Kish. The excavations conducted at this site between 1923 and 1932 also yielded evidence of inundation. But the flood level here lies well within the Early Dynastic Period; that is, considerably later than 3000 B.C. and many centuries later than the Ur flood deposit. The two cannot refer, therefore, to the same catastrophe (see Watelin and Langdon, *Excavations at Kish*, Vol. IV, pp. 40 ff.).

3. The evidence from Fara. During the excavations at this site in 1931 a sterile, alluvial layer some two feet thick was found between the Jemdet Nasr and Early Dynastic layers—thus indicating an inundation at the site which was earlier than the one at Kish and yet much later than the one at Ur (see Schmidt, *Museum Journal*, XXII, 193 ff.).

4. The evidence from Nineveh. The English archaeologist, M. E. L. Mallowan (whose wife, incidentally, is Agatha Christie) describes an alluvial level or levels found at Nineveh during the course of excavations in 1931–32. It is some six or seven feet thick and is composed of thirteen alternating layers of mud and river sand. This interruption in the occupation lies between levels 2 and 3 at the site. Level 2 ends in the Halaf Period, while level 3 is mostly Uruk Period, though it may

---

[1] Woolley seems to have dug some five pits in all down through the early strata of occupation at Ur, but in only two of them did he find evidence of the flood. The logical inference from such a situation is that the flood in question simply did not cover the whole city of Ur, but only a part of it. Dr. Ann Perkins of Yale University, an expert in the early archaeological history of Mesopotamia, in calling my attention to this fact, also pointed to two different series of tombs which the people of Ur had dug in the flood stratum. One would naturally think that these tombs were dug after the flood was over, but Dr. Perkins has collected evidence to indicate that this is by no means entirely certain, and that the earlier series of tombs may have been dug by people who lived elsewhere on the site during a temporary cessation of the flood. It is impossible here to present all the evidence for this conclusion. What is of most importance to us is the fact that the flood apparently did not cover the whole site at Ur, and that therefore its importance as a historical catastrophe has been vastly overemphasized by the excavator for reasons which are unfortunately all too obvious.—Editor.

have covered the Obeid Period in part (see *Liverpool Annals of Archaeology and Anthropology*, XX, 134 and pl. 73). A precise determination of the date of this flood level is impossible, though it may not be far removed in time from the Ur level.

Do any of these levels represent the Flood of Genesis 6–9? It would appear that the answer must be made in the negative. There are several reasons for this. (1) No two of the inundation levels as yet discovered can be dated in the same period (unless it be those at Ur and Nineveh, and even this is far from certain). (2) Further, all seem to be inundations of a purely local character. Sites nearby show no evidence of flooding at all. For example, Woolley's own excavations at el-Obeid, only four miles from Ur, showed no flood level at all, nor did the great tell of Uruk or Warka (ancient Erech) some forty miles upstream and on the opposite side of the Euphrates. The latter site, excavated by a German organization in ten campaigns between 1928 and 1938, exhibited continuous strata from the Obeid Period through the Early Dynastic without break. (3) It should also be noted that at Ur, at least, the levels both before and after the flood level were of the same general civilization. In other words there is no such break in the continuity of culture as would occur if a deluge of giant proportions wiped out an entire population. The Mesopotamian flood strata, then, represent purely local inundations of the type which still occur when the Euphrates river bursts its banks.

We are at least able to conclude, then, that either Mesopotamian archaeology has yielded no trace of Noah's Flood, or else the Genesis narrative is but an exaggeration of a flood of purely local significance. But this latter alternative is difficult to hold in the light of the wide diffusion of the Flood tradition. Unless we are to explain the remarkable similarity between Flood stories from lands as far removed from one another as India and America on the basis of pure coincidence, some diffusion of tradition from a common original, or originals, must be assumed. But the proposal to date the Flood in the 4th millennium makes it impossible for us to account for such a diffusion. It seems to be the consensus that the early settlement of the Western Hemisphere was via the Bering Strait and took place over a long period of time at least as early as the Late Stone Age in Asia (before 5000 B.C.) and probably even earlier. Thus to date the Flood in the 4th millennium is to make it too recent by thousands of years to account for such a process of dissemination.

This concludes the actual archaeological evidence bearing on the Flood. There is perhaps little use in discussing various stories that have received currency from time to time to the effect that the Ark itself has been found. A recent one, asserting that the Ark was seen resting on a shoulder of Mt. Ararat by Russian aviators in World War I, and subsequently examined and described by an expedition sent out by the Czar (unfortunately the Revolution destroyed the records), has achieved wide circulation. It has been published in *Defender of the Faith,* Oct. 1942 (Intercession City, Fla.); in *The King's Herald,* Nov. 1941 (Springfield, Mo.); in *Prophecy,* Mar. 1942 (Los Angeles, Cal.); and also in tract form by the Pilgrim Tract Society, Randleman, N.C. The story is quite without foundation and, inasmuch as at least two of the above publications have printed retractions of it, it deserves no further notice. It may be regarded as a symptom of man's willingness to believe what he wishes to believe.

What then can we conclude about the Flood itself? As a matter of fact, very little. Archaeology has given us no trace of it. It would be quite profitless to speculate concerning its nature and scope, since we do not know enough, and perhaps never will. It would seem, however, that we must regard it as a catastrophe taking place far back in the Stone Age. The only alternative would be to class it as pure myth—a view to which, as one can easily see, any number of objections can be raised. We can hardly regard it merely as an exceptionally bad freshet on the Euphrates sometime in the fifth, fourth, or third millennia B.C.

Archaeology and the Antecedents of the Israelite Flood Story

If archaeology has told us nothing about the Flood itself save in a negative way, it has performed invaluable service in revealing to us more ancient Flood traditions with which the Genesis narrative stands in the closest relation. Most of the diverse traditions of a Deluge have come to us wholly independent of archaeology, collected chiefly through the labors of students of folklore and comparative religion. But our knowledge of the most important of all, the Babylonian (or more properly the Sumerian) we owe almost entirely to archaeology. This material is not new and has long been known to most students of the Bible, but some mention of it is in place here.

1. That the Babylonians had a story of the Flood similar in its details to the Genesis story has been known since ancient times through the writings of Berossus. Berossus was a Babylonian of the third century B.C. who composed a history of his own country on the basis of records and traditions at his disposal. Although his actual work has not survived, fragments of it have been quoted in the writings of later Greek historians. Among these fragments is the Babylonian story of the Flood, in which the adventures of the hero, Xisuthrus, are closely parallel to those of the biblical Noah.

2. It was not, however, until the English excavators at Nineveh in 1853 stumbled upon what turned out to be the palace and library of Ashurbanipal (king of Assyria in the seventh century B.C.) that an ancient version of the story was found. Among the many thousands of tablets of every description there was the Gilgamesh Epic, a long poem in twelve tablets, one of which was the Babylonian story of the Deluge. The discovery of this tablet was first announced by George Smith in 1872 and created unprecedented excitement in the scholarly and religious world.

This story bears the closest resemblance, albeit with numerous differences in detail, to Genesis 6–9. The hero, Utnapishtim, is secretly warned by the God Ea of the purpose of the other gods, particularly Enlil, to send a flood, and is told to build a ship. This he does, daubing it inside and out with bitumen, stocking it with provisions and bringing all his possessions and family, together with the animals and skilled craftsmen, into it. A tempest ensues for seven days, at the end of which time nothing but water can be seen. After twelve days the Ark grounds upon a mountain. Ut-napishtim sends out first a dove, then a swallow, but both return. Then he sends a raven which does not return inasmuch as the water has receded. Leaving the Ark the Babylonian Noah makes a sacrifice of a sweet savor to delight the gods who hover like flies over it. They vow that there shall never again be such a flood, and Ut-napishtim is taken away to live as one of them. Another fragment of the same story, also found at Nineveh, differs in that the hero is called Atrakhasis.[2]

3. The account above presumably dates from the reign of Ashurbanipal (668–633 B.C.) and is thus considerably later than the oldest Hebrew version of the same narrative. But by the end of the last century the discovery of bits of several older versions had forced the conclusion that the text in Ashurbanipal's library was but a copy of much more ancient originals. As early as 1894, the excavations sponsored by the Turkish government under the direction of Père Scheil at Abu Habbah (ancient Sippar) had brought to light a mutilated version of the Flood story, dated by a colophon in the eleventh year of King Ammizaduga—thus in the middle of the first half of the second millennium B.C.

That the story really rests on yet more ancient Sumerian traditions dating back at least to the third millennium B.C. was definitely shown by the excavations at Nippur between 1889 and 1900. Among the 20,000 tablets of all descriptions found there by the American archaeologists, there was one—published by A. Poebel in 1914—which was definitely a Sumerian version of the same Deluge story. Written in Sumerian, much briefer than the one from Ashurbanipal's library, and sadly mutilated, it none the less bears unmistakable likeness to the previously known story of Ut-napishtim. The hero here is called Ziusudra.

To compare the above stories with Genesis in further detail would be tedious. The reader can do so for himself. It is quite clear that the Hebrew story is derived directly or indirectly from the ancient Sumerian. This does not mean, of course, that the Hebrews copied the Mesopotamian story during the period when they were in Exile—as some have maintained in the past—for the Genesis story in its oldest form is centuries older than the Exile. How then did the Hebrews in Palestine get their Flood tradition? Two alternates present

[2] The reader will find handy translations of the various Babylonian flood stories in *ANET*, pp. 42–44, 93–97, 104–6.

themselves. (1) They learned it from the Canaanites in Palestine, who, in turn, learned it from Mesopotamia. While this view has been generally held by scholars, it is becoming increasingly difficult. We now know a great deal about the early traditions of the Canaanites, and as far as we now know they had no tradition anything like this. (2) The second alternative now appears increasingly more probable—the ancestors of the Hebrews in Palestine brought the story with them when they migrated from Mesopotamia in the Patriarchal Age.

The story in Genesis 6-9 is thus but one among many, and is clearly related to yet older traditions. But the most significant thing about it is not its historical antecedents or its archaeological basis. Its actual significance lies in its religious outlook. In Genesis the Flood is not caused by mere chance or the whim of capricious, brawling gods. It is brought about by the One God in whose hands even natural catastrophe is a means of moral judgment. In the biblical story alone is a relation between the Flood and the moral order of our world clearly drawn. To the Israelite writers the telling of the story has become an opportunity of demonstrating and illustrating the righteousness of God. In other words, they have purged it of the base theology that pervades the Babylonian and other stories, and have made it a fit vehicle for the monotheistic and ethical demands of Israelite religion.

4

SODOM AND GOMORRAH

J. PENROSE HARLAND

I. THE LOCATION OF THE CITIES OF THE PLAIN*

Few stories in the Bible are better known than that about the destruction of the "Cities of the Plain" and the transformation of Lot's wife into a pillar of salt. Often has the fate of Sodom and Gomorrah been held up as a warning of what the Lord has done in the past and can do in the future to punish the wrongdoer. Even P. G. Wodehouse, the humorist (who incidentally knows his Bible well), compares the feelings of one of his characters to that of the inhabitants of the "Cities of the Plain" when they became aware of the impending doom. The very expression "fire and brimstone" is familiar to most people and to many connotes the terrible fate of the inhabitants of the cities—despite the fact that the supposedly well-known passage in the Bible (Gen. 19:24) reads "brimstone and fire."

And yet, in spite of the fame—or ill-fame—of these cities no one has yet discovered the remains of those destroyed, or of the fifth, Zoar, which was spared. Of course, there have been surmises as to their location, but so far no actual remains of Sodom, Gomorrah, Admah, Zeboiim, and Zoar have been brought to light. Almost all agree that the Cities of the Plain

* In the text and notes only the author's name will be mentioned unless more than one work of an author has been used. For full citations of the works mentioned see the Bibliography at the end of the article.

were located in the *Ghor* or Valley of the Jordan. It is to be
noted that this designation embraces not only the Jordan valley proper but also the Dead Sea and the bordering land in
this mountain-hemmed region. The five cities are referred to
as the "Cities of the Plain" in Genesis 13:12. In the apocryphal
Book of Wisdom (10:6) the cities are grouped under the
name *Pentapolis,* the Greek word for (a group of) Five Cities.
The usual term in the Bible for what we call the Dead Sea
is the Salt Sea. It is said that the name "Dead Sea" first appears in the works of Jerome in the fifth century A.D. It is
interesting to note that the Arabic name for this body of water
is *Bahr Lut:* that is, the "Sea of Lot."

One would do well to read about this region which is quite
unique and probably not duplicated anywhere else in the
world. The long, narrow, canyon-like depression or rift was
brought about in a remote geological age by a great fault or
fracture in the earth's crust with a sinking or displacement on
one side of the fracture. This great rift runs from Syria southward along the Jordan and the Dead Sea, down through the
Arabah to the Gulf of Akabah (the eastern arm of the Red
Sea); it continues on through the Red Sea across to the upper
Nile valley and on into southern Africa.

The Jordan river, starting from its source at an altitude of
several hundred feet, rapidly descends as it erodes its way
southward in and along this rift. As it enters the Sea of Galilee
it is about 696 feet below sea level, and, winding its 200-mile
course as it traverses the sixty-five miles southward, it empties
into the Dead Sea at 1290 feet below sea level. The Dead
Sea, therefore, is nearly 1300 feet below the level of the Mediterranean, less than sixty miles away. But still more striking is
the difference in altitude between the shore of the Dead Sea
and the mountains which tower on either side. Jerusalem is
about 3700 feet higher than the Dead Sea, and some of the
western wall of mountains are 4000 feet higher. On the east
side, the mountains of Moab tower to even a greater height,
about 4400 feet above the shore. This disparity in height is
the more noticeable because the Dead Sea itself, about forty-
seven and a half miles long, averages only ten miles in width
and the mountain wall on either side is quite steep. It has

been said that no locality on the earth can parallel the geographical setting and geological character of this region.

Our lack of definite knowledge as to the exact location of the Cities of the Plain is not due to any lack of investigation of the problem. Books and articles, both of scientific and popular character, have been written on the subject. The studies of Dr. W. F. Albright, of Dr. Nelson Glueck, and of the consulting geologist, Mr. Frederick G. Clapp—to name a few American works—have done much toward the elucidation of the problem. One is tempted to call it a mystery-story—this search for the answer to the questions: Where were Sodom and Gomorrah? How were they destroyed?

There is practically general agreement that the Cities of the Plain are to be found in the *Ghor*, or Valley of the Jordan and the Dead Sea. The evidence is preponderantly in favor of a location at the southern end of the Dead Sea. However, some have recently held that the remains of Sodom and Gomorrah are to be sought at the north end of the Sea, that is, in the southern part of the Jordan valley proper. Less than ten years ago, a report appeared in the papers that a French scholar had discovered ancient Sodom in the Jordan valley, just north of the Dead Sea. One might cite other writers with similar opinions. Hence it may be worthwhile and of interest to review the evidence from literature, archaeology, and geology, together with the results of topographical or geographical investigations in this area. As will become readily apparent, the biblical scholar must supplement his study of the Bible with evidence from other fields in order to arrive at a solution of the mystery of the disappearance of Sodom and Gomorrah.

Evidence from the Bible

In Genesis 13, we have the story of an episode which has occurred hundreds of times among the nomadic and semi-nomadic tribes in the Near East before and since the time of Abraham. The herdsmen of the latter and those of Lot had been continually fighting with each other, doubtless over pasture land and watering places. There are indications in the Old Testament that such quarrels were not uncommon. Abraham, being the elder as well as the more generous, suggested

that they make a division of the land and he offered first choice
to his nephew Lot.

Standing on a height near Bethel, Lot looked to the east
(and southeast) and "beheld all the Plain (*kikkar*) of Jordan,
that it was well watered everywhere (this was before the Lord
destroyed Sodom and Gomorrah) even as the garden of the
Lord, like the land of Egypt, as thou comest unto Zoar"
(13:10). The Hebrew word *kikkar,* translated "all the Plain"
(American Translation, "the whole basin"), really embraces
the lower, broader part of the Jordan valley and the entire
basin of the Dead Sea. In other words, Lot looked across to
the Jordan-Dead Sea valley and observed that it was well watered and fertile like the famed Garden of Eden or, to use
another comparison, like the land of Egypt; and this fertile
land extended all the way to Zoar.

So Abraham accepted the less fertile, but more stable and
permanent Palestine, eventually settling at Hebron. Lot, on
the other hand, "journeyed east . . . and dwelt in the cities of
the plain and moved his tent as far as Sodom" (13:11–12).

In an earlier chapter of Genesis the land of Canaan is at
least partially delimited or bounded for us: ". . . the territory
of the Canaanites extended from Sidon in the direction of
Gerar, as far as Gaza, and in the direction of Sodom, Gomorrah, Admah, and Zeboiim, as far as Lasha" (10:19). The site
of Lasha is unknown, but nevertheless this passage seems to
favor a location at the southern end of the Dead Sea for the
cities in question. If the writer had had the northern end of
the Sea in mind, one would expect that he would have mentioned Hebron or Jerusalem or both in mapping out this southern boundary line. But with the Cities at the southern end of
the *Ghor,* the line from Gaza to Sodom would be a natural one.

The third piece of evidence for locating the site of the Cities
of the Plain is to be found in that interesting chapter, Genesis
14, which tells of the invasion from the north of four kings,
Amraphel of Shinar, Arioch of Ellasar, Chedorlaomer of Elam,
and Tidal king of Goiim. They "made war with Bera king of
Sodom, and with Birsha king of Gomorrah, Shinab king of
Admah, and Shemeber king of Zeboiim, and the king of Bela
(the same is Zoar). All these joined together in the vale of
Siddim (the same is the Salt Sea)" (14:1–3). As only the

fifth king is not named, it has been suggested that the last line should read "Bela king of Zoar." Defeated, the Five Cities were held in subjection for twelve years and then in the thirteenth year rebelled. The next year the "Eastern Kings," led by Chedorlaomer, returned by the "way of the kings"—a Transjordanian route with a line of settlements which has been discovered by Albright and Glueck—and seem to have gone on past the Dead Sea, possibly as far as the Gulf of Akabah. On their way northward, they met and defeated the five kings and sacked their cities. There may be reason to believe that this war or raid took place before 1800, perhaps around 2000 B.C.

The battle was fought in the "vale of Siddim" which was "full of slime pits" or, as the American Translation has it, "full of bitumen wells" (14:10). The word for slime here is the same as that used in the description of the Tower of Babel which was built of bricks with "slime for mortar" (11:4), and it is well known that bitumen was quite generally used as mortar in early Babylonia. Now bitumen (or asphalt as it is called by the Greek writers) has been found in considerable quantities—in the form of large masses, small flakes, and as mud —on and around the Dead Sea, especially around the *southern* part of the Sea. To this fact both ancient writers and modern travelers bear witness.

In Genesis 19:20-23 Lot escapes from the threatened Sodom to Zoar and eventually becomes the "father" or founder of the nation of Moab. We shall return later to the location of Zoar, but, from the fact that Lot is closely associated with Moab (more than with Ammon), one would expect to find this city located near Moab and hence near the southern half of the Dead Sea. In this connection, it may be of interest to note a remark of Abel (pp. 467–68) that Stephen of Byzantion locates Engaddi (Engedi about the center of the west side of the Dead Sea) near *Sodom of Arabia* and that among the bishops present at the Council of Nicea in A.D. 325 was one Severos, bishop of Sodom. This title, Abel continues, does not appear after this date and had probably been taken by the bishop of Zoara whom one meets in 381. It seems hard to believe that there could have been a Sodom in A.D. 325 and that any bishop should have wished such a title. Zoar, how-

ever, was not destroyed according to biblical tradition and the
survival of the name in this southeastern part of the Dead
Sea valley in conjunction with the remains of successive towns
around the present mouth of the el-Qurahi may be of value
in this investigation.

A final passage which should be noted is Genesis 19:28.
Abraham, on the morning after the catastrophe, looked toward
Sodom and Gomorrah and saw the smoke of the land going
up "as the smoke of a furnace." If there is any historicity in
this narrative (that the smoke of the conflagration was visible
to people at Hebron), a southern rather than a northern location of the cities seems preferable, though not necessarily
required.

Evidence from Greek and Latin Writers

Diodoros, the Sicilian, a late Greek historian of the first century B.C., mentions a large lake in the land of the Nabataeans
(which is, of course, the Dead Sea), and proceeds to describe
it.[1] In particular, he writes of the great masses of asphalt
which are spouted forth from the sea and which float upon
the surface of the water. This reminds one of the valley of
"slime pits" and of the fact that in modern times it is the southern part of the Dead Sea that yields pieces of bitumen or
asphalt.

Of more value is the Greek geographer, Strabo (63 B.C.–
A.D. 19), who mentions the city of Sodom. He devotes considerable space to the Dead Sea and discusses at length the
bitumen which is found on and around it, commenting on the
uses of this substance. After referring to the scorched rock
around Moasada (probably Masada on the west side opposite
Lisan), and the pitch, hot waters, sulphur, and bitumen which
he had noted, he states that according to the people, "there
were once thirteen inhabited cities in that region of which
Sodom was the metropolis."[2] It appears from the context that
Strabo had in mind a southern location for the Cities of the
Plain.

Josephus, the Jewish historian (born A.D. 37), mentions the

[1] Diodoros II. 48. 6–9; XIX. 98.
[2] Strabo XVI. 2. 44.

land and city of Sodom in both his *Jewish War* and *Antiquities of the Jewish People*. Josephus calls the Dead Sea by the name "Lake Asphaltitis," obviously because of the quantity of asphalt which it casts up in black masses. These great lumps of asphalt or bitumen, which float upon the surface, are likened in their shape to headless bulls. That Josephus localized Sodom at the southern end of the Dead Sea is clear from his description of the mountain range which extends southward from Jericho "as far as the country of the Sodomites and the extremities of the Lake Asphaltitis."[3] We shall see also that his account of the pillar of salt into which Lot's wife was transformed indicates his belief in the southern location of Sodom.

Tacitus, the Roman historian (*ca.* A.D. 50–117), mentions the Dead Sea ("Lake") and its habit of throwing up to the surface the bitumen collected by the natives. A plain, not far from this lake, he says, was once fertile and the site of great cities.[4] It seems from the context that the plain and the gathering of the bitumen—and hence the Cities of the Plain—were in his mind located at the southern end of the great *Ghor* or valley of the Dead Sea.

In summary, one may conclude that the evidence from the Bible and from the late Greek and Latin writers indicates a location around the southern end of the Sea. And this localization is supported by other evidence derived from geology, hydrography (study of water supply), and from both positive and negative results of archaeological investigations.

The Pillar of Salt

Disobeying the Lord's injunction, "Fly for your life! do not look behind you, nor stop anywhere in the valley!," Lot's wife could not resist the temptation to turn around to see the "fireworks" (the word which almost literally describes the scene—Gen. 19:17, 24). She looked back and "became a pillar of salt" (19:26). This expression is probably even more familiar to the average person than the "fire and brimstone" or the names of the two chief cities which were destroyed.

Assuming that the site of Sodom is unknown, the Old Testa-

[3] *Jewish War* IV. 479. 453.
[4] Tacitus *Histories* V. vi–vii.

ment does not localize the Pillar of Salt for us. But later writers
of antiquity and modern travelers and explorers are almost
unanimous in associating this legend with the one and only
great, conspicuous salt-mass in the Jordan-Dead Sea valley:
namely Jebel Usdum (Arabic meaning "mountain of Sodom"),
the low mountain flanking the southern end of the west side
of the Dead Sea.

Our first reference to the existence of an actual pillar of salt
is found in Josephus who recounts the story of the destruction
of Sodom and of the transformation of Lot's wife into a *stele*
or pillar of salt. Josephus adds, "And I have observed it for it
still remains even to this day."[5]

Irenaeus, Bishop of Lyons, writing in the second century
(*ca.* A.D. 130–202), likewise tells of Lot's escape and of Lot's
wife remaining "a pillar of salt unto this day . . . no longer
corruptible flesh, but a pillar of salt which endures forever."[6]
And a later poem, *Sodoma,* preserved by Tertullian and Cyprian, relates both the indestructible character of the pillar and
its ability to heal or repair itself, should any damage to it
occur.

Modern writers have recorded the existence of a pillar of
salt on the east face of Jebel Usdum. Lieut. W. F. Lynch
(U. S. Navy), who led the United States' Expedition to the
River Jordan and the Dead Sea, visited this region in April of
1848. As their boat comes off the north end of this Jebel Usdum, he writes (pp. 307–8):

> Soon after, to our astonishment, we saw on the east-
> ern side of Usdum, one third the distance from its north
> extreme, a lofty, round pillar, standing apparently de-
> tached from the general mass, at the head of a deep, nar-
> row, and abrupt chasm. We immediately pulled in for
> the shore, and . . . went up and examined it. The beach
> was a soft, slimy mud encrusted with salt, and a short
> distance from the water, covered with saline fragments
> and flakes of bitumen. We found the pillar to be of solid

[5] *Antiquities of the Jewish People* I. xl. 4. For a similar reference
from the same century, see Clement of Rome *Epistle to the Korin-
thians* I. xi.
[6] Irenaeus *Against Heresies* IV. xxxi. 1–3.

*salt, capped with carbonate of lime, cylindrical in front
and pyramidal behind. The upper or rounded part is
about forty feet high, resting on a kind of oval pedestal,
from forty to sixty feet above the level of the sea. It
slightly decreases in size upwards, crumbles at the top,
and is one entire mass of crystallization. A prop, or but-
tress, connects it with the mountain behind, and the whole
is covered with debris of a light stone colour. Its peculiar
shape is doubtless attributable to the action of winter
rains. The Arabs had told us in vague terms that there
was to be found a pillar somewhere upon the shores of
the sea.*

The diary of one of the party who accompanied Lieutenant
Lynch was edited by Edward P. Montague and published in
1849. Although the salt pillar was seen on the same day, the
writer of this diary gives different dimensions and Montague
proves himself, not more pious, but less scholarly than Lynch.

*On pulling round the shores of the sea, we saw an im-
mense column, rounded and turret-shaped, facing toward
the southeast. This, we were told by our Arabs, was the
Pillar of Salt, in which Lot's wife was encased at the
overthrow of Sodom . . . It was measured, and found to
be sixty feet in height, and forty-five feet in circumfer-
ence. We cannot suppose that Lot's wife was a person so
large that her dimensions equalled those of this column*
(p. 200).

Montague seems to think that Lot's wife actually formed
the core of the pinnacle of crystalline salt which the keeper
of the diary saw. On page 202 he writes:

*My own opinion on the matter is, that Lot's wife having
lingered behind in disobedience to the express command
of God . . . became overwhelmed in the descending fluid,
and formed the model or foundation for this extraordinary
column. If it be produced by common, by natural causes,
it is but right to suppose that others might be found of a
similar description. One is scarcely able to abandon the*

*idea that it stands here as a lasting memorial of God's
punishing a most deliberate act of disobedience . . .*[7]

Concerning Montague's remarks one may note that there is
not even legendary evidence that the salt came from above
and that Lot's wife was "overwhelmed in the descending
fluid." B. K. N. Wyllie, a geologist with the Anglo-Persian Oil
Company, states that the "salt has reached its present position
by intrusion. It has pierced, buckled and raised the sediments
of the earlier Dead Sea" (p. 366). The salt originated in the
remote geologic past (possibly in the Mesozoic or even Palae-
ozoic era) and reached its present position by intrusion as a
semi-fluid. This great salt mass came from below, not from
above.

Secondly, as regards Montague's intimation that the pillar
of salt, seen by his informant on April 26, 1848, was the same
as that which formed about Lot's wife and which was seen
by Josephus, let us quote from that excellent article by the
geologist, Mr. Frederick G. Clapp (p. 332): ". . . it seems
improbable, to judge by the column's geologic position and
its form, that only a single pillar existed approximately for 4000
years on a precipitous hillside in an earthquake region. It is
more likely that sometimes one mass, sometimes another, was
called 'Lot's wife' during intervening millennia."

This interesting geologic structure, Jebel Usdum or Mount
of Sodom, is described by Clapp as a hill, 5 miles long (North
to South), 3 miles wide, and rising 742 feet above water level,
though its top is still 550 feet below sea level. The mountain
is not composed entirely of salt, but is a pure compact crystalline salt mass about 100 feet thick. Above this salt stratum
are marly and clayey (gypseo-argillaceous) strata, topped
with limestone cap-rock. The salt of the lowest 100-foot stratum is deeply eroded, caverned and creviced, which explains
why there has always been a pinnacle to equate with the
famed Pillar of Salt of Genesis.

[7] About twenty years later another traveler, with more imagination, writes: "Suddenly we saw before us among the pinnacles of
salt a gigantic 'Lot,' with a daughter on each arm hurrying off in a
south-westerly direction, with their bodies bent forward as though
they were in great haste, and their flowing garments trailing behind." (*Quart. State.* of the Pal. Explor. Fund [1870], p. 150.)

Since biblical and Mohammedan traditions have associated Jebel Usdum with the destruction of Sodom and with Lot's wife, it would seem that the ancient city was situated in this southern part of the Dead Sea. The folk tale of the transformation of Lot's wife may be connected with a historical event and with a general locality.

Water Supply

The site chosen for a settlement has always been conditioned by the availability of water. Before the days of aqueducts almost every town was located in the vicinity of a spring or a stream. The first settlers doubtless gave as much thought to the problem of getting drinking water for the people and their livestock as to the matter of defense. Hence, if we are to look for the Cities of the Plain in the southern end of the Dead Sea valley, we must find an area that is well watered or that gives signs of having had in the past a good supply of water. Furthermore, there is the tradition that the region of the Five Cities was a fertile and well-watered one (Gen. 13:10).

Because nothing can live in the Dead Sea the prevalent idea is that the land around it in the deep *Ghor* is barren and desert. However, the reports of Albright and Glueck (see Bibliography) show that even today there are fertile fields and orchards in the southeast corner of the valley; that is, along the east shore of the Dead Sea south of the Lisan. According to them and other travelers, the land was even more fertile when attention was given to irrigation. In the Byzantine and Mediaeval period, an organized government kept the irrigation system in good repair and in the southern part of this region there were plantations of sugar and indigo. The Rev. Melvin G. Kyle, who accompanied Albright in the explorations of 1924, describes the luxuriant gardens and orchards through which he passed between Lisan and the southern end of the Dead Sea. These are the results of three streams that pour down from the mountains of Moab and from the little irrigation ditches dug and maintained by some of the Bedouin inhabitants of this region. "Despite the saltiness of the Sea, the whole valley is thus well watered" (p. 83). And he quotes from Tristram's *Land of Israel:* "It was, in fact, a reproduction of the oasis of Jericho, in a far more tropical climate, and with yet more lavish supply of water . . . For three miles we rode through these rich groves, reveling in the tropical verdure and swarming ornithology of its labyrinths."

Albright mentions five streams which flow into the south end of the Dead Sea and form oases in this southeast area of the *Ghor*, but gives particular attention to three: the streams named 'Esal, en-Numeirah, and el-Qurahi. Incidentally, Albright is of the opinion that this area was more fertile and rich in the centuries immediately before and after 2000 B.C. than later, when little attention was paid to water conservation. The prosperity of that period was not equaled until the Middle Ages.

Thus we have a satisfactory site for the Cities of the Plain, but as yet no trace of early habitation. Byzantine, Crusader, and Arab had left their traces in this southeastern area, but not the ancient Canaanite.

Evidence from Archaeology

An interesting discovery and the subsequent investigation by Albright, however, has thrown light on the question. This was the discovery of the site of Bab edh-Dhra' to the east of the Lisan and about 500 feet above the shore of the Dead Sea. It lies on the road which led eastward up to Kerak and seems to be about five miles distant from the present shore line of the Dead Sea.[8]

At Bab edh-Dhra' were found a cemetery and "a great fortress, an extensive open-air settlement with enclosures and hearths, as well as a group of fallen monoliths." The wall of the fortress is built of large field stones and averages 12 feet in thickness and 15 feet in height. Adjoining this fortified stronghold, especially on the south, are the remains of an extensive settlement containing the foundations of round and square enclosures, identified as individual family huts. In each were found a hearth and various stone artifacts, loom weights, millstones, etc. Several minutes' walk east of the fortified camp were the fallen monoliths which were of a stone foreign to this vicinity. They were undoubtedly *maṣṣēbôt* or sacred cult

[8] Albright, *BASOR*, No. 14, pp. 5–7; *AASOR*, VI, 58–62.

pillars "at which the religious rites of the community of Bab edh-Dhra' were performed."

This site was occupied for a considerable time, but the absence of debris shows that it was not continuously inhabited. Albright believes that it "was a place of pilgrimage, where annual feasts were celebrated, and to which people came, living in booths and merrymaking for several days of the year." It was a primitive *gilgal* and the festival was probably in the spring or fall. As to the provenance of the people who came here for a spring or a harvest festival, there can be little doubt that their homes were below, in the valley of the Dead Sea. It would be highly probable that the people from the hot valley would go up to a cooler place, above their home district, and would want also to have protection against the nomads of the Moabite mountains.

The pottery that has been found at Bab edh-Dhra' has been dated in the period *ca.* 2300–1900 B.C. Wright believes that "the end of the first occupation of Moab and Edom can scarcely be placed later than the twentieth century." He adds: "To judge from Glueck's explorations and Albright's work at Bab edh-Dhra' and Ader, sedentary culture did come to an end for one reason or another about the twentieth century."[9]

Thus we have evidence at Bab edh-Dhra' for a people living around 2000 B.C., but archaeology has produced no home-sites for them. By now, however, the reader has been impatient to sail out over the southern part of the Dead Sea in order to look beneath the water for the remains of four of the five Cities of the Plain. For we have seen that all the evidence—from the Bible, the late Greek and Roman writers, from geology and topography, from hydrography and archaeology—has been pointing to the southern embayment (Clapp's term for the part of the Dead Sea south of the Lisan) as the site of Sodom and Gomorrah.

In the light of all the foregoing evidence, two passages become the more significant. In Genesis 14:3, the vale (valley) of Siddim is mentioned as the plain where the Five Cities were located or on which they bordered. Then follows the parenthetical notation "which is the salt sea" or "the same is the

[9] Wright, *BASOR*, No. 71, p. 34; *Pottery of Palestine . . .* , pp. 79 ff.; Glueck, *The Other Side of the Jordan*, p. 114.

Salt Sea," or, as the American Translation has it, "that is, the Salt Sea." In other words, the plain where the four eastern kings defeated the kings of the Cities of the Plain and which was full of "slime pits" (Gen. 14:10), is now submerged under the waters of the Dead Sea.

The same clue is given by Josephus who states that the invaders encamped in the "valley called the Wells of Asphalt; for at that time there were wells in that district, but now that the city of Sodom has disappeared the valley has become a lake, the so-called Asphaltitis" (*Antiquities* I. ix. 174).

The problem is: how account for the submersion of Sodom and Gomorrah under the waters of the Dead Sea?

The Rise in Water Level

There is ample evidence that the Dead Sea has been rising in height of water level and expanding. Lynch in April of 1848 at the mouth of the Jordan saw "one large and two small islands at the mouth of the river; the islands of mud six to eight feet high . . ." (p. 267). Albright may have in mind one of these islands when he writes: "the famous island at the northern end of the Dead Sea, Rujm el-Bahr, has been submerged since 1892." This was the "beautiful island at the north end of the Sea" which Kyle had seen in 1892. Yet in 1924 he passed over that same island in a motor boat in several feet of water.[10]

About 1850 De Saulcy noted that the space between the base of Jebel Usdum and the Dead Sea varied from about 260 to 750 feet; yet according to Albright, the road along here "has been under water since the early nineties, and has long since been absolutely unfordable." Furthermore, this embayment south of the Lisan is quite shallow as compared with the depth of the Dead Sea to the north of Lisan. This is shown clearly on the "Sketch Map of Dead Sea Area Showing Soundings" on page 328 of Clapp's article. The greater portion of the northern part of the Sea is 500 feet deep and almost half of the area has a depth of 1000 feet or more; in one place the sounding reads 188 fathoms or 1128 feet, nearly a half mile below the shore of the Mediterranean Sea only 55 miles away! But soundings taken in the southern embayment re-

[10] Albright, *AASOR*, VI, 54–55; Kyle, p. 135.

vealed only once a depth of 2½ fathoms (15 feet) and for the most part a maximum of 12 feet.

The soundings taken by Lynch in 1848 give a maximum of 18 feet at one point for the area between the south (southwest) tip of Lisan and the west shore just opposite. Farther to the south, at the widest part of the embayment, the depths ran from 7½ to 13½ feet; opposite Jebel Usdum's northern end the depth never exceeded 9 feet and the Sea became progressively shallower as one went south or approached the east and west shores. In fact, Lynch's small boat could not come within 200 yards of the shore of the Pillar of Salt and at the south end of the Sea the men had to wade the last 300 yards because of the shallowness of the water here.

Perhaps the most striking indication that the level of the Dead Sea has been steadily rising is the appearance of dead trees, partially submerged, which are to be seen around the shores of this southern embayment. In 1848 Lynch noted the standing and prostrate dead trees near the base of the cliffs of the Lisan. Kyle comments at some length on the fringe of submerged trees around the lower part of the Dead Sea: "There were trees little and big, from mere saplings to trees a foot in diameter. It was a ghost of a forest once living and green, now dead and blasted a ghostly white by the salt. In places the submerged forest was seen to extend out a mile from the shore on the eastern side and somewhat less from the western side of this narrow arm of the Sea at the southern end" (p. 64). Albright writes: ". . . in the Ghor es-Safi many square miles of former tamarisk groves are now under water, and the naked boughs project in the most uncanny way from the waters of death."

An authority has maintained, not later than 1924, that "the southern basin is fully a third larger than it was a century ago."[11] That the Dead Sea has expanded southwards in the past century is shown clearly by a comparison of the chart made by Lynch in 1848 with the sketch map drawn by Clapp as a result of his investigations in 1929 or 1934.[12] In Lynch's time the Jebel Usdum projected farther south than the lower end of the Dead Sea. But when Clapp visited the site some

[11] Schwöbel, quoted by Albright, loc. cit., n. 152.
[12] Clapp, Fig. 4; Lynch, Map, opposite p. 268.

eighty years later, the Sea had pushed its southern shore line seemingly a distance of about two miles below the south end of Jebel Usdum. Furthermore the rise of the Dead Sea level is definitely confirmed by measurements taken of the water level at different times within the past sixty-four years. While there is some difference in the figures given by the explorers, the annual increase has been at least 2½ to 3½ inches.[13] There does not seem to be a uniform annual rise in level, of course, for as the area increased the rise would be proportionately lessened.

Whatever the rate of the annual rise, it does seem clear that the whole southern embayment was once a plain. In the time of the Cities of the Plain, around 2000 B.C., the south end of the Dead Sea was probably somewhere between the peninsula of Lisan and the opposite side of the *Ghor*.

The Roman Road

Both archaeology and Arab tradition indicate that at some time in the past one could walk, ride, or drive from the peninsula (el-Lisan) across to what is now the west shore of the Dead Sea. In an aerial survey made with an officer of the British Flying Force, Nelson Glueck was able to trace the greater part of the old Roman road which ran from the mountain plateau of Moab through el-Moteh and Kathrabba in a northwesterly direction toward the Lisan. This road in a sense connected two great Roman highways, one of which ran through Kerak (biblical Kir) in Moab southwards to the Gulf of Akabah and the other from near the southeast corner of the Lisan southward along the east shore of the Dead Sea and the east side of the Arabah to Aila on the Gulf of Akabah.[14]

A modern road follows a good part of this Roman road and similarly the latter seems to have followed a more ancient route. Probably the invading "eastern kings" went down along part of this road system when they defeated the kings of the Cities of the Plain.

[13] Wyllie, Fig. 1; Albright, *loc. cit.* The various causes for this increase in level are here discussed.

[14] Glueck, *BASOR,* No. 67, pp. 20 and 28; *AASOR,* XVIII–XIX, 89, 97, 147.

Glueck thinks that a branch of the west road (that along the east shore of the Dead Sea) ran to the Lisan and across this peninsula to the Dead Sea; "it then probably crossed to the west side of the Dead Sea over the ford which used to be passable from the Lisan to the other side." In 1924, Kyle came upon this western Roman road and also a Roman milestone south of Lisan. He noted the branch which forked to the northwest and ran "right down the centre of the Lisan to the point where it reaches the narrow, deep gorge on the western side." This, with other evidence which cannot be discussed here, indicates that there was a Roman road across the Lisan which forded the Sea.[15]

Thus the existence of the Roman road leading to the west shore of the Lisan and also a seemingly trustworthy Arab tradition of a ford between the Lisan and the opposite side, lend further support to the theory that the present embayment south of the Lisan was a plain in ancient times.

This plain, traversed by four or five streams of fresh water for the most part from the mountains of Moab or by one river formed by the confluences of these streams, may with justification be identified with the biblical "Vale of Siddim." In this area, now under water, must be sought the remains of Sodom, Gomorrah, Admah, and Zeboiim and not far from here, therefore, should be found the site of ancient Zoar.

The Location of the Cities of the Plain

In conclusion, let us note Albright's attempt to localize the Cities of the Plain with some exactness. He believes that each stream would have supported just one town, because otherwise a town situated above another on the same stream would divert all the water for its own use. With the advance of the salt water line (and the writer would think of this happening

[15] E.g., Thomsen, p. 58. There is a tradition among the Arabs in this locality that there was once a ford there, used in the early nineteenth century, and Edward Robinson seems to have seen or heard about it in 1838. In 1848, however, Lynch made soundings there and found the water too deep for fording. Considering that the Arab tradition is supported by Robinson and the Roman road, one would hazard the guess that some disturbance had occurred in the unstable rift in the decade before 1848: so also Albright, *AASOR*, VI, 55.

long after the destruction of the Cities), the stream would be
tapped farther and farther back. Albright would locate Sodom
on the lowest course of the Seil (stream) en-Numeirah, which
flows into the Dead Sea today at approximately the center of
the east side of the embayment. Gomorrah he would place
farther north on the Seil 'Esal. This stream empties into the
Sea near the southeast corner of the Lisan. The two less familiar towns, Admah and Zeboiim, are not so definitely located
but it is suggested that they were on two other streams now
submerged.

Both Albright and Glueck would locate Zoar, which seems
from Genesis to have been nearest to Sodom, in the Ghor es-
Safi, the fertile valley at the present mouth of the Seil el-
Qurahi. The Ghor es-Safi was cultivated to a greater extent
in Byzantine and Mediaeval times than now and "supported
flourishing sugar and indigo plantations." Graves have been
found in it which can be dated by the pottery to about 2000
B.C., in the period in which the Cities of the Plain seem to
have flourished. Hence near the Byzantine Zoar in this fertile
district the Zoar of the Old Testament may be found, but,
Glueck adds, "it is probably so covered with accretions of later
ages that it will be found, if at all, only by accident."

Of course, in our present state of knowledge—or ignorance
—as to the character of the original Plain, it would be unwise
to do more than surmise that the "Vale of Siddim" was a fertile
region well watered by four or five streams. Here and there
among the gardens and orchards we may imagine seepages
of asphalt or bitumen, the "slime pits" of Genesis 14. The Cities
may have been scattered about the Plain, each on its own
stream, or situated on a main stream which would have flowed
north to the Dead Sea with whatever water had been left after
the irrigation ditches had taken their quotas. Somewhere in
this Plain was the scene of the victory of Chedorlaomer over
the kings of Sodom and Gomorrah, Admah, Zeboiim, and Zoar.

II. THE DESTRUCTION OF THE CITIES OF THE PLAIN

It has been shown that Sodom, Gomorrah, Admah, and Ze-boiim were doubtless situated in the area now covered by the waters of the southern part of the Dead Sea, and that the site of the fifth city, Zoar, is probably to be sought near the south-east corner of the Sea. This conclusion was reached from a study of the evidence from the Bible (particularly Genesis), from certain Greek and Latin writers, from the study of geology, topography, and water supply, and from both direct and indirect archaeological evidence.

This region, south of the peninsula *el-Lisan* ("the Tongue"), appears to have been a rather fertile spot, watered by four or five streams which today flow into the east side of this southern embayment of the Dead Sea. Here, too, were doubtless the "slime pits," the seepages or wells of asphalt or bitumen, which are mentioned in Genesis 14. It would seem that the Five Cities of the Plain were flourishing in the twentieth century B.C. and that about 1900 B.C. some catastrophic disaster brought an end to the traditionally wicked cities of Sodom and Gomorrah and of at least two of the other cities.

This area, the "Vale of Siddim" of Genesis 14, was subsequently submerged as the water level of the Dead Sea rose, though possibly a faulting or slipping of the rock strata, induced by an earthquake or earthquakes, may have first allowed the waters to escape from the very deep northern part of the Dead Sea into the shallow depression south of *el-Lisan*.

Of equal interest with the location is the manner of destruction of these cities. The expression "fire and brimstone" has become almost stereotyped although few think of the literal translation "sulphur and fire." The destruction has been attributed either to divine agency, or to natural causes, or to both. It must certainly be emphasized at the outset that, whatever may have caused the calamity, something surely happened at the south end of the Dead Sea which was of an extraordinary character. No ordinary conflagration occurred, but a catastrophe so great and so awful, that the memory of it remained fixed in men's minds and the story of it was passed down by word of mouth for centuries before the biblical narratives were written.

Long after the fate of the Cities of the Plain had become a part of the written tradition of the Hebrew people, the appearance of the region served as a reminder of the fearful episode. Paradoxically, the very dead and barren character of the landscape kept alive the story.

As in the case of the study of the location of the Cities, so also for an understanding of the manner of their destruction one must begin with the Book of Genesis, then consult later writers of antiquity, reports of modern travelers, and scientific studies.

The Biblical Evidence

The first reference to the destruction is the parenthetical allusion in the midst of the description of the Eden-like Plain in Genesis 13:10. The *kikkar* or basin of the Jordan-Dead Sea valley "was well watered everywhere (before the Lord destroyed Sodom and Gomorrah), like the garden of the Lord." The wickedness of Sodom is also first mentioned in this chapter and likewise in a parenthetical manner. "And Lot dwelled in the Cities of the Plain, and moved his tent as far as Sodom. Now the men of Sodom were wicked and sinners against the Lord exceedingly" (13:13).

In chapter 18, the patriarch intercedes for the lives of the innocent persons in Sodom and the Lord agrees to save the city if fifty, then forty-five, and finally if even ten good men may be found in Sodom. But, as appears in chapter 19, not even ten men could be called righteous in all of Sodom. It would seem that there was never any question of finding even one good person in Gomorrah or in the rest of the Plain. Abraham makes no plea for Gomorrah, Admah, or Zeboiim. But Zoar, which is reckoned as one of the Five Cities of the Vale of Siddim in chapter 14, seems not to have shared in the ill fame of the other Cities.

The two angels are supposed to have found that the "outcry against" Sodom was justified and to have told Lot that they had been sent by the Lord to destroy the city. On the following dawn Lot is urged to take his wife and two daughters and escape to the mountains. Afraid of the mountains or their inhabitants, Lot obtains permission to seek refuge in Zoar; and "just as the sun rose over the earth and Lot entered Zoar" (19:23), the catastrophe befel the Plain. The next five verses (24–28) may well be reviewed here.

> Then the Lord rained upon Sodom and upon Gomorrah brimstone and fire from the Lord out of heaven;
>
> And he overthrew those cities, and all the Plain, and all the inhabitants of the cities, and that which grew upon the ground.
>
> But his wife looked back from behind him, and she became a pillar of salt.
>
> And Abraham gat up early in the morning to the place where he stood before the Lord;
>
> And he looked toward Sodom and Gomorrah, and toward all the land of the Plain, and beheld, and, lo, the smoke of the land went up as the smoke of a furnace.

The *American Translation* of verse 24 is: "The Lord rained sulphur and fire from the sky on Sodom and Gomorrah." Attention may be called to the fact that the word translated "smoke" here is not the usual word but one that is used in connection with incense and sacrifice. Furthermore, the word "furnace" appears as "kiln" in the *American Translation,* and we may note that the word means a furnace or kiln "for burning lime, or making bricks."

There is clearly something unnatural or extraordinary that is recorded. Abraham, looking from the heights around Hebron, sees smoke pouring upward as if from a furnace or kiln. Of course, in the case of Sodom and Gomorrah, there is no possibility of volcanic activity. Geologists have ruled that out. Despite some theories advanced, Clapp has come to the conclusion that the latest volcanic activity evidenced in the southern end of the Dead Sea valley took place thousands of years before Abraham's time and that no eruptions have occurred in this locality as recently as 4000 years ago.[16]

Possibly the fact that a different word for smoke is used in connection with Sodom may have some significance. It was

[16] Clapp, Frederick G., "The Site of Sodom and Gomorrah," *AJA* (1936), pp. 323–44.

not the characteristic smoke of a volcano, but of another, though natural, source. We may disregard the view that the mist, which the rapid evaporation of the Dead Sea causes to arise from the surface, gave rise to the story of the smoke being seen by Abraham in Hebron. One near Hebron could have seen mist rising almost any day and such a usual phenomenon would hardly have given rise to a comparison between it and "smoke of a furnace." It would seem that on one occasion some great conflagration took place at the south end of the Dead Sea and the volume of smoke which arose, whether it was seen from Hebron or from nearby, impressed itself indelibly on the minds of the people.

Evidence of Later Writers

The Greek geographer Strabo, writing about the end of the first century B.C. or early in the first of our era, has much to say about the Dead Sea and the appearance of the region around its southern end. He comments at length on the asphalt which

> is blown to the surface at irregular intervals from the midst of the deep, and with it rise bubbles, as though the water were boiling . . . With the asphalt there arises also much soot, which, though smoky, is imperceptible to the eye . . . The asphalt is a clod of earth, which at first is liquefied by heat, and is blown up to the surface . . . the source of the fire and also the greater part of the asphalt is at the middle of it (Dead Sea); but the bubbling up is irregular, because the movement of the fire, like that of many other subterranean blasts, follows no order known to us (XVI. 2. 42–43).

He continues in the next section (44):

> Many other evidences are produced to show that the country is fiery; for near Moasada[17] are to be seen rugged rocks that have been scorched, as also, in many places, fissures and ashy soil, and drops of pitch dripping from smooth cliffs, and boiling rivers that emit foul odors to a

[17] Masada on the west side of the Dead Sea, opposite el-Lisan.

great distance, and ruined settlements here and there;
and therefore people believe the oft-repeated assertions of
the local inhabitants, that there were once thirteen in-
habited cities in that region of which Sodom was the
metropolis, but that a circuit of about sixty stadia of that
city escaped unharmed; and that by reason of earth-
quakes and of eruptions of fire and hot waters containing
asphalt and sulphur, the lake burst its bounds, and rocks
were enveloped with fire, and, as for the cities, some were
swallowed up and others were abandoned by such as
were able to escape.

Strabo's vivid description seems to be based on both an
eyewitness' report and on local tradition. It is not impossible
for a striking phenomenon to be retained in the memory of a
people for hundreds of years, especially with such reminders
about one as a seemingly burnt landscape, the presence of
sulphur and bitumen or asphalt. Anyone who has entered
the harbor of the island of Thera (for a while called San-
torin) and seen the wall of the crater of the volcano, which is
now the harbor, will never forget the awe-inspiring sight. If
the habitation of this island has been continuous since the
great eruption, probably in the seventeenth century B.C., it
might not be incredible to hear some feature of the story of
the catastrophe told as it may well have been told over three
millennia ago. The blackened interior of the crater might well
keep alive at least the general account of what happened.[18]

Philo Judaeus, born about 20 B.C., gives a rather lurid, imaginative account of the destruction of the Cities of the Plain
by the fire which rained down from heaven. This is pure fiction

[18] Dr. Nelson Glueck, in commenting on the phenomenon of historical memory as evidenced in the Old Testament, relates an experience which Mr. A. S. Kirkbride had while serving with "Lawrence of Arabia" in 1917. "He told me," writes Glueck, "that on one
occasion, while he was in an Arab encampment, an Arab got up and
related the history of his forbears back to forty generations, and that
there were others in the assembly who obviously could have done
the same, telling who married and who begat whom, and where
they lived, and frequently what they had done, and where they
wandered. Kirkbride said it sounded exactly like a chapter of gene-
alogy out of the Bible" (Newsletter of Nelson Glueck, Aug. 22,
1942).

and is of no aid to the historian. For instance, as clearest evidence of what happened he mentions the smoke which constantly ascends and the sulphur which is dug out. Bits of sulphur are still found in the southern *Ghor*, but his older contemporary, Strabo, and his successor, Josephus, would surely have mentioned the smoke had there been any to see.

Josephus, who seems to have visited the southern end of the Dead Sea in the second half of the first century of our era, recounts the story of the wickedness and punishment of Sodom in his *Antiquities* (I. xi. 1–4).

But of more historical interest is Josephus' description of the Dead Sea, its output of asphalt, and the destruction of the Cities of the Plain, found in his *Jewish War* (IV, 476–85).

> *Adjacent to (Lake Asphaltitis) is the land of Sodom, in days of old a country blest in its produce and in the wealth of its various cities, but now all burnt up. It is said that, owing to the impiety of its inhabitants, it was consumed by thunderbolts; and in fact vestiges of the divine fire and faint traces of five cities are still visible. Still, too, may one see ashes reproduced in the fruits, which from their outward appearance would be thought edible, but on being plucked with the hand dissolve into smoke and ashes. So far are the legends about the land of Sodom borne out by ocular evidence.*

Josephus had apparently visited the site of the catastrophe for he asserts that this story about Sodomitis, the land of Sodom, deserves credence because it is based on what was seen. The thunderbolt or lightning appears to enter the story with Josephus for previous writers spoke of fire coming from heaven. Josephus confirms Strabo's statement that he saw traces of fire or of burning and also remains of the destroyed towns. Strabo had seen ruined settlements here and there while Josephus said that "shadows" or "shades" of the five cities were to be seen. It would seem that at least the entire Plain was not under water in the first century of our era.

The existence of dry land in part of the area now under the waters of the embayment is also to be inferred from the statement of Tacitus whose *floruit* may be placed a little before A.D. 100. Tacitus, to be sure, is not writing as an eyewitness but he was a historian who, at least in matters not directly concerning himself or his political views, displays critical judgment; and he doubtless investigated the information reported to him. In Book V, chapter 7, of his *Histories* he writes:

> *Not far from the lake (the Dead Sea) is a plain which, according to report, was once fertile and the site of great cities, but which was later devastated by lightning; and it is said that traces of this disaster still exist there; and that the very ground looks burnt and has lost its fertility.*

Tacitus proceeds with the story of how plants and flowers wither and crops decay because of the deleterious soil and atmosphere, and admits his willingness to "grant that famous cities were once destroyed by celestial fire." Again we have the reference to the "stroke of thunderbolts"—we would say "bolts of lightning"—but more important is his mentioning the report that cities were destroyed in this region and that traces of this disaster (to the cities, it would seem) and of the fire still existed in his day. Of course, he may have drawn from Strabo, Philo, or Josephus; but from the comparatively lengthy description of the sterility of the region and of the effect upon vegetation, he seems in all probability to have used another source, at least additionally.

Before leaving the ancient sources, mention should be made of the odors emanating from the Dead Sea, which are reported by at least three authors. Diodoros describes the water of the Dead Sea as ill-smelling and bitter and tells how the people are warned of the coming upheaval of asphalt by the odor which, arising from the Sea, carries for many stadia. This odor tarnishes gold, silver, and bronze but the luster returns again after the asphalt has been spouted forth. It is because of the burned character of the surroundings and because of the evil odors that the natives are susceptible to disease and are short-lived.[19]

Strabo mentions boiling waters which emit foul odors to a great distance. Since he speaks later of eruptions of hot waters containing asphalt and sulphur, it may have been a sulphurous

[19] Diodoros *Bibliotheke* II. 48. 7–9; repeated in XIX. 98. 2.

odor which he noticed, if not some gaseous emanation in connection with the asphalt seepages. His statement that "with the asphalt there arises much soot which, though smoky, is imperceptible to the eye" is quite significant as we shall soon see. Incidentally, as in the case of the odor which, according to Diodoros, preceded the rise of asphalt to the surface, so the soot tarnishes the metals and warns the people of the coming up of the asphalt. The two authors seem to have drawn from the same or in part similar sources.

Thirdly, Tacitus, after mentioning the burnt appearance of the ground and its lack of fertility, still does not think that it was the destructive fire which brought about the sterility in this region. On the contrary, the historian believes that "it is the exhalations from the lake that infect the ground and poison the atmosphere about this district, and that this is the reason that crops and fruits decay, since both soil and climate are deleterious."

Some modern writer has attributed the reports about the unpleasant odors to imagination. However, it may well be that such odors at one time did arise from gases emanating from the "Vale of Siddim" or from the bottom of the Sea which eventually covered it, or from the streams passing through, or rising in, deposits of sulphur. Certainly, Diodoros' "odors which tarnish," Strabo's "smoky, imperceptible soot which tarnishes," and Tacitus' "deleterious atmosphere" do suggest the presence of gas, a property which, of course, was unknown to the ancients. In this connection might be mentioned Sir John Maundevile's statement that some call the Dead Sea "the Flom that is ever stynkynge."[20] In recent years the gaseous emanations may have become exhausted or the sulphur washed out.

The barrenness and desolation of the region, stressed by many writers, has possibly to some extent been magnified by imagination, fed by the biblical warnings of the complete destruction wrought as divine punishment. As noted in the preceding article, there are several areas around the south end of the Dead Sea, which are quite fertile. Abandonment of an organized irrigation system may account for the lack of fertility in places rather than the aftereffects of the traditional "fire and

[20] *Flom*—Old English for 'river'—is applied to the Dead Sea by Maundevile. (See note 12.)

brimstone." However, we must bear in mind that in the time of Diodoros, Strabo, and Tacitus, the area south of *el-Lisan* (where we locate the "Vale of Siddim") was for the most part dry land and that these writers or their informants probably saw ruin and desolation in the area now under water.

Fire and Brimstone and Geology

After reading the accounts of the destruction of Sodom, in Genesis and the later classical authors, one comes away impressed by certain outstanding features of the story. They are: the fire from heaven, a great conflagration, the "overthrowing" (or "overturning"), an earthquake, the asphalt seepages or wells, and the great quantities of asphalt or bitumen rising to the surface in ancient and modern times, the odors and the invisible soot which tarnishes metals. Bearing these features in mind, one might reconstruct the story somewhat in this fashion.

A great earthquake, perhaps accompanied by lightning, brought utter ruin and a terrible conflagration to Sodom and the other communities in the vicinity. The destructive fire may have been caused by the ignition of gases and of seepages of asphalt emanating from the region, through lightning or the scattering of fires from hearths.

The earthquake is easy to reconstruct because of the frequency of such phenomena in this rift-valley. The seepages of asphalt or bitumen are evidenced by ancient tradition and modern record. The gas is not pure invention, for Strabo's invisible soot and Diodoros' odors which tarnish metals readily suggest a gas.

Of course, in the layman's mind at least, gas is more often associated with oil or petroleum than with pools of asphalt. But there may well have been, and may be now, petroleum deposits below the waters of the south end of the Dead Sea. On consulting the article by Wyllie,[21] the writer was struck by the notation that Mr. Wyllie was a geologist employed by the *Anglo-Persian Oil Company*. Now oil companies do not send geologists to Palestine purely for biblical research. So

[21] Wyllie, B. K. N., "The Geology of Jebel Usdum, Dead Sea," *The Geological Magazine*, LXVIII (1931), 366–72.

naturally one would be led to believe that oil is expected to be found, or has been located, in Palestine, and this is borne out by the reports of other scientists.

In the ancient and modern evidence which we have reviewed there is no hint as to the presence of oil in the Dead Sea valley, unless we count a few vague or indirect references. Lynch in 1848 noted the slimy black mud, coated with salt and bitumen, and his fellow-traveler, Montague, reported, "We had quite a task to wash from our skin all the oily uncomfortable substance which had clung to us from the Dead Sea."[22] To be sure, neither of these observations prove the presence of oil.

Possibly of more significance is the remark of Josephus in his *Jewish War* (IV. 478): "Another remarkable feature (of the Dead Sea) is its change of color; three times a day it alters its appearance and throws off a different reflection of the solar rays." Commenting on this passage, R. J. Forbes says, "This is probably an allusion to the interferential colours caused by a thin layer of oil on the surface of the water."[23] It may be noted here in passing that as early as 1912 Blanckenhorn had designated this locality as an oil-bearing region and in 1924 Alfred Day is credited by Kyle with the same conclusion.[24] In 1936 Clapp published the results of his investigations and concluded that in certain strata in the Dead Sea area liquid petroleum may have accumulated and that this region has produced bitumen and petroleum since earliest known habitation.[25] Other equally strong evidence will be presented below.

Hence all the materials are present and the conditions met,

[22] Montague, Edward P., *Narrative of the Late Expedition (1847–1848) to the Dead Sea.* From a Diary of one of the Party (1849), p. 188.

[23] Forbes, R. J., *Bitumen and Petroleum in Antiquity* (Leiden, 1936), p. 17.

[24] Blanckenhorn, Max, *Naturwissenschaftliche Studien am Toten Meer und in Jordantal* (Berlin, 1912), pp. 111–29. Kyle, Melvin G., *Explorations in Sodom* (1928), p. 118.

[25] Clapp, "Geology and Bitumens of the Dead Sea Area, Palestine and Transjordan," *The Bulletin of the American Association of Petroleum Geologists*, XX:7 (1936), pp. 881–909, 11 figures; esp. pp. 907 and 909.

which would justify the reconstruction of the catastrophe as outlined above.

The case for a natural, scientific explanation of the destruction of the Cities of the Plain is well presented by Clapp:

> *Exudations of bitumen, petroleum and probably natural gas (since the last-named is generally an accompaniment of these substances), emerging throughout historical times, may have been erratic and have taken place whenever disastrous earthquakes or controlling subterranean pressure impulses were manifested. The seepages, catching fire from lightning or human action, would adequately account for recorded phenomena without necessarily having recourse to supernatural or fanciful theories . . .* (He is "unable to accept 'showers of sulphur'—a substance which is not known in the region in large bulk— or of bitumen.") . . . *Bitumen from the earth is the most probable combustible material, especially as there are voluminous asphalt deposits . . . about a mile west of Jebel Usdum . . . In this spot one still finds seepages of semi-fluid petroleum in the form of soft bitumen saturating tarry conglomerates of late Tertiary or Recent age, which have a reported volume of . . . nearly 750,000 cu. ft. containing 140,000 cu. ft. of asphalt, emanating either from below the surface or from contiguous Senonian limestones.*

In another passage, Clapp writes that "an abundance of evidence suggests an escape of natural gas from the southern Dead Sea depression in the past" and associates the biblical "slime pits" with "existing and historical petroliferous signs" in the south end of the Dead Sea.

> *Considering the bituminous nature of the surroundings, gas in association with salt water has probably emerged within walking distance of Jebel Usdum during historical periods, not in one spot alone, but along several known fault planes on either side of the valley. The gas may have caught fire and facilitated destruction of the five ancient cities.*

Clapp continues:

These ancient settlements . . . were not founded upon rock but on sinking bottom lands of one of the most unstable valleys in the world,—a "rift," which still slips between its bounding planes to some extent on the occasion of every local earthquake. The notorious "slime pits" . . . were . . . probably oil or bitumen seepages, "mud volcanoes" or primitive hand-dug petroleum "wells" (perhaps a complex of asphaltic ground) such as have been observed by travelers in the Soviet Union, Iraq, and Iran during the past century.

The Apple of Sodom

Having discussed the location of the Cities of the Plain and the probable, or at least possible, manner of their destruction, there remains one subject which deserves comment. This is the "Apple of Sodom," the inedible fruit which was considered another memorial of the Lord's punishment meted out to the Cities of the Plain.

In the account of the destruction of Sodom and Gomorrah in Genesis 19:24–25, the Cities and the Plain were devastated along with the inhabitants and "that which grew upon the ground." More specifically, Deuteronomy (32:32) mentions the *vine of Sodom:* "For their vine is of the vine of Sodom, and of the fields of Gomorrah; their grapes are grapes of gall, their clusters are bitter." It would seem that these bitter grapes are not to be associated with the vine of Sodom for the latter is identified with the *colocynth* by the *Cyclopedic Concordance of the Oxford Bible* and the *colocynth* is a vine allied to the watermelon. The *Concordance* describes this plant as having "long straggling tendrils like a vine, and a fruit of tempting appearance, like a beautiful orange, and its bitter nauseous taste—bitter as gall—agrees with the description of the grapes of the vine of Sodom."

In the *Book of Wisdom* (10:7) the fruit has become a tree-fruit: "To their (the Five Cities') wickedness a smoking waste still bears lasting witness, as do trees that bear fruit that never ripens." Strabo does not mention the "accursed fruit," but

Josephus intimates quite clearly that he saw it with his own eyes. After mentioning the "shades" of the Five Cities which were still visible, he writes: "Still, too, may one see ashes reproduced in the fruits, which from their outward appearance would be thought edible, but on being plucked with the hand dissolve into smoke and ashes."

Tacitus, though he does not appear to have seen the Dead Sea region, doubtless received the "report" which he quotes, from fellow Romans who had served in Palestine. After mentioning the traces of the disaster and lack of fertility in the soil, he says, "All the plants there, whether wild or cultivated, turn black, become sterile, and seem to wither into dust, either in leaf or in flower or after they have reached their usual mature form."

Exactly one thousand years after Tacitus, Fulcher of Chartres, the historian of the First Crusade (1095–99), wrote a *History of Jerusalem* in which he describes this peculiar fruit of the Dead Sea region.[26] "Among the other trees there, I saw certain ones that bore apples (*poma*). Wishing to know of what nature they were, I gathered some from the trees and found, when the skin was broken, that the interior was just like black powder, and from inside came forth simply (empty) smoke." (*Poma*, which means a tree- or orchard-fruit, is here for convenience translated as "apples.")

Sir John Maundevile of St. Albans, England, traveled through the Near East (and into the Far East) during the years 1322 to 1356 and wrote what he saw, heard about, and imagined, in a work entitled *The Voiage and Travaile of Sir John Maundevile, Kt.*[27] That he has been rightly called a "veritable Baron Munchausen," is apparent on almost every page. For instance, after saying that nothing, man or beast, which breathes can die in the Dead Sea for it receives nothing into it that breathes life, he adds: "And if a man casts iron into it, it will float on the surface. And if men cast a feather

[26] Fulcher of Chartres, *Historia Hierosolyma*, II, 4 (more accessible in Thackeray's edition—Loeb Library—of Josephus, *The Jewish War*, III, 144–45, in note to Book IV. 485).

[27] The edition of J. O. Halliwell (London, 1866) has been consulted. This is "Reprinted from the Edition of A.D. 1725" as we learn on the title page. Passages, not dealing with the Apple of Sodom, have been translated into modern English from pp. 100–1.

into it, it will sink to the bottom." But he does mention the asphalt which is cast up by the sea in large pieces the size of a horse.

Sir John seems to have visited the southern end of the Dead Sea for he mentions Segor (the mediaeval Zoar) and may have seen this site which he says was set upon a hill and some part of it appears above the water and "men may see the walls when it is fair and clear." He mentions the Five Cities of the Plain and comments on their destruction by the wrath of God because of their sin: "And in that See sonken the 5 Cytees, be Wratthe of God."

He too describes the so-called "Apple of Sodom" after mentioning the Cities "lost, because of Synne." He writes: "And there besyden growen trees, that beren fulle faire Apples, and faire of colour to beholde; but whoso brekethe hem or cuttethe hem in two, he schalle fynde with in hem Coles and Cyndres; in tokene that, be Wratthe of God, the Cytees and the Lond weren brente and sonken in to Helle." Here too we find the fair-colored fruit with ashes and cinders within. Incidentally, "apples" is used as a general term for fruit from trees by Maundevile, to judge by the fact that elsewhere he describes the huge cones of the cedar of Lebanon as "apples."

Lieutenant Lynch does not seem to have come upon the "apples" or tree-fruit in his visit to the Dead Sea in 1848, but he did see and try the other characteristic fruit of the devastated region. On April 26, 1848, he logged the following note,[28] after recording their exploration of Jebel Usdum and the Pillar of Salt: "Some of the Arabs, when they came up, brought a species of melon they had gathered near the north spit of Usdum. It was oblong, ribbed, of a dark green color, much resembling cantelope. When cut, the meat and seeds bore the same resemblance to that fruit, but were excessively bitter to the taste. A mouthful of quinine could not have been more distasteful, or adhered longer and more tenaciously to the reluctant palate." Lynch, of course, had eaten a *colocynth*, but a green one and not the "beautiful" orange-colored, though just as bitter, kind, described above.

[28] Lynch, Lieut. William F. (U.S.N.), *Narrative of the United States' Expedition to the River Jordan and the Dead Sea*, (1849; 9th ed. 1853) p. 308.

Kyle in 1924 experienced both "the disappointing *apples of Sodom* giving us little more than a puff of dust" and the "poisonous melons," that is, the *colocynth*.[29] A rather recent description of the former fruit by Dr. C. Geikie in *The Holy Land and the Bible*, shows that both Fulcher of Chartres and Maundevile had in all probability examined the "apples" for in the main the three descriptions are similar. Geikie writes:

> The "osher" of the Arab is the true apple of Sodom . . .
> Its fruit is like a large smooth apple or orange . . . When
> ripe it is yellow and looks fair and attractive, and is soft
> to the touch, but if pressed, it bursts with a crack, and
> only the broken shell and a row of small seeds in a half-
> open pod, with a few dry filaments, remain in the hand
> (II, 117).

The only scientific observation that the writer has come upon is that by Hasselquist, a student of the great Swedish botanist, Linnaeus. Hasselquist traveled in Palestine and visited the Dead Sea some time around 1750—he died in Smyrna in 1752—and he described the *Poma Sodomica* or "apple of Sodom" which in his time was found in great abundance around Jericho and the Dead Sea. According to this scholar, these "apples" are sometimes filled with ashes, but only when the fruit has been attacked by insects. Then the interior changes to ashes but the skin remains entire and has a very beautiful color. (From a work by Professor Axel Persson of Uppsala, entitled *Med hacka och med spade* [1934], p. 37.)

Notes on the Later History of the Plain

After the catastrophic destruction of the Cities of the Plain, which seems to have been brought about by a great earthquake, concomitant explosions, ignition of natural gas, and the general conflagration, the Vale of Siddim and the rest of the Plain seem to have been left desolate and abandoned. Possibly a subsidence of part of the Plain was caused by the apparent convulsion of nature and a partial submergence of the land may have resulted from this forced extension of the waters of

[29] Kyle, *Explorations in Sodom* (in 1924), p. 82.

the Dead Sea. However, a consideration of the evidence from Strabo, Josephus, and other late writers of antiquity, as well as the existence of the Roman road to the shore of the *Lisan*, lead to the conclusion that the present south embayment is largely the result of forces at work since the Roman Imperial period. Earthquakes and the natural rise in level of the Dead Sea have probably accounted for the submergence of the Plain. As was noted in the previous article, it is thought that the south embayment has increased one-third in area in the last century.

Though a part of this Plain, south of the *Lisan*, may have been flooded at the time of the catastrophe, it would appear that it was largely the devastating results of the conflagration that kept the region from being reinhabited. Of course, it is quite possible that religious reasons entered and caused the district to become taboo. As Albright has well summed up the situation, "Ever afterwards the Southern Ghor was shunned by both races, to whom it was a terrible memorial of human wickedness and the wrath of an angry God."[30]

Ezekiel's prophecy seems to have been only partially fulfilled. Writing sometime between 586 and 570, the prophet (16:53, 55) addresses Jerusalem: "But I will restore their fortune—the fortune of Sodom and her daughters, and the fortune of Samaria and her daughters—and I will restore your fortune along with theirs . . . Then your sisters, Sodom with her daughters, and Samaria with her daughters, shall return to their former state . . ."

The two other sinful cities did rise again, but Sodom appears to have remained totally destroyed and desolate. It remains for a well-organized irrigation system to bring about a rebirth of the city, and that too, in a place some distance removed from the original and now submerged site; this indeed has happened in the modern Israeli settlement, Sedom.

[30] Albright, *AASOR*, VI (1924–25), 66.

BIBLIOGRAPHY

Abel, LeP. F.–M., *Géographie de la Palestine*, II (1938).

Albright, William F., "The Jordan Valley in the Bronze Age," *AASOR*, VI (1924–25), pp. 13–74.

"The Archaeological Results of an Expedition to Moab and the Dead Sea," *BASOR*, No. 14 (1924), pp. 2–12.

Clapp, Frederick G., "The Site of Sodom and Gomorrah," *AJA*, (1936), pp. 323–44.

Glueck, Nelson, "Explorations in Eastern Palestine, II," *AASOR*, XV (1934–35).

"Explorations in Eastern Palestine, III," *AASOR*, XVIII–XIX (1937–39).

"An Aerial Reconnaissance in Southern Transjordan," *BASOR*, No. 67 (1937), pp. 19–26.

The Other Side of the Jordan (1940).

Kyle, Melvin G., *Explorations in Sodom* (Undated. According to Albright, exploration in 1924, publication in 1928.)

Lynch, Lieut. William F. (U.S.N.), *Narrative of the United States' Expedition to the River Jordan and the Dead Sea* (1849; 9th ed. 1853).

Montague, Edward P., *Narrative of the Late Expedition (1847–1848) to the Dead Sea*. From a Diary of one of the Party (1849).

Robinson, Edward, *Biblical Researches in Palestine* (2 vols., 1841). *Later Biblical Researches in Palestine and Adjacent Regions* (1856).

Thomsen, Peter, *Die römischen Meilensteine der Provinzen Syria, Arabia, und Palästina* (Leipzig, 1917).

Tristram, Henry Baker, *The Land of Israel* (London, 1865).

Wright, G. Ernest, "The Chronology of Palestinian Pottery in Middle Bronze I," *BASOR*, No. 71 (1938), pp. 27–34. *The Pottery of Palestine* (New Haven, 1937).

Wyllie, B. K. N., "The Geology of Jebel Usdum, Dead Sea," *The Geological Magazine* LXVIII (1931), pp. 366–72.

5

THE MANNA OF SINAI

F. S. BODENHEIMER

In Exodus 16 and Numbers 11 we find reports of manna in the desert. Some believe that this manna was similar to bread and that it was furnished in quantities large enough to feed a whole people. Others regard it as a natural phenomenon which contributed to the diet of the Israelites in the desert. Only the latter view permits analysis and discussion. Since biblical history often is confirmed by archaeology, why not confirm the reports of manna by existing natural phenomena?

The most widely accepted view in textbooks is that the lichen *Lecanora esculenta* is identical with the manna of the Bible. This lichen grows on rocks and produces fructifications in the form of pea-sized globules which are light enough to be blown about by the wind. The natives of the Irano-Turanian steppes, from Central Asia to the high Atlas plateau, collect these globules for their sweetness ("halvah"). The idea of a manna rain based on this phenomenon is impressive, even though the collected bits remain as delicacies and do not appear in quantities large enough to replace bread. However, these rains of *Lecanora* are rare and unique occurrences and usually happen during the day. The Bible reports that the manna appeared at night, and also strongly indicates a regular recurrence of the event. Another fact which refutes the idea of *Lecanora* as the manna of Sinai is its complete absence in the region of Sinai during the last 150 years when many collections of rock lichen were made. During this same period not one traveler has ever reported a manna rain or heard about it from the local monks or nomads.

The record of the oldest local traditions of Sinai comes from Flavius Josephus and the early monks of the St. Catherine monastery. These reports link the manna with the tamarisk thickets in the wadis of the central Sinai mountains. Here year after year in June appears a granular type of sweet manna from pinhead to pea size. It appears on the tender twigs of tamarisk bushes for a period of three to six weeks. The quantity of this manna fluctuates according to the winter rainfall. The crop may fail entirely in one wadi and at the same time be plenteous in others. Certain wadis such as Wadi Nasib and the Wadi esh-Sheikh are especially famous for their manna production. Usually the annual crop does not exceed several kilograms, but one steady man may collect over a kilogram a day at the peak of the season. This certainly does not allow for the "bread" or daily food of the wandering Israelites. However, we must note that *lehem* does not have an original meaning of bread, but of food in general. Otherwise, it could not have come to mean 'meat' in Arabic. All in all, the nutritive value of these few kilograms of manna could not have been important enough to deserve a recording in Israel's history. There must have been a special quality to justify its inclusion in the chronicle. The special quality was its sweetness.

A chemical analysis reveals that this type of manna contains a mixture of three basic sugars with pectin. One who has wandered with nomads in the desert knows that sweetness is their highest culinary dream. At the time in which the Israelites wandered in the desert, neither sugar beets nor sugar cane was known. Sweet dates had only a limited productivity and may have been unknown or almost unknown in the deserts. Therefore, the sudden discovery of a source of pure and attractive sweetness would have been an exciting event.

This manna was regarded until recently as a secretion of the tamarisk. Ehrenberg, however, about 120 years ago connected it with an insect which he described as *Coccus manniparus*. His description is so mixed in character that we must suppose he described the larva of a lady beetle within the ovisac of a scale insect together with the insect itself. Ehrenberg assumed

that the insect sucked on a plant, and from these sucking holes
or punctures oozed the manna.

In June of 1927 the writer visited the valleys of central Sinai
in order to study this manna. It soon became obvious that
two closely related species of scale insects produce the manna
by excretion. These are *Trabutina mannipara Ehrenberg*, the
short, brown, sticky ovisac of which was described by Ehrenberg, and the *Najacoccus serpentinus Green*, which is easily
recognized by the very long, snow-white, narrow, and cylindrical ovisac. Of these two, the former is the manna producer in
the mountains, the latter in the lowlands. This manna is none
other than the well-known honeydew excretion of so many
plant lice and scale insects. The honeydew drops are excreted
mainly by the growing larva and immature females. Rapid
evaporation due to the dry air of the desert quickly changes
the drops into sticky solids. These manna pieces later turn a
whitish, yellowish, or brownish color. The reason that insects
excrete and waste high-valued foodstuffs in great quantities,
such as pure sugars, can be explained on a physiological basis.
These insects suck great quantities of plant saps which are
rich in carbohydrates but extremely poor in nitrogen. In order
to acquire the minimum amount of nitrogen for the balancing
of their metabolism, they must suck carbohydrates in great
excess. This excess passes from them in honeydew excretion.

Now, we shall compare briefly the biblical report with the
actual manna phenomenon in Sinai. But first, we must make
clear one thing about the biblical report. All the statements
about manna in the early traditions of Scripture (i.e., the Elohim or Yahweh codes), agree closely with our observations.
However, Priestly materials which were added hundreds of
years later and which are based on conjectures or on misinterpretation of the oral tradition, show definite divergences
(cf. F. S. Bodenheimer and O. Theodor, *Ergebnisse der Sinai-
Expedition* [Leipzig, 1929], pp. 79 ff).

We begin with the criteria of space and time. The location
of the manna excretion which is given in the older codes as
beginning at Elim (near Wadi Gharandel) and ending at
Rephidim (the oasis Feiran), agrees well with the northern
limits of the manna excretion in our day. Manna first was discovered on the 15th day of the second month after the Exodus

from Egypt. This would be the middle or end of Siwan, which is late May or early June. This date agrees with the natural season of manna production. The description of manna in the Bible, which likens it to small, light brown cummin seeds and to the stickiness of bdellion resin, is a remarkably suitable description of the tamarisk manna. In the Bible its taste is described as like that of *ṣappîḥît bidbāš*, which easily may refer to the crystallized grains so often found on the surface of honey. Exodus 16:14 and Numbers 11:9 state that the manna fell from heaven during the night. Actually, most of the dropping of manna, or at least its accumulation on the soil, occurs at night when the ants are not collecting it. And in many countries the honeydew of aphids is called "dew of heaven," because the causal connection between the insects and the honeydew is not recognized.

An easy explanation can be offered for the worms and stinking decay of the manna which was collected in excess of need (Exodus 16:20, 21). The manna grains are eagerly collected by ants, and in a primitive tent there is little protection against them. These ants could be called worms, while the addition of stinking decay is a later misinterpretation and interpolation. The Bible has a special word for ant (*nemālāh*), but in this place it uses the general word for worms and vermin (*tôlāʿ*). However, a personal experience may explain this. When I asked our nomad guide for the name of the many manna-collecting ants, he called them *dudi,* which corresponds to the Hebrew *tôlaʿat.* When I asked him if they might be called *nimleh* (*nemālāh*), he answered that it was possible. Since he knew both designations he had used the more general one. This was almost certainly the procedure of the oral tradition.

Exodus 16:21 tells us that the manna was collected early in the morning and that it "melted when the sun grew hot." We must regard the melting as a late and mistaken interpolation. The ants begin to collect the manna only when the temperature of the soil surpasses 21°C. (70°F.). In most of the wadis at the time of our visit the rays of the sun usually accomplished this about 8:30 A.M. This activity of the ants ceases in the early evening. In the lowlands the ants begin much earlier. All those manna grains which drop from late afternoon to early morning remain until the beginning of ant activity in the morning. Then, however, they are speedily collected and carried away.

These and a number of other agreements between the biblical report and the tamarisk manna have led people to connect them since olden times. We have seen that all the eyewitness reports of the Bible can be taken as literal descriptions of the tamarisk manna of Sinai.

However, this tamarisk manna of Sinai is no isolated event. It is not even the most abundant manna known to us. If it were not for the biblical record we would know very little at all about it. "Man" is the common Arabic name for plant lice, and "man es-simma" (the manna of heaven) for honeydew. This confirms our views, because a number of small cicadas (*Homoptera* of various families) are found in Sinai, southern Iraq, and Iran, and are locally called "man." They produce a product in small quantities which is similar to manna and which is used as a delicacy and as an ingredient in popular medicines. The large *Cicada orni* L. produces a like excretion on ash trees in Italy. The most famous manna product of the Middle East is the Kurdish manna which is collected by the thousands of kilograms every year in June and July. It is used for the preparation of special confections which are sold in the streets of Baghdad and elsewhere under the name of "man." This manna is also produced all over the general Kurdistan region in the extensive oak forest by a still undetermined aphid. This plant louse sucks on the oak leaves and copiously excretes a honeydew which solidifies with fragments of the leaves. We were unfortunate in July 1943, when we visited one of the famous manna-producing forests near Penjween in northeastern Iraq, for the manna crop was a complete failure that year. We could not observe even abortive manna production. This type of manna is composed principally of a rare polysaccharide trehalose.

Accordingly, we find that manna production is a biological phenomenon of the dry deserts and steppes. The liquid honeydew excretion of a number of cicadas, plant lice, and scale insects speedily solidifies by rapid evaporation. From remote times the resulting sticky and oftentimes granular masses have been collected and called manna.

6

MUSICAL INSTRUMENTS OF ISRAEL

OVID R. SELLERS

Even to the cursory reader of the Old Testament it is apparent that music played a vital part in the formation and development of Israel. Moses, according to Exodus 15, was concerned about making the songs of his nation as well as about making its laws. Joshua employed music to bring down the walls of Jericho (Josh. 6); Deborah celebrated the important victory of the Israelites over Sisera with a song (Judg. 5); instrumental music was a prophetic device which influenced Saul (I Sam. 10:5) and David's playing soothed him when he was troubled by an evil spirit (I Sam. 16:23). The Israelite empire arose under the leadership of David, who was as skilful at playing a tune or turning out a song, both words and music, as he was at war or statecraft.

In Solomon's temple there was, no doubt, a good deal of musical performance. While the elaborate musical organization described in I Chron. 25 is thought by most scholars to be an idealization, it certainly had a historical basis. Sennacherib in his account of his third campaign in 701 B.C. mentions in the tribute that Hezekiah, king of Judah, sent to the Assyrian capital, Nineveh, "male and female musicians" (*ANET*, p. 288). Evidently these musicians were sufficiently skilled to make an impression on the mighty monarch. So here we have an outside confirmation of the Bible picture. There must have been also a great deal of popular music around the countryside as well as the elaborate and organized music in the temple. When Elisha needed a "minstrel" to help induce the prophetic spirit, the musician was easily produced (II Kings 3:15). The word translated "minstrel" means a performer on a plectrophonic instrument. In the exile the complete dejection of the people is expressed, according to Ps. 137, in hanging their lyres on the trees and refusal to sing one of the songs of Zion. Then in the stories of the restoration, particularly in Ezra 2 and Neh. 7 and 12, we have repeated mention of the "singers," who apparently constituted a highly important section of the temple personnel. Along with the singing naturally came instrumental music (Ezra 3:10; Neh. 12:27, 35, 36).

What were the musical instruments of the Israelites? When we read in Exod. 15:19 that Miriam took a timbrel in her hand what kind of mental image do we form? Do we get a hazy idea of something that jingles or do we know that the dictionary defines the timbrel as a small drum or a tambourine? Naturally there have been many studies and discussions of the Iraelites' musical instruments by eminent scholars, such as J. Stainer, J. Weiss, H. Gressman and W. O. E. Oesterley. J. Wellhausen's volume on Psalms in *Holy Bible, Polychrome Edition* (New York, 1898) has a large appendix, pp. 217–34, on "Music of the Ancient Hebrews." While some of his terminology is obsolete his discussion is highly competent and embellished by numerous illustrations. Sol Baruch Finesinger published an excellent technical study of the terms designating these instruments entitled "Musical Instruments in the Old Testament," *Hebrew Union College Annual*, III (1926), 21–75. The discussion is brought up to date in the fifth section of the comprehensive volume of Curt Sachs, *The History of Musical Instruments* (New York, 1940). Sachs probably is the world's foremost authority on musical instruments. This article leans heavily on the material which he has assembled and on the deductions which he has made.

A great handicap in the study of the musical instruments of the Hebrews is the lack of objective evidence in Palestine. Due to the climate of the Holy Land all the wood, reed, hide, and gut which went into the ancient instruments long ago has disintegrated; and sculptured scenes showing musicians, which have taught us so much about the instrumentalists of Babylonia and Egypt, were forbidden by the Second Commandment. Consequently our knowledge of the instruments which stirred or entertained the ancient Israelites must come almost entirely from the literary references, comparison with known instruments in the surrounding nations, and analogies with present Palestinian instruments which seem to be survivals from antiquity. The English words used in both the Authorized and the Revised Versions are frequently inconsistent and misleading; but that is not surprising, since many of the Hebrew words are obscure.

The Hand Drum

If we are curious about Miriam's timbrel, we find from Young's *Analytical Concordance* that it is a translation of the Hebrew *top*. Then if we look at the index-lexicon in the back of the concordance we see that *top* is translated nine times as 'timbrel' and eight times as 'tabret.' It was played by women (Exod. 15:20; Judg. 11:34; I Sam. 18:6; Ps. 68:25), but also by men (I Sam. 10:5). Most lexicons give 'tambourine' as an alternate translation and this term is used in some passages of the "Chicago Bible." But, while 'tambourine' is better than 'tabret' or 'timbrel' for the ordinary American reader in that it presents a familiar picture, it may be misleading; for when we think of a tambourine we think of the instrument with jingles that is shaken or thumped by the end man in a minstrel show or the percussionist in an orchestra. There are, according to the dictionary, tambourines without jingles, but they are not familiar to us. The *top*, to be sure, may have had jingles; the corresponding Arabic word *duff* means 'tambourine.' But we cannot be sure as to just what the Hebrew instrument was. The term *top* may have been, according to Finesinger, a general term for drums, including tambourines. It is the modern Hebrew word for a drum. Sachs holds that it "was made of a wooden hoop and very probably two skins, without any jingling contrivance or sticks." In that case the sound would be something like that of a tom-tom when beaten by the hand. We may be reasonably sure that the Israelites had a portable drum, possibly of several varieties, that this drum was beaten by women or men, that it frequently accompanied singing and dancing—doubtless to accentuate the beat—and that it some-times was used in conjunction with other instruments. Clearly it was a joyful instrument; most of its occurrences in the Old Testament are associated with merrymaking or praise.

Such was the 'tabret' or 'timbrel.' Laban apparently had in his household one who played it (Gen. 31:27). It was used by Miriam in celebrating the successful escape of the Israelites, by Jephthah's daughter when she came to meet her victorious father, by the company of prophets which Saul joined, by the girls who came out to meet Saul after the slaying of Goliath and made the undiplomatic comparison between the accomplishments of Saul and David as killers. David himself in bringing the ark from the house of Abinadab gave a musical exhibition in which he played on this small drum as well as on other instruments (II Sam. 6:5). It was used for praise in the temple (Ps. 150:4). So this instrument from patriarchal times through the period of the restoration figured in the life of Israel.

The Lyre

Another instrument about which we can be fairly certain is the lyre. Readers of the English Authorized Version, unless they have read some of the recent commentaries, have a mistaken idea about this instrument. The Hebrew term is *kinnôr*, which in all 42 of its occurrences in the Old Testament is translated 'harp.' That is not a good translation; for the harp is the instrument which started as the musical bow and developed into the elaborate affair which we hear exploited at the beginning of many radio programs. We are accustomed to think of David as carrying around something like an Irish harp and performing on it at frequent intervals. A very popular spiritual has the refrain, "Little David, play on your harp." But the instrument on which David played before Saul was not a harp; it was a lyre.

In 20 instances the Septuagint translates *kinnôr* by *kithara* (a kind of lyre) and 17 times *kinura*, which is merely a reproduction of the Hebrew word. The Vulgate has *cithara* 37 times and *lyra* twice. So we may be reasonably sure that the *kinnôr* was the kind of lyre that was called 'cithara' by both Greeks and Romans. The Egyptian word *knynywr*, which from its form shows itself to be a loan word from the Semitic *kinnôr*, means 'lyre.' The "Chicago Bible" in several places rightly has 'lyre' where the Authorized Version has 'harp.'

From the Bible references we know that this lyre was an instrument of joy and mirth. It was hung on the willows in Babylonia, for the captives had not the heart to play it. It was used for accompaniment to singers and often was blended with other instruments. The body of the lyre was made of wood (I Kings 10:12). According to rabbinic sources the strings were made from the small intestines (chitterlings) of sheep.

From Palestine and the surrounding countries there are several illustrations which give us a good idea of the aspect of the Israelite lyre. On the well-known Beni-hasan monument, dated *ca.* 1900 B.C., one of the Semitic nomads shown entering Egypt is playing a lyre. Lyres are not known in Egyptian Old Kingdom monuments; they were introduced by Asiatics coming in from Palestine. So this Semite with his lyre was a novelty in Egypt and probably played a part in the development of Egyptian music. We can see that the strings were stretched across a sounding board, over a blank space, and attached to a cross bar. The performer seems to be drawing a plectrum across the strings with his right hand and with the left fingers deadening the strings that he does not want sounded. Another picture shows an Assyrian relief showing three Semitic captives playing lyres under the eye of an Assyrian guard with drawn dagger. Their lyres seem to be in principle the same instrument as that of the Beni-hasan performer, though proportionally widened considerably at the far end. Probably these performers are Israelites; for they look very much like the Israelites on the black obelisk of Shalmaneser III and those appearing before Sennacherib at Lachish. The player near the guard seems to be drawing his index finger over the strings and not using a plectrum. Sachs believes that the plectrum was used in accompanying song and that a purely instrumental performance was without a plectrum. When David played before Saul (I Sam. 16:23) he "played with his hand." Sachs thinks this means that David played without a plectrum because he did not on this occasion sing. One who has played a guitar or a ukulele will be pardoned for being a bit skeptical about this distinction. From a time between these two pictures

of Semitic lyrists is the picture of an Egyptian girl of the
XVIIIth Dynasty. Except for the curves in the sticks supporting
the cross bar and the arrangement for left-handed playing her
lyre is much the same as those of the Semites. One development may be noted: in the early instrument the strings are
parallel, while in the later examples the strings diverge as they
extend outward. Assyrians seem to have used both forms together.

Jewish coins of the second century A.D. picture later lyres of
Palestine. In modern Hebrew *kinnôr* means 'violin.'

*Left, an Assyrian quartet (hand drum, two kinds of lyres,
and cymbals); right, an Assyrian harpist.*

The Harp (?)

Generally associated with the lyre is the harp. Since it is
clear that the 'harp' of the Authorized Version is really a lyre,
it is in order to inquire whether the Israelites actually had a
harp. In both Egypt and Mesopotamia harps were common
from early days on. It would be strange if the Israelites, who
were great lovers of music and prided themselves on versatility,
had ignored this popular and comparatively elaborate instrument. And there is a Hebrew word, *nēbel*, which can well
mean 'harp.' It is the regular word for skin bottle, but in 27

occurrences it clearly refers to a musical instrument. The Authorized Version translates it by 'psaltery' 23 times and 'viol' four. The Septuagint has *nabla* (a reduplication of the Hebrew) 14 times and *psalterion* eight. The Vulgate uses *psalterium* 17 times, *lyra* four, *nablium* three.

Now the psaltery is a harp. According to Jerome, commenting on Ps. 32:2, the cithara gives its sound from the lower part, the psaltery from above. If the psaltery as Jerome knew it was the *nēbel* of the Old Testament, it would be like the Assyrian harp, which is carried with the sounding box above, rather than like the Egyptian harp, which has the sounding box below and in many instances resting on the ground.

The harp has more and larger strings than the lyre. According to the Talmud they were made from the large intestines of the sheep and the *nēbel* made a louder sound than that of the *kinnôr*. There may be truth in the rabbinic tradition that the harp was called *nēbel* because it had the shape of a skin bottle; for the body was rounded out and covered with a skin.

The Zither (?)

In three places (Ps. 33:2; 92:3; 144:9) the Hebrew word *'āśôr*, which means 'ten,' apparently refers to a musical instrument. Generally it has been taken as another term for a tenstringed *nēbel* (harp) or a word added to show that the particular *nēbel* mentioned had ten strings. In all three cases it is associated with the *nēbel*. The "Chicago Bible" in Ps. 92:3 has 'ten-stringed lyre' and in the other two verses 'ten-stringed lute.' Sachs, however, thinks that the *'āśôr* was a ten-stringed zither. The zither was not used in Egypt and Mesopotamia, but was played in Phoenicia. It was a rectangular instrument with ten parallel strings. It would be unlikely that the Israelites would have a ten-stringed lute, since the necks of the contemporary Egyptian and Assyrian lutes were too narrow to accommodate more than two or three strings.

The Flute

In the English Old Testament the only mention of the flute is in the instrumentation of Nebuchadnezzar's band (Dan. 3:5, 7, 10, 15). There the Hebrew word *mašrôqîtā'* means 'whistle' and hence could be applied to any of the wood winds.

Some have thought that the word *'ûgāb* (Gen. 4:21), translated 'organ' in the Authorized Version and 'pipe' in the Revised Version, really indicates the flute. Generally it is connected with the Hebrew verb meaning 'to be in love' and the idea is that the dove-like sound made by the flute has amorous potency. Sachs, however, suggests that the dark color of the word *'ûgāb* "reflects the hollow *oo*-like timbre of a long, wide, vertical flute." It would not be unlikely that it originally was the name of the flute and then became a more general term for any wood wind.

We can scarcely doubt that the Israelites had a flute. This instrument is pictured in prehistoric, Old Kingdom, and Middle Kingdom Egyptian drawings. It is nothing but a hollow reed pipe with some finger holes drilled near an end. The player holds it in a transverse position and blows. It is strange that the flute is not pictured in any known New Kingdom monument in Egypt. This does not mean that the flute became obsolete. In temple music and in royal orchestras more strident sounds became fashionable, so that the louder reed instruments pushed out the soft-toned pipe. The flute had no more chance than it would in a swing band today. But probably the flute remained in the country. In Babylonia there were early flutes, some of them made of clay.

The simple flute remains throughout the Fertile Crescent today. In Palestine it is called *šabab* and in Egypt *sattawiya*. Shepherds play it in the same manner as it was played by the ancient Egyptians. The author once, near the site of ancient Shechem, met a boy who had fashioned a flute from a piece of a gun barrel.

This instrument must have been in use in ancient Israel. Jubal was the father of all that handle the lyre and the pipe. The pipe in its simplest form is the flute.

The Oboe

While the Hebrew *ḥālîl*, which means literally 'pierced' and is translated 'pipe' in the English versions, generally has been taken to be a name of the flute, Sachs argues that it must have been an oboe. The term is not used in any of the Bible stories until the time of Saul. During the period of the monarchy all the pipers pictured in the surrounding countries were playing the double oboe. The instrument was in some cases a cylindrical pipe and in others a cone, with a double reed as a mouthpiece. It was played in pairs with the ends held apart and each hand fingering a separate pipe. Judging from the positions of the hands in pictures the performer produced two tones; for one hand regularly is higher than the other. This instrument was used for rejoicing and also for mourning.

It is possible that *ḥālîl* is a general term for a wood wind and may include the double clarinet. This consists of two pipes bound together with their finger holes opposite, so that one hand fingered the upper three holes and the other hand the lower three. The mouthpiece was made by cutting three sides of an oblong piece in a small reed, thus leaving a tongue to vibrate. The ancient clarinet and oboe sounded much alike; but the oboes were held apart and had the double reed, while the clarinets were bound together and had the single reed. The double clarinet is called *nay* in both Palestine and Egypt, though the word seems to be originally a Persian word meaning flute.

Ḥālîl is used in modern Hebrew for flute and the rabbis seem to have understood it that way. Archaeological evidence, however, supports Sachs in his opinion that it was the double oboe.

The Trumpet

Trumpets of the Old Testament are of at least two kinds. The first was that made from the horn of the ram or goat (according to the Talmud the cow's horn was not valid). It was called *qeren*, the Hebrew form of the Semitic word from which our word 'horn' is derived, or *shofar*, which meant 'ram' and then 'ram's horn.' *Qeren* is translated 'cornet' four times and 'horn' ten times where it refers to a musical instrument. *Shofar* is translated 'cornet' four times and 'trumpet' 68 times. In all probability, however, the words are two names for the same thing.

It is not unlikely that the method of making the *shofar* for synagogue use today is the same as it was in ancient Israel. The horn of the ram or goat is heated by steam until it is soft; then it is flattened and straightened, and the bell end is bent to form a right angle. There is no separate mouthpiece and the performer blows into the smoother small end. Though a skilled performer can produce a variety of tones the main playing is on two tones, tonic and fifth. The function of the *shofar*, in fact, was not the playing of tunes but the giving of signals. It was used to give war signals by Joshua, Ehud, Gideon, and Joab. It announced the coronation of Solomon (I Kings 1:34, 39). It sounded an alarm when danger threatened the land (Jer. 4:5, 19; Ezek. 33:3; Joel 2:1, 15). It proclaimed the year of jubilee (Lev. 25:9) and the new moon and full moon (Ps. 81:3). By rabbinic times there were refinements: the *shofar* blown on New Year had its mouthpiece overlaid with gold and the one blown at the new moon festival was appropriately a crescent-shaped ibex horn.

At all periods of Israel's history the sound of the *shofar* must have been familiar. Its loud tone was potent. The blasts of the trumpets with the shouts of the Israelite people caused the walls of Jericho to come tumbling down.

The other trumpet was made of metal, the *ḥăṣōṣěrāh*. In the Old Testament the singular is used only once (Hos. 5:8); the plural appears 28 times. In Num. 10:12 Moses is commanded to make two trumpets of silver. Josephus says the trumpet which Moses invented was little less than a cubit long, slightly thicker than a flute, and ending in a bell. This description fits the two trumpets from Herod's temple shown on the Arch of Titus, except that these trumpets are considerably more than a cubit long. Trumpets on Jewish coins of the 2nd century A.D. seem to tally well with Josephus' description.

These metal trumpets also were used to sound war alarms and, in the temple worship, doubtless were presumed to attract

God's attention. These trumpets often were combined with other instruments.

It is interesting to note that the ḥăṣōṣĕrôt come in pairs. Moses made two trumpets; the Arch of Titus shows two trumpets; and the Jewish coins show two trumpets. Though this gemination of trumpets has been known in other lands the Hebrews seem to be its originators; in Egypt the metal trumpet of the same pattern is shown always as a single instrument. There is no reason to believe that the priests played two parts on the trumpets. The priests often functioned in pairs and two priests would need two trumpets. Probably they played in unison, though they may have given some passages antiphonally.

Cymbals

Cymbals in the Old Testament are mentioned first in the list of instruments on which David performed on the occasion of the bringing up of the ark (II Sam. 6:5). The word used here and in Ps. 150 is ṣelṣĕlîm. Elsewhere another word, mĕṣiltayim, from the same stem is the term employed. This occurs thirteen times, all in the writings of the Chronicler (I and II Chron., Ezra, and Nehemiah). Both are related to a verb meaning 'clash,' 'jingle,' 'tingle,' and are onomatapoetic, that is, by their sound suggest the sound of the instrument. In Ps. 150:4 we may have mention of two kinds of cymbals—loud cymbals and high-sounding cymbals as the Authorized and Revised Versions have it, or clanging cymbals and crashing cymbals as the "Chicago Bible" translates. The Hebrew is ṣilṣĕlê šāmaʿ and silṣĕlê tĕrúʿāh. Sachs takes the former to mean 'harsh,' 'noisy,' and the latter to mean 'clear.' He calls attention to the two kinds of cymbals in Tibet and Java. The harsh cymbals are the heavier and are vertically struck, while the lighter clear cymbals are horizontally struck.

While there are no pictures of Hebrew cymbal beaters, the two kinds of cymbals appear in Assyrian reliefs. The harsh cymbal seems to have wooden sticks as handles and the performer is beating vertically. The clear cymbal is being beaten horizontally. We have the good fortune to possess a pair of the latter cymbals from the land of Israel. They are about of the size of their Assyrian counterparts and doubtless were played the same way. Their handles must have been small thongs thrust through the holes in center and knotted on the inside.

The Sistrum

Among the instruments which David played on the celebrated occasion was the *měna'an'îm*, which the Authorized Version mistranslates 'cornets.' The Septuagint has *kymbala* and the Vulgate *sistra*. The Revised Version and the "Chicago Bible" have 'castanets,' but the former in the margin has 'sistra.' Both Finesinger and Sachs think that the instrument was the sistrum.

In Egyptian art we have the sistrum frequently pictured and it was connected with the worship of Hathor. It came in two forms, but the principle was the same. Above the handle, which frequently showed the head of the goddess, was a metal loop with holes through which pieces of wire were inserted and bent at the ends. Since the holes were larger than the wire, the instrument produced a jingling sound when shaken. The Hebrew word comes from a verb which means 'shake'; so it is reasonable to suppose that the *měna'an'îm* were sistra. At Bethel in 1934 there was found the Hathor-headed handle of a sistrum. While it comes from pre-Israelite times and has an image which would be abhorrent to the followers of Yahweh (Jehovah), it shows that the sistrum was known in central Canaan just before the Israelites came in. The sistrum appeared in early Babylonia and was not always connected with the worship of Hathor. So the Israelites may very well have taken it over.

Related to the sistrum is the rattle, which once was a musical instrument and later became a toy. There is no reference to the rattle in the Bible, but at Tell Beit Mirsim Albright found two good examples.

Other Instruments

In Ps. 150:4 the term 'stringed instruments,' Hebrew *min-nîm*, is the name not of any single object but of a family of instruments.

The term *šālĭšîm* (I Sam. 18:6) translated 'instruments of music' in the older versions and 'sistrums' in the "Chicago Bible" is enigmatic. Since it is closely related to the Hebrew word for 'three,' there have been suggestions of the triangle, the three-stringed lute, the triangular harp, and castanets bound to the thumb and two fingers. The triangle may be ruled out, since it does not appear until well along in the Christian era. Sachs on grammatical grounds (unconvincing to the writer) holds that the word cannot mean an instrument and suggests that it is the name of a dance. It could also designate a song pattern. The women who came out to meet Saul with 'timbrels,' with joy, and with *šālĭšîm* sang antiphonally as they played, "Saul has slain his thousands, and David his ten thousands." There are three beats in each half of this line. At present we shall have to leave the *šālĭšîm* as an unsolved problem.

In Dan. 3:5, 7, 10, 15 there is a list of instruments used in the court of Nebuchadnezzar. These instruments are not offered as belonging to Israel. The Authorized Version calls them cornet, flute, harp, sackbut, psaltery, and dulcimer. This part of Daniel is in Aramaic, not Hebrew. The first two names are Semitic: *qarnā* means 'the horn' and *mašrôqîtā* (discussed above in the section on flutes) designates a whistle, according to Sachs probably a double oboe. The other names are Greek: *qatros* is the cithara; *sabka* is from a Greek word, said to be the name of a harp shaped like a siege machine, consisting of a ladder on a boat; *pesanterin* is the psaltery; and *sumponeyah* is the same as our word 'symphony.' Some have thought it meant bagpipe; but, though we may be sure that it signified the blending of sounds, we cannot identify it as an instrument.

In the titles of some Psalms there are obscure words which at various times have been considered musical instruments, such as *nĕgînôt, gittît, šĕmînît*. The last, since it is connected with the word for eight, has been thought related to the musical octave. Now it is generally agreed, however, that these words are names not of musical instruments, but of melodies or styles of singing.

Tunes Still Unknown

We now have a better idea of the instruments of the Israelites than our fathers had and can tell with a reasonable degree of certainty the kinds of noises that came from these instruments. We think we can identify the instruments on which David showed himself skilful and those designated to be used to the praise of the Lord in the final Psalm. But still we cannot have more than hazy notions about the tunes that were played on them. Sachs favors the notion that there was a prevailing pentatonic scale; but of that we cannot be certain. The directions that the rabbis gave are not altogether intelligible to us and moreover they were written after Hellenization had affected the music as well as the architecture and speech of Palestine.

We can only wonder how it sounded when the Israelite musicians played and the congregation sang. Probably it would have seemed discordant to the concert goer of the Victorian age; but those of us who are accustomed to Stravinsky, Sowerby, and Duke Ellington doubtless would think it delightful.

WHAT WERE THE CHERUBIM?

7

WHAT WERE THE CHERUBIM?

W. F. ALBRIGHT

Today we think of a cherub as a tiny winged boy, following the tradition of Renaissance artists. This conception was directly borrowed from pictures of Graeco-Roman "loves" or Erotes, familiar to us from the excavations of Pompeii. The actual appearance of the cherubim of the Old Testament was already forgotten before the time of Christ, and Josephus (first century A.D.) says that "no one can tell what they were like."

Since the veil of the Tabernacle was decorated with embroidered cherubim, and the walls and the religious objects of Solomon's temple lavishly adorned with them, we ought to be able to identify them in contemporary Syro-Palestinian art. The account of the Ark of the Covenant shows that only a creature with wings can be considered. If, therefore, we study all known representations of animals and hybrid creatures, partly animal, we find one which is much more common than any other winged creature, so much so that its identification with the cherub is certain: that is *the winged sphinx or winged lion with human head*. In Egypt the wingless sphinx and the griffin appear; in Babylonia and Assyria the winged bull with a human head prevails; but in Syria and Palestine it is the winged sphinx which is dominant in art and religious symbolism.

The God of Israel was often designated as "He who sitteth (on) the cherubim" (I Sam. 4:4, etc.). The conception un-

derlying this designation is well illustrated by representations
of a king seated on a throne supported on each side by
cherubim, which have been found at Byblus, Hamath, and
Megiddo, all dating between 1200 and 800 B.C. One shows
King Hiram of Byblus (period of the Judges) seated upon his

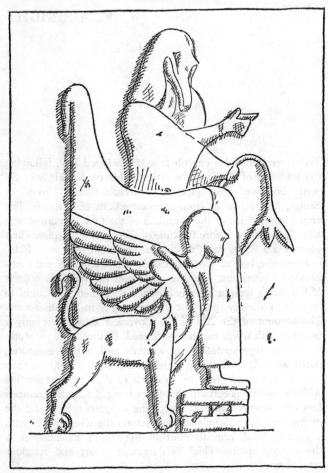

*King Hiram of Byblus seated on his cherub-throne, tenth
century* B.C.   Drawing by A. H. Detweiler

cherub throne. Pottery incense altars found at Taanach and
Megiddo are archaeological parallels to the wheeled lavers
("bases") of Solomon's temple, which were decorated with
lions and cherubs, according to I Kings 7:36.

The primary function of the cherub in Israelite religious
symbolism is illustrated by two biblical passages. A very ancient hymn, found twice in the Bible, has the words, "And He
rode upon a cherub and did fly" (I Sam. 22:11, Ps. 18:11);
the second is Ezek. 10:20. The conception of the deity as
standing or as enthroned on an animal or hybrid creature was
exceedingly common in the ancient Near East, but it was most
common in Syria and Northern Mesopotamia between 2000
and 700 B.C. In Babylonia the figure of a deity is replaced in
certain cases by a winged shrine and later by a thunderbolt.
So in Israelite symbolism between 1300 and 900 B.C., the invisible Glory (Jehovah) was conceived as enthroned upon the
golden cherubim or standing on a golden bull.

8

A NEW LETTER IN ARAMAIC, WRITTEN TO A PHARAOH OF EGYPT

JOHN BRIGHT

The last years of the kingdom of Judah are of peculiar interest to the student of the Bible. From the great (Deuteronomic) reform of King Josiah in 621 B.C. until the last futile resistance to the Babylonians failed in 587 and Jerusalem lay in ruins, there is spun out a drama of tragic significance in the life of the ancient people of Israel. Towering over all the lesser characters in the play are the figures of two of Israel's greatest prophets, Jeremiah and Ezekiel.

With the discovery of the Lachish ostraca in 1935 welcome light was cast upon the final scene of the tragedy's last act.[1] These are a series of letters written in classical biblical Hebrew on broken bits of pottery. All (except one) date from the year before the final fall of Jerusalem, and were sent from a nearby outpost to the garrison commander in Lachish, where they were found. The situation is that of Jer. 34:7 when, of all the Judean cities aside from Jerusalem, only Lachish and Azekah still held out.

Now an additional ray of light has fallen upon a slightly earlier phase of the drama. It is in the form of a papyrus fragment discovered in 1942 at Saqqara (Memphis) in Egypt during the course of excavations conducted there by Zaki Saad

[1] The bibliography on the Lachish letters is rather extensive. Let the reader consult Haupert, *BA*, I.4, pp. 30–32; Albright, *BASOR* No. 70, pp. 11–17, etc.

Effendi. Now in the Museum in Cairo, it was published in 1948 by A. Dupont-Sommer and more recently discussed by H. L. Ginsberg.[2] It is written in Aramaic in a form of the "square" (Assyrian) script, which subsequently displaced the older Phoenician characters as a vehicle for the writing of Hebrew, and with which we are familiar from our Hebrew Bibles. It is a letter from one of the Palestinian kinglets to the Pharaoh imploring his aid against the king of Babylon. Unfortunately the papyrus is badly damaged. It consists of nine lines, which seems to be all that were originally there, but the sheet has been torn in the middle and the left half lost, so that only the first part of each line is present. In addition there are obscurities, line 5 being so badly preserved that only one word can be made out. But we ought, nevertheless, to be grateful; only in Egypt, where the climate is so dry, would such a papyrus fragment have been preserved at all.

I

Following is the text of the letter as given by Ginsberg. It will be realized that the words in brackets represent the missing half of the page and have been supplied from conjecture.

> (1) *To Lord of Kingdoms,[3] Pharaoh, thy servant Adon king of [Ashkelon (?). May X (i.e. the name of a god or goddess), the lord of] (2) heaven and earth, and Baalshemain [the great] god [make the throne of Lord of Kingdoms] (3) Pharaoh enduring as the days of heaven.[4] That [I have written to my lord is to inform thee that the troops] (4) of the king of Babylon have advanced*

[2] A. Dupont-Sommer, "Un papyrus araméen d'époque Saïte découvert à Saqqarah," *Semitica*, I (1948), 43–68; H. L. Ginsberg, "An Aramaic Contemporary of the Lachish Letters," *BASOR*, No. 111 (1948), pp. 24–27. Future undocumented references to either of the above scholars will refer, respectively, to these articles.

[3] Dupont-Sommer reads "to the Lord of the kings," but Ginsberg (note 5) seems to be correct. The title is equivalent to that used by the Ptolemies, *Kurios basileion*, and signifies the ancient Pharaonic claim to be the "Ruler of Upper and Lower Egypt."

[4] The expression is that used in Deut. 11:21, Ps. 89:29, Ecclus. 45:15.

*as far as Aphek and have be[gun to . . . . . (5)
. . . . .] they have taken [. . . . . .] and [. . . . . .].
(6) For Lord of Kingdoms, Pharaoh, knows that [thy]
servant [cannot stand alone against the king of Babylon.
May it therefore please him] (7) to send a force to succor
me. Let him not forsake m[e. For thy servant is loyal to
my lord] (8) and thy servant remembers his kindness,
and this region⁵ [is my lord's possession. But if the king of
Babylon takes it, he will set up] (9) a governor in the
land and⁶ . . . . . . [. . . . . .*

That the letter was sent from Palestine or Syria there can
be no doubt. An appeal to Egypt for help against the Babylonian army would make no sense from any other quarter. Further, the name of the sender, Adon, fits in well with the onomasticon (lists of known names) of both Canaanites and
Hebrews. Presumably it is a hypocoristicon (i.e. an abbreviated writing, the name of the deity, which constitutes the latter
part, being omitted). Phoenician inscriptions give us such
names as Adoni-baal, Adoni-eshmun, etc.; the Bible lists a
Canaanite king called Adoni-zedek (Josh. 10:1), as well as
such good Hebrew names as Adonijah, Adoniram, etc. Besides
this, the only deity invoked in the part of the text that is preserved is that of the active head of the Canaanite pantheon,
Baalshemain (Lord of the heavens). Long known to readers
of the Old Testament as a foreign deity, the Ras Shamrah
texts have now clearly illuminated the place and function of
Baal in the Canaanite religion.⁷ The name of the other deity
referred to as "[. . . . . . lord of (mistress of)] heaven and

---

⁵ Dupont-Sommer, reading different consonants here, gets "this
leader." If Ginsberg (note 4c) is correct, the meaning is literally
"this isle," which is like the expression which Isaiah (20:6) used
of his own tiny land.

⁶ Dupont-Sommer, partly on the basis of a different interpretation of some of the words, partly on conjecture, has "[and they have
punished] the governor with death, and the secretary they have
changed . . . . .[. . . . ." The writer will not attempt to de-
cide, but he feels that the reading is too uncertain to bear the deductions which Dupont-Sommer lays upon it (p. 61).

⁷ To supply a bibliography would be out of place here. The writer
suggests Albright, ARI, chap. iii; or, for a popular treatment, Gordon,
The Living Past (1941), chap. vii.

earth" is not sure. Dupont-Sommer suggests (p. 47) that it is
the Babylonian goddess Ishtar, who is known to have borne
the title "mistress of heaven and earth," and whose worship,
as Ginsberg (note 8) points out, was very popular in contemporary Judah (Jer. 7:18, 44:17–19, "queen of heaven"). But
it is at least equally likely that some Canaanite deity is intended.

Of what city Adon was king we are not told. The text breaks
tantalizingly just at that point. But there is good reason for
the suggestion made by Albright and taken up by Ginsberg
that it is Ashkelon. King Adon states that the Babylonians have
already reached Aphek. Since the Babylonian invasion moved
into Syria and Palestine from the north, it seems likely that
Aphek lay to the north of the city where Adon ruled. The
situation is complicated by the fact that the Bible knows of
at least four Apheks: one in the tribe of Asher (Josh. 19:30),
one east of the sea of Galilee (I Kings 20:26), one in Phoenicia
near Byblos (Josh. 13:4), and one on the plain of Sharon
(Josh. 12:18, I Sam. 4:1, 29:1).[8] It is probable, however, that
this last is the Aphek of our text. It is to be found at Ras el-Ain
(N. T. Antipatris) some 10 miles N. of Lydda. The Old Testament knew it as the base of Philistine operations against Israel,
and it is probably the "Apqu (Aphek) belonging to the territory of the land of Sama(ria)" through which Esarhaddon
marched en route to his invasion of Egypt in 671.[9]

But if the Aphek on the coastal plain is in question, and
Adon's city is to be sought south of it, then the latter must have
been one of the cities of the Philistine plain. Now the five great
cities of the Philistines were Gaza, Ashkelon, Ashdod, Ekron
and Gath. But Gaza had been the Egyptian residency in
Palestine and, even if the Egyptian troops had abandoned it
at the time of Adon's plea for aid, it would hardly have had a
native king of its own. Gath drops from history after its capture
by Uzziah (II Chron. 26:6). Ashdod, ravaged by the Assyrian

[8] Cf. Wright-Filson, *The Westminster Historical Atlas to the Bible*
(Rev. ed., 1956), p. 121; F. M. Abel, *Géographie de la Palestine*,
II, 246.
[9] Cf. the translation of Esarhaddon's inscription, line 16, in H.
Gressman, *Altorientalische Texte zum Alten Testament* (1926),
p. 358.

Sargon (Isa. 20:1) (as was Ekron by Sennacherib), was (according to Herodotus, II. 157) taken by Psammetichus I of Egypt (663–609) after a bitter siege; probably it now lay in ruins (cf. "remnant of Ashdod," Jer. 25:20). This leaves Ashkelon, on the seacoast some 12 miles NE of Gaza, as the most likely possibility, a supposition which, if correct, ties in well with the doom pronounced on Ashkelon in Jer. 47 (esp. vs. 5, 7).[10]

Further support comes from tablets from Babylon published by Ernst Weidner.[11] Here are mentioned, among captives living in Babylon, two "sons of Aga', the king of Ashkelon." Besides these princes there are mentioned "foremen of the Ashkelonians," "Ashkelonian seamen," etc. So we have evidence that princes of Ashkelon, together with skilled elements of the population had been deported to Babylon before 592, just as was done to the people of Jerusalem (II Kings 24:14). No other Philistine city is mentioned in these tablets. It is possible that Aga' still reigned in Ashkelon at the time, the two princes being hostages. If so, Aga' must have been the successor of Adon, set up as a Babylonian vassal, like Zedekiah of Judah, after his predecessor had been made to pay for his loyalty to the Egyptian cause.

II

It is, therefore, possible to place the letter of Adon in its context in history. The king of Babylon can only be Nebuchadnezzar, the Pharaoh in question is almost certainly Necho II (609–593). The letter is thus an additional footnote to the events of II Kings 23–24. When Assyrian power tottered after the death of Ashurbanipal (633), Egypt entertained the dream of re-creating the empire which the Pharaohs of the XVIII Dynasty had held, up to the Euphrates river. For this reason

[10] The editorial note in Jer. 47:1 seems to be in error, as the commentators agree. The foe in question comes "out of the north" (vs. 2).

[11] *Mélanges Dussaud*, II, 298; cf. Ginsberg, note 7 and Albright's comments there. These tablets also yield important evidence concerning the deported king Jehoiachin; cf. Albright, *BA*, V.4, pp. 49–55.

Psammetichus I moved into Palestine as the Assyrians lost control, and subsequently Egyptian troops were sent to aid Assyria against Babylonians and the Medes in the hour of her extremity. The same policy was followed by Necho, whose soldiers aided the remnant of the Assyrian army in an effort to retake Harran in 609. Meanwhile Josiah hoped not only to rule over a free Judah, but also to unite the remains of the defunct northern state under the throne of David at Jerusalem, as the extent of his reform (II Kings 23:15-20) shows. This is why he attempted to head off Necho's army at Megiddo—an effort which cost his life (II Kings 23:28-30). Judah then passed into the Egyptian orbit, Jehoahaz being deposed and led away to Egypt, Jehoiakim made king in his place and the land placed under tribute (II Kings 23:31-35). It may be assumed that the Philistine kings such as Adon had already suffered a similar fate.

All this was reversed by the crushing defeat which Nebuchadnezzar dealt Necho at Carchemish in 605.[12] Although Nebuchadnezzar was prevented from following his advantage at once, owing to the death of his father Nabopolassar, by 603/2 his armies had returned and had rolled the last vestiges of Egyptian power out of Asia. The petty states of Palestine now became vassals of the Babylonian. Jehoiakim of Judah gave in along with the rest, for II Kings 24:1 states that he served the king of Babylon three years before the rebellion that cost Judah so dearly. Adon of Ashkelon, however, appears to have chosen to resist, banking on Egyptian aid which, as always, came too little and too late, if at all. It could, of course, be argued that Adon submitted to Nebuchadnezzar, only subsequently to rebel, as did Jehoiakim. If so, the letter must date *ca.* 600-598. But the tone of the letter, fragmentary as it is, suggests the plea of a loyal vassal of Egypt who fears Babylonian advance, rather than a rebel against Babylonian authority appealing to the Pharaoh for aid. A date *ca.* 603/2 for the letter is, therefore, better.

---

[12] We follow the usual interpretation here, holding that the editorial gloss in Jer. 46:2 is accurate, against Dupont-Sommer (pp. 57 ff.) who, on the basis of a statement of Berossus quoted by Josephus, holds that Necho was crushed in 609. Cf. Albright, *JBL*, LI (1932), 86 ff., on the question.

Had Adon had a Hebrew prophet in his court he would at least have been warned. For always the prophets pointed out the folly of counting on Egypt. Isaiah thought it both foolish and impious during the crisis of 701 when Sennacherib's army "came down like a wolf on the fold" (Isa. 30, 31), as he had previously when Sargon's troops appeared in the vicinity (Isa. 20); Egypt is a bruised reed (Isa. 36:6): if a man leans on it, it will break and pierce his hand. Jeremiah had equally few illusions as his advice to Zedekiah, who was in turn listening to the Lorelei song (this time of Hophra) makes clear (Jer. 37:6 ff.; chap. 27). While the prophets were by no means moved to give their advice merely by a shrewd look at the political weather, it was as political advice, none the less excellent. But poor Adon had no prophet to tell him; maybe he would not have listened anyhow. The kings of Judah certainly did not, as the book of Jeremiah as well as the Lachish letters (III, 14–16, which tells of the mission of Coniah ben Elnathan to Egypt in the last days of Zedekiah) tell us.

III

Our papyrus is important from another point of view. Not only is it (with the possible exception of a mutilated fragment from the Assyrian period, cf. Dupont-Sommer, p. 44) by almost a century the oldest Aramaic papyrus now known, but it is also a new illustration of the international importance of the Aramaic language. Adon presumably spoke some dialect of Canaanite; Pharaoh spoke Egyptian. Yet Adon wrote neither in his own tongue nor that of his lord, but in Aramaic. In this respect the letter is a parallel to the Amarna letters of the fourteenth century, written by Canaanite kings to the Egyptian court in Akkadian cuneiform. It illustrates, then, the fact that Aramaic was already before the end of the seventh century becoming the international language of state.

It has long been known that Aramaic became the official language of the Persian empire, at least in its western part, almost a century later. But until now it had not been dreamed that this development had begun so early. It is true that Aramaic had begun to enjoy wide use as a commercial language in the Assyrian empire since the Sargonids, as Aramaic "dockets" (abstracts of contents) on cuneiform business documents show. It would seem from II Kings 18:36 (= Isa. 36:11) that by the end of the eighth century highly placed personages (in this case Assyrians and Hebrews) might be expected to converse in Aramaic. And an ostracon from Ashur of the mid-seventh century contains the correspondence of one Assyrian official with another—in Aramaic. But this letter of Adon is the first evidence that Aramaic had begun to oust Akkadian as the language of official diplomatic correspondence before the Persian period. The horizon of this development is thus pushed back the best part of a century. Indeed it is probable, though not proved, that the Babylonians administered the western part, at least, of their empire in Aramaic and that the Persians merely took over the existing custom together with much of its machinery.

While the letter here in question does not throw direct or decisive light on the question of the Aramaic portions of the Old Testament, it will perhaps serve as an additional warning against overmuch skepticism. The Aramaic of Ezra (4:8–6:18, 7:12–26), which contains correspondence purportedly with the Persian court and in Aramaic, and which has been branded as a forgery by such able scholars as C. C. Torrey (*Ezra Studies* [1910], pp. 140 ff.) and R. H. Pfeiffer (*Introduction to the Old Testament* [1941], pp. 816 ff.), takes on a more authentic flavor with each such discovery. Again, that courtiers should address Nebuchadnezzar in Aramaic as the story in Dan. 2:4 has it, no longer appears at all surprising. All in all, if Adon was not able to save his royal skin by his letter to the Pharaoh, we remain very glad that he wrote it.[13]

---

[13] Since the above was written, new portions of the Babylonian Chronicle have appeared which furnish more information about the period to which this letter belongs: see D. N. Freedman, "The Babylonian Chronicle," in Chapter 10.

9

KING JOIACHIN IN EXILE

W. F. ALBRIGHT

For twenty-five hundred years the unhappy fate of poor young Joiachin (or Jehoiachin) has moved men to pity. At the age of eighteen he became king of Judah, and he remained under the control of his mother Nehushta until the end of his short reign of three months. During his brief rule the country lay at the mercy of the Chaldeans, against whose king Nebuchadnezzar the young king's father, Joiakim (Jehoiakim), had rebelled. The latter had apparently met a tragic end, probably in a palace revolt, since his body was thrown outside the gates of the city and left to lie there like the carcass of an ass (Jer. 22:18–19; 36:30). Not long afterwards (in 598–97 B.C.) Jerusalem was besieged by the Babylonian army. Prospects seemed so dark that the king, his mother, and the principal officials surrendered and were carried as captives to Babylonia, along with thousands of people, the flower of the land.

Though the men of Judah regretted his departure and many of them are said to have preferred Joiachin and his fellow exiles greatly to the "bad figs" (Jer. 24) which remained in Judah, Joiachin never returned to his native land, but died in exile. Thirty-seven years after his surrender to the Chaldeans he was released from prison by Nebuchadnezzar's son Evilmerodach, and was given preferential treatment: "His chair was set above the chairs of the (captive) kings who were with him in Babylon" (II Kings 25:27–29). The names of seven sons of Joiachin, born "(while he was) a captive" (I Chron. 3:17, Hebrew text), are known; the eldest of them was Shealtiel, father of Zerubbabel.

The first archaeological light on King Joiachin appeared fourteen years ago, when I dug up a broken jar-handle, stamped with a beautifully carved seal inscribed "Belonging to Eliakim, steward of Yaukin." Immediately after the find the eminent Palestinian archaeologist, Father L. H. Vincent, identified the name "Yaukin" as an abbreviated form of "Joiachin," just as the name "Yauqim" of contemporary documents is an abbreviation of "Joiakim" (name of Joiachin's father). In 1930 two more examples of the same stamp were found on jar-handles: one by Professor Elihu Grant at Beth-shemesh in northwestern Judah; the other by my colleagues and myself at Tell Beit Mirsim (Kiriath-sepher) in southwestern Judah, where the first had previously been discovered. All three stamps were made from the same original seal, indicating that Yaukin was a person of very high importance, probably king, since seals bearing a formula of this type have been proved to belong to kings of Judah and surrounding lands. It was possible to demonstrate rather conclusively (in 1932) that Eliakim had been steward of the crown property of king Joiachin while the latter was a captive in Babylonia. During the years 597–587 B.C. Joiachin's uncle Zedekiah was in control, and since his nephew was still considered by many, perhaps most, of the people of Judah as the legitimate king who might return any day (Jer. 28:1–4), Zedekiah would scarcely dare to appropriate his nephew's property. Presumably the Chaldeans themselves blew hot and cold, favoring Zedekiah one year and his nephew the next.

Seven years after the publication of these stamps, a very important discovery was announced by Dr. Ernst F. Weidner of Berlin. Weidner had informed me of his remarkable find several years ago, in a personal letter. More than a third of a century ago the German excavators of Babylon cleared the ruins of a remarkable vaulted building near the famous Ishtar Gate. Just southwest of the building in question lay the ruins of the great palace of the Chaldean kings, called "The House at which Men Marvel." According to the excavators, the vaulted building represents the substructure of the Hanging

Gardens, counted by the Greeks as one of the Seven Wonders of the World. However this may be, there can be no doubt that the vaulted rooms (fourteen in number) represent the substructure of an important public building, probably one of the main depots for the distribution of supplies from the royal storehouses. In favor of this more prosaic interpretation are the location of the building at the Ishtar Gate and the discovery of nearly 300 cuneiform tablets relating mostly to the distribution of sesame oil and barley to individual recipients. These tablets were found in the bottom of a stair well, where they had fallen when the upper stories of the structure collapsed.

The contents of the tablets, in Weidner's résumé, prove to be extraordinarily interesting, since they list payment of rations in oil and barley, etc., to captives and skilled workmen from many nations, all living in and around Babylon between the years 595 and 570 B.C. Among them are Yaukin, king of Judah, and five royal princes, as well as numerous other men of Judah; the sons of Aga, king of Ascalon in the land of the Philistines, together with mariners and musicians from that seaport; mariners and craftsmen from Tyre, Byblus, and Arvad in Phoenicia; Elamites, Medes, and Persians; many Egyptians, who were mariners, shipbuilders, horse-trainers and monkey-trainers (among their names are Necho, Psammetichus, Haryotes and perhaps Apries); Ionian carpenters and shipbuilders, all with Carian or Lycian (localities in Asia Minor) names; and finally a number of Lydians. When all the tablets have been cleaned and published in detail, they will provide rich material for the study of the international relations of Babylonia in the reign of Nebuchadnezzar.

The name of the king of Judah is written in several ways, all pointing to the pronunciation "Yaukin," that is, "Yow-keen," as we know from recent studies of Babylonian spelling and pronunciation. The cuneiform writing of the name thus conclusively demonstrates the correctness of Vincent's identification of the Yaukin of our Palestinian stamps with King Joiachin of the Bible. Yaukin is called "king of the land of Yahud (Judah)." The spelling of the last name proves the correctness of the writer's long-standing contention that the shortened form "Yehud," which later became usual in Aramaic, was already employed instead of the longer "Yehudah" before the Babylonian Exile. In exactly the same way the longer name "Yah-weh" ("Jehovah") had been replaced for some purposes by "Yahu" long before the Exile. After the Exile the latter became the regular form of the divine name among the Jewish colonists at Elephantine in Upper Egypt.

A number of other biblical names occur among the persons receiving rations in these tablets. Shelemiah, Semachiah (both also found in the Lachish Letters[1]), Kenaiah (known from the Elephantine Papyri and from an early Jewish seal), Gaddiel, Or-melech are specifically mentioned by name; Shelemiah is called "gardener." A century later Jews had already become so numerous and so important in the economic life of Babylonia that they figured largely in the business transactions for such houses as that of Murashu and Sons at Nippur.

As pointed out by Weidner, this distribution of rations undoubtedly means that Joiachin was free to move about Babylon and was not in prison. His imprisonment was then a later event, perhaps brought about by an attempt at escape in connection with intrigues or actual revolt in Judah. One such movement is mentioned in Jer. 28:1–4: the prophet Hananiah son of Azariah ("Azur," also mentioned in the Lachish Letters) of Gibeon predicted that Joiachin would be restored to his throne within two years. Since this prophecy is dated 594 B.C. and one of the tablets mentioning Joiachin is dated in 592, it follows that Joiachin's status was not seriously affected by this particular incident. Some later event was therefore responsible for his incarceration.

Almost as significant as the mention of King Joiachin of Judah is the reference to his five sons, who are mentioned three times immediately after his name. Each time they are listed together with their attendant, Kenaiah. Weidner suggests that they may have been brothers of Joiachin, not sons, observing that he was only 23 at the time. Actually, however, he was 24, and he doubtless had more than one wife, like his grandfather, Josiah. Even so, at that age it would be perfectly possible for him to have had six or seven successive children by a single wife. These five princes doubtless included several who lived long enough to be included in the list of Joiachin's

[1] For a description of these documents dating from the last days of the Kingdom of Judah, see *BA*, I, 4, p. 30 ff.

seven sons given by the Chronicler (I Chron. 3:17–18). Among them was certainly Shealtiel, the Salathiel of the New Testament (Matt. 1:12; Luke 3:27), better known as the father of Zerubbabel, who was prince of Judah when the Second Temple was under construction. That Weidner's suggestion is practically impossible is shown by the fact that the princes are always mentioned in the same breath as their father and that they were so young as to be "in the hands of" an attendant who was himself a Jew. Had they been older youths, they would surely have been provided with a Babylonian tutor for the purpose of indoctrinating them thoroughly in Babylonian ways (cf. Daniel 1:3–20).

Incidentally, the discovery that several of Joiachin's seven sons were already born before 592 B.C. makes it necessary to push the birth of the eldest, Shealtiel, back to around 598 at the latest. In this case it becomes probable that his son Zerubbabel was older than commonly supposed in 520 B.C., when the prophecies of Haggai were delivered. (The reader will recall that Zerubbabel was the leader of the returned Exiles of Jerusalem at this time.) This observation has a very important bearing on the interpretation of events following the Edict of Cyrus in 539 B.C. which permitted the Jews to return to Palestine. Since the history of the Restoration has been very obscure and difficult to reconstruct, this new light on Zerubbabel's age is valuable. Moreover, it now becomes even clearer than it was hitherto that the list of Joiachin's descendants down to the seven sons of Elioenai (in I Chron. 3:17–24) cannot come down later than the very beginning of the fourth century, that is, the period immediately after 400 B.C. Every pertinent recent find has increased the evidence both for the early date of the Book of Chronicles (about 400 B.C. or a little later) and for the care with which the Chronicler excerpted and compiled from older books, documents and oral traditions which were at his disposal.

Another by-product of Weidner's discoveries is new evidence for the authenticity of the Book of Ezekiel, sometimes held by recent writers to be a late fiction, or at least historically unreliable. The discovery of the jar-stamp made it possible to call in question Professor Torrey's denial of the authenticity of the dating of Ezekiel's prophecies by years of Joiachin's captivity

(C. C. Torrey, *Pseudo-Ezekiel and the Original Prophecy* [1930], pp. 17 f., 59 ff.). Now we know that Joiachin was not only the legitimate king of the Jewish exiles in Babylonia from their own point of view; he was also regarded by the Babylonians as legitimate king of Judah, whom they held in reserve for possible restoration to power if circumstances should seem to require it. At the same time, no Jewish exile in Babylonia could safely make public acknowledgment of his loyalty to the deposed ruler by dating events in his regnal years, so dating by the year of Joiachin's captivity was the only escape from the dilemma. This system of dating is thus one which could scarcely have been invented centuries afterwards; it is a striking confirmation of the genuineness of Ezekiel's prophecies. The year of our dated tablet mentioning Joiachin is precisely the year in which Ezekiel saw his lurid vision of the idolatrous abominations which were being practiced in Jerusalem (Ezek. 8).

The new documentation brings other confirmations of the authenticity of the Book of Ezekiel—small but none the less significant, especially when added to the accumulated mass of archaeological illustrations of Ezekiel. On pp. 31 f. of his book Torrey insists that Ezekiel paints the material situation of the exiles in impossibly bright colors: the prophet lived in a house; he possessed an iron pan and a balance; he could eat wheat, barley, beans, lentils, millet, and spelt. Quite aside from the fact that such circumstances are far from being luxurious, is the fact that at least one of the Jews listed in Weidner's tablets is expressly termed a "gardener," and that skilled craftsmen were in great demand, since rations for many hundreds of them from all parts of the Near East are recorded on these same tablets. Torrey's statement that the Jewish exiles under Joiachin were "not farmers" and that "artisans (craftsmen) could have found no means of support" are thus directly disproved by our new source of information (cf. II Kings 24:14 ff.).

Another point which Torrey stressed with great confidence (p. 84) is now disproved: he insists that Ezekiel could not possibly have made "casual reference to the Persians before that people had made its appearance on the stage of history" (Ezek. 27:10, 38:5). At that time he was not yet aware that the land of Persia and its king, Cyrus I, were mentioned on recently discovered inscriptions of Ashurbanipal (biblical Asenappar) of Assyria, dating from about 640 B.C. Now we have several Persians mentioned by name on one of the new tablets; they are said to come from the land of Parsuwash, the regular form of the name of Persia in older documents. Three Persians and only one Mede appear in our new texts.

The discoveries of Weidner thus have an importance far beyond the mere mention of the name of King Joiachin. Again we realize that every new archaeological discovery touching the Bible affects our understanding of it as a whole, and is not limited to the illustration of a single point.

SOME PERTINENT LITERATURE

Albright, W. F., "The Seal of Eliakim and the Latest Preexilic History of Judah, with Some Observations on Ezekiel" *JBL* (1932), pp. 77–106.

——, "The Date and Personality of the Chronicler" *JBL* (1921), pp. 104–24.

——, *ARI* (1942), pp. 165–68.

Koldewey, Robert, *Das wieder erstehende Babylon* (1913–   ), pp. 90–100.

Koldewey and Wetzel, *Die Königsburgen von Babylon* (1931), pp. 38–64, especially p. 49.

Weidner, Ernst F., "Jojachin, König von Juda, in babylonischen Keilschrifttexten," *Mélanges Syriens offerts à M. René Dussaud*, II (1939), 923–35.

10

THE BABYLONIAN CHRONICLE

DAVID NOEL FREEDMAN

On the 2nd of Adar, in the 7th year of his reign, Nebuchadnezzar, king of Babylon, captured Jerusalem. The precise date, March 16, 597 B.C.,[1] which has been the subject of much debate among scholars, has now been supplied in a newly published tablet of the Babylonian Chronicle,[2] along with other fascinating details of the international power struggle in which the kingdom of Judah was caught and perished. D. J. Wiseman, Assistant Keeper in the Department of Egyptian and Assyrian Antiquities, is to be congratulated upon a splendid achievement. The Trustees of the British Museum are to be commended for bringing to completion the publication of the tablets of the Babylonian Chronicle in their possession: a process which began in 1907 with the appearance of L. W. King's *Chronicles concerning Early Babylonian Kings.*

The present volume contains all the extant tablets of the Babylonian Chronicle for the years 626–556 B.C., including four hitherto unpublished texts, and one that had appeared

---

[1] The Babylonian like the biblical "day" extended from sundown to sundown, thus overlapping two of our days. In transferring dates to the Julian calendar, it would be more accurate to give two successive days: thus, 2 Adar 7 Nebuchadnezzar = 15/16 March 597 B.C.

[2] D. J. Wiseman, *Chronicles of Chaldaean Kings: (626–566 B.C.) in the British Museum* (London: Trustees of the British Museum, 1956), pp. xii, 100, and XXI plates.

previously, but is now out of print.[3] Together with the
Nabonidus Chronicle, published by Sidney Smith,[4] these constitute the surviving formal record of the Neo-Babylonian Empire (626–539 B.C.). As such, and in spite of several sizable
gaps, they are of great interest and importance.[5]

The tablets presumably were copied during the Persian period from older documents, which were compiled from the official annals (i.e., detailed yearly records) of the Babylonian
kings. They constitute a summary but most trustworthy source
for the reconstruction of the historical era which they describe.[6]

B.M. 25127

The first tablet of the Chronicle covers the years 626–623
B.C., and describes the beginnings of the new Babylonian kingdom. As the text opens, Nabopolassar, the leader of the in-
surgent Babylonian forces, has defeated the Assyrian army
outside the gates of Babylon. To celebrate their independence,
the Babylonians enthroned Nabopolassar as their king on Nov.
23, 626 (a new fixed date in Babylonian history). While the
Assyrian empire was disintegrating in the east, there were dangerous stirrings in the west also. Egypt, long since free of Assyrian suzerainty, was scheming to recover its long-lost Asiatic
provinces.[7] Even Judah, doubtless spurred by reports of Assyrian confusion and defeat, was preparing for its day of freedom. Already Josiah had moved into effective control of the

---

[3] C. J. Gadd, *The Fall of Nineveh* (London, 1923).

[4] *Babylonian Historical Texts* (London, 1924).

[5] The gaps are for the years 622–617, 594–557, and 556–555.

[6] There is an interesting parallel between the Babylonian Chronicle and the two "Israelite Chronicles": the so-called Deuteronomic
History comprising the books from Deuteronomy through II Kings,
was compiled at the end of Judah's independent existence from a
number of sources including the Annals of the Kings of Israel and
Judah; the Chronicler's History (I & II Chronicles, Ezra, Nehemiah)
is a similar compilation made about 200 years later from a variety
of records including the Deuteronomic History.

[7] Paradoxically the Egyptians were to fight as allies of the Assyrians, their age-old enemies, against the greater threat of the Medo-
Babylonian alliance.

northern provinces, though still nominally a vassal of Assyria.[8]

During the following years, the Assyrians made unsuccessful attempts to regain control of Babylonia. Nabopolassar, on the other hand, was not yet strong enough to go on the offensive. The Chronicle for the years 622–617 is missing.

B.M. 21901

This tablet, already published by Gadd in 1923, now re-edited by Wiseman, deals with the events of 616–608. The Medes have now made their appearance as leaders of the anti-Assyrian coalition; the Egyptians, on the other hand, have joined forces with the weakened Assyrians, to offset the overwhelming threat of the Medo-Babylonian alliance. In 614, the Medes under Kyaxares their king, captured the ancient Assyrian capital, Assur; Nabopolassar arrived with his forces after the fall of the city. There the two kings met, concluded a treaty of mutual assistance, and departed. With the Medes leading the way, the allies attacked Nineveh in 612. After three months of siege, the city was captured and destroyed. The masters of siege operations had been mastered.[9] While Medes and Babylonians divided the spoils, fragments of the Assyrian army and bureaucracy fled to Harran, where under Assur-uballit II an attempt was made to reconstitute the kingdom. In spite of extensive Egyptian help, the attempt proved unavailing. Assur-uballit had to abandon Harran in 610; a combined attack on the Babylonian garrison there in 609 failed. To what extent Josiah's interposition at Megiddo in 609 delayed or diverted the main forces of Pharaoh Neco from their rendezvous with the Assyrian army in that year at the Euphrates is difficult to determine. But it may be that the suicidal Judahite action contributed materially to the triumph of Medo-Babylonian

[8] Extensive operations occurred in Josiah's 12th year (*ca.* 628/7), in anticipation of the final break with Assyrian authority in the 18th year (622); cf. II Chron. 34:3–7. F. M. Cross, Jr., and David Noel Freedman, *JNES*, XII (1953), 56–58.

[9] A vivid description of the anticipated fall of the city which had dominated the world for centuries is found in the book of Nahum. The end of the ancient oppressor was greeted with universal rejoicing; cf. Nahum 3:7, 19.

arms.[10] In any case, the Assyrians disappeared from the picture, their position in North Syria being taken by the Egyptians.

B.M. 22047

The events leading up to the historic battle of Carchemish (605), are described in the next tablet, newly published B.M. 22047. During this period, the Babylonian armies—Nabopolassar and Nebuchadnezzar the crown prince had separate commands—campaigned against the mountain people on the Urartian border, to prevent raids on the former Assyrian provinces. They also reconnoitered against the Egyptians, who were firmly entrenched at Carchemish on the Euphrates. Efforts to contain the Egyptian army by garrisoning towns below Carchemish in the years 607–606 were frustrated by strong Egyptian thrusts at Kimukhu and Quramati, both of which were captured. Nabopolassar returned to Babylon at the end of the year 606/5 (= Jan.–Feb., 605); he did not again leave the capital, until his death in August.

B.M. 21946

The next tablet in the series covers the important years 605–594. It opens with the battle of Carchemish. Nebuchadnezzar, now in sole command of the Babylonian army, marched swiftly to Carchemish where he engaged the Egyptian forces directly. The Chronicle goes on to say: "He (Nebuchadnezzar)

[10] The biblical accounts of the affair at Megiddo (II Kings 23:29–30, II Chron. 35:20–24) make it clear that Pharaoh Neco had urgent business with the Assyrians at the Euphrates, and did not wish to be delayed by the Judahites. Although the account in II Kings implies that Neco's intentions were hostile toward the Assyrian king, we know from the Babylonian Chronicle that Neco was coming as an ally. It is reasonable to conclude that Josiah was an ally (or vassal) of the Babylonians, and that his action at Megiddo was part of a concerted plan to pin down the Egyptian forces, while the Medo-Babylonian army disposed of the Assyrians. There was a long-standing tradition of friendship between Babylonians and Judahites, going back at least to the days of Merodach-Baladan and Hezekiah, who schemed together against Assyria (cf. II Kings 20:12 ff.) just as their successors were to do a hundred years later.

accomplished their defeat and to non-existence [beat?] them. As for the rest of the Egyptian army, which had escaped from the defeat (so quickly that) no weapon had reached them, in the district of Hamath the Babylonian troops overtook and defeated them so that not a single man escaped to his own country. At that time Nebuchadnezzar conquered the whole area of the Hatti-country (i.e., Syria-Palestine)."[11]

Important for determining synchronisms between Babylonian and Judahite history and establishing the absolute chronology of this period is the date of the battle of Carchemish. While the precise date is not given, the battle must have taken place after April (= Nisan, the beginning of the regnal year) and before August (= Ab) when Nabopolassar died, and Nebuchadnezzar had to return to Babylon. According to Wiseman's calculations, May–June, 605 is the most probable date for the battle.[12] Jer. 46:2 provides a synchronism with Judahite history, dating the battle of Carchemish to the 4th year of Jehoiakim. This in turn fixes the year 609/8 for the commencement of Jehoiakim's reign, as well as for the death of Josiah, and the three month rule of Jehoahaz (cf. II Kings 23:31–34).[13] Having been placed on the throne by Pharaoh

[11] B.M. 21946, obverse, lines 5–8, following Wiseman's translation, *op. cit.*, pp. 66–69. Both the Bible and Josephus refer to the battle and its important consequences for the history of the Near East. Cf. Jer. 46:2 ff., and *Antiquities of the Jews* X.6. Noteworthy is the striking agreement between Josephus and the Babylonian Chronicle (cf. Wiseman, *op. cit.*, pp. 24 f.).

[12] Wiseman, *op. cit.*, p. 25.

[13] It is most probable that regnal years were reckoned in Judah at this time in accordance with the Assyro-Babylonian "post-dating" system. According to this method the period between the king's actual accession and the beginning of the next calendar year (in April) was called the "accession-year." The first "regnal year" began with the New Year's Festival. Thus Nebuchadnezzar was enthroned on Sept. 6, 605. His "accession-year" extended until April, 604, when his "first year" began. So also Jehoiakim's 4th year commenced in April, 605, the year of Carchemish. His first regnal year began in April, 608, and his "accession-year" from his actual enthronement in 609/8 until April, 608. Josiah's last year began in April, 609; he was killed at Megiddo, probably during the summer months. To this we must add the three months of Jehoahaz, and arrive at a date late in 609, or possibly early in 608 for the actual accession of Jehoiakim.

Neco, Jehoiakim served him as vassal for four years. As a result of Nebuchadnezzar's victory over Neco, Jehoiakim transferred his allegiance (cf. II Kings 24:1).[14]

Nabopolassar died on Aug. 16, 605. On receiving the news, Nebuchadnezzar hurried back to Babylon to be crowned king on Sept. 7, 605. From then until the following April is designated his "accession-year." Then in April, 604, during the *akitu* or New Year's Festival, the official "first year" of his reign began.[15] During the early years of his reign, Nebuchadnezzar's chief military activity, according to the Chronicle, was to pacify the newly acquired western territories. Most of the time it was sufficient to parade the Babylonian army through Hatti-land in order to collect the annual tribute. Occasionally, punitive action was required, as in the case of a city, probably Ashkelon, toward the end of 604.[16] Then in Dec., 601, Nebuchadnezzar marched against Egypt. A fierce battle ensued, with heavy casualties on both sides. Neither place nor date is given, but the battle must have occurred near the Egyptian border between Dec., 601, and April, 600, the beginning of Nebuchadnezzar's fifth regnal year. Jehoiakim's rebellion against Babylon is related to this event, since the three-year period of submission ended in 601/0 (cf. II Kings 24:1). In all likelihood the act of rebellion was an independent move following the Babylonian defeat (though there is always the possibility of Egyptian encouragement).[17]

[14] The occasion of Jehoiakim's submission to Nebuchadnezzar was probably the triumphal sweep through Hatti-land in 604/3: "In the first year of Nebuchadnezzar in the month of Sivan he mustered his army and went to the Hatti-territory; he marched about in the Hatti-territory until the month of Kislev. All the kings of the Hatti-land came before him and he received their heavy tribute" (B.M. 21946, obv., ll. 15–17; Wiseman, *op. cit.*, p. 69).

[15] Cf. note 13.

[16] An Aramaic letter dating from this period contains a plea to the Pharaoh for help against the Babylonians; it may reflect the same situation described in the Chronicle. For a brief account of this letter cf. John Bright, *BA*, XII (May, 1949), 46–52.

[17] Jehoiakim, whatever intrigues with Egypt may have been under way, would have made no overt action until after the defeat of Nebuchadnezzar. Nebuchadnezzar would not have undertaken an invasion of Egypt unless the Judahite flank were secure. If Jehoiakim had been in open rebellion, Nebuchadnezzar would first have crushed resistance in Judah before attacking Egypt.

The Babylonian army suffered such serious losses that Nebuchadnezzar returned home immediately, and spent the whole of the following year in reorganizing his military forces. Not until Dec., 599, did he set forth to the west again. The Egyptians must have suffered badly also, because they made no overt move to establish themselves in Syria-Palestine. While the great powers were licking their wounds, Jehoiakim and Judah enjoyed freedom briefly. Nebuchadnezzar, however, countered the rebellion by enlisting the help of Judah's neighbors.[18] These measures proved insufficient, so Nebuchadnezzar led the main Babylonian force against Judah in Dec., 598.

The Capture of Jerusalem

The siege and capture of Jerusalem are described as follows: "In the seventh year, the month of Kislev, the king of Akkad mustered his troops, marched to the Hatti-land, and encamped against the city of Judah and on the second day of the month of Adar he seized the city and captured the king. He appointed there a king of his own choice (lit. heart), received its heavy tribute and sent (them) to Babylon."[19] There can be no doubt that the captured king was Jehoiachin, while the appointed one was Zedekiah. We thus have a fixed date not only for the capture of Jerusalem, but also for the chronology of the last kings of Judah: 2 Adar 7 Nebuchadnezzar = 15/16 March, 597 B.C.[20] Jehoiachin's brief reign of three months ended on March

---

[18] II Kings 24:2. Arameans, Moabites, Ammonites are mentioned along with Chaldean garrisons as the attackers. If this took place in 600/599, it would fit well with the Chronicle's statement that Nebuchadnezzar remained in Babylon with the main army during his 5th year. On the other hand, the guerilla action may have followed the campaign of 599/8 in which Nebuchadnezzar subjugated the Arab tribes of the west. On his return to Babylon in March, 598, he may have left Babylonian garrisons behind to cope with the Judahite rebellion, aided by such native levies as could be mustered.

[19] B.M. 21946, reverse, lines 11–13, following Wiseman's translation, op. cit., p. 73.

[20] A long-standing debate among scholars concerning the chronology of the last years of Judah may now be settled. Many have favored the sequence 597 for the capture of Jerusalem, and 586 for its destruction; others, 598 for the capture, and 587 for the de-

16, 597.[21] His accession is to be dated in Dec., 598, which also marks the death of Jehoiakim.[22] The latter's official regnal years include 608–598, with his accession in the year 609/8.[23]

Computing in the other direction, the end of Jehoiachin's reign also marks the beginning of Zedekiah's rule.[24] Zedekiah's first regnal year began the following month, April, 597. His eleventh and final year began therefore in April, 587; his reign terminated with his capture just before the destruction of Jerusalem, in July of the same year.[25] The new chronological information may be conveniently incorporated into a table of the last kings of Judah:

King	Length of Reign[26]	Accession[27]	Regnal Years[28]	End of Reign
Josiah	31	640/39	639–609	609
Jehoahaz	3 months	609	—	609/8
Jehoiakim	11	609/8	608–598	Dec., 598
Jehoiachin	3 months	Dec., 598	—	March, 597
Zedekiah	11	March, 597	597–587	July, 587

struction. It is to be remembered that these figures are only approximate, since the Babylonian (and Judahite) year extend from April to April, thus overlapping two of the modern (Julian) years. Properly speaking, the patterns mentioned should be set down as 597/6 (8th of Nebuchadnezzar) and 586/5 (19th of Neb.), or 598/7 (7th of Neb.) and 587/6 (18th of Neb.). The Chronicle now establishes the first date (March, 597) in the 7th of Nebuchadnezzar; therefore the second date is in the 18th of Neb. (July–August, 587). The first sequence proposed is wrong, while the second is confirmed.

[21] II Kings 24:8. II Chron. 36:9 gives 3 months and 10 days, which may be a more accurate figure.

[22] He died in the same month that the Babylonian army set out against Judah (see above). The exact manner of Jehoiakim's death remains a mystery. It is difficult to reconcile the accounts in Kings, Chronicles, Josephus (cf. Jer. 22:18–19). The Chronicle shows that he died before the siege began, supporting the statement in II Kings 24:6 (cf. vss. 10 ff.).

[23] Cf. note 13. Jehoiakim reigned 11 years (II Kings 23:36). His first regnal year began in April, 608, his 11th and last in April, 598.

[24] Zedekiah's accession must have taken place in the same month, March, 597 (the last of the year), since the Babylonian Chronicle records the event in the 7th year of Nebuchadnezzar.

[25] II Kings 25:2–7 = Jeremiah 52:5–11.

The following synchronisms between the kings of Babylon and Judah can also be established:

Battle of Carchemish (May–June, 605): 4th of Jehoiakim = 21st of Nabopolassar.

Capture of Jerusalem (March, 597): 11th of Jehoiakim = 7th of Nebuchadnezzar.

Fall of Judah (July, 587): 11th of Zedekiah = 18th of Nebuchadnezzar.

The synchronisms with the 7th and 18th years of Nebuchadnezzar agree with certain biblical references, but disagree with others. It is difficult to explain the discrepancy. On the one hand, Jer. 52:28–29 dates the first captivity in the 7th year of Nebuchadnezzar, and the second in the 18th year.[29] On the other hand, II Kings 24:12 places the first captivity in the

---

[26] In calculating the reign of a king, the biblical historian added the number of regnal years (i.e., full years beginning with the first of the new calendar year, plus the final partial year; the accession year was considered part of the previous king's reign in the numerical computation). Different procedures were followed at earlier periods in Israel's history.

[27] The "accession-year" includes the portion of the year remaining after the death of the reigning king, and before the beginning of the next year in April. Thus Josiah's 31st year began in April, 609; on his death, Jehoahaz succeeded to the throne. The latter's accession-year is therefore the remaining months of 609/8 until the beginning of the new year in April, 608. Jehoahaz, however, failed to finish his accession-year being deposed after three months. The remaining months to April, 608 then constitute Jehoiakim's accession-year; his first regnal year commences in April, 608.

[28] Regnal years are calculated from the beginning of the year following the accession of the king. Since neither Jehoahaz nor Jehoiachin reigned long enough to reach April of the year following their accession, they are not credited with any regnal years. Zedekiah, on the other hand, whose actual reign can be fixed at 10 years and 4 months, is credited with 11 regnal years, the final partial year being added to his total.

[29] We may infer from the documentary character of this excerpt (contrast the precise figures for the number of captives with the round numbers of the account in Kings) that it was copied from an official record kept in Babylon, and which therefore followed Babylonian chronology accurately. A third captivity five years later is presumably to be connected with the punitive expedition sent to Judah after the assassination of Gedaliah (cf. II Kings 25:22–26, and Jeremiah 40–41).

8th year of Nebuchadnezzar; and II Kings 25:8 dates the second in the *19th* year.[30]

Various suggestions have been made with regard to the discrepancies. In view of the statement in II Chronicles 36:10 that Jehoiachin was brought to Babylon at "the turn of the year," Wiseman infers that there was some delay in rounding up the captives so that the exile did not actually begin until after the end of the 7th year and the start of the 8th year of Nebuchadnezzar. Thus the capture of Jerusalem is to be dated in the 7th year, but the captivity in the 8th.[31] This procedure, however, only accentuates the discrepancy, since Jer. 52:28–29 dates the *captivity* in the *7th* year, while II Kings 24:12 dates the *capture of Jerusalem* in the *8th* year. While it may be granted that the larger number of exiles did not arrive in Babylon until the 8th year, it is altogether probable that Nebuchadnezzar and the chief captives reached Babylon in time for the New Year's Festival.[32] Since the events described took place at the turn of the year, they might with some propriety be assigned to the 8th year, though strictly speaking, 7th is correct. The difference is not great, only a month in fact, and may explain how this discrepancy arose. In the case of the second captivity, however, the Bible specifies a month in the middle of the year; so the discrepancy here is a full year (i.e., July–August, 587 or 586).

A second suggestion explains the discrepancy as the result of a difference in methods of reckoning. The two principal methods used for calculating reigns were the post-dating (which has already been explained), and the ante-dating. According to the post-dating method used in Babylon, Nebuchadnezzar's first regnal year began in April, 604, on the completion of his accession-year. His 7th year began in April, 598 and ended in March, 597. According to the ante-dating system, however, the

[30] Also Jer. 52:12; other references in Jeremiah follow the same chronology.

[31] Cf. Wiseman, *op. cit.*, p. 34.

[32] It was the regular practice of the Babylonian king to return to his own land before the end of the year, as repeated entries in the Chronicle show. Note the references for the early years of Nebuchadnezzar: for the years 1, 3, 4, 6, and 8, his return to Babylon, generally in the last months, is specified; in 2 the lines are missing, and in 5 he remained in Babylon all year.

accession-year was reckoned as the first regnal year, so that each succeeding year of the reign is assigned a number one higher than is accorded it by the post-dating method. Thus Nebuchadnezzar's first regnal year (official post-dating system) is equivalent to the second year (ante-dating system) though the calendar year is the same, 604/3. The year 598/7 is Nebuchadnezzar's 7th (post-dating) or 8th (ante-dating); his 18th (post-dating) is equivalent to the 19th (ante-dating), but in either case it is April 587–March 586. In short, there is no discrepancy in the biblical figures; the difference is simply due to variant methods of calculation. If there were any positive evidence that the ante-dating method was in use in Palestine at this time, the proposal would make the most satisfactory solution. We know, however, that the post-dating method was official in Babylon, and it appears certain that the same method was used in Judah for reckoning regnal years. It would therefore be quite strange if the regnal years of a king of Babylon were recorded by a Judahite historian according to the *ante-dating* system.

A third suggestion follows the main lines of the second in equating the two patterns of dates. However, the assumption of an ante-dating system is rejected as improbable, and a different explanation for the pattern 8th and 19th of Nebuchadnezzar is sought.[33] It is possible that the Palestinian historian, without using an ante-dating system, nevertheless reckoned Nebuchadnezzar's reign from the year 605 rather than the official 604. By 605, Nabopolassar was no longer active in the field. At the battle of Carchemish, Nebuchadnezzar was in sole command of the Babylonian army, and may well have been recognized in the west as *de facto* king.[34] For the Judahite historian then, Nebuchadnezzar's first regnal year would have been 605/4, equivalent to the accession-year of the offi-

[33] This suggestion comes from Professor W. F. Albright. I am grateful to him also for many valuable comments on the Wiseman publication.

[34] Jer. 46:2 may reflect this point of view: ". . . Concerning the army of Pharaoh Neco, king of Egypt, which was by the river Euphrates at Carchemish, which Nebuchadnezzar, *king of Babylon*, defeated in the fourth year of Jehoiakim. . ." Styling Nebuchadnezzar as king of Babylon may not be merely a minor anachronism.

cial chronicle. The other equations would follow as in the previous hypothesis.[35]

The merit of suggestions two and three is that they deal not only with the negligible difference of a month with respect to the first captivity, but with the more serious disagreement of a full year in connection with the second. They also take into account all of the relevant data, biblical and non-biblical. It is not always possible to reconcile divergent biblical data; at the same time a discrepancy of a single year in the chronology of events which occurred more than two-and-a-half millennia ago is rather a tribute to the accuracy of the biblical editors and scribes. It is to the credit of modern biblical and Near Eastern scholars that they are able to pin down chronological data of such antiquity with precision, and that a slight discrepancy can be the subject of serious debate.

The Last Years of Judah

After the account of the 7th year, the remaining entries on this tablet are brief and fragmentary. Of interest is the notice of the 10th year (595/4), when Nebuchadnezzar remained in Babylon to deal with a local rebellion. It was quickly suppressed, and all was apparently peaceful when the king set out on his annual tribute-collecting journey to the west. Nevertheless, news of the insurrection must have traveled quickly; in spite of the revolt's failure, it must have added to the false hopes for an early collapse of the Babylonian kingdom. Within the year, Hananiah the prophet openly announced that God had broken the yoke of the king of Babylon, and that within two more years, the exiles would return, and Jehoiachin be restored as king of the land.[36] With patriotic zeal whipped up by the false prophets both in Judah and in exile, there was

[35] We must also reckon with the possibility of a numerical error in the calculations of the Deuteronomic editor. As previously suggested the source of the error may lie in the fact that the first capture of Jerusalem took place at the *end* of the 7th year. Then the second figure was erroneously calculated from the 8th year, instead of the 7th, and the 19th was arrived at, whereas 18th was correct.

[36] Hananiah's speech (Jer. 28:1 ff.) is dated in the 4th year of Zedekiah (594/3).

also a good deal of undercover activity on the part of the Jews. Diplomatic intrigue with Egypt, and the smaller nations of the west was the order of the day in Judah;[37] the Jews in Babylon undoubtedly provided information about Nebuchadnezzar's difficulties at home, and may even have had direct connection with the Babylonian plotters against the king. By putting together various data—the unavailing struggle of prophets like Jeremiah and Ezekiel to keep their people from revolting against the authority of Babylon; the continuing power and influence of Egypt in Asiatic affairs, even after the defeat at Carchemish; the Babylonian insurrection against Nebuchadnezzar—we can better appreciate the extent and depth of anti-Babylonian activity throughout the empire, and the rather substantial basis for the hopes of independence and restoration which appear repeatedly in the biblical record of this period. We may also understand more fully the formidable odds against which the prophets Jeremiah and Ezekiel had to contend in trying to persuade their people to be submissive to Nebuchadnezzar.[38] In the long run the prophets failed; Judah rebelled. But in its overwhelming defeat, the prophets and their message were vindicated.

B.M. 25124

After tablet 21946, which ends with a notice of the 11th year of Nebuchadnezzar, there is a large gap in the series, extending from 594/3 down to the third year of Neriglissar

---

[37] The roster in Jer. 27:2 ff. shows that most of the western vassals were involved in negotiations with the Judahite king. Contacts with Egypt are frequently mentioned. An Egyptian army did come to the aid of Judah during the final siege of Jerusalem (cf. Jer. 37:11, 34:21).

[38] It is noteworthy that the prophets emphasize moral obligations in urging the king of Judah to keep his covenant with the king of Babylon, rather than realistic military and political considerations. It appears now that these latter may have favored the rebels. The picture is no longer that of a tiny, decimated group in isolated revolt against a monolithic, all-powerful empire. Rather, the empire seems less than solid; Judah is in league with many dissident groups within the empire; and there is a strong enemy without, Egypt, ready to mix in at any time. Choosing between true and false prophets was not an easy task.

(557/6). The events of this year are described in a new tablet, B.M. 25124. It records Neriglissar's campaign against Appuashu, king of Pirundu (West Cilicia), who had invaded Hume (East Cilicia), territory under the protection of the Babylonians. The campaign was successful, and is described at greater length than is usual in the Babylonian Chronicle. The tablet, however, does not have the dramatic contact with biblical events which is the case with the previous ones in the series. There is no reference to the people of Judah either in Palestine or Babylon.

Conclusion

The four new tablets of the British Museum, together with others previously published, provide a fairly continuous account of the Neo-Babylonian Empire from it inception in 626 B.C. to the 11th year of Nebuchadnezzar (594/3). After a gap of 37 years, the final phase from the 3rd of Neriglissar to the fall of Babylon (539) is also available on tablets.[39] A number of new facts are presented, as well as more precise chronological data for the history of this epoch. While we could wish for more details and background information in the chronicler's terse reports—and the gaps, large and small, are especially frustrating[40]—nevertheless we have vivid glimpses of the empire, and general impressions of its structure and strength. It displaced Assyria as the imperial power in the Near East. Since its northeastern flank was protected by treaty with the powerful Medes, Nabopolassar and Nebuchadnezzar were able to devote their chief attention to the western regions, and the ancient foe, Egypt. While Carchemish was a decisive victory, and the Egyptians were driven out of Asia for good, it was not conclusive. Behind their own borders, the Egyptians remained dangerous; and they could stir up trouble in Palestine and Syria. They were able to inflict grievous damage on the Babylonians (601; a hitherto unreported battle). During

---

[39] Cf. the Nabonidus Chronicle, for the years 555–539, B.M. 35382 published in Sidney Smith's *Babylonian Historical Texts*, pp. 98–123.

[40] E.g., an account of the destruction of Jerusalem and the second captivity would be especially desirable.

the early years of Nebuchadnezzar's reign, an uneasy balance between the rival kingdoms was maintained: Babylon ascendant, but Egypt strong and active. The critical predicament of Judah, caught between them, is more easily appreciated in the light of the new material. Political realism and the false prophets might advocate alliance with the closer power, Egypt, especially after the success in 601 against Nebuchadnezzar, but the true prophets were not primarily concerned with military prowess. They saw in Nebuchadnezzar the chosen servant of God, through whom the divine purpose for Israel and the world was to be accomplished. They held fast to their position regardless of the setbacks which the Babylonians experienced.

The tablets also reveal that all was not peace and quiet within the Babylonian empire. Nebuchadnezzar had the usual troubles with vassal states, i.e., tribute was not always delivered in full or on time. So he had to parade his army regularly through the Hatti-land to intimidate the subject peoples; and on some occasions he had to resort to force. There was also difficulty at home: e.g., the hasty trip back to Babylon to claim the throne upon the death of his father, and the reported rebellion of the 10th year.

The historical information in the tablets fills out the picture of Judah's last years. The chronological data are of immediate value for fixing specific dates in biblical history. The two key dates are the Battle of Carchemish (May–June, 605) and the Capture of Jerusalem (March 16, 597). From these the regnal years of the last kings of Judah, and the date of the destruction of Jerusalem can be calculated with a high degree of probability.[41]

[41] See the chronological table above.

11
NEW LIGHT ON THE ELEPHANTINE COLONY

EMIL G. KRAELING

An archaeological mystery story reached its final denouement when it was revealed that a hoard of Aramaic papyri had come to light in the Brooklyn Museum. These papyri proved to be fresh documents of the Jewish colony at Elephantine, and were actually not only the first such documents found at that site, but the first major find of Aramaic papyri ever made. Coming from Jewish sources and from the fifth century B.C., they possess great interest and significance for the student of Jewish history of the time of Nehemiah.

Yeb and Syene

"But where is Elephantine Island?" some of our readers may well ask. Let Strabo, the famous Greek geographer who lived about the beginning of the Christian era, give the answer. After enumerating the towns of Upper Egypt, as one ascends the Nile from Thebes, he says, "Now follow Syene and Elephantine, the former on the borders of Ethiopia (i.e., Nubia) and a city of Egypt, the latter an island lying half a stadium (or *ca.* 100 yards) in front of Syene with a temple of Khnouphis (i.e., the God Khnum) and a Nilometer as in Memphis." The Egyptian name of the island was Yeb, which was translated in Greek times to 'Elephantine'; it appears in the papyri under its old name, while Syene is called Sewen, 'mart'—a word that has survived in its modern name Assuan. It is popularly believed that certain rocks on the southern tip of Elephantine island, which look like elephants, gave rise to its name, but that view receives no credence from Egyptologists, who hold that it applied originally to a larger region extending southward and noted for the ivory trade.

Syene was known to biblical writers. That fact is obscured in the Authorized Version, but discernible in the revised versions and modern renderings. Thus Ezekiel, pronouncing an oracle against Egypt, says, "I will make the land of Egypt an utter waste and desolation from Migdol to Seveneh, even unto the border of Ethiopia" (29:10; cf. 30:6). Migdol (probably Pelusion) and Seveneh (Syene) are here mentioned as the northernmost and southernmost points of Egypt, just as Dan and Beersheba are often used to describe the limits of Palestine, and Seveneh is explicitly localized on the Nubian frontier. It is barely possible, though not certain, that the author of Isaiah 49:12, too, has Syene in mind when, in hailing the return of the Jewish exiles to Zion he singles out those from the land of Sinim (Dead Sea scroll: Siniyites), which, according to the context, lay either far to the south or to the east. Syene was thus an important frontier outpost—a place that had to be guarded to prevent inroads into Egypt, a jumping-off place for expeditions into the Upper Nile country, a terminus of boat-traffic, owing to the First Cataract just above it, and last, but not least, the source of a red granite much in demand by kings and princes of Egypt for their sculptures, obelisks and buildings. The mineral name "Syenite" still preserves to this day the remembrance of ancient Syene.

Elephantine in Egyptian History

Occupation of the strategic place by Egyptians thus must be very ancient. There may have been a fortress there as early as the Third Dynasty. Certainly they were well established there in the Sixth Dynasty, when Elephantine became the residence of powerful princes who exercised some control over the wild "land of the bow." On the west shore of the Nile opposite Elephantine are still to be seen the tombs of some of these mighty men, with inscriptions recording their deeds of war and their expedition to the South.[1] The Jews of the fifth century, whose houses lay on the western rim of the island, must often have looked across the river to that hill of the tombs, where slept "kings and counselors of the earth who built up waste places for themselves" (Job 3:14).

Famous Egyptian Pharaohs had also interested themselves in this locality. Early in the Twelfth Dynasty, Sesostris I (ca. 1970 B.C.), proceeding up the river from this point, defeated the "miserable Cushites" of central Nubia, and Sesostris III (ca. 1887 B.C.) firmly established Egyptian control over them and their southerly neighbors. Through the First Cataract, just above Elephantine, the latter ruler had constructed a canal which made river-traffic possible as far as the Second Cataract. This was a difficult engineering achievement, involving the cutting of a channel about 260 feet long, 34 feet wide, and nearly 26 feet deep. Charles Edwin Wilbour was the first to note (in 1889) the inscription recording this feat, as well as another inscription commemorating the repair of the canal (ca. 1490 B.C.) under Thutmose III.[2]

In the time of Amenophis I (ca. 1550 B.C.) all Nubia was made a province called "Cush." There followed the succession of powerful "Viceroys of the Southern lands," whose sovereignty lasted late into the period of the Ramessides. Egyptian influence in Nubia seems to have survived the unrest that marked the period including the Twenty-first to the Twenty-fourth Dynasties (ca. 900–712 B.C.), but then we suddenly find independent "Kings of Cush" reigning in Napata and finally even extending their rule over Egypt and constituting its Twenty-fifth Dynasty (712–663 B.C.)[3] For these, Syene and Elephantine must have formed an important key for keeping open the door to the land of the Pharaohs.

A change in the status of Elephantine must have come about with the Assyrian conquest that culminated in 663 B.C., with the fall of Thebes (No-Amon of Nah. 3:8). Once more it

---

[1] See H. W. Müller, *Die Felsengräber der Fürsten von Elephantine* (Glueckstadt, 1940).

[2] See C. E. Wilbour, "Canalizing the Cataract," *Recueil de Travaux*, XIII (1890), 202 ff.

[3] On the preceding see especially T. Säve-Söderberg, *Ägypten und Nubien* (Lund, 1941).

formed an important frontier post facing Nubia, for the Assyrians did not aspire to the task of policing and governing that far-flung region: they even controlled Egypt itself through local kings of native origin. One of these, Psammetichus of Sais, waxed increasingly powerful and finally set himself up as Pharaoh. By 645 he had gained control of the entire land. From the Egyptian point of view (which ignores the Assyrian occupation) the Twenty-sixth, or Saite, Dynasty was already established by the grandfather of Psammetichus, Necho I. It lasted for over a century, until Cambyses conquered Egypt in 525 B.C. The Persian monarch and his successors constitute the Twenty-seventh Dynasty of Egypt's rulers. Presumably they took over the garrisons of the Saitic kings, including the one at Elephantine, and therewith the Jews of this area transferred their loyalty to the occupying power. The favors shown their people by the Persian kings, notably permission to re-establish the community in Judaea, must have gained their enthusiastic support of the new order.

An Archaeological Mystery Story

Our archaeological mystery story concerns documents from this colony. It began with Charles Edwin Wilbour, an American scholar who spent his winters in Egypt in the eighties and early nineties of the last century, cruising on the Nile in a sailing vessel, or *dahabiyyah*, which he called "The Seven Hathors." He took pains to study ancient Egyptian and such a scholar as Brugsch expressed a high opinion of his knowledge of it. He kept a detailed diary of the things he saw and of objects offered to him for sale.

In Jan.–Feb., 1893, Wilbour, according to an entry in his journal, was at Assuan. On the *kom* (the ruin mound) of Elephantine he acquired some papyri from Arab women—doubtless diggers after *sebakh*, or fertilizer. He said nothing about the matter—perhaps intending to study the papyri himself. He died in 1896 and his possessions, including a trunk containing numerous papyri carefully wrapped and deposited in tin biscuit-boxes, were sent to America. The trunk ultimately found its way into a New York storage warehouse where it stayed until the death of Wilbour's daughter, Theodora, who bequeathed it to the Egyptian Department of the Brooklyn Museum. When it was opened, it was found to contain, in addition to important Egyptian papyri, the largest collection of Aramaic papyri to be found anywhere outside Cairo. There were eight intact rolls with the seals and strings still about them and the "endorsements," or brief comments as to what the texts dealt with, visible on their surface. In addition there were boxes containing broken papyri and an envelope of tiny fragments. This envelope bore a question in Wilbour's handwriting: "Is not this authentic Phenician?" A reply in another hand—apparently British rather than American—gives the following answer: "It is Aramaic, passing into Palmyrene and Hebrew, like the Carpentras text. It should all be carefully copied." It seems, therefore, that Mr. Wilbour sent these fragments to a Semitic linguist for an opinion on their nature; his own guess, that they were Phoenician was in line with what had been thought about the few known papyrus fragments of this character up until a decade or so previously. But his informant gave the right answer: the writing was Aramaic.[4] However, it seems unlikely that Wilbour informed him of the unopened papyri and larger fragments in his possession. In any case, Wilbour himself died without having divulged his discovery.

First Published Elephantine Discoveries

But in the meantime additional documents were discovered at Elephantine and several were sold by dealers; one important, though incomplete document, the full import of which only became clear through later finds, came to Strassburg in Germany and was published by J. Euting in 1903; another was acquired by A. H. Sayce and also was published in 1903 by A. Cowley. In 1904 a considerable number of new papyri turned up in the hands of dealers at Assuan. Five and one-half were acquired by Sir Robert Mond and three and one-half by Lady Cecil. Howard Carter, later to win fame as discoverer of the tomb of King Tutankhamon, was then Director of Antiqui-

---

[4] Publication of the photo of the letter led to the identification of the handwriting as that of A. H. Sayce. See A. Sachs, "The Answer to a Puzzle," *BA*, XV:4 (1952), p. 89.

ties in Egypt, and at his request the papyri were turned over
to the Cairo Museum. They were subsequently published,
along with a tenth papyrus that Sayce had acquired for the
Bodleian, by Sayce and Cowley in 1906.[5]

This collection made it fully clear that there was an Aramaic-speaking Jewish colony at Elephantine in the days of the
Persian (Achaemenid) kings, and that they even had some
sort of religious edifice (*'egora*) dedicated to the god Yahu on
that island. Many held at that time that it could not be a temple but was only a sort of meetinghouse, though the name was
explained by leading scholars as an Assyrian loan word (from
ekurru 'temple'). Scholars were eager to get more such documents. Sayce, who was closer to the situation than anyone else,
believed that the papyri were not found on Elephantine but
rather on the mainland of Assuan (hence the title given the
publication).

Up the river from the Fayyum, where he had been digging
for Greek papyri for the Berlin Museum, now came Dr. Otto
Rubensohn. He induced local Arabs to show him where the
papyri had been found and was persuaded of the truth of the
story that the documents came from the island and from a
certain spot pointed out to him. The Department of Antiquities
gave him an excavation concession for the western half of the
kom of Elephantine. Within a few yards of the spot indicated
to him, and close to the surface of the ground, Rubensohn in
his second campaign of 1906 made a great find of Aramaic
papyri, outstripping in importance anything contained in the
collection of Sayce-Cowley. When Eduard Sachau published
three of these texts (two being duplicates) in a preliminary
publication in 1908, the story of the Jewish temple at Elephantine was revealed.

There could no longer be any doubt that the *'egora* was a
real temple with an altar for bloody sacrifice. The papyri told
how the priests of Khnum had this Jewish temple destroyed in
410 B.C. and how the Jews sought to get it rebuilt, even sending letters to high authorities in Palestine in 408 B.C., appealing
to them to use their influence. The texts left the question open
as to whether they succeeded in their purpose. The full col-

[5] A. H. Sayce and A. E. Cowley, *Aramaic Papyri Discovered at
Assuan* (London, 1906).

lection, which contained numerous other documents, many of them fragmentary, but among them part of an Old Aramaic Book of Aḥiqar and of an Aramaic version of Darius' Behistun inscription, was published by Sachau in 1911.[6] Some of the remaining texts threw light on the Jewish religion as observed at Elephantine, but no further information was afforded concerning the fate of the temple. Eduard Meyer who wrote a valuable little book on the Elephantine colony, thought it unlikely that it was ever restored, since he held that Persian rule must have ended with the accession of Artaxerxes II in 404 B.C.[7]

The German campaign on Elephantine was carried on for three seasons and the explorers, though only commissioned for a papyrus-hunt, sought to clarify the general situation on the *kom*. The western part of the north wall of the temple of Khnum, primarily dating from Hellenistic times, was uncovered and followed to the boundary of the concession. It led across the line of the concession to a point where it intersected a line that would lead south at right angles to the portal of Alexander II, visible from afar as the outstanding landmark of Elephantine island. North of the wall of the temple ran a street, on the opposite (north) side of which were houses. They were of a later period, but beneath them structures of the Persian era with some Aramaic papyri came to light. In one building at the border of the concession numerous large jars, some with Aramaic and some with Phoenician inscriptions had been stored.

Meanwhile an expedition of the French Académie des Inscriptions had taken up the concession for the eastern part of the *kom*. Clermont-Ganneau, noted Semitic epigraphist, its leader, was imbued with the hope of finding papyri and particularly of locating the site of the Jewish temple. His expectations were disappointed; he found only a few insignificant fragments of papyrus, though he did recover a large number

[6] E. Sachau, *Aramäische Papyrus und Ostraka* (Berlin, 1911). All known papyri were re-edited in convenient handbook by A. Cowley, *Aramaic Papyri of the Fifth Century B.C.* (referred to as *A.P.* and the text numbers). Cf. also A. Ungnad, *Aramäische Papyrus aus Elephantine* (1911).

[7] E. Meyer, *Der Papyrusfund von Elephantine* (Leipzig, 1912). The religion of the colony was exhaustively discussed by A. Vincent, *La religion des Judéo-Araméens d'Eléphantine* (Paris, 1937).

of Aramaic ostraca, which he did not live to edit and whose long-delayed publication by M. Dupont-Sommer may soon be expected. Clermont-Ganneau became convinced that the Jewish temple was in the northern part of the site, just over the line in the German concession and in the very spot which the Germans had made a dumping ground for their rubble. However, it seems unlikely that his theory as to the site of the Jewish temple was correct. The evidence of the Brooklyn Museum papyri points in a different direction.

In 1918 the Fathers of the Pontifical Biblical Institute in Rome carried on a dig at Elephantine, primarily re-excavating part of the ground dug over by the Germans, but going to a greater depth and carefully screening the soil. Only a rough sketch plan and a brief itemization of finds was published, together with a general preliminary report. A few scraps of Aramaic papyri were discovered, but a small raised inscription, apparently in Canaanitic letters and an inscription on stone in an unknown script (both unpublished) were the chief reward of their toil.

Since that time silence has descended upon Elephantine. The Egyptian government has been guarding the desolate scene, so that the unauthorized digging has ceased. The situation is not conducive to anyone's sinking more money into a site so confusing and so much dug over. The only untouched parts of the ancient town, furthermore, are either covered by workers' houses or, where the land is vacant, full of recent Arab burials. It seems likely, therefore, that the Brooklyn papyri may be the last Aramaic records to come from the palm-studded isle.

Preparation of the Wilbour Papyri

When the Trustees of the Brooklyn Museum assigned to me the task of preparing the Wilbour Aramaic papyri for publication, most of the papyri had not yet been opened. Mr. Anthony Giambalvo, the technician of the Egyptian Department, evolved his own method of preparing these papyri. A roll like that illustrated is not much larger than a cigar and the papyrus material is sometimes not much thicker than the wrapper of a cigar. Since it would crumble under the fingers in its dried out condition, it is necessary to subject it to moisture before trying to open it. This was done by setting it on a rack above a dish of water and covering it with a bell jar. After forty-eight hours or more (depending on the papyrus) it was removed and opened. (The photograph reproduced in this book represents a particularly nerve-racking moment for the technician, for owing to the time-lag and the heat engendered by the photographic procedure the papyrus is starting to curl and threatening to break apart). The papyrus was then placed between sheets of blotting paper and weighted down with a pane of glass. The blotting paper was changed several times until the papyrus was perfectly dry. It was always a great moment when Mr. Giambalvo uncovered a papyrus and I had my first glance at a text that no one had read since it was written and sealed more than two millennia ago. The writing looked as fresh as though it had just been composed yesterday.

Each fully dried and complete papyrus was put between panes of glass and sealed up. It was different, however, with papyri that had to be reconstructed from a mass of fragments. The efforts of Mr. Cooney, Curator of the Department of Egyptian Art, and Mr. Giambalvo resulted in the recovery of four further papyri, which were put under glass, but not sealed; this preliminary labor was then supplemented by the efforts of Mr. Giambalvo and myself to assort and place the numerous small fragments, most of which belonged to these four. It was doing jig-saw puzzles of a most fascinating kind. Misplacements had to be corrected and often what we thought had been finished had to be done over again. It was necessary to understand the import of the papyri before some of the fragments could be properly placed. Several significant fragments fell into place at the very last moment, when No. 7 was reversed (a difficult operation) before sealing. In the end only a small residue of fragments remained, none important enough to warrant expenditure of more of the technician's time. But the result of our labors is gratifying, and scholars must be thankful to Mr. Charles Nagel, the Director of the Museum, and to Mr. John D. Cooney for the understanding shown for a task of this nature, which really interferes with normal functions of a museum staff.

Contents of the Papyri

The *Brooklyn Museum Aramaic Papyri*, which form a collection larger than the Sayce-Cowley collection, were published by the author under the above title by Yale University Press in 1953. There are in all seventeen numbers, though 14 to 17 represent fragmentary texts. Papyri 1 to 12 constitute the bulk of the material. In them the main personage whose family presumably preserved the texts, is a man named Ananiah (or Anani) bar Azariah, who bears the title of "servitor of the god Yahu." An earlier papyrus fragment published by Sachau shows that his father Azariah held the same office before him (*A.P.* 63:9. 12). The papyri are arranged in chronological order. Nos. 1–10 give both Babylonian and Egyptian months and days.[8]

Papyrus No. 1 shows Ananiah bar Azariah receiving a piece of property which a certain Mika bar A(gur?) has been compelled by law to cede to him for its price. This text had to be reconstructed from fragments, but is virtually complete except for a name or two. It was written in the reign of Artaxerxes I, July 6, 451 B.C. In No. 2, written two years later, July 13, 449 B.C., we find Ananiah marrying Tamut, the slave of Meshullam bar Zakkur, a prominent member of the Elephantine community, known from previously published texts. It is an important marriage document and, in conjunction with texts still to be mentioned, proves that a slave was not necessarily liberated when given in marriage to a freeman. Her owner still had title to her and even to her children. In this case Tamut already has a son (by Ananiah?), and Meshullam pledges not to reclaim him except under certain conditions. In No. 3, of September 14, 437 B.C., Ananiah bar Azariah buys a house across the street from the temple of Yahu; this document thus is of considerable interest for the location of this temple. In No. 4, of October 30, 434 B.C., Ananiah gives his wife Tamut a half-interest in the house he had bought three years earlier, pledging furthermore that their two children Palti and Yehoyishma are to inherit his portion. No. 5

[8] S. H. Horn and L. H. Wood, "The Fifth-Century calendar at Elephantine," *JNES*, XIII (1954), 1 ff.

of June 12, 427 B.C., is an extremely important text—a manu-
mission document. In it Meshullam bar Zakkur makes what is
known to Greek papyrology as a *paramone* arrangement; he
liberates Tamut and her daughter Yehoyishma but in a manner binding them to serve him during his remaining years and
to serve his son Zakkur after him. Their liberty is thus not
complete until Zakkur's death. There is reference to an interesting ritual of liberation. No. 6, of July 11, 420 B.C., is fragmentary. In it, Ananiah bar Azariah gives his daughter Yehoyishma a house (or an apartment in a house?) adjacent to his
own residence. In No. 7, of October 2 in the same year, we
find Ananiah's daughter Yehoyishma marrying a man named
Ananiah bar Haggai. This document, more elaborate than the
Sayce-Cowley marriage document, "G" (*A.P.* 15), had to be
reconstructed from fragments in months of laborious effort. It
contains much that is new. The bride's father does not appear
in the document at all—it is Zakkur her "brother" who acts on
her behalf and receives the *mohar* or "price" given by the
groom. Evidently Meshullam bar Zakkur was no longer alive,
but his son Zakkur still had a vested interest in both Tamut
and Yehoyishma. No. 8 stands apart somewhat from the family archive of Ananiah; it concerns Zakkur bar Meshullam,
who gives a slave-boy named Yedoniah to Uriah bar Mah-
seiah, who presumably is the brother of the woman Mibtahiah
of the Sayce-Cowley marriage document referred to above.
Uriah is to adopt this boy as a son and is forbidden to re-
enslave him. The text is dated either September 22 or October
22, 416 B.C. (the scribe having made a mistake in either the
Egyptian or the Babylonian month name). All the texts so
far enumerated antedate the sacking of the Jewish temple,
which, according to the letter of the Jews to Bagoas, governor
of Judaea, written in 408 B.C., took place in 410 B.C., as stated
above.

Nos. 9–13 and Their Historical Importance

The papyri Nos. 9 to 12 have a peculiar importance owing
to their dates. When I began to study them I placed them first
chronologically because they were dated in the first, third and
fourth years of Artaxerxes. I naturally thought that the king

referred to was Artaxerxes I, since Persian rule in Egypt was
held to have ended with Darius II. However, the family history
of Ananiah bar Azariah can be understood only if Nos. 9 to
12 are later than the other texts, and from this it follows that
the Artaxerxes of these three texts must have been Artaxerxes
II. The synchronism of the double dates in Nos. 9 to 12 provides still further proof if that were needed. Thus the dates
of texts attain a historical significance: they prove that the
Persian rule over Egypt continued until the end of 402 B.C.,—
the winter before the rebellion of Cyrus the younger and the
anabasis of Cyrus made immortal by Xenophon. After the
death of Cyrus, the leaders of the Greek expeditionary force
offered their services to the Persians for a campaign against
Egypt to assist in reducing it; the Persian supreme commander is described as being more incensed at the Egyptians
than at other rebels (Xenophon *Anab.* 11. 1; 14. 5, 13). It
seems certain therefore that Egypt shook off Persian allegiance
only when the revolt of Cyrus was imminent or in full swing.

But how shall we understand the fact that a reign of six
years was assigned to Amyrtaeus by the ancient chronologers?
The tradition is substantiated by the Aramaic Papyrus *A.P.*
35, dated in the summer of his fifth year. We must suppose
that Amyrtaeus himself stressed the idea that his sovereignty
had begun with the end of the reign of Darius II. But this is
idealism rather than realism. He may have held power from
December 405 to December 402 over a part of lower Egypt
from a haven in the Delta such as that described by Herodotus
(II. 140), which allegedly remained undiscovered "until the
time of Amyrtaeus" (the rebel of 455 B.C., and perhaps the
grandfather of the king of whom we here are speaking). The
Brooklyn Papyri prove that until the winter preceding the
anabasis of Cyrus in 401 B.C., the military colony at Elephantine still owed allegiance to Artaxerxes II, and that apparently
signifies that the communications from Palestine to Egypt and
up the Nile were in Persian hands at the time.

Papyrus No. 9 is dated November 5, 404 B.C. In it Ananiah
bar Azariah gives his daughter Yehoyishma a part of the house
he had bought years ago. It is a long, beautifully written and
perfectly preserved papyrus. No. 10 of March 9, 402 B.C., represents another gift of a house to his daughter. It, too, is well

written and perfectly preserved. Of a different nature is No. 11, dated December 2, 402 B.C. It records a loan of grain made by Yehoyishma's husband, Ananiah bar Haggai from a man named Pakhnum (Egyptian: 'The one of Khnum'). No. 12, written soon afterward, December 13, 402 B.C., records the sale, by Ananiah bar Azariah and his wife, of the house bought in No. 3 to their son-in-law Ananiah bar Haggai. Therewith the family archive breaks off, though there is an endorsement preserved from a lost papyrus (No. 15) in which this son-in-law presumably transferred a part ownership in his house to his wife Yehoyishma.

Of an entirely different character is No. 13. It is a letter in a very distinctive handwriting. It was broken into several fragments and their proper arrangement was difficult. While it has been impossible to guess every word of which traces remain, that which can be read and understood is of real importance. For this letter alludes to the capture (and death?) of King Amyrtaeus and the accession of Nepherites I, founder of the Twenty-ninth Dynasty, at Memphis in the month of Epiphi. The letter bears only a month date "Fifth of Epiphi," but if Nepherites' official reign began in December 399, it must date from October 1, 399 B.C. The writer, Shewa bar Zekariah (known from previously published texts) is writing from somewhere in Egypt to a man named Yişlaḥ (bar Nathan?) at Elephantine about business matters and acquaints him with this new military and political happening. It is this letter which in all probability sounded the death-knell for the Elephantine colony. The Jews had been apparently left undisturbed by Amyrtaeus, as is shown by the papyrus A.P. 35, dated under him (June 19, 400 B.C.). The rise of a new dynasty under Nepherites, however, was an ominous event. For the Twenty-ninth Dynasty came from Mendes, where the ram-god was supreme, and it stands to reason that it took great interest in the ram-god Khnum of Elephantine and gave heed to the wishes of its priesthood. The Yahu temple was thorn in their flesh; they had sought to get rid of it in 410 and punishment had been meted out to the conspirators. It is plausible to suppose that the existence of the Jewish colony was terminated soon after the rise of the new dynasty and that it is for this reason that no later records have come to light from Elephantine.

Origin of Jewish Colony of Elephantine

But how, the reader may well ask, did it come about that a colony of Jews existed on the remote Ethiopian frontier in the fifth century B.C., and even had a temple of Yahu? The Brooklyn Museum documents give no help in answering this question. They confirm the fact that individual members of the colony belonged to a *degel* or 'troop' named after its commanding officer (a Persian or Babylonian), though there is no evidence that Ananiah bar Azariah, the servitor of the god Yahu and leading figure in the Brooklyn texts, himself was affiliated with one. It is obvious from the fact that many persons drew rations from the government, that they were soldiers of the garrison guarding this frontier outpost. It was but natural that a foreign occupying power like the Persian should employ a considerable number of foreign soldiers and not depend too strongly on native Egyptians. But the Jewish colony, according to the testimony of previous published papyri, antedates the Persian conquest. When Cambyses came down to Egypt, so the letter to Bagoas states, he found the temple of Yahu at Elephantine already in existence, and did it no harm, though he destroyed the Egyptian temples. The Jewish colony must thus have been founded in the days of native Egyptian rulers. Just when that was remains uncertain. The practice of supplying Egyptian rulers with Jewish manpower is already reflected in the Deuteronomic Law, promulgated, as many hold, in the time of King Josiah of Judah, about 622 B.C. This law enjoins the Jewish king as follows: "He shall not multiply horses to himself, nor cause the people to return to Egypt, to the end that he should multiply horses" (Deut. 17:16). This peculiar ordinance must be understood as referring to the dispatch, by previous Judean rulers, of detachments of Jewish soldiers to Egypt, in return for horses, of which there was a great dearth in Judah ever since northern Israel and Aram had been overwhelmed and annexed by the Assyrians. Eduard Meyer argued that this passage mirrors the origin of the Jewish military colony at Elephantine, which thus may have gone down to

Egypt prior to the time of Josiah. However, one may well doubt that the colony is so ancient. It is equally possible and perhaps more probable that it was recruited from Jewish elements that came to Egypt after the fall of Jerusalem in 586. Had the Yahu temple in Elephantine been in existence when Jeremiah harangued the Jews of Pathros (the region north of Elephantine) he would hardly have declared in the name of Yahweh, "Behold I have sworn by my great name, saith the Lord, that my name shall no more be named in the mouth of any man of Judah in all the land of Egypt . . ." The group that put Jeremiah's prophecy to shame, was moreover, not as deeply sunk in paganism as the one confronting the prophet at that occasion. Possibly the inner strength of the Yahweh religion had reasserted itself in later decades, when the demoralization of the catastrophe of 586 had passed, and the ministry of Jeremiah (who disappears from the scene with the aforementioned address) may have contributed to that result.

It has been suggested that the Jewish Elephantine colony was founded under Pharaoh Apries, the Hophra of Jer. 44:30, (588–570), for a rebellion of troops at Elephantine is recorded from his reign in the inscription of the Elephantine official Nesuhor[9] and could have led to a change of garrison. This view received strong endorsement by Albright.[10] But an even later date, in the early years of Pharaoh Amasis, (569–526) may well be advocated owing to the absence of documents of the colony antedating Darius I, and to allow for a resurgence of Yahwism among the Jews of Egypt, as noted above, in speaking of Jeremiah, and for their absorption by an Aramaic-speaking environment. The founding of a Yahu temple at Elephantine must have been permitted because it was ordered by the government. The Egyptian priests may have been instructed to regard Yahu as a visiting god, paying homage to Khnum, while the Jews may have considered their temple a refuge for their God, who had departed from Jerusalem (Ezek. 11:22 f.).[11]

[9] J. H. Breasted, *Ancient Records of Egypt*, IV, 989.
[10] W. F. Albright, *Archaeology and the Religion of Israel* (Baltimore, 1942), p. 168.
[11] C. H. Gordon, "The Origin of the Jews in Elephantine," *JNES*, XIV (1955), 56 ff., would derive the Elephantine Jews from a

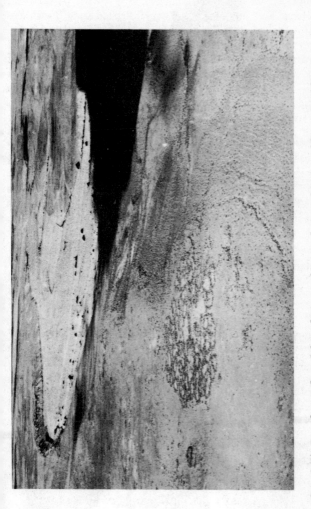

Site 345. Circular and oval foundations of conical stone houses of large Middle Bronze I village above the Wâdi Hafir. *Photo: Israeli Air Force*

Broken Iron II vase from Ezion-geber: Elath, decorated with painted and burnished slip. *Photo: HUC-JIR*

Iron II, handmade bowls from Tell El-Kheleifeh (Ezion-geber: Elath). *Photo: HUC-JIR*

Large, originally roofed-over Nabatean-to-Byzantine cistern in the Negev showing steps leading down into it and remains of pillar which supported the roof. *Photo: Nelson Glueck*

Judean kingdom cistern in the Negev, still watertight.
Photo: Nelson Glueck

A manger from a government stable for horses of the time of Solomon. Found at Megiddo and now in the Palestine Archaeological Museum, Jerusalem, Jordan. *Photo: G. Ernest Wright*

Two Assyrian scribes writing at dictation, tabulating the booty of a captured city. The first writes with stylus on a clay tablet, the second with pen on leather. *Photo: British Museum*

Letter written on a portion of a pottery vessel from a local commander to the Judean general at Lachish in 589 or 588 B.C., near the beginning of Nebuchadnezzar's campaign against Judah. *Courtesy Wellcome Trustees*

A reconstruction of the Ishtar Gate, Babylon, showing a procession of King Nebuchadnezzar entering the city. At the right are
the Hanging Gardens, one of the "seven wonders" of the world
Photo: Oriental Institute

The tower of Babel. *Photo: Dombart, Der babylonische Turm*

An Egyptian group of musicians, with harp, lute, and double oboe. *Photo: Oriental Institute*

Impression from an ancient cylinder seal found in Mesopotamia. Here are shown a primitive reed-shrine and an altar-like structure being transported on a decorated boat.

Photo: Oriental Institute

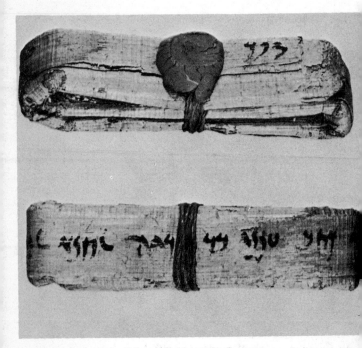

An unopened papyrus roll from Elephantine.

Courtesy Brooklyn Museum

"Politics makes strange bedfellows," as the saying goes, and change of politics brings awareness of the incongruity. When the Jews after 525 B.C., took service with the Persian oppressors of Egypt their status and that of their temple doubtless underwent a change in Egyptian eyes. In the course of time this developed into a desire to be rid of the Yahu temple and led to its destruction in 410 B.C., as described in the letter to Bagoas.

The Restoration of the Jewish Temple

The previously published Elephantine papyri left unanswered the question whether the Jewish colony succeeded in getting its temple restored. The recommendation of Bagoas and Delaiah, the son of Sanballat of Samaria, held that it should be done, but with a thinly veiled implication that bloody sacrifice should not be permitted there. However, the interim between 408 (the date of the Bagoas letter, A.P. 30) and the supposed end of Persian rule seemed so short that Eduard Meyer could express doubts as to whether the temple was reopened. The new Brooklyn papyri establish the fact that the temple was rebuilt, for we find it in existence in the latest of the fully dated documents (No. 12 of December 402 B.C.). Not only does this text mention the temple of Yahu but it speaks of Yahu as "the god who dwells in Yeb the fortress," a statement just like that in Ps. 135:21 where Yahweh is described as the one "which dwelleth at Jerusalem." Where a deity has his "dwelling" a cult is naturally in full operation. The important list on the temple contributors (A.P. 22) is dated in the fifth year of an unspecified king, who, in my opinion, is to be identified with Amyrtaeus, and thus further substantiates the existence of the temple as late as the summer of 400 B.C.[12]

The new papyri, then, cover a period from 451–399 B.C. These dates correspond rather closely to the journeys of two

---

Judean enclave in Aram. He does not consider or discuss the explanation given above, which is far more simple. There is no need of "forcing" the Elephantine Jews to learn Aramaic.

[12] On the location of the temple see the writer's discussion in The Brooklyn Museum Aramaic Papyri, p. 76 f.

famous men. One was the father of history, Herodotus, who must have made his journey to Egypt about 450 B.C., and who even visited Elephantine Island (that being the point farthest south reached by him).[13] There can be no doubt that he saw some of the men mentioned in the papyri and that they in turn saw the tourist from "Yawan." The end of the period covered by these papyri brings us close to the time in which recent scholarship would put the journey of Ezra to Palestine:[14] the seventh year of Artaxerxes II (exactly as in the case of the Brooklyn papyri Nos. 9 to 12 mentioned above). Ezra would then have arrived in Jerusalem, July 31, 398 B.C.[15] If we are right in our belief that the Elephantine colony and temple came to an end in the reign of Nepherites I (December 1, 399–November 29, 393) it may be said to have expired at an appropriate moment, when a drill-sergeant of righteousness, backed by Persian political authority, was about to subject his people to a fateful legislation which forever made impossible the old, easygoing life of the Jews of Elephantine and the existence of a temple and cult such as theirs.

[13] The rebellions of 460–450 were over; he mentions a battle of 459 B.C. in III. 20.

[14] Cf. H. H. Rowley, "The Chronological Order of Ezra and Nehemiah," in his volume The Servant of the Lord and Other Essays on the Old Testament (London, 1952), pp. 129 ff.; and O. Eissfeldt, Einleitung in das Alte Testament (2nd ed., 1956), p. 686.

[15] Following the tables in R. A. Parker and W. Dubberstein, Babylonian Chronology 626 B.C.–A.D. 45, ("Studies in Ancient Oriental Civilization," No. 24 [Chicago, 1942]).

12

THE SIGNIFICANCE OF THE TEMPLE IN THE ANCIENT NEAR EAST

For what purpose did the ancient temple exist, and what role did it play in community life? What was thought to be the relation of Deity and people to it? How are the modern church and synagogue related to it and yet different from it? Two articles are here presented (Parts I and II) on the Egyptian and Mesopotamian temples by the late Professor Harold H. Nelson and by Dr. A. Leo Oppenheim of the Oriental Institute of the University of Chicago. These are followed by Part III on the temple in Canaan and in Israel by G. Ernest Wright and by Part IV on the Herodian Temple, the synagogue, and the church in the period of the New Testament by Professor Floyd V. Filson of McCormick Theological Seminary.

It will be seen that temples were originally constructed as homes for the deities in whom the people believed. Just as king and commoner lived in houses, so did the gods. Temples, therefore, were exceedingly important in community life because they were the point where the Divine touched the human, where the transcendent became immanent, and where the ultimate source of power became available to alleviate human weakness and need. Man's duty, people then believed, was to provide for the physical needs of a god: that is, food, water, and innumerable delicacies. In return for these services the god was confidently expected to provide for human necessities, give directions for the conduct of daily life, and furnish the stability necessary for a community's prosperity.

A study of the articles of Drs. Nelson and Oppenheim will reveal that a fundamental difference existed between Egyptian and Mesopotamian conceptions as to the way in which the divine power was manifested in human life. This difference can largely be traced to the variant conceptions of kingship in the two countries. In Egypt the king was himself a god, the son of Amon-Re who was the chief deity of the land; and the divine blessings to the country were largely mediated through his person. In Mesopotamia, on the other hand, the relationship between god and people was more direct. The king was not a god. He humbly sought the divine instructions for his life as did any other man, though to be sure his position in the community entitled him to certain special privileges and favors.

The Mesopotamian conception was basic to the whole of the Fertile Crescent, including Israel. Yet in Israel it was inevitable that the fundamentally different conception of Deity should arouse questioning about the meaning of the temple. Solomon's structure was commonly called the "house" of God, just as were other Oriental temples; but Israel was not content to leave the matter there.

With the destruction of the Temple and the Dispersion something new appeared on the scene. That was the synagogue, differing radically from the temple in meaning and function. The early Christian Church followed with a complete repudiation of the whole temple-idea. It is in this setting that the full significance of the words of Paul to the Athenians is understood: "God that made the world . . . dwelleth not in temples made with hands; neither is worshipped with men's hands, as though he needed any thing" (Acts 17:24–25; cf. also John 4:20 ff.). In both modern Judaism and Christianity, however, the temple-idea is still occasionally to be found, especially in subtle forms.

G. E. W.

I. THE EGYPTIAN TEMPLE

with particular reference to
THE THEBAN TEMPLES OF THE EMPIRE PERIOD

HAROLD H. NELSON

The Egyptian temple was originally a house for the god, just as an Egyptian dwelling was a house for its human master. It was a simple affair of a single small room, a hut, apparently little more than a *naos* or shrine, a frame with matting or wattle sides or possibly constructed entirely of wood. Before it stood a symbol of the god while the whole was enclosed in a fence or low wall. As time went on the god's house was expanded with the addition of rooms and halls before and on either side, but the shrine, developed into the holy of holies of a temple complex, still remained. It had become a room, secluded far in the rear of the building, but lying on the main axis of the temple. There in mysterious shadow stood the sacred image, shut off from the profane sight of the outside world by a series of doors which closed portal after portal along the great central passage running from the main entrance through the pylon back to the "great place" (as the Egyptians called it), the god's peculiar quarters. At most of the great city temples, the chief seats of the leading deities, the principal god of the town had his own temple which belonged to him exclusively or which might contain minor accommodations for the other two members of his holy family. At Karnak, Amon, Mut, and Khonsu, the Theban Triad, had each his or her own temple with apparently no provision for the reception of the other two deities. These were their special dwellings and belonged to each alone although Amon figured prominently on the walls of all the buildings. In the reliefs the

king is shown officiating before other gods who belonged to
Amon's Ennead or circle of associated powers, but there seems
to be no place within the temple itself reserved for the worship
of such divinities. The inscriptional evidence, on the other
hand, speaks of the sanctuaries of the Ennead as found within
the temple, so that we must presume that they existed there.
Outside the main temple were numbers of minor shrines dedicated to various gods such as Ptah, Osiris, Maat, etc., and
there we know that services in their honor were regularly
celebrated.

There are two other groups of buildings to which this description does not fully apply, namely, the processional "stations" and the temples "on the west," as the Egyptians designated them. The former were used in connection with the
periodic processions which the god made from place to place
in his temple grounds. Under the early 18th Dynasty each of
these stations consisted of a raised platform reached at opposite ends by a low stairway, little more than a ramp. On the
platform was a structure consisting generally of a single room
with a door at either end, sometimes surrounded by a colon-
nade. When the portable bark-shrine containing the image of
the god and carried on the shoulders of priests reached one of
these buildings, which were numbered in regular order of succession, it was carried up the gentle slope of the stairs into the
cella and deposited upon a support in the middle of the room.
There are reliefs showing the bark of Amon within such stations where the accompanying inscription reads, for instance,
"resting or stopping in station no. 5, called 'Maat-ka-Re receives the beauty of Amon.'" After the completion of the ceremonies customary at one station, the god proceeded on his way
to that next in order and ultimately returned to his "great
place" from which he had set out. In these early 18th Dynasty
buildings and in the reliefs of that period provision is made
only for the bark of Amon which seems alone to have taken
part in such processions within the temple compound. By the
19th Dynasty (after *ca.* 1320 B.C.), however, the bark of
Amon was accompanied by those of Mut and Khonsu and the
stations built by Seti II and Ramses III, now included in the
first court of the Amon temple at Karnak, have accommodations for all three barks which no longer entered and left the

building by different doors but came out by the same door by which they entered.

Aside from the great temples of particular gods and the processional stations associated with them, we have still another group of temples which were known as those belonging to the West, or "on the West of Thebes," "on the west of Abydos," etc. Whether or not they should be termed "mortuary temples" is largely a matter of definition. The West was the region of the dead and of Osiris. The goddess of the West welcomed the dead to his tomb, and also figured in the reliefs on the temple walls where the king is shown as an Osiris. Moreover, they seem to furnish the only substitute for the tomb chapel, a regular part of an Egyptian sepulcher but conspicuously lacking in the tombs of the kings in the hills just behind the Theban mortuary temples. That these latter were intended, in part at least, for the service of the dead king is evidenced by such statements as that made by Ramses II regarding the temple of his father, Seti I, at Abydos which was left unfinished when Seti died and was completed by his son. The latter addressing his dead father says, "Behold I am making thy name to live, I have protected thee, I give attention to thy temple, thy offerings are established. Thou restest in the other world like Osiris, while I shine like Re for mankind. How happy for thee, who begat me—since thou comest as one living again. I have fashioned thee, I have built the house thou lovest, wherein is thy statue in the cemetery of Abydos, region of eternity. I have endowed offerings for thy statues, the daily offerings come to thee."[1] While these temples served the king when he was dead, they began to function while he was yet alive. At the same time they were dedicated to the great god of the locality. Thus at Thebes the temples on the West, each built by a different Pharaoh, were all Amon temples. At Medinet Habu, Ramses III in most instances appears upon the walls as the living king. Ramses says of this temple: "I built for thee (Amon) my house-of-millions-of-years in the necropolis of Thebes. I fashioned thy august images dwelling in its midst while the great Ennead are in shrines in their sanctuaries." The king then goes on to say that he has arranged the cult of

[1] Breasted, *Ancient Records*, Vol. III, ¶ 272.

the temple, provided for the proper observance of the regular
feasts, organized its priesthood and set the whole institution in
motion. Here is the living king building the temple and officiating in it while alive but at the same time he says to Amon:
"I give all things to my father Amon-Re, that he may [benefit
from] them *in after years*, and that he may give therefrom to
my image and my statue while I rest beside him receiving
offerings."

In these temples on the West, provision was made for the
service of other gods besides Amon, such as Re, Osiris, Monthu,
Sokar, Ptah, etc. One of their chief functions as is constantly
stated in the inscriptions is to serve as a resting place for the
bark of Amon when he visited the necropolis in "his beautiful
Feast of the Valley." During this feast the sacred bark was
transported to the necropolis and spent the night in the temple
of the reigning Pharaoh or in that of the most recently built
of the temples there. In this feast not only the living king but
the dead Pharaohs as well took part. At Karnak we have a
relief showing the bark of Amon setting out for the temples
on the West of Thebes with the living king burning incense
before it and his dead predecessor walking behind the bark
accompanied by an inscription stating that he is "following his
father, Amon, in his beautiful Feast of the Valley."

The Symbolism of the Egyptian Temple

The very simplicity of the primitive shrines of early times,
which only later developed into the great temples of the Empire and Ptolemaic periods, argues against any very elaborate
mystical interpretation of their significance. As time went on,
however, and the house of the god became more and more
complex, the Egyptian began to see cosmic reflections in the
temple building in which the god resided and in which he
came into closest contact with the world of men. The priesthood of the various temples indulged their fancy in mystical
and metaphysical explanations of the divine dwelling, which
speculations naturally took the form of envisaging within the
limitations of the physical building the limitless world in which
the deity moved. The temple was thus pictured as a microcosm
of the world, the realm of the god. I can find no indication

that this interpretation of the temple plan was other than secondary. At any rate, the cosmological significance ascribed to the temple did not determine its form. The structure came first and the interpretation dealt with what already existed. Moreover such concepts seem to have had no bearing on the relation of the temple to society, or on the daily service observed within it.

The Egyptian constantly applied to his temple figures of speech drawn from the physical world. Thus its pylons reach to the height of the heavens: its beauty illuminates the surrounding area with its brightness: it is like the horizon where Re is born again every day: it is the lord of silver and the mistress of gold. The temple also becomes a reflection of the world. Its ceiling is painted blue for the sky and is studded with a multitude of golden stars. Across this "sky," in a long line down the central axis of the building leading up to the "great place," there flies with outstretched wings the vulture goddess. She is shown in a succession of representations so that, as the king or the god in his portable shrine proceeded along the sacred way, he was under the shadow of the protecting deity's wings. The floor of the temple is similarly conceived as the earth out of which plants grow. These take the form of the lotus or papyrus columns which spring from the sacred soil on which the building stands.[2] The Holy of Holies where the god's image rested in its shrine is regarded as the mound which first rose from the primeval waters, the hill where Re first appeared out of chaos. Along the bases of the walls, normally left undecorated in the earlier temples, runs at times a dado of lotus or lily stalks, each crowned with its bud or open flower, growing like the columns from the holy ground. Here too appear the long lines of small human figures bearing as gifts to the temple the various products of the land. These are the personified Nile, or the canals, lakes, fields, vineyards, nomes, and districts of Egypt. They stand close to the earth from which their offerings come. In some temples, the side walls of the narrow rooms below the stairs that lead up to the temple roof and which form right triangles with the hypotenuse determined by the ascending lower surface of the stair-

[2] Borchardt, *Die ägyptische Pflanzensäule*, pp. 53 ff.

way, show these Nile gods as though rising from the earth
and moving towards the door leading out into the temple halls.
The two pylon towers are the hills of the horizon between
which the sun-god rises, and the platform above the gate between the two towers where the sun first penetrates into the
temple each morning is frequently decorated with reliefs of
the morning and evening solar barks in which Re sails through
the sky each day. In late times the pylons are likened to the
goddesses Isis and Nephthis who are shown in the reliefs lift-
ing up the sun in the morning to begin his journey through
the sky. A text at Edfu, speaking of the two towers of the
pylon, states: "One is like Isis, the other like Nephthis as they
lift up Behedety (the sun-god of Edfu) when he shines on the
horizon." Even the interior of the temple is said to resemble
the heavens. In later times a visitor to one of the early tombs
which he mistakenly took for a temple has left his impressions
of the building thus: "The scribe, So-and-so, came to see the
beautiful temple of King Snefru. He found it within like the
heaven, for Re rises therein, and he said: 'The heaven rains
fresh myrrh, it drops incense upon the roof of the temple of
King Snefru.' "[3] Ramses III, speaking of his temple at Medinet
Habu states: "When Re rises, he shines into its midst. When
he sets, he touches its beauty. Its form is like the horizon of
the heavens." Speaking to Amon-Re, he adds: "Happy is my
temple if thou dwellest therein to eternity, and it shall abide
forever."

Deity and Temple in Egypt

Though the god was spoken of as "dwelling" within the
temple, he was not thought of as circumscribed by time or
place. Amon had his chief residence in *Ipet-sut,* 'the select of
places,' the name of this great shrine at Karnak. But he was
immanent in a multitude of other temples both in Egypt and
in other lands over which the Pharaoh ruled. His daily service
was celebrated each morning in all his temples and his morning
and evening meals, to which his priest summoned him, were

[3] Spiegelberg, "Die Auffassung des Tempels als Himmel," *Zeitschrift für ägyptische Sprache und Altertumskunde,* LIII
(1917), 99.

set out for his enjoyment in all of his numerous dwellings. The king, standing before a row of identical divine figures, is said to be addressing Amon "in every place in which his Ka is." In each town where one of his temples stood he might be spoken of as Amon of this or that place, but these were merely names of the same god. The litany of Amon in the first court of the Luxor temple shows the king standing before the deity and the accompanying text begins: "Making incense to Amon-Re, king of gods," "in each of his names," or "in all his names." Then follows a list of these names such as Amon-Re in Thebes, or in Hermopolis, or in Heliopolis, or in foreign lands. More interesting are such designations as Amon-Re: "in all his forms, in all his figures, in all his appearances, in all his beings, in all his births, in every place where he desires to be, in all his likenesses, in all his monuments."[4] Elsewhere he is "lord of the sky, of the earth, of the underworld, of the water, of the desert." Men also call upon Amon who is "in the south lands, in the north lands, in the west lands, in the east lands." The king, speaking to the god, terms the city of Thebes "thy peculiar, or special, house." While it might be the god's favorite dwelling, at the same time he also dwelt in every one of his temples. The sun-god, Re, first acquired this universality. It was difficult for the sun-god to be localized exclusively in any one town or sanctuary, though Heliopolis was regarded as his special dwelling. The immanence of other deities in any place where their worshipers were found might be reinforced by combining them with Re. The identity of the deity was, therefore, somewhat fluid as the result of this tendency to merge two or more gods under one hyphenated name. Thus we have Amon-Re-Harakhte-Atum, or Khonsu-Re-Horus-Thoth, or Mut-Saosis-Sekhmet-Bast, though these combinations were generally of deities who already had much in common.

The question of whether the god might be approached in only one place or in every place simultaneously apparently never arose in the Egyptian's mind. The god was simply there where the worshiper sought him. He was not confined to any place or any image however sacred. The Egyptian says: "He

[4] Daressy, "Litanies d'Amon du Temple de Luxor," *Rec. du Trav.*, XXXII, 63 f.

[the god] is one who confoundeth by what is seen of the eyes [i.e., by his outward form in his statue]. Let the god be served in his fashion [i.e., according to the proper requirements] whether made of precious stones or fashioned of copper, like water replaced by water. There is no stream that suffereth itself to be confined: it bursteth the dyke by which it is confined." Breasted points out that this statement "is obviously an effort to distinguish between the god and the conventional temple image. As water bursts the dyke, so the being of god cannot be confined within the visible image," but "is as elusive as one body of water merging into another."[5] In other words the Egyptian did not confuse the deity with his image any more than he identified the dead man with his mummy or his statue in the tomb. When a man died he passed into the other world, into the realm of Osiris. There he carried on his life much as he did in this world, but he never entirely severed his connection with the world of living men. To retain his identity his name must be preserved, and to take part in the ceremonies at his tomb, which were perhaps his chief link with the living, his mummy or his statue which also stood in the tomb must, by proper magical rites, be vitalized and made capable of occupancy by his soul or Ba. Just as these physical entities must be made available to the unseen dead, so the statue of the god, by the same magical rites, had to be animated, that the deity might use it to manifest himself in his temple. Moreover, these rites had to be repeated again and again. They serve at least to demonstrate that the Egyptian god was not the temple image.

Temple and Community in Egypt

It was apparently through the image that the deity could make his will known. While embodied in it he pronounced oracles affecting the lives of men. These expressions of the divine will were effected by the image nodding its head in approval of one of two alternatives laid before it, or by other physical acts. In this way the god decreed the erection of buildings, selected his favorites for office, rendered decisions as to the guilt or innocence of the accused, gave his blessing to plans

[5] Breasted, *The Dawn of Conscience*, pp. 157–58.

for warlike undertakings, etc. The maintenance of the vitality of the temple image was thus a matter of prime necessity.

With the actual daily service of the temple the mass of the people had little or nothing to do, although there was a considerable body of lay priests who, in monthly rotation, carried out duties along with the regular priesthood. The temple service was conducted by and for the king, that he might obtain life, health, abundance, power, and a multitude of other blessings. But his prosperity was also that of his land and its inhabitants. He became, as it were, a channel through which the divine blessings might flow not only for his own happiness and satisfaction but for that of his people as well.

The king may have been originally the "servant" of the god. The same word in Egyptian means both 'servant,' and 'majesty.' But in actual fact in historic times the servant idea as applied to the monarch had become much weakened. The ruler was himself a god, the son of the deity who dwelt in the temple. The relationship between them was one of mutual advantage, that of a father and his eldest son. Though the wording of the temple service speaks of the king prostrating himself before the deity and kissing the ground, just as do the captives taken in war who beg for mercy, the reliefs showing such acts of the cult depict the Pharaoh either standing, or at most kneeling, before the divine image. The use of magic which played so large a part in Egyptian ritual gave the officiant a measure of equality with the deity who, if approached with the proper formulas and gestures, might be practically coerced into doing what was desired. Moreover, the king, being already of divine parentage and destined to become a full-fledged deity on his death, would perhaps find it difficult to assume the humility which the wording of the service seemed to require.

The ordinary man came nearest to the deity perhaps on the occasion of the great feasts when the god was carried outside his temple precincts and either went in procession through the town or journeyed to visit his divine neighbors in other temples, traveling in his gorgeous *dahabiyeh* on the river while the populace ran rejoicing along the banks or swarmed upon the water in their own small craft, chanting the god's praises and joining in dances and games. As the feasts celebrated in any temple were fairly numerous, the god was, probably, not so remote from the sight of his people as we would sometimes imagine. The king might be the one who approached the god in his holy sanctuary, but the ordinary man could still address his prayers even to the mighty king of gods. In fact one of the epithets of Amon is "he who hears petitions and answers prayers." One imagines that the farther down the social scale he stood, the less assurance did the petitioner feel that his prayer would be heard. Possibly for some such reason there was a tendency to appeal to the god nearer at hand. While, as we have seen, the official religion held that the god was one, though with diverse names and dwellings, the common people apparently developed the conception of a distinct individuality attached to the local form of the god who dwelt in their own locality. Such a tendency among the ignorant is not unknown in Christianity, where the Virgin of one district will find her champions against the claims of a rival Madonna in a neighboring town. In the letters of late times we find the writer calling down upon his correspondent the blessings of Amon-Re, king of gods, of Mut, of Khonsu, and of all the gods of Thebes, of Re-Harakhte when he shines and when he sets, of Amon, United-with-Eternity, of Amon of Jame, of Amon of the throne of the Two Lands, of Amon Userhet,[6] etc., as though these latter were separate divinities like Mut, Khonsu, and Harakhte. Undoubtedly the ordinary citizen felt nearer to the form of Amon who was connected with his local shrine than he did to the more remote and august deity who lived in grandeur in his imposing fane at Karnak, a conception which would undoubtedly be encouraged by the local priesthoods to enhance their own prestige and, perhaps, emoluments.

The temple impinged upon the life of the common man in its economic aspects with increasing force as time went on. From the beginning, the tribute paid to temples through their royal endowments must have laid a considerable burden on a large section of the population. Until the time of the Empire we have little statistical data bearing on this subject, but beginning with the 18th Dynasty we can see a steady increase in the growth of the temple wealth. Thutmose III, who seems

[6] Cerny, "Late Ramesside Letters," *Bibliotheca Aegyptiaca*, IX (1939), *passim*.

to have gained power largely through the assistance of the priesthood of the Amon temple at Karnak, repaid their help by pouring into the god's treasury much, if not most, of the wealth derived from the plunder and tribute of his Asiatic conquests. From his time on the power of the great Theban deity grew to alarming proportions. The revolt against the position of Amon that took shape in the religious movement under Akhnaten, may have been directed as much against the economic dominance of the priesthood as in support of a theological concept. After the collapse of that movement, the gods, and especially Amon, recovered their lost power with great rapidity and moved on to secure a still stronger hold on the country until, in the end, the very throne itself crumbled before the power of the great priesthood at Thebes. The recently published Wilbour Papyrus, a sort of Doomsday Book of the estate of Amon under the later Ramessides, together with information derived from the great Papyrus Harris and numerous temple inscriptions contemporary with it, give a still more vivid picture of the dangerous influence exercised by the Amonite ecclesiastical institution under the 20th Dynasty. The register of Amon's vast landed possessions, coupled with our knowledge of the control possessed by landlords over the bodies and souls of the peasants who work their estates under such an economy, clearly show the stranglehold that the priesthood had acquired on the life of the country by the eleventh century B.C. This is undoubtedly not the situation throughout the whole course of Egyptian history, but that the economic power of the temple institution always had a tendency to increase in more prosperous times is certain. It happens that under the 20th Dynasty our knowledge of this aspect of Egyptian life is fullest.

Like the Egyptian fellah of today, the peasant of Pharaonic times bore his burden of poverty and toil, of injustice and tyranny, with submission and considerable cheerfulness. And just as today, escape from his social prison was closed by circumstances to all but the few. He bowed to necessity but trusted to a better life in the world after death where he too might share some of the pleasures and, perhaps, some of the ease of the Osirian hereafter. However, he was probably pleased to be called to the attention of the god when he was

shown on the votive scale his master erected on the sacred
soil of Osiris at Abydos, even though he were there depicted
performing his humble offices for his earthly lord. He might
be debarred from too close approach to the great deity who
resided at Thebes, or Heliopolis, or Memphis, but he did utter
to them his petitions in times of difficulty and entertained hopes
of a better lot when the troubles of this world were over.

II. THE MESOPOTAMIAN TEMPLE

A. LEO OPPENHEIM

In the marshy canebrakes of Lower Mesopotamia worshipers
of still undetermined ethnical affinities constructed boats,
fenced off sacred enclosures, wove dais-shaped windscreens
and elaborate reed-huts to house their images and other worshiped objects as long ago as the fourth millennium, B.C. The
rare pictorial representations allow us only a few glimpses of
the religious activity enacted in these reed-sanctuaries.[1] This
aquatic past left sundry traces in the ritual practices, the sacred
furniture of the later temples, as well as in the material features of their architecture.[2] To this we trace back naval processions, the use of reed-huts for certain rites, altars made of
reed, and other customs.

With the invention of sun-dried bricks was ushered in the
epoch of monumental temple-architecture. The oldest extant
brick buildings were devoted to the gods. On a mound of clean
earth a rectangular and symmetrical temple was lifted high

[1] Cf. the article of L. H. Vincent, "La représentation divine
orientale archaïque" in *Mélanges Dussaud* (Paris, 1939), pp. 373 ff.
[2] Cf. e. g. E. Heinrich, *Schilf und Lehm, ein Beitrag zur
Urgeschichte der Sumerer* ("Studien z. Bauforschung," Vol. VI,
[1934]).

above the level of secular human life; three naves and, most probably, a second story feature an imposing structure in whose white-faced walls numerous doors opened in three directions. Yet, this temple was still an experiment, an attempt to create a sacred building to shelter the deity, its worshipers and their cult. Though the architectural technique—rectangular and symmetrical planning, recessed brick-walls, colored facing, etc.—was accepted as normative for all future edifices of that type, the characteristic features of the building itself (that is: location on a mound, accessibility through numerous doorways, and arrangement of the rooms) seem nevertheless to have been rejected as inadequate expressions of the religious concepts of the community. Whether it was because this concept was still in actual evolution or because there were successive ethnic or political changes in the community, new types of temple-architecture appear and disappear in Mesopotamia[3] until, towards the end of the third millennium, the perfect expression was finally achieved by the creative religious genius of the temple-builders. A pattern was thus set to be followed conscientiously by all Babylonian architects until this civilization disappeared.[4]

The Typical Mesopotamian Temple

The old sanctuary was replaced by two buildings: one aloft on the mound, the dimensions of which were considerably increased and which was to become the marvel of the Near Eastern world, the other on the level soil. The tower (*siqqurratu*) was destined to receive the deity alighting there in its descent from heaven, while the lower building, with the ground plan of a typical South-Babylonian private house, was to be the abode of the god when staying on earth. None of the small sacred structures erected on top of the stage-tower has survived, exposed as they were to the inclemencies of the weather and to the inevitable decay of this part of the build-

[3] The article of V. Müller "Types of Mesopotamian Houses" in *JAOS*, LX, 151 ff., will inform the reader with regard to these questions and the pertinent literature.

[4] The short-lived innovations which appear very rarely in the period of the Cassite rulers are not discussed here.

ing. No literary evidence describes clearly their function so that
we have to rely on Herodotus' perhaps fanciful information
that the lofty sanctuary contained a beautifully decked-out
bed and a golden table, but no image, and that a priestess
chosen by the god slept there.[5] Archaeological evidence in-
forms us furthermore of monumental stairways leading to the
upper parts of the tower while historical inscriptions of later
periods describe the uppermost stage as faced with blue-
colored enameled bricks, and adorned with mighty copper
horns indicating, perhaps, that an altar was the model for that
story of the temple-tower.[6]

In the lower temple we have a central court surrounded by
groups of rooms of which the principal one, situated on the
shady south-front, contained the image. Here, in the reproduced living room of the Babylonian private house, the sacred
image stood on a low threshold-like step before a door-shaped
recess in the wall and in front of the main door of the transverse room. This door led through one or two other transverse
anterooms to the main court, where the worshiping crowd
gathered to look through a monumental doorway, which presented the characteristic architecture of a city-gate, to the
beautifully dressed image glowing in the darkness of the sanc-

[5] Both features of this description seem to have appealed to
Herodotus; the absence of an image and the concept of sexual inter-
course between a god and a human female. The first information
was certainly reliable because the temple harbored only one image
of its god; as to the second we have to bear in mind that Herodotus
very likely had some fixed ideas about "Oriental mysteries" as can
be seen from sundry colored details in his descriptions of Babylonian
and Egyptian customs. It is likely that he (consciously or uncon-
sciously) transferred the information he received of the "Bed-
Room," i.e., the part of sanctuary where the rite of the "Sacred
Marriage" was enacted, to the mysterious shrine on top of the tower.
[6] The idea that the deity alighted on the tower when descending
from heaven to perform its epiphany before the "false door" in the
lower temple lacks the support of any sort of architectural connection between these two buildings. Yet, it should not be dismissed for
that reason, which only appeals to our type of logical thinking. The
Assyrians to whom the ṣiqqurratu-idea was originally alien, unmistakably stress this connection in the temples built in Asshur, Kar-
Tukulti-Ninurta, Kalhu and Khorsabad. It seems that these architects were free to express a relation which their Babylonian colleagues could not materialize, bound as they were by their traditions.

tuary. Only the servicing priests and those sacerdotal officials, termed "[those allowed to] enter the house," had access to it. Exception was made for the king of Babylon who entered the naos of Esagila (main temple of this city) once a year, at the New Year's festival, yet stripped of his regalia and as a humble and devout penitent. When, for example, the Assyrian king Shalmaneser III (858–824 B.C.) came to Kutha in Babylon to worship the god Nergal he referred in his inscriptions[7] to the pious act: "He humbly made the prostration at the door of the temple, offered his sacrificial lamb and gave the [required] gifts."[8] Obviously the king was not permitted to enter the shrine.

The Assyrian temple has another origin and lacks—in its earlier and genuine forms—the central court holding the worshiper. The visitor to the house of god had to enter the room itself where the deity permanently dwelt. He stepped into the oblong sanctuary through a door in the longer wall, near the farther end of the room on the shorter wall of which the image was placed. Consequently, he had to turn to his right or left to behold the god enthroned on a platform and separated from the main room by a small partition formed by wall-ledges. Under Babylonian influence the entrance was sometimes provided with flanking towers (imitating a city-gate) or placed in the shorter wall, creating thus—against the spirit of the building—a sequence of rooms strung on one central axis: anteroom, main room for the worshiper and adyton with the image.

The Assyrian deity was enthroned in the place of honor, far away from the entrance and not to be seen from the outside. As the master of the house it there received the visitor who reverently entered its room. The resulting intimacy was somewhat counteracted by the division of the main room, but was undoubtedly so intended by the architect. In this context

[7] Cf. Luckenbill, *Ancient Records of Assyria and Babylonia*, Vol. I, No. 624.

[8] This description covers the typical features of a visit to the sanctuary. The frequent personal names of the type *pan ili amaru* 'to see the face of the god' (cf. J. J. Stamm, "Die akkadische Namengebung," in *MVAG*, XLIV, 85 f.) show the religious import of such visits while the scarcity of personal names referring to temples (cf. *loc. cit.*, 85 f., 203) squares with the conclusions reached in the present article.

it should be stressed that the Assyrian image seems to have been confined to its shrine, while the Babylonian gods quite frequently left their sanctuaries to be shown to the admiring crowd in the spacious temple-yards and in the streets. That the Assyrian images were kept in their abodes is expressly indicated, for example, by a passage of an inscription of Ashurnasirpal II (883–859 B.C.) who warned his successors not to bring the holy image of Ishtar (whose temple he had restored) to the profane light of day.[9]

Before discussing the construction and appearance of these temples, short mention should be made of their most famous representatives. In the first place we have Esagila, the Marduktemple (Tower of Babel) in Babylon of Bible-fame; the Ezida in Borsippa, whence Nabu, the son of Marduk, came annually to pay homage to his father; the Shamash-temples (called Ebabbar) of north and south Babylonia in Sippar and Larsa respectively, while Uruk (the biblical Erech) harbored the famous temple of Anu and Ishtar, the Eanna. The temple of the national god of Assyria stood in Asshur among many other shrines dedicated to Assyrian and Babylonian deities; a famous Ishtar-sanctuary in Arbela seems to have been a place of pilgrimage at the time of its revelling festivals.

The very heart of the temple was the place where the image had to stand; it was distinguished by deep foundations of kiln-fired bricks or clean sand, and protected by numerous magic figures imbedded in brick-cases. The orientation of the building[10] was determined by the setting of the *libittu makhritu* ('first brick') which was placed ceremoniously on clean earth, surrounded by precious beads and anointed with perfumed oil. This brick was conceived as harboring the protective numina of the building, the 'god,' 'goddess,' and 'genius' (*ilu, ishtaru, Lamassu*) with which the temple was endowed like any living human being.[11] In case of the desecration of the sanctuary, by repair-work or reconstruction, the *libittu makhritu* had to be taken from its location by the temple-architect

[9] Cf. Budge-King, *Annals of Assyrian Kings*, p. 165, rev. 5.

[10] For this problem cf. G. Martiny, *Die Kultrichtung in Mesopotamien* ("Studien z. Bauforschung," Vol. III [1932]).

[11] Cf. the texts published by F. Thureau-Dangin, *Rituels accadiens*, for the details mentioned above.

and brought to a ritually clean and secluded place in the open air. Here, penitential songs, continuous aspersions, and fumigations were enacted for the sustenance of this "temple in exile" till it could be put in place again.

Architects and surveyors with their ropes and rods determined the outlines of the *temennu* (Sumerian: *temen;* cf. Greek: *temenos*), the foundation-platform in which was also to be deposited the foundation-document. In case of a rebuilding of a ruined temple the architects had to follow exactly, "neither projecting nor recessing a finger's breadth," the outlines of the old *temennu,* a custom of great advantage to the modern excavator, who finds layers upon layers of such foundations, like the pages of a book, laid by scores of pious generations.

The walls of sacred buildings were consistently made of sun-dried bricks, although the advantages of kiln-fired bricks were well known. The latter were frequently employed in secular buildings, but the conservatism of sacred architecture tended here, as everywhere, to retain antiquated techniques. The roof of the temple was made of timber stretched over the rooms, thus determining their width, since the temple-architects did not favor the use of supporting devices, such as columns, etc. Its inner side was magnificently decorated with metal inlays and incrustations. The last stage of the construction-work was reached when the door-openings were skilfully framed. Then the heavy doors, coated with sheets of copper or precious metals which the artist had engraved or embossed, were set in their hinges, and provided with heavy locks and strong ropes for their manipulation. The brick-walls were faced on both sides with white coatings often decorated with colored washes or other, more costly, mural decorations (mosaics, enameled bricks, etc.).[12]

When the work was completed, the image was brought into

[12] It might not be amiss to stress here the perishable nature of all that sumptuousness. Thorough and constant repair-work was vitally necessary to maintain the roof-cover and the protective coating of the brick-walls in good condition, but it was not able to prevent the deterioration and the final ruin of the temple, a situation which the kings so eloquently describe in their reports on the reconstruction of ruined sites.

its new house in a solemn and jubilant procession. As a rule
each image dwelt in a separate sanctuary: the principal god
in the main room, the members of the divine family or the
officials of the divine court in smaller shrines. Statues of kings
and of private persons,[13] in worshiping attitudes with pious
dedicational inscriptions, sumptuous votive-offerings praising
both the god and the donator, filled the sanctuary, together
with multifarious sacred furniture such as altars, sacrificial
tables, portable shrines, canopies, etc.[14]

The deity was conceived as living in the sanctuary just as
the king lived in his palace. This is unmistakably expressed
by the fact that the throne-rooms of the Babylonian and Assyrian palaces correspond exactly in their architectural features to the sanctuaries of the region. In Babylonia we have
transverse rooms with the king visible from the court through
a central door. In Assyria there were longitudinal rooms with
the throne on the smaller wall. The daily life of the image is
also patterned after that of the king. In this regard we are
fairly well informed by the ritual texts of the Seleucid period,
and by the numerous administrative documents from Neo-
Babylonian temple-archives. There is good reason to assume
that the picture which these sources yield is also valid for the
daily life of the king, of which we know little.

After having been awakened by a ceremonious assembly of
minor deities, the image is furnished water for its morning
toilet, then clothed and decked out with sumptuous garments,
crowns, etc., according to the requirements of the day's ceremonies; it is served twice or three times a day a plentiful repast on exquisite and precious plates; it receives the visits of
the members of its family or court, and was led on festival
occasions through the streets of its town to rites performed in
out-of-door sanctuaries, or carried in a festive cortege to nup-
tials with its divine spouse. It was not even refused the truly
royal pleasure of hunting in its game-cover.[15]

Many, and certainly the most impressive, of these scenes
were enacted by the priests before throngs of admiring wor-

---

[13] Cf. the passage *KAR* 214:19–20.
[14] The importance and role of the so-called "symbols"—special objects of religious worship in the temple—cannot be discussed here.
[15] Cf. the Assyrian letter Harper, *ABL*, p. 366.

shipers which saw the beautifully decorated golden or wooden images carried around on magnificent platforms in huge processions with appropriate musical accompaniment. The priests were well aware of the propaganda value of such a display of wealth and pomp. As a matter of fact the entire architectural setup of the Babylonian sanctuary is actually based on the very same trend of thought. The image is effectually displayed to the gaze of the worshiper by placing it in a shallow room opposite a monumental door shaped like a city-gate in order to create a magnificent frame for the statue.

For the worshiper, however, this priestly concept of the relation between the divine and the human had serious consequences. Though he could admire with religious awe the glamor of the image displayed in the background of the sanctuary, he was forever separated from it by the unsurmountable barrier which excluded him from the shrine.[16] Though he was able to enjoy in the thronging crowd some fleeting glimpses of the age-old statues carried hither and yon in elaborate but unintelligible ceremonies, he could only expect to be asperged by the priests with some drops of the water which was sanctified by the supposition that the image had touched it when washing its hands after the repast. Apart from that he could take part only in the collective and periodical ecstasy of joyous festivals of thanksgiving and in the traditional mournings where there was no room or time for the intense subtlety which links the individual to his god. No deeply spiritual bond could emerge under the circumstances just described. The "house of god" was separated from the fostering soil of individual religious intensity, and the same chasm gaped between the temple and the worshiper as between the king's palace and the mass of loyal subjects.

Temple and Community in Mesopotamia

But the sanctuary was not the only building of the extensive temple-complex. The latter contained within its girdle-walls the living-quarters of the numerous priests who directed and performed the ceremonies, accompanied them with song and music, manufactured the costly utensils of the cult, and cared

---

[16] Cf. note 8 for the importance of the optical impression.

for the maintenance of the sanctuary itself. Furthermore there
were schools and libraries where the young priests were
trained and prepared for their duties and there the scholars
worked, copying old tablets and keeping the lore of their calling alive. Besides all this there were large warehouses, workshops, granaries, and stables where the immense wealth of the
deity was stored, administered, and increased by a special
body of competent priests. This part of the temple meant far
more to the average Babylonian than the admired splendor
of the sanctuary, and interfered far more with his daily life.
The economic weight of this institution was a tangible reality
in the city-state, and its powerful influence was felt in every
domain of the political, social, and economic life of the community.

It is beyond the scope of this article to discuss the development of the temple as an economic institution. Suffice it to
state that its tap-roots disappear in the darkness of the prehistoric period, into that protoplasmic state of Mesopotamian
social organization where the offices of the king and the
(high-) priest were still united in the same person. The ensuing schism left the temple provided with enough land and
serfs to ensure its economic prosperity, yet to a certain extent
subject to the secular royal authority. The latter is clearly
borne out by the fact that from a very early period the Babylonian king appointed the high-priest of the city's temple, although he himself was only permitted to enter the sanctuary
once a year and then after having been humiliated by the very
same priest. It is furthermore remarkable that, until the last
period, the board of sacerdotal officials which ran the temple-
organization, had to include a representative of the king. It
was the latter's duty to control the transactions of the temple
and to pay the royal taxes or else to obtain special charters
from the king granting freedom of taxation for the sanctuary
and its possessions. Although this peculiar relation between
the secular and the religious authorities might have caused
friction or at least created tension between them, it can be
stated that they lived in harmony throughout the two and a
half millennia recorded in the extant texts. Though this impression may be partly caused by our restricted knowledge of

Babylonian history,[17] the basic attitude between palace and temple was obviously that of collaboration and mutual ideological assistance.

Economically, the temple fared very well: a steady stream of royal gifts (partly spoils of war) and endowments, together with the offerings brought in by the pious poor extended more and more the landed property of the temple, filled its warehouses, added glamor to its sanctuaries, and lightened the burden of taxation. An efficient administration, controlled by a highly developed and extensive bureaucracy, could not but increase the accumulated wealth. On the fertile soil and fat pastures the countless serfs and slaves of the temple were working. In the efficiently equipped workshops they produced not only for the needs of the deity and the priests but manufactured also export-goods in order to buy in foreign countries coveted precious metals, stones and timber which nature had denied to Babylonia. It is easy to imagine how such a thriving and ambitious institution influenced the economic life of its city by creating the pattern and showing the effects of international trade and commercial efficiency, not to speak of the work and money it procured for the merchants, craftsmen, and artists of the city.

Another and equally influential side of the temple's activities deserves notice here. Owing most probably to their common roots the temple felt and accepted, just as the palace did, the responsibilities incumbent upon it by virtue of its social and economic predominance. It therefore endeavored to correct in some ways the grievances of the economically underprivileged. It attempted to standardize the system of measurements whose irregularities constituted a severe burden on farmers and other debtors. It tried to reduce the rate of interest, the fluctuations of which were constantly in favor of the creditor, or at least to set an example of what should be normal. It also tried to regulate the money-market by granting loans without interest in special cases. Without the backing of legal enforcements these reformative trends were certainly as inefficient as the corresponding efforts of the kings to control

[17] Beyond a thin and not even always coherent network of king-names and a meager array of historical facts (of varied importance) only little is known of Babylonian history.

the prices of the standard commodities. Yet, such postulations, theoretical and propagandistic though they actually were, bear eloquent witness to a concept of social responsibility.

The reader of the preceding pages in which we have tried to outline the tenor of the relations between the temple (as a religious and an economic institution) and the individual, will certainly have observed that we were dealing for the most part with the situation in Babylonia. The important question now arises whether the archaeological and literary data of the Assyrian region offer the same picture.

With regard to the ground plan of the genuine Assyrian sanctuary we have already shown that it was basically different from that of the Babylonian. Instead of the stage-like display of the image, the Assyrian architects wanted to shelter the god in the remotest part of the oblong sanctuary, thus inviting the worshiper to enter the divine abode. There, one room enclosed both the god and the man, endowing this meeting between the divine and the human with an unmistakable atmosphere of intimacy. Such an atmosphere, created by the architect and willed by the worshiper, betokens the altogether different Assyrian concept of the relations between the "house of god" and its visitor.

As to the literary evidence, it unfortunately offers only scarce information for two reasons: first, the administrative documents of the temple-archives, which constitutes our foremost source of information in Babylonia, are all missing and the extant rituals offer little insight into our field of interest. Secondly, a consistent and steadily increasing process of Babylonization has produced a nearly solid overcast which hides most of the specifically Assyrian features, especially in the realm of religious thought. Only two salient facts can be mentioned here without too much detailed discussion: the fact that the Assyrian king was also the high-priest of the national god, thus linking palace and temple by means of his person; and the fact that the Assyrians did not believe that the sanctuary was the only place of divine presence. They offered sacrifices and prayers to divine beings dwelling on mountain-tops, in sacred groves, and near the sources of rivers.

All this betrays the existence of a specific Assyrian religiosity of which little is yet known and which definitely differs from the religious concepts of the Babylonians. It seems to have been pervaded with the same intensity that patently animates the impetuous energy of the entire Assyrian civilization, so different from the reclusive stability and equipoise of the Babylonian.

III. THE TEMPLE IN PALESTINE–SYRIA

G. ERNEST WRIGHT

From Parts I and II which dealt with the temples of Egypt and Mesopotamia we have gained or may infer the following information:

1. In the pagan world of ancient times men could scarcely believe in the Divine as an all-pervading Spirit. Divinity did not reveal itself at any time or in any place chosen by the worshiper. The common man could pray, but his prayers were more likely to be heard when they were uttered *in particular places* where a divine being was believed to have manifested itself in times past. In other words, certain places on the earth had become sacred or holy, and worship was largely confined to them.

2. At these holy places it was customary, when resources permitted, to build temples, sacred buildings, to the god or gods there worshiped. Modern churches and synagogues are the temple's successors, but their function is very different. The modern church building is a place where worshipers assemble to participate in acts of corporate devotion, praise, and confession, and to be instructed in the things pertaining to God and his service. By contrast, the temple was erected as the house or palace of a deity, comparable to the palace of a king or noble. No such word as "temple" existed, but the divine

abode was called by the same names (i.e., "house" or "palace") as the abode of a king. Being the divine dwelling place, it was holy and was erected in a special compound which separated it from the outer world. The common man could never enter it for religious assemblies; that was not the building's purpose. The rites of worship carried on in a temple by specially ordained priests took the form of ministrations to the physical needs which a god was believed to have: that is, food (sacrifices and offerings), drink (oblations), incense, etc. Man's duty was to supply divine wants, and in return for the service thus rendered, he could hope for divine rewards.

3. In no country, however, as far as we know, were thinking people naive enough to believe that a god could be confined to a particular building. Re (Sun) in Egypt, for example, not only had various abodes (temples) as did kings and nobles, but he was a cosmic god who was believed to control the times, seasons, and destiny of earth. His palace, therefore, naturally reflected the cosmos as it was then understood. "Its ceiling is painted blue for the sky and is studded with a multitude of golden stars . . . The floor . . . . is similarly conceived as the earth out of which plants grow" (Nelson, Pt. I, p. 151). The same is true in Babylonia where the most elaborate cosmic symbolism was employed in a temple's construction. Most characteristic in that country was the temple-tower. This type of structure originated as an artificial platform, the purpose of which was to raise the temple above the water level and preserve it from the danger of floods. As time went on, however, the original purpose was forgotten, and the tower was built higher and higher in order to lift the temple on top of it toward the sky (cf. Gen. 11:4). The main temple was now built at the base of the tower, while the building at the top "was destined to receive the deity alighting there in its descent from heaven" (Oppenheim, Pt. II, p. 159). Thus while a god "dwelt" in the earthly palace built for him, he was not confined to that building. Instead it became a symbolic microcosm of the deity's world.

4. In all ancient temples the proof of the deity's presence was his statue, which somehow was thought to house his essence. In neither Egypt nor Mesopotamia did religious leaders, at least, believe that the statue *was* the god, or that it

confined him. Nevertheless, he was believed to be *in* the statue. Such a careful distinction, however, was probably not understood by the ordinary worshiper (Nelson, Pt. I, pp. 153–54).

5. The great temples and their services of worship were largely aristocratic or upper-class affairs; and the poor peasant could hardly afford to participate in them to any extent. In common practice, therefore, the religion of the common people concerned itself chiefly with lesser deities who were closely connected with a farmer's daily life. The Divine was not one, as we believe, but many. Nature was alive, and its powers and forces since time immemorial had been personified and worshiped. The official pantheon of the gods might be accepted by all and elaborately systematized by theologians; but the religion of the common people was certainly far less sophisticated, preserving many more primitive attitudes and beliefs. This point may be overstressed, as it has often been in the past, but it does explain many of the contradictory currents of thought which are common in every age and so clearly seen, for example, in the Old Testament. Thus country shrines, sacred trees, stones, mountains were the common heritage of the ancient world, having survived from the life of prehistoric times.

6. Inevitably, the temples of the great gods were a source of tremendous power in community life. Here were the points where the divine touched the human, where the sources of ultimate power were available to alleviate human need, and from which directions were issued for the conduct of life's affairs. The whole stability of the social order was dependent on the temple. This situation is vividly illustrated by the names given temple-towers in Babylonia, some of which are as follows: "The house (which is) the link of heaven and earth"; "the house (which is) the mooring-post of heaven and earth"; "the house (which is) the foundation-platform of heaven and earth"; "the house (which is) the destiny [i.e., divine prefiguration] of heaven and earth."

Temples were also centers of the economic life of a community. In both Egypt and Mesopotamia they were heavily endowed with landed properties and received a tremendous income. At certain periods they probably owned nearly all the land of the country and acquired almost an economic stranglehold over the people.

The Temple in Canaan

Turning now to Syria-Palestine in pre-Isrælite times, we find that the role of the temple was basically similar to that in Egypt and Mesopotamia. The temple as abode of a god was called the god's 'house' or 'palace' (*hêkāl*), and precisely the same words were used as in Babylonia.

The most popular god in whom the Canaanites believed was one familiarly called Baal ('Lord'; his proper name was Hadad). In the religious texts of Ras Shamrah Baal, like the Lord of Isræl in David's time (II Sam. 7), had no "house," though other gods and goddesses did have them. So with the permission of El, the father of the gods, an elaborate structure was completed. This suggests that while such a house was not absolutely required by Baal, it was something he greatly desired.

Baal, moreover, was believed to be the god of the storm, the controller of rain, and the giver of all fertility. He was called the "Rider of the Clouds," the "Lord of Heaven," the "Lord of Earth." He reigned over gods and men, and his kingdom was "eternal, to all generations." This god could certainly be no more confined to a physical building as his sole dwelling than could the great gods of Egypt or Babylonia. As a result, the many temples built for him were undoubtedly conceived to be his abode in the sense that they were the mirrors of the cosmos in which he moved.

There appears to have been in Canaan, however, a sharper conflict than in Egypt and Mesopotamia between the official views regarding the oneness of such a god as Baal and the views of the common people. We are told in the Old Testament, for example, that "the children of Isræl did that which was evil in the sight of the Lord and served Baalim" (that is Baals, Judg. 2:11)—as though there were many Baals about the country. From the same source we learn of some of these Baals: the Baal of Peor in Moab, Baal-zebul of Ekron, Baal-hazor, Baal-hermon, Baal-meon, Baal-tamar, etc. (the last four are names of towns). Thus, though theoretically Baal was one, in practice his being became split up into many, each locality having its own shrine or temple. The same can probably be said with regard to the chief goddesses in whom Canaanites believed, particularly Asherah (the mother-goddess) and Ashtoreth (the goddess of fertility).

It is legitimate to suppose that the geography of Syria-Palestine may have had something to do with this situation. Canaan possessed no geographical unity. Instead, the mountains and valleys tended to accentuate local differences. As a result, the city-state system was the political organization developed, and each city-state had its rival temples to the Canaanite deities. In Egypt and in Babylonia (and in Israel too), during periods when there was a strong centralized government, there was a central temple or temples for the chief god or gods. But a unified Canaanite state never came into being. The result was that no one temple of Baal, for example, could be said to be his main abode.

The attempt, then, to localize a god's accessibility in a sacred building, and the geographical disunity which encouraged the erection of rival shrines and temples to any one god *without a counter tendency toward centralization*—these two factors appear to have resulted in a greater tendency toward splitting up and localizing divine beings than was the case in Egypt or Mesopotamia. Thus it could happen, as stated in the books of Deuteronomy and Judges, that the more Israelites took over Canaanite beliefs and practices, the greater the weakening of the national unity and the accentuation of local differences.

Probably to counteract this situation the so-called "plural of majesty" came into being among the Canaanites. Thus the name for Ashtoreth frequently appears in the plural (Ashtaroth). An important town in Transjordan was so named (Deut. 1:4, etc.). It is most improbable that a city would be named "Ashtoreths." This plural name must have had another significance. One of the common names for God in the Old Testament is Elohim, also a plural meaning 'gods,' though when used of Israel's Lord it certainly meant one God. It is now recognized that this plural word used to designate a singular

being was thus employed in Canaan before it was in Israel.[1]
Such plural names when referring to deities, therefore, must
often have designated the totality of a god's appearances or
attributes. Ashtaroth would mean the sum total of all the appearances and attributes of the goddess Ashtoreth. Such a
usage would arise in all probability only as a result of an attempt to counteract the popular tendency to believe in numerous Ashtoreths. (For a somewhat similar problem in
Egypt, see Nelson, Pt. I, p. 153 ff.).

Temple-Form and Ritual in Canaan

It is comparatively simple to describe the physical features of the Canaanite temples, since a considerable number of them have been found. Among the earliest are one
at Jericho and one at Megiddo dating *ca.* 3000 B.C., and
three at Megiddo dating *ca.* 1900 B.C. All except possibly the
Jericho structure are of the broad-house type: that is, they
have a single long room with door on the long side. One of
the most extraordinary and one of the finest examples of architecture recovered in Palestine is a building at Ai which has
been called a palace. There can be no doubt, however, that
this too was a temple; and it belongs to the same type as those
just mentioned at Jericho and Megiddo. Later temples, at least
after 1500 B.C., tend to be square, with a special vestibule or
portico for entrance provided. At Beth-shan the most interesting addition was a special room or cubicle at the rear, raised
above the main room and reached by steps, in which the divine
statue or statues were placed. In other words we have here the
beginning of the *děbîr* or 'Holy of Holies' which is a main
feature of the Solomonic Temple and also present in the tem-

[1] See Albright, *Archaeology of Palestine and the Bible*, pp. 166 f.;
and Kittel, *Geschichte des Volkes Israel*, I (5th–6th ed.), 173.
Albright calls my attention to one of the important proofs of this
point in the *Tell el-Amarna* letters of Canaanite kings to the divine
Pharaoh of Egypt. In them Canaanite (or Semitic) scribes address
the Pharaoh as "my *ilani* (i.e., my gods), my sun-god," while non-
Canaanite scribes use the singular of this word. Yet the Pharaoh was
one, not many. Thus *ilani*, 'gods,' here can only be a translation of
Elohim, and used as a "plural of majesty," or better a plural designating the totality of the deity's personality and attributes.

ples of Egypt and Mesopotamia. In the main sanctuary room were benches on which offerings were placed, a small altar before the raised shrine on which incense was probably offered, a libation stand or stands, and lamps. Outside was the court and the main altar for burnt offerings.

The only Phœnician temple recovered from the period following 1000 B.C. is a small one at Tell Tainat in Syria. This, together with the earliest Greek temples which were influenced by Syrian models, indicates that the general plan of the temple of Solomon was typical for the age: that is, a long narrow structure with entrance at one end and with the "Holy of Holies" at the other.

It was the duty of both king and commoner to provide for the upkeep of the temples, as in Egypt and Mesopotamia. The sacrifices and oblations provided food and drink for the gods; as the Ras Shamrah texts put it poetically, "The gods eat the offerings; the deities drink the offerings." Temple ritual was apparently elaborate. Judging from such information as we have in the Ras Shamrah texts, the Old Testament, Phœnician, and other archæological sources, we may presume that this ritual was in major essentials that described in the early chapters of Leviticus, though more elaborate. The mythical background of the ritual, however, was far cruder than anywhere else in the Near East at the time. The primitive nature and the brutality of the mythology are surprising. In addition, there were cultic practices of an especially degrading nature: "human sacrifices, long given up by the Egyptians and Babylonians, sacred prostitution of both sexes . . . , the vogue of eunuch priests, who were much less popular in Mesopotamia and were not found in Egypt, serpent worship to an extent unknown in other lands of antiquity."[2]

The Temple in Israel

When we turn to Israel, we note first of all that the worshipers of the LORD, like their pagan neighbors, believed that worship must take place at holy sites and not in any spot

[2] Albright, "The Role of the Canaanites in the History of Civilization," *Studies in the History of Culture* (Menasha, Wis., 1942), pp. 28 f.

chosen by the worshiper. Before the Deuteronomic reform in
621 B.C. (II Kings 22–23) the particular places where God
revealed himself were numerous: Mt. Sinai, Kadesh-barnea,
the Tabernacle, Shechem, Mamre, Beersheba, a place between
Bethel and Ai, Shiloh, Mizpah, Gibeon, etc.

Some of these places (Shechem, for example) were probably Canaanite holy sites before the days of Israel. But the
important point to notice is that such places were not conceived primarily as dwellings of the Lord. Rather they were
places where he revealed himself. This is especially clear in
Genesis, and is an important point of difference between Israel
and the surrounding peoples. Thus there was no real localizing
of Deity in the various shrines, as appears to have happened
in popular Canaanite religion. The danger of splitting up the
Divine Being into numerous local manifestations was thus
avoided.

In Israel the consciousness that the being of God was opposed to confinement in any one place was evidently stronger
and more explicit than elsewhere. The dynamic character of
the Lord meant that he used even Canaanite holy places for
his revelation. At the same time, however, his favorite place
was believed to be Sinai. And at least as early as the tenth
to ninth centuries, the people believed that his real dwelling
was in the heavens (Gen. 24:3, 7; 28:12, 17; cf. 11:5; 18:21;
Exod. 19:11, 18, 20).[3] While there was a tendency on the
part of some to believe that the LORD was confined or at least
especially connected with his own land,[4] yet there appears to
have been a more general belief that he heard and answered
prayer (i.e., was present) wherever his people were. He revealed himself to Moses and Israel in Egypt and Sinai, to
Abram and Eliezer in Paddan-aram (Gen. 12:1 ff.; 24:10 ff.),
and to Absalom in Geshur (II Sam. 15:8).

In early Israel, therefore, two tendencies, the one counter-
balancing the other, appear to have been in operation. The
one, emphasizing the immanence of God, localized his appear-

---

[3] See also Eichrodt, *Theologie des Alten Testaments*, I, 44 ff.
[4] Cf. II Kings 5:17 where Naaman is said to have requested some
Israelite earth for transport to Damascus, so that he might build an
altar on it and worship the God of Israel.

ances in particular places, though it did not regard these places as his "dwellings." The other, emphasizing the transcendence of God, believed in his omnipresence and in his heavenly abode (cf. the similar conflict in Canaan, noted above). As a result of the first emphasis, it was possible for sacred trees, high places, pillars, etc., to play a role in religious life just as they did in Canaan, though as the issues became clearer such things were vigorously denounced by prophets and priests (cf. Deut. 7:5; 16:21–22; I Kings 14:23–24; etc.). The greater the extent of this particularizing influence, the greater the tendency for Israelites to forget their covenantal relation with God, indeed the very bond which held them together.

The Tabernacle

These two opposing tendencies in Israelite conceptual life are seen in sharper focus in the tabernacle and in the temple of Solomon. During the wilderness wanderings the central religious focus of the people had been the portable "tabernacle." This English word is used to translate the Hebrew *miškān*, which properly means 'tent-dwelling':[5] that is, the tabernacle was God's dwelling. We are immediately reminded of the pagan temples which were conceived to be divine abodes. But the tabernacle was also called the Tent of Meeting: that is, a place before which people assembled to meet God. In addition, when Moses and the people did meet God at the tabernacle, we are told that the Lord *descended* on the structure and enveloped it with his glory or pillar of cloud (Exod. 33:9; 40:34; etc.). Thus, on the one hand, the tabernacle was thought to be God's dwelling; and yet, on the other, it did not confine him because his proper abode was in the heavens above. He descended to this earthly building as a gracious condescension to the people's needs, giving himself thus to direct and guide their journey (Num. 9:15 ff.). This gracious element in the Lord's dealing with Israel was fundamental to the latter's thought of God, and is one which does not receive a similar emphasis in the conceptions of deity held by surrounding peoples.

[5] On the basis of Ras Shamrah evidence. See below chap. 14.

The Temple of Solomon

During the early days of the settlement in Palestine Israel seems always to have had a central holy place where the tabernacle was erected. Best known was Shiloh, though this town was destroyed by the Philistines *ca.* 1050 B.C.[6] According to II Sam. 7 David consulted the prophet Nathan about his desire to build a permanent "house" for the Lord. But Nathan did not appear at all enthusiastic about the idea. He said that God had been quite satisfied with the tabernacle up to that time and placed no requirement upon his people to build him a temple. Later, when the Chronicler wrote about David's plans, he was confronted by an accomplished fact; the temple had been built. So his explanation was that God would not permit David to build the structure because the latter had been a man of war and had shed much blood (I Chron. 22:8; 28:3). Nathan's lack of enthusiasm for the temple is paralleled by the purist reactions against the course of events to be seen among the conservative, tent-dwelling Rechabites (cf. Jer. 35) and perhaps in the early prophetic movement as a whole.

The temple was built by Solomon according to Phœnician designs (I Kings 5 ff.). There were three parts to it: the vestibule ('porch'), called the *'ûlām;* the main room or 'Holy Place,' called the *hêkāl;* and the 'Holy of Holies' or 'oracle,' called the *dĕbîr.* The last mentioned was an unlighted room in which were placed two huge olive-wood cherubim or winged sphinxes. Beneath their outstretched wings the Ark of the Covenant was placed. On them the Lord was believed to be invisibly enthroned. It is clear, therefore, that there was to be no statue of God in this temple. Instead of a podium with statue characteristic of the "Holy of Holies" in pagan temples, a different symbolism was used for which we have no parallel in temple arrangements. The cherubim with their outstretched wings bearing the invisible God must certainly refer to the belief in the cosmic, omnipresent Deity, and they presuppose a somewhat different situation from that in known Canaanite and Babylonian temples. In the latter the image of the god was raised upon a platform in a special little room in such a

6 See Albright, *ARI*, pp. 103 f.

way as to signify his kingship (cf. Oppenheim, Pt. II, p. 160).
The differing symbolism in the closed and dark *dĕbîr* of Solo-
mon's temple undoubtedly was occasioned in large part by the
Israelite prohibition against images of God.[7]

The name for the whole structure was simply "House of
the Lord" (I Kings 6:1, etc.). The term "house," as previously
noted, was also used by Canaanites and Babylonians. Albright suggests that since Solomon's temple was a Canaanite
product, the names for the three parts of it, *'ûlām*, *hêkāl*, and
dĕbîr were also borrowed from Canaan. Before the fifteenth
century, when the average Canaanite temple was a single-
roomed structure, it was called both "house" and *hêkāl*, 'palace'
(see above). After the addition of the other rooms, the term
hêkāl continued to be used for the central or main room. No
specific name or term was ever applied to the Solomonic
"House" as a whole, and in this respect we may contrast the
situation in Babylonia where temples were given proper names
(see Oppenheim, Pt. II, p. 162). But for Israel the godhead
was one; there was no pantheon of deities on the same level.
Thus there was only one sacred "house" and this became "The
House."[8]

[7] Occasionally scholars have maintained that there was a golden
image of the Lord in the temple, but this view scarcely rests on
solid, objective evidence. Others claim that images of Yahweh must
certainly have existed. Considering the fact that so many of the common people in Israel fell into idolatry, it would be surprising if an
occasional image were not made. But the fact remains that whereas
male idols occur in nearly every excavation in known Canaanite
ruins, only one to my knowledge has ever been unearthed in the vast
amount of debris moved by excavators from Israelite towns. This
fact has to be reckoned with. It can only mean that deeply engrained
in Israelite religion from the time of the settlement in Palestine on
there was a strong belief that the Deity was simply not to be hon-
ored or worshiped in this fashion. While male images may turn up,
the evidence is already overwhelming that they were exceedingly
rare.

[8] Of course, after the division of the kingdom, North Israel had its
rival royal shrine at Bethel. But as far as we know, there was no
elaborate building ever erected there comparable to the Solomonic
temple in Jerusalem.

"The House of the Lord"

The very fact that the temple was called "the House of the Lord" indicates that the structure, under Canaanite influence, was an attempt to localize God. But in what sense was it his abode?

A study of the symbolism clarifies this point. The large bronze 'sea' (I Kings 7:23 ff.) closely resembles the Babylonian *apsu*, a word used both as the name for the subterranean fresh-water ocean from which all life and fertility were derived, and also as the name of a basin of holy water in the temples. The great altar for burnt offerings was built in stages like a Babylonian temple-tower, and the lowest stage or foundation of both was named "bosom of the earth."[9] The uppermost stage of the altar was crowned with four horns at the corners (as were Babylonian temple-towers) and was named *har'ēl*,[10] explained most convincingly by Albright as meaning 'mountain of God,' and to be compared with the meaning of the Babylonian word for temple-tower (*ṣiqqurratu*), which meant 'mountain-peak.' Old Sumerian names of temple-towers in Babylonia often designated them as cosmic mountains. This and other evidence indicates that the temple and its paraphernalia were rich in cosmic symbolism, just as were Babylonian and presumably Canaanite temple installations.

It is clear, therefore, that Solomon's temple was to be the abode of the Lord in the sense that it was the earthly representation of the heavenly abode; or, in the words of Nelson in describing the Egyptian temple, the physical building envisaged "the limitless world in which the deity moved. The temple was thus pictured as a microcosm of the world, the realm of the god."[11] Numerous passages in the Old Testament support this view. Thus the perennial problem of the distant, transcendent God and the knowledge of and desire for his nearness or immanence was solved in Solomon's temple, as in

---

[9] Ezek. 43:14 which the R. V. misunderstands as "from the bottom upon the ground." For these points see Albright, *op. cit.*, pp. 148 ff.

[10] Ezek. 43:15 where R. V. has "upper altar."

[11] See also Eichrodt, *loc. cit.*

the temples of surrounding peoples, by means of a rich, sacramental symbolism which possessed deep significance for those who understood its meaning. It is probable that this interpretation of the temple's significance remained the dominant one, at least in Israel's priestly circles.

The evidence that there was a conflict in some Israelite minds over the idea that the temple was in any sense God's dwelling is first encountered in the writings of the Deuteronomic school. Perhaps the clearest example (though cf. Deut. 12) occurs in Solomon's prayer of dedication at the temple's completion (I Kings 8). This is a remarkable prayer, though scholars generally believe that its present form represents an expanded edition prepared by the Deuteronomic editor of the books of Kings. It would be difficult to say, however, just when many of the conceptions contained in the prayer first appeared in Israelite thought. Whatever their precise date, we have in the prayer these words (vv. 27–30):

> But will God really dwell upon the earth? Behold, neither the heavens nor the heaven of heavens can contain thee; how much less this house that I have built! Yet do thou turn unto the prayer of thy servant and to his supplication, O Lord my God . . . . that thine eyes may be open toward this house night and day, even toward the place whereof thou hast said, "My name shall be there" . . . . And do thou hearken unto the supplication of thy servant and of thy people Israel, when they shall pray toward this place. Yea, hear thou in heaven thy dwelling place; and when thou hearest, forgive.

In other words, there is a clear rejection of the whole attempt to localize God or to consider the temple as his dwelling. What is the temple's significance then? It is the place where God's name is.

The importance of names in the ancient Near East is well known. In Mesopotamian literature great stress was laid upon the names of gods, buildings, and objects. Somehow people could scarcely believe in something, or conceive what it was, until it was identified with a name. Frequently, a name had of its own right some independent mythological significance and could be reverenced.[12] Thus this emphasis upon the name of God had a long history in the religious thought of the ancient world. But here the old usage has been transformed in a new setting. The temple is not important because it is God's dwelling, but because it is the bearer of the name of the Lord. It is his building only because he has chosen to regard it so and because he has allowed it to be known by his name.

This interpretation of the significance of the temple, not as God's dwelling, but as the bearer of his name, represents a most important solution of the problem of immanence and transcendence with regard to the temple in the Old Testament. It bridges the gap most satisfactorily between the distant heavenly God and the desire for and knowledge of his nearness. The temple was important in the eyes of God, not because it was his palace, but because humble prayer besought him so to regard it. He had no need of a temple; the importance of the structure in his sight was an accommodation to the needs of the people, a gracious consideration for human necessity.

Though it is not generally recognized, at this point the Old Testament attains an extremely high level of religious thought. Indeed, it may be a clearer witness to truth than some modern conceptions of churches as "houses of God." It is an assertion of the centrality and sovereignty of God, who is not confined or bound by human wishes. Canaanite worship which supplied the physical needs of a god and pleased him with the erection of temples to the end that the capricious and unpredictable being might look favorably upon the worshiper's desires—all that is here discarded and superseded.

The origin of this viewpoint in Israelite life is unknown. Since it belongs to the Deuteronomic literature (Deuteronomy through II Kings), the theology of which seems to have come to Judah from North Israel, we presume that it belonged to certain northern circles of Israelite faith. The Jerusalem priesthood, with their sacramental emphasis, did not adopt it. In-

---

[12] Compare our modern tendency to be satisfied once we have a large clinical or psychological label for some malady, even though the name does not advance our understanding one whit. The very fact that we have a name somehow makes it more familiar to us.

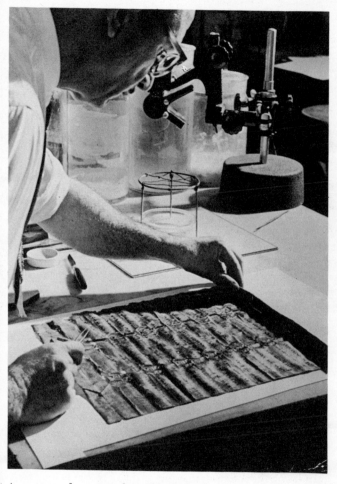

A papyrus document from Elephantine after it has just been unrolled for the first time in 2500 years.

A small temple found at Megiddo, dating *ca.* 3000 B.C.
Photo: Oriental Institute

The plan of a Canaanite temple of *ca.* 1200 B.C. at Beth-shan, Palestine. *Photo: Rowe, Topography & History of Beth-shan*

A reconstruction of the temple of Solomon by C. F. Stevens, from specifications of W. F. Albright and G. Ernest Wright.

The altar of burnt offering at the Jerusalem temple, as described by Ezekiel (43:13-17), drawn by C. F. Stevens.

Mosaic floor from a synagogue at Beth Alpha, showing the signs of the zodiac. *Courtesy British Academy & Oxford University Press*

Scene from a papyrus marsh in ancient Egypt. The flowers and
vertical lines of the relief represent papyrus. From the south
wall of the Tomb of Mereruka. *Photo: Oriental Institute*

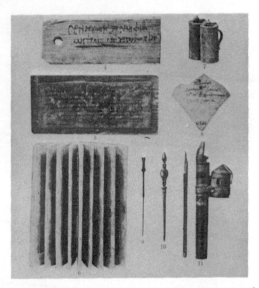

Writing equipment from ancient times. No. 5 is a wooden tablet with a wax surface; No. 6 shows wooden tablets bound together into a "codex"; No. 8 is an ostracon; Nos. 9-10 are forms
of stylus; and No. 11 a reed pen with penholder and inkwell.
Photo: Schubert, Einführung in die Papyruskunde

A painting of a young woman with stylus and wooden tablets found in the ruins of Pompeii, Italy.

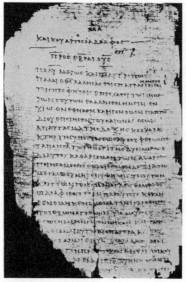

First page of the Book of Hebrews in a Chester Beatty Codex of Paul's Letters, written about A.D. 200.

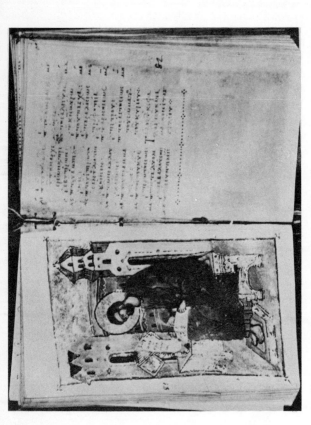

A complete Greek New Testament of the eleventh century A.D., recently found in the Greek Patriarchal Treasury in Jerusalem, Jordan. A portrayal of the Evangelist Mark appears before his Gospel. *Courtesy Library of Congress.*

stead, they developed a special terminology to express the mystery of God's presence. To be sure God did not "dwell" on earth, but it is a sign of his grace that he has chosen to "tabernacle" in the people's midst. As Frank M. Cross, Jr., was the first to point out (see pp. 225–27), this special use of an old nomadic word 'to tent,' or 'tabernacle,' was a technical theological term of the Jerusalem priests, expressing their awareness of the gracious mystery of God's immanence, without which, they believed, there would have been no Israelite nation.

The Temple in Community Life

Space does not permit an extended discussion of the temple's significance in Israelite life. Jerusalem was captured by David, made his personal property, and called "The City of David." The temple was erected primarily as a royal chapel, adjoining the king's palace, as were many temples in other countries. It had, of course, a national significance throughout its history, but during the Divided Monarchy a rival shrine of some sort existed at Bethel in North Israel, as is clear from the statement of the Bethel priest to Amos (7:13). Only with the fall of Israel and with the reforms of Hezekiah and Josiah did the Jerusalem temple assume paramount importance as the religious focus of the national life.

The chief priests in Jerusalem were all of the line of Zadok (I Kings 4:4). They were not independent of the king and therefore his rivals for power, as was the case in Egypt. Instead, they were actual members of the successive royal administrative cabinets. "By identifying the religious focus of the tribal confederacy of Israel with the court of the king, David and Solomon forestalled the most serious threat to national unity, and prevented the high priest from setting himself up as the head of the state."[13]

It seems highly probable that the religious practices described in Leviticus were substantially those used in the temple. Both this and Deuteronomy prescribe tithes for temple support (Lev. 27:30–33; Deut. 14:28–29). From the days of the settlement when the land was parceled out among the

[13] Albright, op. cit., p. 139.

tribes, there was a strong belief that ancestral property must not be sold to those outside the clan or family. Probably for this reason the temple was supported not by large grants of land, as happened in Egypt and Mesopotamia, but by the system of tithes. Such gifts to the temple service, together with the numerous vessels and instruments employed in the sacrificial ritual, must have required considerable storage space. The three stories of small rooms or vaults around three sides of the temple were undoubtedly used for this purpose.[14]

In Israel as in other countries the temple was a center where learning and literature were cultivated. Priests had to be educated. Careful records had to be kept. Both the First and the Second Temples played an exceedingly important role in the editing, compilation, and preservation of the literature of the Old Testament that it later might be transferred to synagogue and Church.

[14] In an article in the *Journal of Near Eastern Studies* (II [1943], 284 ff.) Professor Leroy Waterman rightly emphasizes the importance of these vaults. But he vastly overworks the point by maintaining that the temple was originally erected to serve as the royal treasury and was only later converted into a temple. This surely exceeds the evidence. In fact, it is probable that we should minimize the importance of these vaults as the royal or state treasury, because when subsequent kings found it necessary to pay tribute, they stripped the treasuries of both the king's house (governmental headquarters in the palace) and the temple of their valuables (cf. I Kings 15:18; II Kings 16:8; 18:15)—as though the palace and temple treasuries were distinct entities.

IV. TEMPLE, SYNAGOGUE, AND CHURCH

FLOYD V. FILSON

The temple was never an adequate expression of the religious life of Israel. Although the temple at Jerusalem gave that city a convenient place of worship, communities at a distance from the capital city were left without sufficient means of corporate worship and religious training. Thus the centralization of worship in the time of Josiah, while animated by the worthy purpose of stamping out the paganism of local shrines and high places, left an empty place in the life of the people.

Furthermore, the temple never corresponded to the distinctive features of the religion of Israel. This religion centered in the revealed will of God for all of existence. It had a healthy application to moral and social life. No system of sacrifice and ritual could provide the instruction and stimulus needed for the mature knowledge of God. The Mosaic and prophetic streams were the distinctive elements of the religion of Israel, and the temple did not adequately express and cultivate them.

A suitable supplement to temple worship does not appear to have arisen before the Exile. Such a supplement could not come by multiplying temples. To be sure, in the days of the divided monarchy the rulers of the Northern Kingdom naturally provided places of worship within the borders of their realm (cf. I Kings 12:26–29), but high spiritual leadership did not mark the priesthood of the Northern Kingdom. In the sixth century B.C. some Jews at Elephantine in Egypt built a temple for their worship, and when it was destroyed at the end of the fifth century B.C., it apparently was rebuilt but was not to have animal sacrifices offered in it. Later in the second century B.C. another Jewish temple was built at Leontopolis in the same country. These, however, were isolated events which had no wide support.

More in keeping with the best in the religious life of Israel were prophetic expressions of the will of God for the people. These often took place near the central sanctuary, but such was not always the case. Religious leaders of prophetic spirit spoke to communities wherever and whenever they were impelled to do so.

Origin and Growth of the Synagogue

The actual origin of the synagogue as an institution for regular worship and instruction is usually dated in the Exile. The temple had been destroyed, and the people of Israel had no center of worship. They desperately needed fellowship, comfort, and instruction. Moreover, those in exile were the real leaders of the people, possessing native resourcefulness and initiative. It is quite reasonable to conclude, therefore, that the synagogue did arise during this period, although the need for such an institution existed as soon as Israelite worship was centralized at one temple.

Under Cyrus, Persian conqueror of Babylon, the exiled Jews received permission in 539 B.C. to return to their native land and re-establish their worship. The more devoted and daring of the group went back and promptly restored the sacrifices upon the altar (Ezra 3:2). The rebuilding of the temple, however, was delayed for eighteen years (Ezra 4:24; Hag. 1:1-4). The delay was due to the poverty of the Jewish community, local resistance, and the fact that the people, having altar sacrifices, were content until a better time for rebuilding presented itself. This Second Temple, begun in 520 B.C. and completed four years later, was by no means the equal of that of Solomon. It no doubt adopted the location and basic plan of its predecessor, but of the details of its appearance and equipment we are not informed.

The synagogue, however, continued to function after the temple was restored. The exiles still needed a place of worship and fellowship, as did Jews in Palestine who did not live near the temple. Moreover, the latter was the special precinct of the priesthood; it did not give the continual instruction in the

Law and the common participation in worship which the synagogue provided. As time went on and the priesthood became
heavily involved in political life, the temple ministry proved
unable to satisfy the hunger of the people for spiritual leadership and help. The synagogue assumed the temple rites, and
did not seek to displace them. It even kept alive a loyalty to
the temple on the part of people who could never or rarely
visit it. Yet increasingly the synagogue played a role of its own.
By the first century A.D., every town in Palestine must have
had its synagogue. Jerusalem itself is reported by Rabbinical
sources to have had 394 or 480. Even when we discount these
figures, we know that the number of such buildings in the
metropolis was very large. In every Gentile center where loyal
Jews were found there was also to be found a synagogue.

Archaeological evidence for the synagogue prior to the first
century A.D. is meager. At Alexandria in Egypt a synagogue
inscription has been found which dates from the reign of Ptol-
emy III (246–221 B.C.). On the island of Delos, in the southern Aegean Sea, excavators uncovered the remains of what
appears to have been a synagogue. The conclusion is supported by the discovery of an ornate seat which may be regarded as the Seat of Moses (cf. Matt. 23:2). This structure
may be dated in the late second century B.C. Later synagogue
buildings on the island of Aegina and at Miletus and Priene
in Asia Minor testify to the Jewish practice of establishing a
synagogue wherever they settled in any numbers.

At Corinth a fragmentary inscription reads "(Syn)agogue
of the Hebr(ews)." This inscription is in Greek, but appears
to identify the building as the synagogue of Aramaic-speaking
Jews. The building itself has not been found, but it may well
have been standing when Paul visited the city. At Dura-
Europos, on the Euphrates River, a synagogue of the third
century A.D. has been excavated. It was made by remodeling
a private house, but later was reconstructed and decorated
within, not only with botanical and geometric designs, but
most strikingly with mural paintings of biblical scenes.

As Professor May has pointed out in his instructive article,
"Synagogues in Palestine," (pp. 229 ff.) the earliest archaeological evidence for a Palestinian synagogue is the Theodotus inscription of the first century A.D. This synagogue was for Greek-

speaking Jews and included guest-rooms for pilgrims. The earliest remains of synagogue buildings date from the (second or) third century A.D.

The function of the synagogue in Gentile lands may have been more important than in Palestine itself. It was in no sense the dwelling place of the deity. Instead it was a building in which Jews could assemble and hear the reading and exposition of the Law. Thus it symbolized the religious faith and loyalty of the isolated Jewish communities. It was a rallying point to sustain and unite Jews in the midst of a pagan civilization. *And as a place of worship it was a radical departure from anything the world had yet seen. Here religious exercises were carried on without benefit of sacrifice or Holy of Holies, and without requiring the presence of a priest.*

There was still no thought of displacing the temple, whose importance in the minds of loyal Jews was seen in the Maccabean period. For a time (*ca.* 168–165 B.C.) the Syrian king, Antiochus Epiphanes, controlled and desecrated it. After three years the Jews regained it and the Feast of Dedication, on the twenty-fifth day of Chislev (approximately December), so impressed them that it has always remained one of the festival days of the Jewish calendar.

Herod Rebuilds the Temple

In view of this loyalty of Jews to the temple, it is not surprising that Herod the Great, king of Palestine under Roman supervision from 37 to 4 B.C., undertook to rebuild the structure on a more imposing scale (*ca.* 20–19 B.C.). He thought thereby to please the Jews as well as win recognition for himself. He avoided the risk of offending Jewish feelings concerning the sanctity of the temple by using specially trained priests to do the work. To provide a fitting setting, he enlarged the temple area by building heavy retaining walls which enabled him to extend the level court over the natural slope of the hill.

The rebuilding of the temple itself was completed with the greatest possible dispatch, in order to interfere as little as possible with the Jewish rites and worship. The time required, Josephus says, was eighteen months (*Antiquities* XV. 11. 6). Reconstruction of the other parts and buildings of the sacred area lasted for decades. In fact, Herod did not live to complete it. To this longer process the Gospel of John refers when it says, "Forty and six years this temple has been under construction" (2:20). It continued, with interruptions, until A.D. 64; the full project was thus finished just before the Jewish revolt which ended with the building's final destruction.

From Josephus (cf. *Wars* V. 5. 1–7), the Mishnah (tractate *Middoth*), and other sources a fairly clear conception of the ground plan of Herod's temple can be formed. The entire sacred area was marked off by a heavy outer wall, which had military strength. Just within this wall a portico extended around all four sides of the area. The wider porch on the south side was called the Royal Porch. On the east was Solomon's Porch, to which reference is made in John 10:23; Acts 3:11; 5:12. On the northwest corner, stairs led down from the nearby Tower of Antonia to the portico and temple court. This tower, a strongly manned citadel, gave the civil ruler a means of controlling what went on in the sacred area. However, as events in the Jewish revolt of A.D. 66–70 proved, the stairs could be cut and the temple isolated. From this tower the Roman captain and soldiers ran down to rescue Paul when the mob was trying to kill him, and from the stairs leading up to the tower, Paul addressed the angry crowd (Acts 21:31 ff.). Josephus also tells of an underground passage which Herod built from Antonia to the eastern gate of the "inner temple" area (*Antiquities* XV. 11. 7). It was intended to aid the military control of the temple, but probably was easily blocked.

Entrance to the temple area was also possible by at least eight gates, four on the west, two on the south, one on the east, and one on the north. These entrances led into the large outer court, the only one which Gentiles could enter. Notices placed at the gates leading into the inner courts warned Gentiles not to proceed further. Two of these inscriptions have been discovered. They read as follows: "No foreigner is allowed within the balustrade and embankment about the sanctuary. Whoever is caught (violating this rule) will be personally responsible for his ensuing death." It was the charge that Paul had taken a Gentile companion into one of the inner courts which precipitated the riot against the Apostle.

In this large outer court groups could meet; the early Chris-

tian brotherhood gathered in Solomon's Porch (Acts 5:12).
Other uses of the outer court, less religious in character, were
common. Worshipers planning to make sacrifices or gifts
needed unblemished animals, acceptable doves, and proper
Jewish coins. The most convenient place to find them was in
the outer court, and the priests not only encouraged but even
controlled and profited by such traffic. It was the resulting
confusion which aroused Jesus on the occasion of his last trip
to Jerusalem. Such disturbances were particularly serious in
the mind of those who wanted the temple to be "a house of
prayer for all the nations" (Mark 11:17; cf. Isa. 56:7). This
goal was possible only if the one court open to Gentiles was
free from distractions.

By an ornate gate in the eastern part of the area, probably
called the Beautiful Gate, Jews could go up into the Court of
the Women. Here were receptacles for gifts of charity (cf.
Mark 12:41). Jewish women could go no further. Jewish men
could ascend another stairway and enter the Court of Israel,
which appears to have been on the same level as the court
around the altar, but marked off from it by a definite barrier.

At the altar of burnt-offering the priests ministered in turn.
Their storerooms and workrooms were mainly on the north
side of this area. The altar, a large structure on which daily
burnt offerings and other sacrifices were offered, was probably
located where the famous Dome of the Rock, a Mohammedan
mosque, now stands. Some scholars hold that the huge rock
which today lies under the Dome was the site of the Most
Holy Place of the ancient temple. This rock, however, is so
large (58 x 51 ft.) that it would have extended beyond the limits of the Most Holy Place. We therefore conclude that the
rock probably marks the site of the ancient altar; to locate
the Most Holy Place at this point would push the altar court,
the Court of Israel, and the Court of Women so far east as
to locate the Beautiful Gate at the eastern edge of the temple
area.

The temple building proper was approached by steps which
led up to a porch flanked by a large pillar on either side. A
curtain was hung between the Porch (vestibule) and the Holy
Place. Into the latter the properly chosen priest could enter
to perform the prescribed ministries (cf. Luke 1:8). It con-

tained the seven-branched candlestick, the altar of incense, and the table of shewbread. A "veil," consisting of two parallel curtains, likewise separated the Holy Place from the Most Holy Place (cf. Mark 15:38), into which the High Priest entered alone once a year, on the Day of Atonement (cf. Heb. 9:6 f.). Store chambers or treasuries were in the north, west, and south sides of the temple building. They were used as a kind of bank or safety deposit vault.

The implication of the increasing sense of sanctity which was felt as one moved towards the inner precincts might seem to be that the Deity resided in the Most Holy Place. This conclusion would have been generally denied in the first century. The Most Holy Place was unlighted and empty. This was probably true even of the Second Temple, and Josephus, a priest, explicitly states (*Wars* V. 5. 5) that such was the case in Herod's temple. A dark and empty room can hardly have been meant as a reproduction of the heavenly home of God. However, the absence of any image is a negative witness to a spiritual conception of God, and the panorama of the heavens which Josephus tells us (*Wars* V. 5. 4) was embroidered on the curtain before the Holy Place appears to suggest that here was worshiped the one God of earth and heaven. Probably it would have been said that God was approachable in the temple and especially in the Most Holy Place and had decreed that worship of him should center there.

The positive significance of the temple must not be underestimated. It was a necessary center for the fulfilment of Pentateuchal injunctions to offer sacrifices. Every good Jew was bound to seek the fulfilment of these laws. Moreover, the temple offered opportunity for those near at hand to attend services of worship and for those living at a distance to deepen their religious life by special pilgrimage. Furthermore, the temple stood as a center and rallying point of the devotion and loyalty of all Jews. Human beings are creatures of space and time, and the visible temple served as a useful symbol and expression of unity in faith. By payment of an annual tax each Jew took his part in the upkeep of the services and felt himself part of the united people.

Nevertheless, the temple was never the most fitting or adequate expression of the distinctive features of Judaism. It

rather laid stress on the things which Judaism had in common
with many other cults, and was compromised by elements
which made its worship imperfect and incomplete. It was a
military stronghold, and its involvement in affairs of war
blurred its expression of spiritual devotion. Built by Herod the
Idumaean, it did not embody solely the consecration of Israel
to the ancestral faith; it also expressed the ruler's cultural interest and political pride. Indeed, the architecture reflected
Hellenistic motifs to some degree, and one of the tense times
in Herod's reign came (4 B.C.?) when two rabbis cut down
the golden eagle which Herod had placed over the gate of the
temple (Josephus *Antiquities* XVII. 6. 2.). The temple was
under foreign domination much of the time, and the priesthood, who, as civil rulers, collaborated with Rome, became
worldly and were compromised by these connections. The
maximum service of the temple was to the local community;
it could never supply fully the religious needs of those at a
distance. Accidents of sex and tribal connection determined the
opportunity to take a prominent place in the worship; the consecration and obedience of the individual was not basic in determining the worshiper's status and privileges.

The most important fact is that the temple, bound as it was
to animal sacrifice, was permanently unable to rise to the
heights of pure spiritual worship. The modern visitor to Jerusalem sees the huge hewn stones which formed part of the
western outer wall of the Herodian temple area. Through
many generations Jews visited that wall to bewail the loss of
the temple and pray for its restoration. With such feelings any
sensitive Gentile should have great sympathy. Yet he cannot
but remember that apparent calamity is often the stern prel-
ude to spiritual growth. The fall of Jerusalem in 587 B.C.
brought on the destruction of the temple, the exile of Israel's
most able leaders, and immense agony of spirit to the entire
people. Spiritual blessings resulted, however, not only in the
growth of the synagogue idea but also in the development of
prophetic vision in chosen leaders. Later, in A.D. 70, the apparently ruinous loss of the temple gave Judaism deliverance
from the primitive and spiritually inadequate practice of animal sacrifice. The supreme calamity which Judaism could suf-

fer today would be to have its temple restored and its prescribed system of animal sacrifices re-established.

The Role of the Synagogue

The future of Judaism was in the synagogue. During the
centuries since its origin its worship had developed. Its meaning to the Jews had increased; of this the existence of so many
synagogues in Jerusalem itself is ample evidence. Thus when
the temple was destroyed, the synagogue was ready for a more
inclusive role than it had sought, and it proved able to provide a more complete spiritual ministry than the temple could
ever offer. It is therefore important to study the role of the
synagogue.

1. For practical purposes the synagogue replaces the temple. It did not disown the temple. While the latter stood,
the synagogue kept alive loyalty to the sacrifices and other
services by reading the laws concerning those rites. When the
temple was destroyed, the hope of its restoration was kept alive
in the synagogue, and the Law which called for a sacrificial
system continued to be the synagogue's basic Scripture.

Yet in practice the synagogue succeeded to the role of the
temple. Perhaps the reading of the Law concerning the sacrifices was early regarded as an acceptable substitute for actual
sacrifice; the Rabbis later explicitly said this, and such passages
as Ps. 51:16 f. may be an early expression of this view from
the time of the Exile. As time went on, the synagogue gathered
to itself much of the loyalty which had been given the temple.
This process was never completed. To great numbers the temple is still a mental rallying point and its ancient site a geographical expression of the unity of Judaism. But the synagogue
became the practical substitute for the temple in the religious
life of the Jews.

The suggestion has been made that the architecture and
plan of the synagogue was a conscious imitation of the temple.
Lack of any evidence from the days when the temple was
standing hampers discussion of this hypothesis. Later evidence
may be misleading; after the temple had been destroyed the
idea of reproducing temple features in the synagogue might
have occurred much more readily than before A.D. 70. For ex-

ample, the Ark of the Law became almost a substitute for the Most Holy Place of the temple. However, the synagogue was always basically different in plan from the temple. The latter was not entered by laymen. But the synagogue differed radically in that the assembly was held *inside* the building. It was basically a gathering place of laymen. It replaced rather than imitated the temple.

2. The synagogue gives Jewish worship a new focus by making the Law rather than the sacrifices the center of thought and devotion. It is true that the sacrifices were performed to fulfil the Law, and that the study of the Law led to loyalty to the sacrificial system. But it is also true that the center of attention is decidedly different in the synagogue, which stresses the study and daily practice of the Law.

3. This means that in the synagogue regular instruction and discussion of God's will for daily life have an importance which they could never have in the temple. That features resembling those of the synagogue service were introduced into the temple during its later period is true, but they were of minor importance and not essential to the temple system. Instruction in God's revealed will and reverent common worship are basic in the synagogue way of life.

4. The priest is not essential in the synagogue. When present, he is shown deference and given prominent parts in the service. But he is not needed. The synagogue was essentially a lay institution. In fact, it is the greatest and most durable system of lay leadership and lay education in religious history. Any ten Jewish men could form a synagogue and hold services. Any Jewish man could read the Scripture and, if gifted, speak to his comrades in the faith. This radical departure from the priest-controlled religious life of antiquity was unique and permanently significant.

5. The synagogue frees the Jewish religion from geographical limitation. A synagogue can be built in any city in any country. There is no rule about its location, although in the earliest period for which we have archaeological evidence the choice of a site was influenced by elevated situation or convenient access to water supply. But these things were not mandatory; the Dura-Europos synagogue was established at first in a private home in the midst of a group of houses. The

specific place is not essential. In this as in the respects already noted the synagogue is the institution fitted to play a permanent role in Judaism and to express the high spiritual and ethical aspects of that faith.

The Church and the Temple

The Apostolic Church was related to both temple and synagogue, but it did not find either adequate to its needs for a place of worship and fellowship. It had relations with the temple both in life and thought. Jesus himself had a deep feeling of loyalty to it. If we accept the witness of the Gospel of John, he made several trips to Jerusalem during his ministry to attend feasts of the Jews (2:13 f.; 5:1; 7:10, 14; 10:23; 12:12). The Gospel of Luke states (2:42) that he visited the temple at the age of twelve, when he entered upon the duties of a man in Jewish religious life. The fact that at the time of his last visit he blazed with indignation at the graft and confusion in the temple shows that he thought of it as a place where God was to be worshiped (Mark 11:15–17). It is true that he predicted its destruction (Mark 13:2), but as a judgment rather than as a welcome advance.

In like manner the earliest Christians began their work in the Church with an attitude of loyalty to the temple. They went there at the hour of prayer (Acts 3:1). They gathered in the outer court (Acts 5:12). Some years later even the Apostle to the Gentiles, Paul, undertook to fulfil a vow in the Temple (Acts 21:26). The Church was seeking to win the remaining Jews to believe in Christ, and their purpose was not to renounce Judaism but to convince the non-Christian Jews that Christianity was the full and true Judaism. They therefore did not ignore the rites and institutions of Judaism; they may have looked for judgment on the temple but they did not seek at once a religious practice without sacrifice. Later the Jewish rejection of the Christian message and the rebellion against Rome which broke out in A.D. 66 prepared the Christians to listen to an oracle (a saying of Jesus or of some early Christian prophet?) which directed them to flee the city and thus break with the temple and its sacrificial system entirely (Eusebius *Church History* III, 5).

It may trouble some Christians that the earliest Christians did not break at once with the temple. The fact is, however, that a new movement must have time to find its proper form through the outworking of its nature. Christianity in its early days found in the temple a place of worship. But forces were at work to alter this situation. Jesus had predicted the destruction of the temple (Mark 13:2). The coming of Gentiles into the Church raised the general question of the necessity of Jewish rites; under the leadership of Paul the Church came to the position that a Christian was not required to keep the ceremonial law to be a full Christian (cf. Gal. 2:16; Rom. 10:4). This in principle undermined the temple's prestige. Moreover, Christians thought of the death of Jesus as a sacrifice. The result was that for his followers the temple could no longer take the central place it had had in the past, and the writer of the Epistle to the Hebrews could argue (chaps. 9, 10) that the sacrifice of Jesus marked the end of the sacrificial system. The Lord's Supper eclipsed the temple rites. These facts, coupled with the important fact that within a few decades the Church became prevailingly Gentile and thus was made up largely of those who had no emotional attachment to Judaism, operated to eliminate the temple as an essential part of Christian thought and worship. Temple imagery continued to be used in Christian thinking, but both the events of history and the considered thought of the Apostolic Church led the Church to a position where the temple was no longer a necessity in Christian worship.

The Church and the Synagogue

There is far more connection between the Church and the synagogue. It was the custom of Jesus to attend the latter (Luke 4:16) and teach there whenever permitted to do so. The first Christians in Jerusalem taught in synagogues; Stephen probably first encountered Paul in one (cf. Acts 6:9). That Paul began his work in every city by visiting the synagogue is well known (e.g., Acts 13:14; 14:1).

It has been argued that the earliest Christians at Jerusalem formed a synagogue of their own. Ten Jewish men could do this. More likely, however, the Christians entered existing synagogues to teach other Jews about their faith. Moreover, they could meet there Gentiles as well as Jews, and particularly in Gentile lands this proved the strategic starting point of mission work. Present at synagogue services might be not only full proselytes, i.e., Gentiles who had become full adherents of the Jewish faith, but also "God-fearers," Gentiles attracted by the spiritual and moral aspects of Judaism but unwilling to become circumcised and keep the ceremonial law. Particularly among the "God-fearers" a fruitful field of evangelism was found.

The Christians thus used the synagogues for worship and especially for missionary appeals, and took over for their own later use the basic elements of the synagogue service of worship—Scripture reading, prayer, and preaching. Nevertheless, the Christian movement was not bound to the synagogue any more than it was to the temple. Just as it had broken with Jerusalem and the temple before they were destroyed in A.D. 70, so, when the synagogue group in a city proved unresponsive or hostile, the Christian leaders felt free to withdraw and continue missionary work and worship elsewhere. In other words, the Christian movement soon proved free of any geographical center and independent of any existing institution. But of the Jewish institutions, the Church was most closely related to the synagogue.

The Church in the Home

It could be argued with much force that the Christian Church grew out of the home rather than out of the temple or synagogue. There is both literary and archaeological evidence for this statement. In the Book of Acts, the first disciples joined other Jews in temple and synagogue, but when they wished to have their own worship and fellowship, they met either in the outer court of the temple (5:12) or in the homes of the more well-to-do members of their group (2:46; 12:12). The home was the center of the specifically Christian worship, fellowship, and planning. It was particularly important as the place of the common meals.

This seems to have been true in Gentile lands as well. At times Paul rented a public hall for his preaching (Acts 19:9),

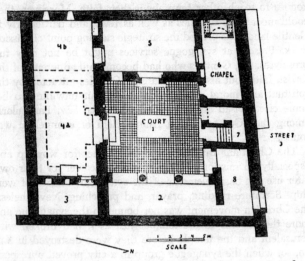

*Plan of the earliest Christian church thus far found,
located at Dura-Europus on the Euphrates. The building
dates from the mid-third century* A.D. *Courtesy Yale
University*

but the home was widely used for Christian meals, teaching,
and worship. The specific references to Churches in homes
(e.g., Philemon 2) clearly indicate where the early Gentile
Church centered. This use of the home was inevitable. With
no temple, with the synagogue closed sooner or later to Christian preachers, with no other institution meeting the need for
a quiet and private place of common worship and meals, the
home was the key location of the young Church. This is a
remarkable proof of the Church's freedom from dependence
upon a separate sacred sanctuary.

The close connection of the place of worship with the scenes
of daily life follows from the fact that the early observance of
the Lord's Supper appears to have been connected with a
hunger-satisfying meal in which the members of the Christian
group participated (Acts 2:46; cf. I Cor. 11:20, 21). In a
home large enough to accommodate the members a meal was
shared, and a definite remembrance of the Last Supper was

early, if not from the beginning, connected with this meal. The home was thought a fit place for the most sacred observances of the Church.

Archaeological data support this view. There is some evidence that the later Church of St. Clement in Rome was built upon the site of a home which was an early meeting place of Christians. But the most striking evidence is the discovery, at Dura-Europos on the Euphrates River, of an early Christian Church. Since Dura was destroyed shortly after the middle of the third century A.D., the developments now to be traced must all be prior to that date. A room in a home had been used for Christian worship. Later, it appears, an enlarged room was prepared for such gatherings, and the entire first floor was dedicated to specifically religious purposes. There was not only a place of meeting but also a baptistry, and walls were decorated with paintings of religious character. Two points emerge from a study of this "house church." The use of the home for worship is confirmed. In the second place, the growth of the church can be traced, and the tendency to add church features, such as the baptistry, and to make use of ornamentation, shows how the development resulted in the separate church building.

For the ancestry of most elements of early church worship we must look to the synagogue rather than the home. Moreover, it is not to be denied that the temple and synagogue influenced the development of the church building. This was particularly true in later days. Nor need it be denied that features of pagan temples and other structures found their way into Christian acceptance. But the evidence cited above agrees well with the information of Acts and the letters of Paul, and shows that the home was of the greatest importance as an early place of meeting for the Christians.

Later Trends

We cannot trace here the later development of the church building. In general, it is clear that the Roman Catholic Church, which has always made use of special objects and places, has drawn on many ideas derived from the temple. In particular, the conception of the mass as a sacrifice reminds one of the temple, and the concentration of ministry and leadership in the hands of the priesthood is consistent with this view. Recent years have seen the Roman Catholic Church give more emphasis to ideas which we associate more with the synagogue than the temple and which formerly distinguished Protestant churches: an example is the recent Roman Catholic emphasis upon Bible reading. But the general observation remains true that the Roman Catholic Church strongly resembles the temple in the main elements of its worship.

The Protestant churches, with their rejection of the mass and their inclusion of lay leadership in the control of the Church, obviously resemble the synagogue rather than the temple. To the extent that they emphasize the sacraments and the priesthood of the ministry, they recall features of the temple type of worship, but in their stress upon Scripture, common prayer, and preaching, in their large use of lay leaders and teachers, and in their greater independence of specific places and object-aids to worship, they are in line with the synagogue. If consistent they cannot have a temple, though in recent years many have been attracted by features of temple worship and symbolism. Thus a number of groups which earlier would have rejected temple ideas have now made the "altar" rather than the Bible the focus of attention in the Church edifice.

13

THE PRIESTLY TABERNACLE

FRANK M. CROSS, JR.

1. Traditions about the tabernacle in the latter part of Exodus are no longer of interest to the casual student of the Bible. Scholars from time to time delve into the tedium of the tabernacle installations, but by and large theologians and preachers look elsewhere for biblical insights. In past generations this was not true. Few students of the Bible were without ideas as to how the tabernacle should be reconstructed from the biblical data. Its attendant theological concepts were heralded as setting forth the ideal age of Israel, the prototype of the Kingdom of God, and the typology of the New Covenant.

One of the causes for the eclipse of these traditions has been the general acceptance of the findings of the great biblical critics of the nineteenth century which cast grave doubts on their historicity. Perhaps the name of Julius Wellhausen more than any other has come to typify this line of scholars. His brilliant treatise, *Prolegomena zur Geschichte Israels* (1878) remains an important and constant companion of biblical scholarship, and his reconstruction of Israelite history continues to dominate much of the historical and critical study of the Bible. A rough sketch of his basic ideas will help to set the present study of tabernacle traditions in perspective.

2. Fundamental to the thinking of the Wellhausen school is the history of the cult. According to the older sources of Judges and the so-called JE materials of the Pentateuch, many

altars and cultic establishments existed in early Israel. But with the promulgation of the Book of Deuteronomy in the Josianic Reform (622 B.C.), the dogma of a central sanctuary and one official altar for the whole of Israel was laid down. In the Priestly materials of the Pentateuch, however, the tabernacle is assumed to be the central sanctuary and the only official place of worship. Such a situation cannot be squared with the Mosaic era but presumes the conditions of the post-Exilic community.

The sacrificial system is said to follow a similar pattern of evolution. In the ancient sources, sacrifices were carried out simply. They consisted primarily of spontaneous 'peace-offerings' (šĕlāmîm), accompanied by feasting and joy. The Deuteronomic materials provide a transition period from spontaneity to formality. Beginning in the Exilic writings of Ezekiel, however, the sacrificial cult has become elaborate, stereotyped, overburdened with the consciousness of sin, and bent on expiation. The tabernacle traditions seem to reflect the culmination of this development. Incense, a cultic feature only of highly sophisticated peoples, according to Wellhausen, found its way into Israelite usage after the Exile. Yet it is to be found in the ritual of the tabernacle. Wellhausen in similar manner traces the history of the clerical orders, finding the concept of hereditary priesthood, the sharp dichotomy between priest and Levite, and the office of the high priest to be post-Exilic anachronisms in Priestly legislation.

Israelite political and ideological history followed the same line of evolution according to this school. In the time of Moses and the Judges, Israel as a nation did not exist. Individual tribes, free and autonomous, went their several ways, worshiped their various gods, and were finally banded together by Saul and David, only under the duress of Philistine oppression. In the time of the monarchy, Yahweh (in particular) became Israel's national God. In the days of Josiah, the doctrine of the covenant was promulgated in definitive form. With the centralization of cult came henotheism as a corollary. But only after Israel had been scattered in Exile were the historical conditions propitious for Israelite writers to rise to the concept of a single universal God. The tabernacle tradition, however, describes the formation of an Israelite amphictyony (a confederation of tribes about a central shrine) at the foot of Sinai. Under Moses, God chose Israel and established an everlasting covenant with her. According to the Wellhausen reconstruction of history, such monotheistic and theocratic motifs can reflect only the period of the post-Exilic Jewish Church. Thus the tabernacle legislation, rather than describing an actual political theocracy established by Moses, presents an unreal idealization of the golden past. The Priestly Code is a utopian constitution drawn up by a downtrodden religious community to serve as a substitute for a political state.

The Wellhausenist states unequivocally that the description of the Priestly tabernacle found in Exodus 25–31 and 35–40 is a pious fraud. On the basis of ancient passages such as Exodus 33:7–11, it may at most be conceded that there had been a primitive tent-shelter for the Ark in the desert. It was Wellhausen's conclusion, however, that the Priestly tabernacle (*miškān*) was demonstrably the fancy of the post-Exilic Priestly writers; or more precisely, a description of the Temple in flimsy desert disguise.

The New Outlook on Israelite History

3. In recent years the Wellhausen reconstruction of history has undergone sweeping revision. As long ago predicted by Rudolph Kittel, revolutionary progress in biblical research had to await the advance of biblical archaeology and philology. This is not to underestimate the contributions of such scholars as Kittel himself, Gunkel (the deviser of the technique of *Gattungsgeschichte*), Driver, Gressmann, and others whose basic work was completed before the major phase of the archaeological revolution.

While the basic outlines of biblical criticism were drawn in the nineteenth century, archaeological research has established itself as a scientific tool in the hand of the Old Testament student only in the twentieth century. Only in our generation have archaeological data reached such proportions as to affect seriously the conclusions of literary and historical research.

Today the Old Testament lies in a new setting. The horizons of ancient Near Eastern history have been pushed back. Israelite history can no longer be made to climb the three-flight staircases of Wellhausen's Hegelian reconstruction. While the broad outlines of the Documentary Hypothesis (JE, D, and P) remain intact, and in fact have been strongly supported by the implications of biblical archaeology, the history of Israel requires thorough reinterpretation.

4. Unfortunately only a few of the results of archaeological and philological research which are of particular importance for a revaluation of the Priestly source of the tabernacle traditions can be given in our limited space.[1] We begin with the Patriarchal Age.

Data dug up by the spade, documentary and non-documentary, in the period between the wars have transformed our knowledge of the second millennium in Near Eastern history. The milieu of the Patriarchs is no longer shadowy.[2] The Amorite or Proto-Aramaean connections of the patriarchs in the region of Harran and Nahor (*Naḥur*) can no longer be doubted. The Cappadocian Tablets (nineteenth century), Babylonian documents from the First Dynasty of Babylon (The Age of Hammurabi, *ca.* 1830 to the fall of Babylon, *ca.* 1550), and especially the Nuzi Tablets (fifteenth century) and the archives of Mari (eighteenth century) have given remarkable parallels to the mores, the religious practices and background, and the names of the Patriarchs.

Of particular interest are the occurrences of the name Abram in contemporary Babylonian records, and the longer form of the name Jacob (Ya'qub-el) in the records of Chagar Bazar (eighteenth century).[3]

The religion of the patriarchs has also been illuminated. The appellations of gods found in the narratives of Genesis indicate that they worshiped old Northwest Semitic deities: primarily

[1] For recent syntheses of the historical background of the Old Testament, see particularly Albright, *From the Stone Age to Christianity* (Baltimore, 1940) and Frankfort, Frankfort, Wilson, Jacobsen, and Irwin, *The Intellectual Adventure of Ancient Man* (Chicago, 1946).

[2] Cf. the recent review of De Vaux, "Les patriarches hébreux et les découvertes modernes," *RB*, LIII (1946), 321–48; LV (1948), 321–47; LVI (1949), 5–36.

[3] The element *Jacob* also appears in the name of a Hyksos chieftain (Ya'qub-har), and in a contemporary Palestinian place name recorded in Egyptian lists.

El, the head of the pantheon, and Hadad, the mountain and storm deity called more commonly by his appellation Baal, both well known from the Canaanite epics of the fourteenth century from Ugarit. The name of the patriarchal god, *El Shaddai* (A. V. "God Almighty"), recorded only in the Priestly strata, accords perfectly in the context of Patriarchal religion in flat contradiction to the views of older scholars (cf. §7). *Šadday* 'Mountain One' must be associated with similar appellations: *Har* 'Mountain (-god),' an element in the names of Hyksos chieftains who ruled Egypt in the second quarter of the second millennium, and *Ṣûr* 'Crag' or 'Mountain' known both from the Mari letters and Babylonian records as elements in personal names—and found in the Priestly lists of princes (see §7).

Alt, Levy, and Albright have pointed out characteristics of the religion of the patriarchs which are particularly significant for Mosaic religion. One of these is the feeling of actual kinship of some sort which linked the patriarch or clan to its god. A second is closely related: the practice of a clan or individual to choose a (special) god and enter into a type of contract or covenant with him.

The old traditions of Israel preserved the coloring—political, social, and religious—of this era in remarkable fashion. While the oral tradition and old Priestly written records cannot be taken as historical in any literal fashion, since tribe and individual often blend and exchange, and since the folkloristic elements common to all ancient folk epics adorn them, they nevertheless, have proved to have an historical aspect.

5. The portion of the Hebrew tribes which found itself in Egypt in the third quarter of the second millennium B.C. had passed into an even more sophisticated age and culture. It was a period of mass identification of the gods of one pantheon with those of similar attributes in another. It was an age in which Accadian served as a *lingua franca* of Near Eastern diplomacy. It was the era in Egypt which produced the solar monotheism of the Akhenaten heresy.

Moses and the leaders of Hebrew elements in Egypt, to judge from their Egyptian names, had become comparatively assimilated into this Egyptian culture. Whether or not Moses was reared as an Egyptian prince, there can be little doubt that he was a cosmopolite of Tanis, the capital city of Egypt.

Perhaps a few general comments about the desert sojourn are now in order, a subject to which we shall return below (§6). The desert wanderings of Israel lay in the era before the effective domestication of the camel, as Albright has shown at length. The Israelites by necessity had to live on the fringes of civilization and could never live the isolated life of the true bedouin. At the end of the wilderness wanderings, at least a portion of the tribes under Joshua stormed Canaan in concerted effort, as shown most recently by Wright.[4] Their settlement was rapid and general. Such broad considerations based on archaeological fact are fast making primitivistic views toward early Israel and its religion untenable.

A great deal of light has been thrown on the life of Israel in the period of the Judges. The admirable monographs of Alt[5] and especially Noth[6] have shown definitively, in the view of the writer, that Israel during the period of the Judges was organized in a twelve-tribe league around a central Yahweh sanctuary. Such an organization has close analogues among the ancient peoples of Greece, Italy, and Asia Minor; and, as Albright has pointed out, there were central shrines at Nippur in Babylonia, Nineveh in Assyria, the temple of Sin in Harran, etc. Noth argues that the unity of the tribes of Israel which becomes highly evident in their uniting under Saul, may be traced clearly to the earliest days of Joshua's conquest. This unity is not to be attributed to the need for defense against the Philistines purely, for many of the tribes were not hard pressed. Nor is it to be attributed to the worship of Yahweh alone. There must have been some outward, concrete expression and center of Yahwism before any unity could have come from the religious factor. Even if they had worshiped a common Yahweh in various localities, such a practice would not have been a uniting force, but rather a separating one. The

[4] G. Ernest Wright, "The Literary and Historical Problem of Joshua 10 and Judges 1," *JNES*, V: 2 (1946), 105–14.

[5] A. Alt, *Die Staatenbildung der Israeliten in Palästina* (Leipzig, 1930).

[6] M. Noth, *Das System der zwölf Stämme Israels* (Stuttgart, 1930).

conclusion must be drawn that the religious unity of the Israelite tribes was based on a common cult at a common sanctuary.

The application of new knowledge drawn from Phoenician and Israelite orthography, and the application of comparative material drawn from the Ugaritic mythological tablets, provide radically new procedures for the analysis and dating of the earliest Old Testament poetry. This method was first applied by W. F. Albright to the Oracles of Balaam, which in their original form are shown to date from the thirteenth or twelfth century. In a similar way, the Song of Deborah (Judges 5), the Song of Moses (Exodus 15), the Blessing of Moses (Deuteronomy 33), Psalm 18 (= II Samuel 22), Genesis 49, Psalm 68, *etc.*, may be shown to antedate the great prophetic movement of the eighth century, and in the case of the first three mentioned, to antedate the United Monarchy. The utility of such scientific means of dating must not be overlooked. It grants scholarship a corpus of literature which reflects Davidic and pre-Davidic theology, and which can be contrasted with the early prophets, presumably the creative and formative minds in the history of Israelite theology. The results of the theological analysis of this early literature make several conclusions necessary. As long maintained by Kittel, Gressmann, Eichrodt, Albright, and other critics of evolutionary historicism, the basic tenets of prophetic religion are already present in this earlier age: the concept of the covenant, a lofty ethical level (in contrast to the essentially amoral religions of contemporary Canaan), a conception of God as righteous Judge, as cosmic Lord of nature and history; and most striking of all, a consistent tradition of the Mosaic and desert origins of Yahwism. Wellhausen admittedly had considerable difficulty in explaining the historical roots of the prophetic movement. But in light of the above mentioned results, not to mention other lines of evidence, how can such a phenomenon as early Yahwism be explained as it suddenly appears amidst the naturalistic polytheisms of the ancient Near East?

The increasing knowledge of ancient Near Eastern lawcodes, together with the use of Form-criticism in analyzing

Israelite law,[7] grants yet another fresh avenue of approach to early Israelite religion. While the customary law of Israel fits in well with the codes of ancient Near East, and probably reflects both Canaanite jurisprudence and the long-accumulated decisions of judge and priest throughout Israel's stay in Canaan, the so-called apodictic law (the unqualified commands of Yahweh typified by the form, "Thou shalt") has at best indirect parallels. Its antiquity and conceptual pattern point to the desert as its place of origin. Moreover, as Alt has pointed out, such law seems to have been preserved and administered primarily in the covenant sanctuary of the confederacy.

The Ras Shamrah tablets, the Marseilles Tariff, and South Arabic Inscriptions have given new perspective in studies of the sacrificial system of Israel. Scholarly opinion now indicates that the Israelite system described in the tabernacle legislation of Leviticus probably goes back in its basic outlines to common Semitic practice.

6. We are better prepared now to turn to a consideration of the desert experiences of Israel, the period to which the tabernacle traditions are attributed. A few generations after the Israelites had left Egypt and stormed Canaan, they were organized in a loose confederation, indeed in a primitive theocratic system, around a central sanctuary. Both their religion and their organization were sufficiently strong to overpower, not only the decadent Canaanites and their religion, but in time also the powerful opposition of the Philistines. Moreover, Israel's religion appears, even in our earliest sources, as a new construct. Its God, its characteristic covenant law, its system of land-tenure, and its political organization are in radical contrast to the religion and social forms of its neighbors.

Such circumstances lead to but one conclusion: the desert era was the creative and normative period of Israel's political and religious history, and this development was fomented and led by a revolutionary religious spirit, no doubt that of Moses. Such evidence has brought leading scholars of the present day to a new recognition of the scope of the Mosaic revolution. Under Moses, Israel came to worship a new God. Yahweh was

[7] See particularly, A. Alt, *Die Ursprünge des israelitischen Rechts* (Leipzig, 1934).

a righteous and living God among the capricious and dying gods of the Near East. He was cosmic in power and abode. He possessed no consort and was of such stature that other gods were reckoned on a secondary level.

It would be incredible in the age in which we are dealing to suppose that Yahwism could be established and transmitted unless Moses had instituted a nuclear cultic system, and organized his tribes or clans into some manner of religious and political structure.

The Historical Status of the Priestly Tradition

7. The conclusions reached above find their primary biblical witness in the Priestly strands of the Pentateuch. While the J stratum strongly emphasized the revelation at Sinai, and E describes both the disclosure of Yahweh's name and the formation of the covenant in the desert, it is particularly the tabernacle traditions which maintain that Yahweh was first worshiped in the desert, and that the cultic institutions and the formation of the state (which P correctly identifies as being one) find their origin under Moses in the desert. While the Priestly account is schematized and idealized, and while the Priestly writers read the theological interpretations and historical developments of later ages into their system, nevertheless, Priestly tradition must be deemed an important historical witness to the Mosaic Age.

Some of the detailed information of the lists and genealogies of P must not be passed over lightly. Often the Priestly scribes placed their ancient sources in wrong contexts; but the day when their work could be universally rejected as "pious fraud" has passed. Examples are the census lists in Numbers 1 and 26 (originally a single document). Moreover, Noth is no doubt correct in regarding the framework of Numbers 26 as premonarchial in its historical origins.

Similarly the lists of cities of refuge and the Levitic cities (Joshua 21 and II Chronicles 6) have recently been shown by topographical and archaeological studies to reflect a system of the Davidic era, but which had its roots in the earlier system of Israelite land-tenure going back to the first days of the twelve-tribe system.[8] Wellhausen is probably quite right in pointing out that there is no trace of the system in later Israelite history. No doubt it was always in part ideal and passed out of existence by the time of the Divided Monarchy. The extended lists of boundaries in Joshua 12–20 have been shown by similar methods[9] to reflect the age to which they are assigned, while the interwoven document dealing with the cities of Judah and Benjamin are probably to be assigned to the early Divided Monarchy.[10]

Even more striking is our increasing knowledge of ancient onomastica, which may be applied to the study of Priestly proper names. Such a document as the list of princes, underlying Numbers 1, 2, 7, and 10, may be used to illustrate our contention. Gray in his *Studies in Hebrew Personal Names*, the standard work of the previous generation, rejected the document as a fiction on grounds which archaeological data have now shown to be false or inapplicable.

It will be instructive to describe briefly how his arguments have been refuted. Names with a *Šadday* element, which appear no less than three times in this list and nowhere else in the Bible, were rejected as artificial constructions without archaeological parallel. We have noted in § 4 the place which *Šadday* assumes in the religion of the Patriarchs, but more striking evidence is found now in the occurrence of the name *Šadday-ʿammî* ('Shaddai is my kinsman') in an Egyptian inscription of the fourteenth or early thirteenth century.[11] *Šadday-ʿammî* seems to have been a Semite, roughly contemporary with Moses in Egypt! The name is almost identical with the *ʿAmmî-Šadday* of the Priestly list. In a similar way the element *Ṣûr* 'Mountain' was regarded as unlikely in personal names owing to the lack of ancient parallels. Those parallels have now been furnished. Gray maintained that the proportion of names with the element *El* far exceeded the proportions of the use of

[8] See Albright, "The List of Levitic Cities," *Louis Ginzberg Jubilee Volume* (1945), pp. 49 ff.

[9] Cf., especially, Noth, *Das Buch Josua* ("Handbuch zum A. T." [Tübingen, 1938]), pp. ix–xv.

[10] For the assignment of the sources of the Joshua lists, cf. ¶ 12.

[11] M. Burchardt, *Die altkanaanäischen Fremdworte und Eigennamen in Ägyptischen* (1909). The name was called to my attention by Prof. Albright. Cf. *From the Stone Age to Christianity*, p. 185.

the name in early Israel, but matched the proportions of late times. However, the various onomastica of the second millennium had a superabundance of names with the element *El*, as our new evidence amply shows. The curve of usage which Gray drew actually reflects a resurgent popularity of the name-element. Hence the proportion of *El* names in our list now supports its antiquity! Moreover, the majority of the single elements in the Numbers lists occur in combination in the milieu to which tradition ascribes them.[12] The elements *'am* ('people,' *i.e.*, 'kinsman'), *'aḥ* ('brother'), and *'ab* 'father,' all referring to the link of kinship felt with a god, are most common appellatives of deity, both in our list and in the Amorite onomasticon from the middle of the second millennium. As Amorite names from the Mari tablets continue to be published, the evidence grows stronger and stronger. While we are still unable to fix the precise historical origin of the name list, it is an old document which accurately reflects the name usage of Mosaic times.

W. F. Albright has recently defended the antiquity of still another old Priestly document, the list of spies in Numbers 13:4–16.[13] While the archaeological documentation of these names is not so striking, it nevertheless must be fitted into the earlier period.[14]

Martin Noth has shown that the Priestly list of stations involved in the Exodus (Numbers 33:2–49) rests on an old document quite independent of the JE narrative of the Exodus and journey to Canaan.[15] This old record seems to come from the time of the early monarchy at latest, and may, as Noth gives good reason to believe, have been developed from a standard list of stations on a pilgrimage route from Canaan to Sinai. If such be the case, it is understandable how Priestly writers took such traditional stations, reversed their order, and

[12] Reuel (*Re'um-el* in the Mari Letters) meaning 'God (El) is a Shepherd,' is a particularly interesting example of a congruent name.

[13] *ARI*, p. 201, note 13.

[14] In this same connection, it may be pointed out that the name Bezalel (one of the traditional fabricators of the tabernacle) now has good parallels from old Amorite usage.

[15] "Der Wallfahrtsweg zum Sinai," *Palästinajahrbuch*, XXXVI (1940), 5–28.

used them as supplementary data for the route of Israel from Sinai to the Promised Land.

The antiquity of these dozen or so Priestly documents warrants closer attention on the part of scholars to other written sources of P. This is especially true in the case of such a document as the tabernacle description, whose doublets and conflate condition reveal a long history of transmission (cf. § 11).

The History of the Tabernacle Institution

8. With the formation of a covenanted league under Moses in the desert, suitable institutions for its functioning were created. The central institution, according to the unanimous witness of the sources, was the Tent of Assembly (cf. § 16), which was utilized both for religious and political gatherings. The "Aaronic" priesthood and a sacrificial cult (derived no doubt from the patterns of worship to which the people were accustomed) were instituted. The essential covenant law was no doubt proclaimed and fixed in liturgical forms at this period and added to from time to time when Yahweh proclaimed his will directly or through sacred lot.

There is good reason to believe that Moses instituted the aniconic tradition of Israel as argued persuasively by Wright and Albright, so that we may assume that the Ark, understood as the throne of an invisible God, was also instituted in the days of Moses. Such traditions best perpetuate themselves when embodied in concrete form.

The sources are at variance as to the place of the tabernacle in Israel's encampment. Gressmann holds that the tent-sanctuary and its precious Ark could never have stood unprotected outside the camp of the Israelites. Rather, drawing upon well-known representations of Egyptian[16] and Assyrian battle-camps, and familiar notices of Diodorus relating to a tent-shrine in the center of the camp of the Carthaginians, he concludes that the Priestly accounts are more accurate in placing the sacred cult installations in the center of the camp. How-

---

[16] Especially contemporary reliefs of Rameses II (1300–1234), presumably Pharaoh of the Exodus, which shows the Egyptian camp drawn up in rectangular form with the tent of the divine king and various sacred objects in the center.

ever, under different circumstances, both traditions may be accurate. The heavily idealized camp of the Priestly tradition, with priests and tribes grouped in systematic order in protective array about the tabernacle, may reflect the battle formation of Israel in the ritual of 'Holy War.' On the other hand, the Tent may have been pitched in partial seclusion among the peaceful encampments of Israel, and there is good reason to believe that the Ark led Israel as they made general migrations (cf. § 13).

9. Little is known about the early history of the tabernacle as an institution in Canaan. If Noth and Alt are correct, the first locus of the central sanctuary was at Shechem, as suggested by early records in Deuteronomy and Joshua, where the desert covenant was renewed and extended to the twelve tribes who made up the later nation of Israel (Joshua 8:30–35; 24; etc.). However, the official sanctuary during the major phase of the period of the Judges was no doubt at Shiloh. Such is the consensus of the sources, early and late. Moreover, the fact that Shiloh is given such prominence despite its insignificant size and out-of-the-way location in Palestine reinforces tradition. Shechem, on the other hand, seems to have remained under strongly Canaanite influence during most of the Period of the Judges.

At Shiloh the house of Eli continued the hereditary priesthood preserving even some of its Egyptian background in the names Hophni and Phinehas. Shiloh remained the central sanctuary until its destruction at the hands of the Philistines after the Battle of Ebenezer (*ca.* 1050 B.C.), when the Ark was captured. The destruction of the central sanctuary is amply corroborated by the excavations of Kjaer and Schmidt,[17] as well as by notices in later tradition (Jeremiah 7:12; 15:1; 26:6; Psalms 78:60, etc.). The earlier sources refer to the sanctuary at Shiloh as a temple (*hêkāl*), while later sources refer to it as a tent. When the old fabric of the original tabernacle disappeared, no one can tell. Perhaps it fell apart during the vicissitudes of the Conquest.

The period following the destruction of Shiloh is largely a blank in the history of the central sanctuary. Saul's establish-

[17] Albright, *ARI*, p. 104.

ment of the sanctuary at Nob, only two miles from his residence in Gibeah, seems to have been an attempt to draw the
strands of the old amphictyonic system together under his
surveillance as well as to identify it with his own proto-mo-
narchial system. The blood purge of Nob priests after their
traffic with David is particularly indicative that certain sover-
eign powers, derived from the strong tradition of the old
theocracy, still resided in the Nob sanctuary.

Whatever may have been the subsequent history of the institution after the fall of Shiloh, it finds its culmination in
David's "Tent of Yahweh." We get ample evidence of David's
political sagacity as well as his religious devotion—or that of
such advisers as Nathan (II Samuel 7)—in connection with the
establishment of the Jerusalem sanctuary. David brought together the Ark, chief cult object of the covenanted tribes, the
hereditary northern priesthood, and the desert-born tradition
of Israel's tabernacle, to form his official cultic institution in
the neutral city of Jerusalem. The nimbus of the old sanctuary,
the loyalty to the old system, and the cherished memories of
the desert tradition were thereby transferred to the Tent of
David, giving legitimacy and security to the Davidic monarchy.

10. It is well to recognize that the "tabernacle" became the
symbol of the institution of the central sanctuary in later
biblical thought. By telescoping tradition, the institution which
served as Israel's sanctuary was conceived *ipso facto* to be the
tabernacle. For this reason, one is justified in terming not only
the desert tent, but also the Shiloh structure (whatever its form
may have been), and particularly the Tent of David, 'the tabernacle'; for in these resided the one, continuous, central religious institution of early Israel. The motifs of the desert tent
maintained themselves in these sanctuaries, arising out of the
desert era, continuing into the time of David, and projected in
ideal form in the later religious thought of Israel. These sanctuaries were characteristically seats of normative Yahwism;
each contained the Ark; each was a center of covenant law and
judgments. They were the focus of pilgrimage customs, a
dominant priestly house, and, in varying degrees, the center of
a political system.

The Promulgation of the Tent Ideal

11. New vistas in the ancient history of the tabernacle institution require a reinterpretation of the character and date of the Priestly materials which promulgated the tabernacle ideal in later times. Priestly tradition seems never to have taken the form of an independant "Code". It is most easily described as a commentary or rather a systematizing expansion of the normative JE tradition in the Tetrateuch (Gen., Exod., Lev., Num.). Evidently priests of the late pre-Exilic and Exilic period collected and edited ancient written (sic!) documents, perhaps salvaged from temple or government archives, and thus produced what they considered a more precise and detailed picture of the desert period. That is to say, they were continuing the prophetic tendency to regard the desert era as normative for Yahwism, but were interested more in its cultic establishment.

An Exilic date for the major Priestly work seems almost certain now. Its language can scarcely be post-Exilic, since there are no Aramaisms. Its theology is clearly reflected in the writings of the oldest post-Exilic prophets, particularly Zechariah (cf. 2:5, 10 ff.; 8:3, 11; and *passim*). The Nethinim, singers, and other orthodox institutions of the Restoration have no place in its pages. It must be closely connected with the work of Ezekiel.

The theology of the Priestly strata fits into this period perfectly. The downfall of the nation with its ensuing captivity was a catastrophe with tremendous implications for its faith. The covenant was "broken." Monotheism was threatened. The doctrine of election seemed directly repudiated. The sacrosanct temple had been sacked, and the inviolable city lay in ruins. The great historical tenets of Yahwism needed emphatic restatement. The future of Israel's religion rested upon the ability of the faithful to explain and answer the crises and problems of the time. Out of the Exile came reformulation of the faith. Ezekiel pointed the way. The Priestly writers looked to the pre-temple era, to Israel's normative Mosaic institutions, and provided a reinterpretation of the past which later became authoritative. In contrast, Second Isaiah (Isa. 40 ff.) heralded the

Restoration; he was not only concerned with the return of Israel to Jerusalem, but primarily with the victory of Yahweh. He exulted over the vindication of the covenant faith. He restated the role of the Chosen People, and effectively described the meaning of the captivity. A powerful doctrine of election permeates Ezekiel, P, and Second Isaiah. In all three the memory of the golden desert era is evoked. Ezekiel and the Priestly strata, especially, are desperately concerned with the sin of Israel, which has precipitated the captivity, and they search for means of atonement. All three emphasize the cosmic and holy nature of Israel's God. Second Isaiah, however, adds a new mood in his victory paean: he sings of the downfall of the idol-gods and of the universal sovereignty of his vindicated Lord.

12. The most recent trend in the literary criticism of the Priestly writings is represented by the work of G. von Rad (*Die Priesterschrift im Hexateuch,* 1934), and M. Noth in his monumental *Ueberlieferungs-geschichtliche Studien* (1943). Von Rad splits P into two separate sources, one older, less priestly, and more historical; the other comparatively late, priestly, and artificial. He is followed by Galling and in part by Noth, but has not gained general acceptance. Noth's work seeks to eliminate P from Joshua, cutting away all accretions to leave a source, largely narrative, which concludes with the death of Aaron and Moses. Noth's treatment, however, overlooks P's character as commentary formed from sundry old records in his insistence that P be a logical unity, later split up to form the framework of the Tetrateuch. Noth is probably correct in regarding JEP and the Deuteronomic books as separate entities. And yet, even if this is true, the Joshua lists, for example (cf. § 7), must derive from the same circle of documents, extant in the pre-Exilic period, as many of those in the Priestly portions of the Tetrateuch.

These recent attempts to seek out the "nuclear" Priestly stratum reflect a new respect for the historical core of P. The conflations, doublets, and additions which allow separation of Priestly materials into two or more parts also testify to the age of its sources, but at the same time to the heterogeneous character of its origin. We cannot use the Priestly materials uncritically. Priestly tradition in its present form is dogmatic and late; nevertheless, it is a valuable historical witness, often more reliable in detail than the older oral sources. In the last analysis, it can in no way represent pious fraud, but rather the best efforts of priestly scholars who tried to piece together the golden past from materials available to them.

The Archaeology of the Tabernacle

13. Old Testament scholars, taking their cue from students of Arab life, as early as the turn of the century, began to compare the tabernacle and the Ark with nomad tent-shrines surviving into modern times. Gressmann, in *Mose und seine Zeit* (1913), compared the Ark to the Ruwala *'utfah,* following Musil and older scholars. In 1918, Hartmann published a study of the tabernacle and Ark[18] in which he drew on the parallel institutions of the *'utfah, mahmal,* and *qubbah.* A most valuable study was that of Henri Lammens, which appeared in 1919,[19] and treated particularly well the pre-Islamic history of the *qubbah.* The most recent collection and treatment of modern and ancient parallels is that of Morgenstern, "The Ark, the Ephod, and the Tent."[20]

The *'utfah* is a class of tribal palladia still surviving among the modern nomad tribes. Its best known representative is the *markab* of the Ruwala. It takes the form of a camel saddle in modern times, is made of a wooden framework, decorated with ostrich feathers, and more or less resembles a tent. Traditionally, it accompanied tribes into important military encounters and led them in migrations. Some manner of "holiness" pervaded the *'utfah.* Originally, no doubt, it was associated with the tribal deity(s). Sacrifices are still made in connection with it, at which time blood is sprinkled on it.

The *mahmal* is a highly revered tent-like structure, which until very recent times was carried in various processions to Mecca. It too was borne on camel back. It was usually fabricated from highly decorated silk on a boxlike framework with

---

[18] *ZAW,* XXXVII, 209 ff.

[19] "Le culte des bétyles et les processions religieuses chez les arabes préislamites," *Bulletin de l'Institut Français d'Archéologie Orientale,* XVII (1919), 39–101.

[20] *Hebrew Union College Annual,* XVII (1943), 153–265; XVIII (1944), 1–52.

a domed top. There is evidence that it was regarded formerly as having some kind of supernatural sway over the camel which carried it, so that it could guide caravans through the deserts.

Going back into the pre-Islamic period, we come upon the highly significant *qubbah* which seems to be the ancestor of the *maḥmal* and *'uṭfah*. The *qubbah* was a miniature red leather tent with a domed top. Some *qubbahs* were suitable for mounting on camel back, others larger. The *qubbah* generally contained the tribal idols or betyls.

The characteristics which have been noted in the *'uṭfah* and the *maḥmal* were far more explicitly characterized in the usage of the *qubbah*. In times of war it accompanied the tribe, generally being set up close by the chieftain's tent. It had the power of guiding the tribe in its wanderings. It possessed a peculiar sacredness or physical holiness second only to the betyls which it contained. It was both a palladium and a place of worship. Moreover, priests used the *qubbah* as a place for giving oracles.

Lammens observes that the red leather of which they were constructed is most extraordinary. Black tents were characteristic from oldest times. Moreover, red exposes the military camp and the station of the chieftain. The custom is strange and implies a strong conservative religious tradition.

A number of representations of the *qubbah* come from Syria, as well as a specific mention of the institution in an Aramaic inscription. Of particular interest is the bas-relief from the temple of Bel in Palmyra (third–first centuries B.C.) portraying the *qubbah* with traces of red paint still adhering to it.

Morgenstern has pointed out that even earlier evidence for the custom of tent-shrines comes from the fragments of the Phoenician history of Sanchuniathon (*ca.* seventh century B.C.) where reference is made to a portable shrine of undisclosed character pulled by oxen. The shrine was presumably in the possession of Agroueros, a semi-mythical figure who lived in primordial times. Better evidence for Phoenician tent-shrines, however, comes from Diodorus, who tells of a tent of sacred nature pitched in the center of a Carthaginian battle camp with an altar near by (cf. § 8).

The Priestly traditions also have specific mention of the

qubbah in Numbers 25:8. The passage is somewhat obscure; but the context suggests that it is a reference to the tabernacle, or as Ingholt suggests, to the sacred enclosure.

These parallels lend striking corroboration to the Priestly tradition that the tabernacle had a covering of ram's skin, dyed red; and no doubt we must conclude that the *qubbah* institution among the Semites sheds light on the origin of the tabernacle. We must suppose that the portable red leather tent was one of the oldest motifs in Semitic religion. Thus it goes without saying that the tabernacle and the Ark have historical connections with their Semitic past. On the other hand, we have no right to push such parallels too hard as has been the tendency of some scholars, particularly of Morgenstern. As the *qubbah* was radically reinterpreted by Mohammed, so no doubt the ancient Semitic tent-shrine was transformed in early Israel to suit the purposes of Yahwism.

Reconstruction of the Priestly Tabernacle

14. The Priestly tabernacle as it appears from descriptions in Exodus 26 and 36 is a portable temple. Two motifs run throughout its structure and installations. One derives from the desert and suggests its origin in a tent-shrine. Under this category are the tent curtains, especially the covering of red leather; the acacia wood similarly is a product of the desert, and stands in contrast to the olive and cedar wood which characterized the temple of Solomon. The other principle clearly represented in the tabernacle points to the influence of Syro-Phoenician temple architecture. The division of the tabernacle into two sections, a "Holy Place" and a "Most Holy Place" or *děbîr*, and the substantial structure of frames (*qěrāšîm*) and pillars over which the curtains were draped, are particularly suggestive of temple form. It will be pointed out at a later time that some of the tabernacle furnishings surely suggest the influence of the environment of Canaan.

The tabernacle *par excellence* consisted of two great tent curtains (in turn composed of five smaller curtains each) made of the finest linen beautifully embroidered with winged sphinxes (cherubim). One of the curtains formed the main hall of the tabernacle, the Holy Place; the second covered the

Most Holy Place, including the back of the tabernacle. Over these curtains, three protective coverings were spread, the outer of finely treated, imported leather,[21] a second of red-dyed ram's hide, and a third of goat's hair.

The curtains were spread on a framework of *qĕrāšîm* which A. R. S. Kennedy on the basis of biblical evidence has translated 'frame' (A. V. 'board'). As scholars have long realized, the *qĕrāšîm* could scarcely have been solid timbers or 'boards.' Their ponderous size and weight alone would eliminate them from reason. The *yādôt* of the 'frames,' then, would be the vertical arms and presumably they were joined together by cross-pieces to make a latticework.

The tablets of Ugarit have given additional confirmation to the theory of Kennedy. Here the *qrš* refers to the throne-room of El at the source of the primordial rivers and the fountains of the two oceans (deeps). Presumably the throne-room was a trellised pavilion.[22]

Again we have evidence of the dual nature of the Priestly tabernacle. Apparently the *qĕrāšîm* framework has historical connections with the abodes of deity in Canaanite mythology. Probably the conception of the *tabnît*, the 'model' (Exodus 25:9), also goes back ultimately to the idea that the earthly sanctuary is the counterpart of the heavenly dwelling of a deity. There is no reason to assume with most scholars (most recently Galling) that the tabernacle framework is the fiction

---

[21] *Tahaš* leather (A. V. 'badger skins') has caused unending speculation on the part of scholars. An Assyrian word supposedly meaning 'sheep-skin' seemed to satisfy for a time. However, Landsberger has maintained that the word in question, *taḫšu*, is to be read *dušu* 'sheep-skin' (?). Efforts to etymologize on the basis of Arabic *tuḫas* have led to weird results, the latest being that of Aharoni who concludes that *taḥaš* means *monodon monoceros* 'narwhale'! By far the most reasonable suggestion is that of Bondi who connects *taḥaš* with Egyptian *tj-ḫ-s*, Middle Kingdom *t-ḫ-s*. As Albright pointed out to the writer, the phonetic equation is quite proper, and the word was borrowed during the second millennium to judge from the laws of phonetic change, thus fitting perfectly into the desert milieu. Egyptian *tj-ḫ-s* is found as early as the Old Kingdom meaning 'to stretch or treat leather.' This would suggest then that the mysterious *taḥaš* skins were actually an imported (?) specially finished leather.

[22] The occurrence of the word in Ugaritic was called to my attention by Prof. Albright.

of late writers who wished to make the tabernacle conform more closely in structure to the temple.

The frames were to be 15 feet high and two feet three inches in breadth. As is to be expected in the case of frames, no thickness is mentioned. Forty-eight of the frames were to make up the structure, twenty frames for each side, and eight for the back, making the dimensions of the tabernacle forty-five feet long by fifteen feet wide by fifteen feet high. The Most Holy Place was to be closed off from the Holy Place by a tapestry veil hung on four acacia wood supports, and in turn, the entrance was to be protected by an embroidered screen hung on acacia supports.

The symmetry of the tabernacle is clarified by the notice that the veil is to be hung under the hooks that join the two great inner curtains (Exodus 26:33). The tabernacle consisted thus of two rooms, the Holy Place of twenty by ten by ten cubits (30 x 15 x 15 feet), and the Most Holy Place, a cube ten cubits to the dimension. The Ark was to be placed in this sacred cube; the Table of Presence Bread, the Altar of Incense, and the Lampstand were to adorn the Holy Place.

The tabernacle is described as being enclosed in a court, shut off by linen curtains, one hundred by fifty cubits in size (approximately 150 x 75 feet). The Altar of Burnt Offering and the Laver were set up in the Court, no doubt standing before the entrance to the tabernacle.[23]

The Tabernacle and the Davidic Tent

15. A number of considerations have led the writer to the opinion that the Priestly tabernacle account reflects the Tent of David. Such an opinion cannot, of course, be demonstrated, but evidence points increasingly in that direction.

It seems evident that P does not give a precise description of the tent which Moses built in the wilderness. Logically, it would seem that the Mosaic tent was simpler and more conformed to its Semitic prototypes. Moreover, it must have been

[23] For the best recent attempt to reconstruct the tabernacle from the biblical data, see A. R. S. Kennedy, "Tabernacle," *Hastings Dictionary of the Bible*, IV, 653–68. Kennedy takes up the many tedious problems not mentioned here.

almost inevitable that the Priestly writers draw their tradition of the tabernacle from the highest and most elaborate *development* of that institution (see § 10).

The dual motifs pointed out in the tabernacle description support the same conclusion. In particular the proportions of the tabernacle must almost necessarily be connected with the plans of such temples as have been excavated at Beth-shan, Tell Ta'yinat, and of course the temple of Solomon. The acacia wood, the tent-curtains of red leather no doubt stem from the desert tradition, but the *qereš* structure which converts the tent into a portable temple seems to have Canaanite connections. Some of the cultic implements and some of the decorations of the Priestly garments in particular suggest Phoenician influence. These dual motifs are not to be explained away entirely by supposing them anachronisms reflecting the temple of Solomon. Some influence of the temple upon the P account is undeniable. Certain parallels in measurement are best explained as resulting from the scribes' knowledge of the temple dimensions; such influence might easily come to bear if certain tabernacle dimensions were vague. It seems totally unnecessary to dissolve the dualism of the tabernacle, however, if we assume that the Priestly sources are describing the culminating development of the tabernacle institution.

Mention has already been made of the large number of old records incorporated by the Priestly writers which are traceable to early times, particularly to the reign of David (§ 7). There can be no doubt that David organized an elaborate administrative and secretarial staff, and it may well be that certain written documents from this time were available to the priests from temple or government archives. Our suggestion is that the tabernacle account also is some such document.

The Priestly tabernacle fits in very well with what little we know of the Davidic tabernacle from earlier sources. We know that it contained "a proper place" for the Ark (II Samuel 6:17), presumably a *děbîr*. In its proximity was an altar of burnt offering (II Samuel 6:17) and there seems to have been a second horned altar inside the Tent.[24]

---

[24] I Kings 1:50; 2:28–30. The words "come out" seem clearly to suggest that the altar was within and thus may have been either an altar of incense or a Table of Presence-bread. It is possible, how-

Finally, the wealth of the Davidic court and the important part which the tabernacle played in David's political strategy (§ 9) would lead us to believe that the Davidic tabernacle was richly and ornately fabricated, in which case it would agree well with the Priestly descriptions. That is not to deny that the extreme lavishness in the tabernacle adornments (and the reckless use of gold in the Solomonic temple) may be due in part to the tendency of tradition to exaggerate.

In this connection it would be well to make some comments on the most recent reconstructions, particularly that of Galling.[25] Galling, following von Rad's separation of the Priestly tradition into two strands (cf. § 12), segregates all the solely desert characteristics of the tabernacle, attributes them to the earlier source, and proposes by that means to arrive at the historical Mosaic tent. He considers the original account to have included different dimensions (later suppressed) and to have consisted only of the outer covering. This he drapes over poles allowing no credence to the division into Holy Place and *dĕbîr*. The framework of the tabernacle, the inner curtain, and a large part of the cultic equipment he ascribes to the imagination of the later, less reliable Priestly strand.

By isolating the desert motifs in the tabernacle Galling may well reach something resembling the actual Mosaic tent. However, to throw out the remainder of the description as later fabrication is unnecessary and goes against what we know of Near Eastern scribal procedures in general, and the Priestly sources in particular.

Light on Tabernacle Terminology

16. '*Ōhel Mô'ēd* ('Tent of Meeting'), the name of the tabernacle which is found in the JE account in Exodus 33 and often in the Priestly tradition, has been explained by the occurrence of the word *mô'ēd* in the Tale of Wen-Amun (*ca.* 1060 B.C.).[26]

ever, that Benaiah was calling from outside an enclosed court, in which case the altar would have been an altar of burnt offering. Neither possibility injures the parallel to the Priestly Tabernacle.

[25] Beer-Galling, *Exodus* ("Handbuch zum A. T.," [1939]), pp. 128 ff.

[26] The discovery was made by Wilson and was published in *JNES*, IV (1945), 245.

In this context it refers to the city assembly of Byblus called
together to consider a petition of the Tjekel (a group of the
Sea-Peoples who settled around Dor) for the extradition of
Wen-Amun. The passage may be compared with Isaiah 14:13
which refers to the mount of 'assembly' (mô'ēd) in the far
reaches of the north. The reference is to the assembly of the
gods,[27] well known from the myths of Ugarit.

From such passages we gather that the Tent of Meeting, or
properly the Tent of Assembly, originally referred to the
amphictyonic or political aspect of the tent. However, the
Priestly interpretation is not to be dismissed too lightly: speaking of the Tent of 'Meeting,' Yahweh says, "I will meet with
you to speak there unto you. And there I will meet with the
children of Israel . . ." (Exodus 29:42, 43; 25:22; and 30:36).
This interprets the 'Ōhel Mô'ēd primarily as a tent of revelation. However, it is to be observed that in the amphictyonic
gatherings, Yahweh was considered to be the head of the
covenant assembly, and it was He who made the important
decisions in war and peace (through oracle, or by human
mediation). There was no separation of church and state in
early Israel.

Noth has shown that nāsî' (A. V. 'prince,' cf. § 7) often
employed by the Priestly writers is another technical term de-
noting a tribal leader who took part in the amphictyonic assembly ('ēdāh) of early Israel's twelve-tribe system. Many
other examples of the Priestly source's use of archaic terminology could be presented; however, we shall confine ourselves
to two other terms which bear particularly on the theology of
the tabernacle tradition.

17. The typical Priestly designation of the tent-sanctuary is
the term miškān 'tabernacle.' Evidence from Ugaritic and the
thirteenth-century Balaam Oracles, especially, makes it virtually certain that the term originally meant simply, 'tent.' Later
it became a poetic, elevated designation of a tent. In the
Priestly materials it is restricted to the tent par excellence, the
tabernacle. Still later the term was used figuratively in references to the temple.

[27] Cf. J. H. Patton's discussion of the assembly of the gods, and
parallel usages of mô'ēd in the Psalms (Canaanite Parallels to the
Book of Psalms [1944], p. 24).

The associated verb, *škn* (A. V. 'dwell'), has an even more interesting history.

Underlying the massive detail of the Priestly strata is one dominant theme. This theme may be expressed as follows: under the conditions of the desert covenant, Yahweh will "tabernacle" in the midst of his people Israel (Exodus 25:8; 29:45, 46; 40:35; and often: cf. Leviticus 26:11). The term translated "to tabernacle" (in lieu of a better rendering) is *škn*. It is generally thought to indicate a literal abode on earth. Scholars have assumed that the Priestly writers follow a grossly primitive doctrine of divine immanence. It is asserted that though they reach sublime heights in their conception of creation at the hand of God, and indeed describe their Deity in the most exalted terms of transcendence, yet they fall to a crass particularism when describing the manner in which God is present in their tent-sanctuary. By the same token, *miškān* 'tabernacle,' has often been translated 'dwelling.'

The early usage of *škn* is closely parallel to the usage of *miškān* 'tent.' It occurs in the Balaam Oracles, the Song of Deborah, the Noachic Oracle, Jacob's Blessing, the Blessing of Moses (all pre-tenth-century sources), in the earlier traditions of the Yahwist (J), in the Keret Epic of Ugarit, etc. In fact there is scarcely an ancient poem dating from the tenth century, or earlier, sources which does not contain this term. In ancient poetry, *škn* is used to picture nomadic life, and clearly means 'to encamp' or 'to tent.'[28] So also it is used in the earlier

---

[28] The writer hopes to publish a treatment of the etymology and specialization of the stem *škn* at an early date. A few remarks may be made here. *Šakânu* in Old Akkadian is already a true root meaning 'to place' or 'to set down.' In Assyrian it is often used in idiom to mean 'pitch or set up camp' (esp. with *mâdaktu*, but also with *karâšu*, etc.). From comparable usage, the derived noun *maškanu* seems to have been specialized in *Northwest Semitic* to mean camping-place or, particularly in the plural, 'encampment.' Hence the singular, 'tent.' It is interesting to note that *maškanu* in East Semitic was specialized to mean 'a grain storage place' or 'grain shed' (so Albright in modification of Goetze) which was later borrowed in Hebrew in the form *miskĕnôt* 'storage places.' The two specializations of the derived noun are almost identical in semantic development to German *Lager*, 'encampment' or 'storage-place.'

The specialization of the verb *škn* in Northwest Semitic probably did not derive directly from such idioms as mentioned above. Rather

J traditions to describe the nomadic habits of the Patriarchs, and in the Keret epic to mean 'encamp.' In contrast to the abundant use of the word in materials of great antiquity—all of which appear to reflect a desert setting—we find that the term *škn* 'to tent' falls into disuse in the bulk of biblical writings until it is met again in the Priestly strata.

In the Priestly strata, the term *miškān* applies to the one tent, the Mosaic sanctuary. The word has become a proper name. So too, P restricts the meaning of the verb *škn*. Taking its connotations from a nomadic background, and more directly from the sacred *miškān*, it is used by the Priestly writers when they wish to speak of God manifesting Himself on earth in the midst of Israel. Thus in P, *škn* is used invariably and solely to specify the 'tabernacling' of Yahweh—the earthly presence of Yahweh—for the purposes of revelation and atonement. Even in cases where Yahweh's Glory or Cloud settles on Sinai or before the tabernacle, this word, *škn*, is used.

Such usage reflects the Priestly effort to go back to a normative desert tradition for terminology. This expression becomes even more significant when we observe that not only does P always use this term to express the concept of Yahweh's immanence, but it never uses the term *škn* in any other sense. Priestly tradition has taken a concrete, archaic term, associated with Israel's desert tradition, and used it as an abstract term to express a theological concept.

Still another line of evidence can be drawn upon. The common word in the Priestly materials, and throughout the Old Testament, which means 'dwell' or 'inhabit' is *yšb*. P uses the term *yšb* whenever it wishes to speak of men 'dwelling,' but never of Yahweh or any manifestation of Yahweh to Israel. Moreover, this distinction is held more or less throughout the Old Testament. When Yahweh is said to 'dwell,' (*yšb*), the place of dwelling is never on earth, in the temple, or in the tabernacle, but *in heaven alone*. The only exceptions, apparently, are in places where *yšb* or its derivatives are used in the sense, 'to enthrone,' or 'throne,' particularly in the expression, "He who is enthroned on the cherubim."

---

it seems to have derived its nuances in denominative fashion from the use of the noun *maškanu* or *miškān* 'tent,' and hence came to mean 'to tent' or 'to encamp.'

The Priestly writers were struggling with the problem of divine immanence and transcendence, in other words, the problem of the covenant-presence of Yahweh in the sanctuary. Israel's cosmic and omnipotent God could not be confined to an earthly sanctuary. Yet the supreme object and benefit of the covenant relationship—of Israel's election in the great events following the Exodus—was God's new "closeness" in the tabernacle. It seems clear that this old word *škn* has been taken as the technical theological term to express this paradox. The Priestly writers retrieved a "desert" terminology that was genuinely archaic. Yahweh does not "dwell" on earth. Rather he "tabernacles" or settles impermanently as in the days of the portable, ever-conditional tent.

We may observe in passing that the Deuteronomists sought in a different way to solve the problem of the covenant-presence of a transcendent God. They bluntly state that Yahweh's abode is in the heavens, not in the temple. Rather, His "Name" may be said to be in the temple (see esp., I Kings 8:27–31).[29]

Confirming the Hebrew evidence is the usage of the Septuagint. There the term *škn* is generally translated by *kataskēnoun* 'to encamp,' or *skēnoun* 'to tent,' and *miškān* is commonly translated *skēnē* 'tent.' This is particularly the case among the more literal translators. Allusion should also be made to the *šĕkînāh* doctrine which grew up shortly after the Old Testament writings were completed. *Šĕkînāh* probably is an older word, however, and is to be very closely related with the Priestly use of *miškān* and *škn*. In early intertestamental writings, the *šĕkînāh* is the restricted or local manifestation of Yahweh, later coming to have a wider meaning. It also plays a part in the theological background of the New Testament.

Conclusion

18. In the preceding pages, we have endeavored to describe the place of the historical tabernacle, both in its relation to the desert origins of Israel, and as it played the role of covenant sanctuary in Canaan. We have found it to be the seat of Mosaic institutions, the preserver of vigorous desert Yahwism, and the center of an inherently theocratic political

[29] Cf. Wright, pp. 181–83.

system. With these concepts as a background, we have turned to the tent ideal of later times, particularly the Priestly description of the tabernacle. The Priestly tabernacle appears in this perspective to be the culminating tradition—schematic and ideal to be sure—of themes which had seminal beginnings in the Mosaic tent.

As for the contemporary and future generations to which the Priestly writers addressed themselves, no doubt the tabernacle account was to be an explanation for the past and a plan for the future. Theologically speaking, they strove after a solution to the problems of covenant theology; the means through which the breached covenant might be repaired, and the conditions under which a holy and universal God might "tabernacle" in the midst of Israel. It may be added that the writers of the New Testament were intimately concerned with the same themes, that is, the forgiveness of sin and the self-revelation of God. Christian theology may thus be said to continue, and, from a Christian point of view, to resolve these Priestly problems of the Old Testament, through the Word which "became flesh and 'tabernacled' among us full of grace and truth . . ." (John 1:14).

14

SYNAGOGUES IN PALESTINE

HERBERT GORDON MAY

Both Christian church and Mohammedan mosque, in their origins, were indebted to the synagogue. Occasionally we find that synagogues have even been transformed into churches and mosques. At Gerasa in Transjordan a synagogue was rebuilt as a church, and at Eshtemoa, south of Hebron, one was turned into a mosque. The New Testament records the importance of the synagogue in the beginnings of Christianity. Because of these things, and because of the significance of the synagogue in ancient and modern Judaism, there is a natural interest in the earliest synagogue discoveries.

Synagogue Origins

The origins of the synagogue are shrouded in the mists of the past. Synagogue is a Greek word meaning 'assembly.' The Hebrew form meant 'the house of (the) assembly.' Although our first actual knowledge of the synagogue comes from the third and second century B.C. (in the Greek period) it may have been the result of a long development from informal meetings for prayer and worship in the private homes of the Jews of Palestine and the Diaspora. It has been maintained that even before the destruction of the temple there were prayer gatherings under prophetic guidance, and that out of these gatherings there grew the more definitely institutional-

ized synagogues, which played an important role in the Mac-
cabaean period of the second century B.C.[1] It is strange that
there are no indubitable references to the synagogue in the
Old Testament. The most probable is Ps. 74:8, which may
come from the Greek period, and where the expression "assemblies of El (= God)" is usually translated 'snyagogues.'
Very improbable is Ezek. 11:16, where an obvious mistransla-
tion produces 'a little sanctuary,' i.e., a synagogue. Some think
that many of the Psalms were written for use in the synagogue,
and it has been suggested that the priestly legislation in the
Pentateuch was written for reading in the synagogue as a substitute for temple sacrifices, but there is no direct evidence for
this. The place of origin of the synagogue, whether in Palestine
or among the Jews of the Diaspora, is as obscure as its time
of origin.

The Earliest Synagogues Unearthed

Our discussion of synagogue archaeology will be limited to
Palestine, with one reference to Syria, although early synagogues are known at other places, such as on the Greek islands
of Delos and Aegina, or at Miletus and Priene on the eastern
coast of modern Turkey. The earliest excavated synagogues
in Palestine belong to the late second, the third, and the fourth
centuries A.D.[2] The reason why none from the first century
has been recovered may be that they were quite completely
demolished during the two violent rebellions against Rome in
A.D. 66–70 and A.D. 131–35. In the first of these both Galilee
and Judaea were subdued by the Emperor Vespasian, and
Jerusalem, with its temple, was burned in A.D. 70 by the
Romans under Titus, Vespasian's son. The Jerusalem Talmud credits Vespasian with the destruction of four hundred

---

[1] See Louis Finkelstein, "The Origin of the Synagogue," *Proceedings of the American Academy for Jewish Research* (1930),
pp. 49 ff.
[2] There are otherwise a first century A.D. synagogue inscription
from Jerusalem, to be discussed later, and a few fragments of Jewish
architecture which might have belonged to a synagogue, and are
to be dated before A.D. 130, possibly before A.D. 68, found in the
fallen debris around the large arch south of the village of Jerash
in Transjordan. See *BASOR*, No. 87 (1942), pp. 10 ff.

eighty synagogues in Jerusalem (*Megillah* III. 1). The extant synagogue ruins come from after this period, but we may assume that their general plan conformed to those in the first century, although they differed in certain architectural features and ornamentations. Each town and city had its synagogue, sometimes more than one. Although we cannot give credence to the tradition that there were four hundred eighty at Jerusalem, the tradition that there were at one time thirteen at Tiberias is plausible (*Berakoth* I. i. 8a; IV. vii. 30b). There were several synagogues at Damascus (Acts 9:20). Acts 6:9 may imply that at Jerusalem Jews from various countries worshiped in synagogues with men from the same country. Synagogues in Galilee are mentioned frequently in connection with Jesus' preaching there. In view of the frequency with which synagogues occurred in ancient Palestine, it is not surprising that their remains have been found at more than forty places in the Holy Land. The larger number of them come from the Galilee district and vicinity. Occasionally more than one has been found at a single site, as at *Kefr Bir'im* and Gischala.

Roman Period Synagogues in Palestine

These Galilean synagogues were the first to attract the attention of explorers almost a hundred years ago, when they were identified by Edward Robinson at *Tell Hum, Meron, Kefr Bir'im,* and *Irbid.* The most recent discovery occurred at *Sheikh Abreiq,* the rabbinic site Beth Shearim, ten miles west of Nazareth, where important Jewish catacombs have also been found. The synagogues excavated in Palestine may be roughly classified into two major types. The first may be illustrated from the remains at *Tell Hum,* the site of Capernaum, from *Kerazeh,* the site of Chorazin (cf. Matt. 11:21; Luke 10:13), and from *Kefr Bir'im;* and they belong to the third and fourth centuries A.D. Chorazin was destroyed by the first half of the fourth century, but Capernaum and other sites were occupied longer. Their architectural ornamentation, about which more will be said later, is characteristic of this period. Father Orfali, who has attempted a partial reconstruction of the Capernaum synagogue, has without success maintained a first century A.D. date for the earliest parts of this synagogue.

In view of the New Testament associations, one would like to be able to claim an early date for it. Located on the northern shore of the Sea of Galilee, its white limestone superstructure contrasts sharply with the black basalt of which most of the city's buildings were made. It is a basilica, with rows of columns supporting a gallery which ran around the north, east, and west sides of the building. The entrance is on the side of orientation, where there are a main portal and two side entrances. The interior is paved with flagstones, and around the walls on three sides run two benches, one built above the other. The gallery was for the use of the women, while the men sat on the benches or on mats in the central nave, facing the entrance. The women entered the gallery from a staircase which was attached to an annex near the northwest corner. In front of the Capernaum synagogue was a platform, while a columned porch graced the façade at *Kefr Bir'im*, and probably also at Chorazin. On the east of the Capernaum synagogue was a trapezoid court with a portico. Besides the three main entrances on the façade, there were several windows, including a large open arch with an iron grating above the central portal.

One who visits these ruins is impressed and surprised by the ornate, almost baroque style of ornamentation. He finds Corinthian capitals, and cornices, pediments, and lintels which are decorated with reliefs. Among the designs he sees the egg and dart pattern, garlands, rosettes, acanthus leaves, vine branches, grapes, ivy, date palms, shell designs, pentagrams, hexagrams, amphorae, lions, eagles, an animal suckling its young, birds, cupids, centaurs, sea-horses, and zodiac signs. He will also note the seven-branched candlestick, pomegranates, etc. In the Capernaum synagogue recent excavations have disclosed the Bema (or pulpit), the platform where the lessons were read, in the southeast corner of the nave, next to the pillar (cf. Luke 4:16 ff.). The central feature of the synagogue was the Ark or Torah Shrine in which were kept the scrolls of the Law. The Ark was at first portable, and during the services placed inside before the central portal. Later a permanent Ark was placed there, and the doorway blocked up. Fragments of miniature architecture from such an Ark were discovered at Capernaum, as well as fragments of two stone lions which stood on either side of the Ark. Remains of two such stone lions associated with the Chorazin synagogue were recovered, and also a fragment of one from *Kefr Bir'im*.

The Beth Shearim synagogue consisted of an interior court and a basilica, with a terrace in front and various side-courts and side-chambers. Near the steps to the terrace a male skeleton was found. The man apparently had been killed by a blow on the chest, probably at the time of the destruction of the synagogue. Like the other Galilee synagogues, it was oriented towards Jerusalem, in this instance, southeast. Three entrances led into the court and two into the basilica, and between the two was the site of the Ark, while the stone platform of the Bema (pulpit) was near the northwest wall of the nave, occupying a space enclosed by walls. Marble slabs, from the walls above the benches and from the floor, were decorated in relief, some being part of a zodiac design. The inscriptions showed that the synagogue was also used as a court house. It dates from the third and fourth centuries A.D., and there was some evidence that it was preceded by a more simple structure in the second century.

The Synagogue at Dura-Europos

Before we turn to the second type of synagogue, our readers should be invited to two superimposed synagogues outside of Palestine, at Dura-Europos on the middle Euphrates. The earlier synagogue was a private house which had been transformed and reconstructed about A.D. 200. Unlike most synagogues, it was in the midst of other dwellings. The long narrow entry led into a colonnaded court, in the corner of which was a cesspool, used as a drain for the laver basin. Originally there had been three doors leading into the main chamber, but one was blocked up, and now there were two, one from the court and one from a side chamber. Benches ran along all four sides, and the wall opposite the main entrance doubtless contained a niche for the Ark, as did the later synagogue. The walls of the side chamber, which may have been used by the women, were decorated with foliage, fruit, and flower designs, while the main chamber was decorated geometrically. The later synagogue belonged to the period A.D. 245–56. The main room

was enlarged and the courtyard extended, and also a house
to the east was used as a synagogue precinct with a court. The
plaster columns of the colonnaded court supported a portico,
and in the northwest corner was a laver basin. Two doors led
into the main room, which was furnished with two tiers of
benches along the walls. The main entrance was for the men,
the women using the smaller door to the left. The benches between the two doors and along the left wall, which were without foot-rests, were for the women. The niche for the Ark was
in the opposite wall, and beside it the elder's seat. A canopy
over the niche supported the curtain or veil before the Ark.
The ceiling was tiled, and on the tiles were fruit, flower, animal
and bird designs, signs of the zodiac, Greek and Aramaic inscriptions, etc.

More striking were the murals on the walls. They are as yet
unique in synagogue art, although the decoration, apart from
the subjects, may be compared with that in contemporary
pagan temples. Above the niche were depicted the temple
(alternatively interpreted as a Torah Shrine), the seven-
branched candlestick, and the story of Abraham offering Isaac
on an altar. In facing the niche, the worshipers turned towards
Jerusalem, and saw this picture of the temple and the scene
which, according to popular tradition, took place on the temple
mount. It may not be without significance that two other representations of the temple are on this same wall, equally distant from the niche to the right and left, one glorifying the
Aaronic priesthood, and disclosing the Ark within the temple
(cf. Rev. 11:19). The murals around the walls represent scenes
from the careers of Jacob, Moses, Aaron, Solomon, David,
Elisha, and Esther, and incidents connected with the Exodus
and the Ark. The lowest zone on the walls was decorated with
masks, leopards, lions, or tigers in circles. The scenes on the
murals are titled in Greek and Aramaic, and to some of them
are appended inscriptions in Pehlevi. Kraeling, Du Mesnil,
Goodenough, Rostovtzeff, and others have added to our understanding of the significance of these murals for interpreting
synagogue religion and Jewish art, but here we cannot go into
detail concerning this. Rather we turn to the type of synagogue
which is particularly characteristic of the Byzantine period.

Byzantine Period Synagogues in Palestine

In contrast to the first type of synagogue we discussed, the Dura synagogue had its entrance on the side opposite Jerusalem, and the Ark was placed at the side opposite the entrance. This is particularly characteristic of the synagogues built after the middle of the fourth century A.D. and later, of which the best example comes from Beth Alpha, near Bethshan, to the south of the Sea of Galilee. To the same category belong the synagogue in Transjordan at Hammath-by-Gadara (*el-Hammeh*) on the Yarmuk River and the synagogue discovered near ancient Jericho. We shall have occasion to refer to others on Mt. Carmel at *'Esfiyeh,* at Naaran (*'Ain Duq*), a few miles northwest of Jericho, and at Gerasa (*Jerash*) in central Transjordan. This type is also characterized by an apse, on the side opposite the entrance, in which the Ark was placed, and by mosaic floors. It is usually a basilica.

The Beth Alpha synagogue had on the north a large open court, from which, by two doors, one entered into a narrow vestibule, and from this three doors led into the main room. All were covered with mosaic floors. The Bema stood on the mosaics near the southeast corner of the nave, and can be seen in the plan. An annex on the west, poorly preserved, contained the staircase mounting to the women's gallery. The mosaic floor in the nave was divided into three panels, especially significant for early synagogue art. The top panel, which was nearest the apse, shows us something of what the congregation saw when they looked toward the apse. We see in the center the Ark or Torah Shrine, from the gable of which hangs the *nēr tāmīd,* the Eternal Light. On each side are two lions, recalling the images of lions found at Capernaum, Chorazin, and *Kefr Bir'im,* and whose prototypes were the Old Testament cherubs. The birds, which are found at other times in early Jewish art with the representations of the Torah Shrine, are less easily interpreted. There are also the two candlesticks on each side of the Ark, one of them more properly a lampstand with oil lamps on the branches. At the sides we see the curtains or veil with the draw-cords. The sockets for the posts holding the veil were actually found on the edge of the platform of the apse. Among other objects on this panel are the *shofar*, the ram's horn which was blown at New Year's, and the *lulab* (palm branches), and *ethrog* (citron) used at the Feast of Tabernacles. The central panel shows the zodiac circle, with the chariot of the sun in the center, and four winged figures, representing the four seasons, in the corners. Similar panels were found at 'Esfiyeh and Naaran.

Of special interest is the lower panel, depicting the story of the sacrifice of Isaac, which we have already noted at Dura over the niche. Hebrew inscriptions identify Isaac and Abraham, and the legend beside the ram reads, "And behold! a ram" (Gen. 22:13). Beside the hand of God (top center) as it reaches down from heaven appear the first words of Gen. 22:12, "Lay not (thy hand)." The hand also appears in the Dura scene. The two servants with the ass during the sacrifice (Gen. 22:5) occupy the left side of the panel. Two other biblical scenes appear on floors of Palestinian synagogues. At Naaran there was the poorly preserved scene of Daniel in an attitude of prayer, with a lion approaching from each side, and the legend "Daniel—Peace." It was Daniel in the den of lions, as told in Dan. 6. The mosaic in the vestibule of the synagogue at Gerasa pictured the departure from the ark after the flood. It was badly preserved; but above the heads of Shem and Japheth were their names in Greek, and above this the dove with olive branch in its mouth. Birds of the air, beasts of the field, and creeping things of the earth are grouped in pairs in three rows. On the border can be seen a bear, lioness, leopard, birds, and other figures, along with plants and flowers, perhaps to indicate a wooded scene.

To the suggested interpretations of the three biblical stories as they appear on the mosaics of the synagogues, the writer would add one more. They may be related to the central conceptions of the Law and the Covenant. The rescue of Isaac suggests God's fulfilment of his covenant with Abraham (cf. Gen. 17). After the animals left the ark, God made a covenant with Noah (Gen. 9:9 ff.). The idea of the covenant and the Law are brought together in the Ark of the Covenant at Dura and Beth Alpha. Daniel, we recall, was thrown to the lions for being faithful to the Law of his God (Dan. 6:5). Doubtless no single interpretation will explain fully the meaning of these scenes to the worshipers in the synagogues concerned, for each scene is a complicated symbol of many things.

The plan of the Hammath-by-Gadara synagogue illustrates well the numerous rooms which may have served as guest-chambers and school-rooms. The mosaic design is more simple. In the top panel two lions stand on either side of a wreath, in which there is a memorial inscription in Aramaic. The synagogue was built not later than the first half of the fifth century, perhaps in the late fourth century. The Jericho synagogue has a small porch supported by two columns before its single entrance. The floor design showed the ark and the seven-branched candlestick with palm branches and ram's horn, and below it an inscription reading "Peace unto Israel." Partly on the evidence of coins, the Jericho synagogue was dated to the beginning of the eighth century. Among the Naaran mosaic designs was a panel showing the Ark with seven-branched candlestick on either side. The synagogue belongs perhaps to the fifth century. The synagogue at Gerasa was succeeded by a church, built in A.D. 530-31, in the reign of Justinian (527-65), as shown by a mosaic inscription. It was probably built in the preceding century or the late fourth century, being in use long enough to require extensive repairs. Anti-Jewish riots in the reign of Justinian may have brought this synagogue to an end, as also the synagogue at 'Esfiyeh, which was destroyed by fire. The Hammath-by-Gadara synagogue was also destroyed and burned. The Beth Alpha synagogue is dated by an inscription on the mosaic floor to the reign of Justin (518-27).

In contrast with these synagogues is the one discovered at es-Samu', the site of biblical Eshtemoa, south of Hebron (cf. Josh. 15:50; I Sam. 30:28, etc.). Like the Dura synagogue among others, it is a broadhouse type. The mosaic pavement was almost wholly destroyed. A porch in front was supported by two pillars, and the entrance on the east had the usual three doors. The building belonged to two periods, Roman and Byzantine. The north wall in the early period contained three niches, at a height about seven feet from the floor. It is suggested that the central niche was for the Ark, and the smaller side-niches for the candlesticks. In the later period there was a single niche near the floor-level.

A Jerusalem Synagogue Inscription

We may conclude this part of our survey with a synagogue inscription which comes from Jerusalem and belongs to New Testament times. In excavating on Ophel in Jerusalem, the archaeologist Weill discovered a Greek inscription. It states how Theodotos, son of Vettenos, priest and archisynagogos (= head of a synagogue), son and grandson of an archisynagogos, constructed the synagogue for the reading of the Law and the teaching of the commandments, built its inn, chambers, and water installations for housing needy strangers. It concludes with the statement that the synagogue had originally been built by his fathers and the elders (presbyters) and one named Simonides. Many think that this inscription comes from the synagogue of the Libertines (= freedmen) in Acts 6:9. The name Vettenos seems to indicate that Theodotos was once a slave in the Roman family of Vettius, but had been freed. In all probability it does come from the New Testament period, and with the fragments of architecture from Jerash mentioned in footnote No. 2, constitutes our only synagogue remains from Palestine dating in the formative days of the Gospel.

Temple and Synagogue

Our general discussion of the nature of the early synagogues in Palestine may perhaps be made more meaningful to the general reader if it takes the form of a treatment of analogies and contrasts between the Jerusalem temple and the synagogues. Analogies do not necessarily indicate any direct relationship, but they may perhaps assist us in our understanding. We should keep in mind particularly the Solomonic temple, and the Herodian temple. The synagogue has frequently been called an "Ersatz" (= substitute) for the temple. This could be understood more literally by those who conceived the synagogue to have developed soon after the destruction of the temple in 586 B.C. and in the Diaspora. It is true that, in function and arrangements, the synagogue had much in common with the temple, but there were also many differences.

The temple ritual, in contrast to that of the synagogue, centered around the sacrificial system. Prayer and the reading and study of the Law, symbolized by the central position of the Torah Shrine, characterized the synagogue. The Talmud represents Rabbi Eleazar as quoting Isa. 1:11 in support of the statement that "greater is prayer than sacrifice" (*Berakoth* V. i. 32b). That the prophetic attitude toward sacrifice had influence on the religion of the synagogue (as, to a lesser extent, it influenced the temple) is abundantly evidenced. Of course, synagogue religion did not deny the importance of the temple, nor the significance of the sacrificial system for the temple. The worshipers faced the temple in prayer. Yet part of the synagogue ritual was considered a substitute for sacrifice, indeed, a sacrifice. The morning and afternoon *Tefilloth* (Daily Prayers) were reckoned a substitute for the continual offerings in the temple. So Rabbi Judah held that the morning *Telfillah* could be said until the fourth hour, because the morning continual offering could be brought until the fourth hour (*Berakoth* IV. i. 26a, b. Cf. Exod. 29:38 ff.) It was argued that the patriarchs had been the ones to institute the *Tefilloth*, but the Rabbis subsequently found a basis for them in the sacrifices (*Berakoth* IV. i. 26b).

The teaching function of the synagogue was also important. The Theodotos inscription declared the purpose of the synagogue to be the reading of the Law and the teaching of the commandments. The Jerusalem Talmud affirmed that each of Jerusalem's four hundred eighty synagogues had a Beth Sepher (schoolhouse) and a Beth Talmud, the former for the text of the Scripture, and the latter for the Mishna (*Megillah* III. i). Side-chambers in the synagogues described above were doubtless used frequently as places of study. The Talmud frequently mentions the synagogue and the house of study, and often they were doubtless in the same building (cf. *Berakoth* IX. v. 64a). In the New Testament there are many references to Jesus and others teaching in the synagogues on the Sabbath and to the reading of the Scriptures (Mark 1:21; 6:2; Luke 4:16, 31; 6:6; 13:10; Acts 13:14, 27, 44; 15:21; etc.).

Orientation of Synagogues

The synagogues looked towards the temple. In general, the façade of the early type of synagogues was on the side towards Jerusalem. In the later type the entrance was on the side opposite Jerusalem, but one might say that the apse on the side towards Jerusalem reached out towards the Holy City. The orientation was not always exact; but in general, the Galilee synagogues were oriented towards the south, those below Jerusalem towards the north, and those in Transjordan toward the west. The background of this general orientation towards Jerusalem is the tradition that prayer should be directed towards the city, a tradition that perhaps appeared first with the Deuteronomic reform at the time of King Josiah. The exiles in Babylonia apparently prayed three times a day before windows opened towards Jerusalem (cf. Dan. 6:10). From Dan. 6:5 we may assume this was a part of the oral law.

The Synagogue Façade

Certain aspects of the façade of the early type of synagogue were possibly interpreted in the light of the fact that the synagogue looked toward the temple. The façades were abundantly supplied with window openings, and one may wonder whether in the minds of the worshipers they served merely to let the light inside, or whether they may not also have been thought to permit the synagogue, the 'Assembly,' to look towards Jerusalem and its temple. At Capernaum there were at least three windows in the façade, besides the large arched window supplied with iron bars above the central entrance. Quite pertinent is a passage in the Talmud (*Berakoth* V. i. 31a) where, we are told, Rabbi Hiyya b. Abba said: "A man should always pray in a room which has windows," and reference is made to Daniel praying through a window open towards Jerusalem (Dan. 6:11). It will be remembered that, although there were no windows at Dura, the Assembly looked toward three prominent representations of the Solomonic temple. Now it is of course true that the windows and arched openings were not unique to synagogue buildings, for they could be found in contemporary pagan architecture. Yet we are justified in believing that these details possessed some symbolic value for the worshipers, as doubtless did also the complex motives used in the ornamentation of the synagogues, even though much of it was typical of pagan Syro-Hellenistic art.

The same may be true of the three doors in the façade of the synagogues, which may possibly have been regarded as having as their prototype the gates of the temple, although they are characteristic of pagan Hellenistic-Roman architecture. It has been suggested that the form of the façade was not functional, and that these doors were not normally used for entrance, there being side or back doors which the congregation used.

Porch and Courts

The porch, a feature of the temple, was frequently a part of the synagogues. It may be found, for instance, at Chorazin, *Kefr Bir'im*, Eshtemoa, Jericho, *Umm el-Qanatir*, etc. Sometimes there is an unroofed platform, as at Capernaum, Gischala, etc. Often, instead of a porch, there is a vestibule, as at Hammath-by-Gadara, Gerasa, Naaran, Beth Alpha, etc. The porch has a long history in Palestinian-Syrian architecture, and can be traced in buildings of megaron type to before the third millennium B.C.

The synagogue also had its court or courts, sometimes with a portico arrangement, as at Capernaum and Dura-Europos. The conjecture has been made that the porticoed court adjacent to the sanctuary of the synagogue may have been used in part to accommodate "God-fearers" or proselytes, in which case it would have had a function somewhat comparable to that of the Court of the Gentiles in the Herodian temple. Sometimes laver basins for ritual ablutions, such as hand-washing before prayers, have been found in the courts. The water installations mentioned in the Theodotos inscription were doubtless both for ritual and the usual cleaning purposes. An inscription from the Sepphoris synagogue mentions a laver (basin), and one may be mentioned on a Naaran inscription. We recall the lavers in I Kings 7:38 ff., and that in the Herodian temple in the Court of the Priests there was a laver for ceremonial washing before offering the sacrifice (*Middoth* III. 6). In the columned forecourt at Gerasa's synagogue, stones with channels for water pipes were found, and it is supposed that there may have been a fountain or laver of water there. In the center of the court of Capernaum's synagogue there was a fountain. The water-vessel for hand-washing had been in the center of the court at Beth Alpha. Of course lavers and fountains were common also in pagan temples.

Separation of Women in Worship

The women in the Herodian temple worshiped in the Court of Women, and were prohibited from entering the inner court, the Court of Israel. This women's court is thought by some to be a later addition; it is mentioned first by the Mishna and Josephus. There were balconies in the Court of Women, from which the men were excluded (*Middoth* II. 6). We may compare the balconies in the synagogues, although we may not assume that they were in imitation of the temple, since the balconies in the Court of Women, for all we know, may have been patterned after those in the synagogue. It is probable, however, that the separation of men and women in the synagogue goes back to temple precedents, and that even before the construction of the Court of Women the women stayed outside the Court of Israel. Philo of Alexandria is evidence for the separation of men and women in the synagogues of the first century A.D. Since the first churches were in the synagogues, we may wonder whether there may not have been some such separation in early Christian worship, and whether in this may be found background for I Cor. 14:34, 35, where women are told to keep silent in the churches, and if they want to learn anything to ask their husbands at home. Paul talked to the women at Philippi outside the synagogue (Acts 16:13).

Location of Synagogues

According to the Talmud, the synagogue should be on the highest site in the town (*Shabbath* 11a: *Tosephta, Megillah* IV). It was said that a city whose roofs overtop the synagogue is given over to ruin. The sacred mountain on which the tem-

ple was situated, Mt. Zion, was important in the thought of
the Hebrews, as we see in Ps. 48:1, 2; Is. 2:2; Ezek. 40:2,
and many other places. There is in Josephus (*Ant.* XIII. vii.
215–17) a tradition that in 142 B.C. Simon, the Maccabee,
leveled the mountain on which the Jerusalem citadel stood, so
that the temple might be higher than it; and it took him three
years. It was natural that a high place be selected as the site of
a sanctuary. The synagogue at Gerasa stood on very high
ground, overlooking the temple of Artemis. The 'Esfiyeh
synagogue was on Mt. Carmel. The Hammath-by-Gadara synagogue was on the crest of *Tell Bani,* which stood from sixty-
five to eighty-five feet above the level of the plain. In search-
ing for the synagogue at Eshtemoa, the archaeologists looked
first and successfully at the highest point of the village. This
rule was, however, not always followed, as, for instance, at
Dura. Synagogues were sometimes built near the water (cf.
Josephus, *Ant.* XIV. x. 258). Capernaum is the outstanding
example of this. To judge from Acts 16:12, 13, the synagogue
at Philippi stood near the river.

The Ark, or Shrine for the Law

One of the most striking analogies between temple and synagogue is in the use of the Ark, candlesticks, and veil. The post-
Exilic temple had no Ark within its Holy of Holies. Where in
the Ark of the pre-Exilic temple there had been, according to
Hebrew tradition, the two tablets of the Law, there were in
the Arks of the synagogues the scrolls of the Law. This Ark
or Torah Shrine, like the pre-Exilic Ark, took the form of a
miniature building. As synagogue religion centered around the
Law, the Ark was central in the synagogue. In the Talmud
we are told that nine people and the Ark may be reckoned
together for a quorum (*Berakoth* VII. ii. 47b). The Ark was
at first portable, then stationary; eventually a special niche or
apse was provided for it in the center of the wall of orientation.
To judge from the data from Capernaum, Chorazin, and *Kefr
Bir'im,* it was flanked on either side by statues of lions, which
probably had their prototype in the cherubs. It may be that
in the later synagogues, as at Beth Alpha, the lions had become only a graphic feature, represented in pictorial art on

either side of the Ark. It has been suggested that the lions in the upper panel of the Hammath-by-Gadara mosaic were thought to be guarding the Ark in the nearby apse. At Dura on the lowest zone of the murals two lions (?) flank the niche. Representations of the Ark are known to us from ancient Jewish gilt glass from Rome, where, as on the Beth Alpha mosaic, we also have the two lions, the two birds, candlestick, ram's horn, palm branches, and citron, as well as other figures. The Ark is not only known to us from the murals at Dura and from the synagogue mosaics; it is found twice at Capernaum ornamenting the stonework, once on a cart, while other reliefs come from Chorazin and Pekiin. Also, at Capernaum fragments of miniature architecture came from a double Torah Shrine. The Ark appears on the catacombs at Beth Shearim, accompanied by a lion. Sometimes there was a veil or curtain before the apse or niche, as so clearly indicated at Dura and Beth Alpha, and we remember that a veil was before the Holy of Holies of the temple (cf. Exod. 26:31 ff.; Matt. 27:51, etc.). Sometimes the apse was separated from the prayer-hall by a marble or limestone screen.

Candlesticks

The seven-branched candlestick was to be found in both temple and synagogue. In I Kings 7:49 there are mentioned ten golden lampstands, five on the right and five on the left of the entrance to the Holy of Holies. Jer. 52:19 describes their despoliation in 586 B.C. In Zech. 4:2 ff. is a lampstand with a bowl on top, and on its rim are seven seven-lipped lamps, each of which would have borne seven lights. In I Macc. 4:49 we are told how, at the rededication of the temple in 165 B.C., the lamps on the lampstand were lit—the story of the origin of the Feast of Dedication, Hanukkah. The candlestick of the temple and early synagogues was called, in Hebrew, a Menorah. The seven-branched candlesticks normally appear with small oil lamps at the top of the branches, and are, more properly, lampstands. At the Dura synagogue the Menorah above the niche clearly supports snouted lamps, while the ones on two other panels more probably support cylindrical lamps, although they have been interpreted as

candles. On the mosaics at Beth Alpha and 'Esfiyeh one of a
pair of Menoroth is shown obviously with lamps, and one, apparently, without. That in the latter case candles are intended,
is not certain. In the synagogue at Hammath-by-Tiberias a
stone lampstand was found, and on the upper surface were
seven grooves hollowed out to contain seven pottery lamps.
The branches are carved in alternating pomegranate and
flower designs. Among the finds at the Beth Shearim synagogue was the marble base of a seven-branched lampstand. In
the synagogue the lampstand was placed on either side of the
Ark, and we have a representation of the lampstands inside the
synagogue on a limestone plaque from Jerusalem. This is obviously the inside, and not, as has been assumed, the façade
of the synagogue. A relief showing the seven-branched lampstand of the temple appears on the Arch of Titus at Rome,
and depicts the spoil from the temple at its destruction in
A.D. 70.

There is a certain analogy between the synagogue arrangements (with the elders seated beside the Ark and the lampstands) and the symbolism of Revelation 5:2–8, where the enthroned deity is surrounded by elders, and seven lamps, the
spirits of God, burn before the throne, around which are four
animals. The common prototype may be the ancient conception of God (El) enthroned in the heavenly courts in the midst
of the divine assembly. We have seen that just possibly in Ps.
74:8 the synagogue is called an "Assembly of El."

Seating Arrangements

In contrast with the temple building, the synagogue was a
place inside which one assembled for prayer and study. The
benches for seating have been already noted. In Matt. 23:2 ff.
the scribes and Pharisees are criticized for liking the best places
at dinners, and the front seats of the synagogues, and for having taken "Moses' seat." The front seats were perhaps those
nearest the side of orientation, or, as in some synagogues such
as at Dura and Beth Alpha, the benches on the side of orientation, to the right and left of the niche or apse. These latter
were the seats for the elders, and according to Jewish tradition, the elders sat with their faces towards the people and

their backs to Jerusalem (*Tosephta Megillah* IV. 21). The
"Seat of Moses" was for the most distinguished elder (presbyter) of the synagogue, and apparently placed closest to the
Ark. We have seen that there was such a seat at Dura, probably occupied by Samuel, son of Jedaiah, described both as
priest and as elder of the Jews, who founded the synagogue.
"Seats of Moses" have been found in Palestine at Hammath-by-
Tiberias and Chorazin, the latter bearing a memorial inscription.

The Priest

We find the priest mentioned occasionally in synagogue inscriptions, as at Dura, where Samuel was priest and presbyter,
and in the Jerusalem inscription in which Theodotos is both
priest and *archisynagogos*. At Naaran a memorial inscription
mentions Phineas the priest, who gave a mosaic and a basin
for the synagogue. These would be descendants of the Jerusalem priesthood. If priests and Levites were present in the
synagogue, they took precedence over others in the reading of
the scripture lesson: the order was "priest, Levite, Israelite
. . . for the sake of peace" (*Gittin* V. 8). A part of the service
was the blessing of the priest (*Megillah* IV. 3). The head of
the synagogue was the *archisynagogos*. This official is mentioned several times in the New Testament. Jairus, whose
daughter Jesus healed, was an *archisynagogos* (Mark 5:22;
Luke 8:41). So also was Crispus, converted by Paul (Acts 18:
8). The *archisynagogoi* summoned Paul and Barnabas to
preach (Acts 13:15). The word simply means "head of the
synagogue," as did its Hebrew equivalent. Such an official had
care of the external order in public worship and the general
supervision of the concerns of the synagogue.

Synagogue Inscriptions

Memorial and other inscriptions in Aramaic and Greek are
found frequently in the synagogues. The most common formula begins with the words "Remembered be for good," and
there follows the name of the donor and his gift to the synagogue. Those who gave columns, basins, mosaics, money,

cloths, lintels, scrolls, and candlesticks are thus memorialized.
A Naaran inscription is a petition that Benjamin the Steward
(Parnas), son of Jose, be remembered, as well as anyone who
shall lend his support and give or has given to the synagogue
gold, silver, any precious thing, or any contribution whatever.
At the Jericho synagogue the mosaic inscription is a plea that
the entire holy community, elders and youths, who exerted
themselves and made the mosaic, be remembered and their
names written in the Book of Life. One at Hammath-by-
Gadara is in memory of a family of six, whose acts of charity
were everywhere, and who gave here five *denarii* (a coin mentioned in Matt. 18:28; 20:2, 9, 10, 13). At Beth Alpha it was
prayed that "the craftsmen who carried out the work, Mari-
anos and his son Hanina, be held in remembrance." The inscriptions recall to mind the prayer of Nehemiah: "Remember
me, O my God, concerning this, and wipe not out my good
deeds that I have done for the house of my God, and for its
services" (Neh. 13:14). Professor Sukenik has found in these
memorial synagogue inscriptions the prototype of a prayer recited today in the synagogues on Sabbath morning.

Pictures and Figures in the Synagogue

The Solomonic temple was decorated with cherubs, palm
trees, and opening flowers. As archaeological researches have
shown, these motives were not original with the Hebrews, but
were characteristic of pagan art. Likewise much of the elaborate ornamentation of the synagogues was characteristic of
pagan Syro-Hellenistic art, and many of the motives possessed
religious symbolism. As the cherubs and the palm tree certainly had religious meaning for the Hebrews of the time of
Solomon, so also, we may be sure, many of these apparently
pagan motives had religious meaning for those worshiping in
the synagogue. Goodenough argues with reason that these designs were not all purely decorative, but had symbolic meaning.[3] Some of the designs are more traditionally Jewish, such
as the candlestick, ram's horn, palm branches, pentagram (=
"Seal of Solomon") and hexagram (= "Shield of David"). We

[3] E. R. Goodenough, "Symbolism in Hellenistic Jewish Art," *JBL*,
LVI (1939), 103 ff.

find this representation of animal, bird, human, and mythological figures in strange contrast with the Second Commandment or the prohibition of images in Deut. 4:15–19. Josephus, criticizing the golden eagle placed by Herod over the great gate of the temple, adds that "the law forbids those that propose to live according to it, to erect images or representations of any living creature" (*Ant.* VI. ii. 151). But as a result of archaeological discoveries we are receiving a new appreciation of Hebrew art. Certain passages in Jewish literature are consonant with this fact. We will here quote only the Pseudo–Jonathan Targum at Lev. 26:1, where we read, "A stoa, carved with pictures and figures, you may attach to the borders of a sanctuary, yet not in order to pray to it, for I am the Lord your God." There were occasional iconoclastic reforms against this pictorial representation. The first was probably sometime after A.D. 300, since it did not affect Chorazin, but did result in the mutilation of the animal and human figures at other synagogues, as at Capernaum. The second resulted in the mutilation of the mosaics, perhaps two or three centuries later.

We may mention here but one important type of symbolism. We have noted the use of zodiac signs at Beth Alpha, Naaran, 'Esfiyeh, er-Rafid, Kefr Bir'im, Dura-Europos, and Beth Shearim. The zodiac circle at the first three of these sites calls to mind the relief from a Nabataean Arab temple of the first century B.C. and A.D. at *Khirbet et-Tannur* in Transjordan. In the center is Tyche, surrounded, like the sun-chariot on the synagogue mosaics, by a circular panel containing the cycle of the zodiac. Sukenik has pointed out the close parallels to the representation of the four seasons in pagan Roman art. Josephus and Philo suggest something of the manner in which this pagan symbolism was adapted by the circle of Jews in which they moved. Josephus, ascribing a cosmic significance to the tabernacle, its furnishings, and the garment of the priest, says of the twelve stones: "Whether we understand by them the months, or whether we understand the like number of the signs which the Greeks call the Zodiac, we shall not be mistaken in their meaning." The origin of this symbolism is ascribed to Moses, as also, for instance, the fact that the seven lamps on the candlestick "referred to the course of the planets, of which that is their number." (*Ant.* III. vii. 181–87.) Philo also finds zodiac symbolism in the twelve stones on the priest's breast-plate, in the twelve wings, six each, of the cherubim, in certain aspects of the candlestick, in the twelve springs of Elim, etc.[4] While these biblical associations may have been characteristic of the more enlightened, the general populace may have taken this type of symbolism in a more crudely astrological sense.

We may conclude, as we began, with a word regarding the relation of synagogue and church. One might say that as the New Testament is integrally related to the Old, so the church is integrally related to the synagogue. The church drew upon the synagogue for much of its symbolism, and much of early Christian art is indebted to Jewish art in a way that we cannot attempt to describe here. Both the church and the synagogue buildings were of the basilica type. As Crowfoot has remarked in his description of the "synagogue church" at Gerasa, it was an easy matter to convert a synagogue into a church. The place for the Torah Shrine in the west was removed, and the eastern end was adapted to the Christian liturgy. The synagogue was oriented westward towards Jerusalem, and the church toward the east. Thus the vestibule of the Gerasa synagogue lay beneath the apse of the church. The columns of the synagogue were left standing on the synagogue level, but were now used to support the church, with two columns added. The close relation of church and synagogue may be well illustrated by a photograph from Gerasa, which shows the columns resting on the synagogue floor, and the mosaic floor of the church but a few inches above that of the synagogue. In view of the fine cooperation of Jews and Christians in archaeological research, it is perhaps fitting that this archaeological study of the ancient Jewish synagogues by a Gentile end on this note.[5]

[4] E. R. Goodenough, *By Light, Light* (New Haven, 1935), pp. 98, 112, 113, 209, etc.

[5] Selected bibliography: S. Krauss, *Synagogale Altertümer* (Berlin-Vienna, 1922); H. Kohl and C. Watzinger, *Antike Synagogen in Galilaea* (Leipzig, 1916); E. L. Sukenik, *Ancient Synagogues in Palestine and Greece* (London, 1934). E. R. Goodenough, *Jewish Symbols in the Greco-Roman Period* (New York, 1953–54): "The Synagogues of Palestine," I, 178 ff., "The Synagogues of the Dias-

pora," II, 70 ff., "Symbols from the Jewish Cult," IV, 65 ff. E. L. Sukenik, *The Ancient Synagogue of Beth Alpha* (London, 1923). H. F. Pearson, C. H. Kraeling, *et al.*, "The Synagogue," in *The Excavations at Dura Europos*, VI (New Haven, 1936), ed. M. I. Rostovtzeff. C. H. Kraeling, *ibid.*, VIII, Pt. 1 (1956). R. Wischnitzer, *The Messianic Theme in the Paintings of the Dura Synagogue* (Chicago, 1948).

15

THE EARLIEST CHRISTIAN BOOKS

C. C. McCOWN

Unexpected discoveries of very early New Testament manuscripts during the last thirty years have astonished biblical students almost as greatly as have the Qumran documents. With other new light on early book manufacture and publication they have necessitated marked changes of opinion as to the form in which the New Testament writings originally appeared. With these changes go others which modify and enrich our conceptions of early Christian life and literature. The interesting subject of publication and the book trade in antiquity is beyond the scope of this article, but is taken for granted. It is the subject of manufacture which is here under discussion. Two problems are involved: (1) the form in which books were published, whether in the roll or the leaf book, in technical language the *codex;* and (2) the materials used, whether papyrus or parchment.

Books and Writing Materials

It had long been taken as established that all literary works published in the first centuries of the Christian era were written on rolls. The first great New Testament manuscripts, such as Vaticanus and Sinaiticus of the fourth century, were, indeed, leaf books of parchment, written on both sides of the page and made up of what are now called signatures, quires, or gatherings, bound together like modern books. But only rolls made of papyrus were supposed to have been used before about A.D. 300, and, naturally, it was assumed that all of the New Testament books were originally written on rolls, or, in the case of the very short ones, such as Philemon, 2 and 3 John, and Jude, on single sheets of papyrus.

Papyrus sheets were made from the reed-like papyrus plant, which grew in great abundance in the marshes by the Nile, in Sicily, and elsewhere about the Mediterranean. (It is now cultivated for its decorative value in American and European gardens where water is plentiful.) The pith of the stalk was cut into thin slices which were laid close together in two layers crossing each other. When pressed, dried, and smoothed off, this became a thin sheet much like good modern paper, but more durable and slightly more fibrous. Although there was much variation, sheets of standard size were ten inches high, more or less, being thus somewhat smaller than our customary letter-size paper. The sheets were pasted together at the sides to make long rolls, and "paper" was ordinarily purchased in the roll. The practiced scribe wrote on one side only in fairly narrow columns (two to three inches wide), and then cut off from the roll the portion used.

In Graeco-Roman times the "volume" (i.e., roll) rarely ran to more than thirty-five feet in length. Apparently ancient works were divided into "volumes" for convenience of handling. Manifestly the length depended upon the size of letter used. A magnificent copy of the *Odyssey*, Book III, in the British Museum was so written that it would have required only seven feet. Since a volume was unrolled by the right hand and rolled up again by the left, as column after column was read, a "big book [a long roll] was a big evil," then even more than now. Moreover, written thus on one side only of the roll, a relatively small book made a big roll.

Other writing materials besides papyrus were widely used. Clay tablets in Babylonia, Assyria, and related lands, stone slabs for monumental purposes, broken fragments of pottery (*ostraca*) for receipts, short letters, and other temporary purposes, pieces of wood, leaves, bark, and even bones, are among the materials which nature placed at hand in some abundance. But the only materials which could adequately serve business purposes, aside from papyrus, were wooden tablets and skins, or leather. The latter, the *diphthera* of the Greeks, *membrana* to the Romans, had long been in use, and examples as early as the fifth century B.C., written in Aramaic by Persian officials in Egypt, have recently come to light. According to a Roman tradition, rolls of vellum, or parchment, made, that is, of carefully prepared sheets of leather, were beginning to be popular at least as early as 200 B.C. While in Egypt, the land of papyrus, where alone such perishable stuff could be preserved, parchment was not fashionable until the fifth century A.D., it was doubtless in much more common use in other lands which had to import papyrus.

Leaf Books, or Codices

How early leaf books, or codices, came to be used is still a moot question. It seems fairly certain that they originated out of the use of the other chief writing material, wood. That wood ever competed with papyrus as a material for making books is not to be supposed. But wooden tablets (*tabellae*), covered with a coating of wax within a slightly raised margin, were in wide use all about the Mediterranean for many kinds of writing. The businessman used them for his accounts and records, the politician and literary man for notes and diaries. Apparently they were once used for public records of all kinds. They were commonly employed for letters. The lover wrote on a tablet to his ladylove. She read the note, erased it from the wax with the broad end of the stylus, wrote her reply on the smoothed wax, and sent it back to her suitor. The poet wrote the first drafts of his poems on wax tablets, which allowed him unlimited opportunities of erasure and correction.

It was customary to bind several wax-covered tablets together and thus make them into a sort of book. It is significant that *codex*, or *caudex*, in Latin means primarily the trunk of a tree, possibly because the original from which the leaf book was imitated was a series of strips of wood which, when bound together, look like a portion of a tree trunk. The evidence for this practice of binding tablets together and for its connection with the codex of papyrus or parchment is to be found in explicit statements of various Latin authors, in actual codices of

wooden tablets found in Egypt, and in pictures of women with
a small codex of tablets in one hand and a stylus in the other.
The little set of bound tablets, which we might call a pocket
notebook, the Roman called a "fist book" (*pugillaris*). Both
pictures and literary allusions go back to the first century B.C.
and the literary references presume a long previous history for
the custom.

Literary Works in Parchment Codices

All of this applies to the use of the codex for practical purposes. It can hardly be denied even by the most conservative
that parchment and papyrus codices, made by folding wide
sheets in the middle and binding them together along the fold,
were an imitation of the wooden codex. When they came into
use and especially when they were first employed for literary
works is a question still under debate. Definite statements of
the Roman writer Martial, made about A.D. 84, show that the
practice of using codices of parchment for literary works had
already begun. He alludes to the works of several writers as
having been put into what have been referred to as pocket
editions, and used as gifts at the time of Saturnalia, that is, as
"Christmas presents." They are on parchment and in pages.
In the *Aeneid*, Vergil's picture appeared on the first *tabella*,
which naturally means "page." Martial seems to be especially
enthusiastic over their conveniently small size.

Many scholars have held that Martial's statements imply
that the use of the parchment codex, the leaf book, for literary
works was something new. It may well be, however, that it is
the small size of these editions that was remarkable. Professor
Henry A. Sanders of the University of Michigan, who assembled all of the evidence, believed that such leaf books were
already in use in the time of Augustus and may well go back
to the time of Cicero. Caesar probably wrote his "commentaries" (diaries) on the Gallic war in parchment codices. It seems
hardly likely that he would have carried with him on his campaigns enough wooden tablets to have served for so long a
work, while papyrus rolls would have been scarce. Moreover
Suetonius says definitely that Caesar adopted the pages of a
diary as the medium for sending reports to the Senate. Since

ink could be erased from parchment, a codex of that material would serve almost as satisfactorily as wax tablets for first drafts of literary works, and various allusions seem to establish the fact of such use in the first century B.C. Even if parchment codices were not fashionable for the publication of literary works before the time of Martial, it can hardly be doubted that long before any New Testament book was written, they were in common use for all the purposes that the wooden waxed tablet had served. This means that, when the earliest books of the New Testament were being written, the roll was no longer the only medium even for the publication of books, and that the use of the parchment codex was still more widely known outside of literary circles.

Christian Codices

Within perhaps a half century after Martial wrote his epigrams on the book trade proclaiming the advantages of the parchment codex, Christians were publishing their sacred books in papyrus codices in Egypt. Of this we have contemporary ocular evidence. One of the most unexpected discoveries of recent years in this field was a scrap of a single page of a papyrus codex of the Gospel of John (chap. 18) that practically all competent scholars declare to have been written before A.D. 150. This oldest New Testament text belongs to the John Rylands Library in Manchester. Earlier than A.D. 150 is a papyrus codex of Numbers and Deuteronomy that doubtless came from Christian hands, for it was found with Christian documents (to be described in a moment) and also because Jews did not use the codex for the Scriptures. To mid-century belong three leaves of a hitherto unknown apocryphal Gospel now in the British Museum.

About 1930 there came on sale in Cairo a considerable group of biblical manuscripts of which portions found their way to the universities of Michigan and Princeton and elsewhere, but the greater part was purchased by Mr. Chester Beatty, an American living in England, and was placed in the British Museum. They have been called the most significant discovery for the text of the New Testament since 1844, when Tischendorf discovered the Sinaiticus codex of the Bible in St. Catherine's monastery at Mt. Sinai. The Numbers-Deuteronomy codex is the oldest now known, and, aside from some small fragments of a roll of Deuteronomy, written in the second century B.C., it was the oldest known copy of any biblical text. The Qumran, or Dead Sea Scrolls, now outshine all other witnesses to the Old Testament text. As to manuscript form, they merely confirm the Jewish preference for the roll. There is not a codex among them, according to Professor F. M. Cross, Jr.

The oldest of the Chester Beatty codices contains the letters of Paul from Romans through Thessalonians, including Hebrews after Romans. It is dated at A.D. 200, or a little earlier, and for twenty-five years has been regarded as the earliest considerable New Testament text. In 1956 however, the Bibliotheca Bodmeriana of Cologny, Switzerland, announced the approaching publication of a papyrus codex of John 1–14 that is to be dated between A.D. 150 and 250. The carefully written and well-preserved pages of Bodmer II, and the 176 pages, also clearly written and well preserved, of the Chester Beatty Paul, with 60 pages of the Gospels and Acts from the early third century and 20 pages of Revelation written before A.D. 300, provide extremely valuable evidence as to both text and manuscript form nearly a century and a half before the writing of Vaticanus and Sinaiticus, on which our New Testament text so largely depends. To these is now to be added a part of a page of a parchment codex containing portions of Romans 4 and 5. It was recently purchased in Cairo by Professor L. C. Wyman of Boston University and is dated by the veteran palaeographer, Professor W. H. P. Hatch, about, perhaps a little before, A.D. 300.

The few scholars who, for half a century, had been insisting that the early Christians all along had showed a marked preference for the codex over the roll have been completely justified by the recent discoveries. Also comparative studies of the data regarding copies of other ancient books and those of the Christians establish the fact that the codex, the leaf book that we now use, owes its origin to Christian practice. Whether the papyrus codex was "the book of the poor," as some have claimed, is still uncertain. It clearly was not at first the book of the literary world of leisure, but of practical men who widely ... used and ... literature ... in a more ... easily accessible form.

Of the ... biblical manuscripts written below, 12 are opisthograph, that is, written on the backs of already-discarded ... I am now inclined to ... preference for the literary ... reference to ... Christian ... documents. Only one is left, a ... No New Testament practice has yet been ... among the rolls.

... these New Testament fragments, and the content ... of ... Christian literature. Besides, the Greek ... had been in use for ... Dura ... an exodus from ... manuscript ... Beatty ... belongs to the second century and contains ... Numbers, a leaf of ... and ... Ezekiel and Esther which antedate ... or ... Over against these Christian codices ... Over ... non-Christian codices now known ... and only two on papyrus and two on vellum ... In this very large number of non-Christian literary works ... written on rolls which have been found ... before us in the books. Especially important is the ... a contrast ... significant in the two succeeding centuries. Various ... on rolls and codices of literary works found ... so far discovered made from ... Beatty ... a complete ... which contains ... twenty (by precentory) five interest of ... codex ... numbers based on ... the latest census now before us ...

ROLL AND CODEX IN BIBLICAL AND NON-CHRISTIAN MANUSCRIPTS

Form of Manuscript	Century II		Century II-III		Century III		Century III-IV		Century IV	
	No.	P.c.	No.	P.c.	No.	P.c.	No.	P.c.	No.	P.c.
BIBLICAL										
Papyrus Codex	8	100	3	100	34	82			34	50
Parchment Codex					8	18			34	50
Codex Total	8	100	3	100	42	100			68	100
NON-CHRISTIAN										
Roll	465	97.7	208	97.1	297	83.2	28	51.9	25	26
Papyrus Codex	9	1.9				(5.1)				(42.6)
Parchment Codex	2	0.4				(1.3)				(22.7)
Codex Total	11	2.3	6	2.9	60	16.8	26	48.1	71	74

The above table is based upon figures in Mr. Colin H. Roberts' latest article. I have added two recent manuscripts—the Wyman Romans reported by Professor Hatch and the Bodmer II of John reported by the Reverend Georg Madfeld (see Bibliography). Exact correlation of the shifting and growing data is impossible. Percentages in parentheses are from the previous article in the Biblical Archaeologist, VI (1943). It should perhaps be noted that the above data apply only to Egyptian practice.

wished to have their highly prized, though not yet sacred, literature in a compact, easily accessible form.

Among the biblical manuscripts written before A.D. 400, 12 are rolls: 3 certainly Jewish, 3 more probably so, and 5 are opisthograph, that is, written on the backs of already-discarded "scratch paper." They indicate no preference for the literary roll, but the desire of some poor, or thrifty, Christian for a copy of his religious documents. Only one is left, a copy of the Psalms. No New Testament passage has yet been found on the recto (inside) of a roll.

Along with these New Testament fragments must be counted other examples of early Christian literature. Besides the British Museum apocryphal Gospel and the Chester Beatty Numbers-Deuteronomy, there is an Exodus-Deuteronomy fragment in Baden which belongs to the second century and two other Chester Beatty codices, a leaf of Jeremiah and several from Ezekiel, Daniel, and Esther, which are late second or early third century in date. Over against these Christian codices are to be placed only four non-Christian codices now known to belong to the second century, two on papyrus and two on vellum. In view of the very large number of non-Christian works of this century written on rolls which have been found, the number of Christian leaf books is significant. The relative numbers are equally significant in the two succeeding centuries. Various enumerations of rolls and codices of literary works found in Egypt (the only region thus far discovered, aside from the Judean desert and Negeb, with a climate in which considerable numbers could be preserved) give interesting evidence. The accompanying table, based partly on the latest "census," by Mr. C. H. Roberts, exhibits the data.

Several significant facts are revealed by the comparison. The contrast between Christian and non-Christian custom in the second, third, fourth centuries and the rise of the codex, especially the parchment codex, in favor are notable. In passing, it may be observed that the drop in the number of non-Christian literary works in the fourth century is to be marked as indicating the victory of Christianity. The use of papyrus, rather than vellum, in the earliest Christian codices is no doubt due to their Egyptian origin. As vellum, or parchment, became fashionable, Christians adopted that more durable, probably more expensive, material.

Conclusions and Inferences

After this brief summary of the facts, their interpretation and the conclusions to be drawn are demanded. It is still to be granted that literary works in early Christian times were usually published on rolls of papyrus. But it is clear that, as early as the first century, the parchment and probably the papyrus codex was in use, not only for business and private purposes, but also for publication of literary works.

Since diaries were commonly written in parchment codices and also notes and records were kept in codices of wooden waxed tablets, there is every reason to suppose that the first collections of the sayings of Jesus were jotted down, either on the one or the other type of codex. Some businessman or housewife may have made the first records of Jesus' words along with business or household accounts. Out of such jottings in Aramaic and Greek some earlier "Matthew" or "Luke" may have compiled the "Sayings of Jesus" which were used in the teaching sections of the first and third Gospels. Mark may have noted his translations of Peter's sermons *in membranis,* as Martial would say, that is on the pages of a parchment "fist book."

There is no reason to suppose that the finished books, in most cases, would have been written in rolls. Since the Bible has so long been one of the choicest specimens of literature in the Western world, it has been forgotten, even by many scholars, that originally the New Testament books were not literature at all, even to their own writers and first readers. Paul was writing what, for him and his converts, amounted to business letters discussing pressing problems of church administration and Christian practice. They were neither theology nor literature. Neither he nor his readers dreamed that they would be preserved and elevated to the rank of literature. They were written, not in literary Greek, but in the language of ordinary people. Mark was writing sermons, whether Peter's or not; Matthew, a book of Christian instruction.

The one New Testament book which was almost certainly

published in the roll form was Luke-Acts. Each of the two books would reach about the maximum size of the roll, thirty-two to thirty-five feet. They manifestly are one work. Possibly the first draft was written as one in a codex, with no introductory passage at the beginning of Acts, for they would easily go into such a book. The unevenness of construction in the first verses of Acts may be due to the later division into two of what was originally one book, written in first draft in a codex. On second thought, this history of the beginnings of Christianity, which has so many marks of literary composition and intention, may have been divided and published in two rolls in order to gain the attention of people of "honorable estate," like Theophilus.

Other attractive hypotheses, not yet demonstrable, may be based on the probable use of the codex for the earliest Christian books. Since the codex was so well known in Rome, it may be taken as almost certain that the first draft of the "Roman Gospel," Mark, would have been written *in membranis* and probably also the earliest copies would have been made in codices. One may doubt whether it was ever distributed in roll form. The codex form would explain the loss of the ending of the Gospel. In rolls it is usually the beginning of the book which has suffered damage, since that usually is outside. In the codex the last leaf was most likely to suffer.

A peculiarity of Luke's Gospel may also be explained on the same assumption. Luke's "great omission" of Mark 6:44 to 8:26 has puzzled students of the Synoptic problem. If Mark was published as a codex, the loss of a few leaves from Luke's copy would explain the omission. In many early codices, the gatherings consisted of but one sheet, folded so as to make two leaves, or four pages. That is the case in the Chester Beatty Codex I, the Gospels-Acts, volume. It is also the form of the codices of all of the papyri found by the Colt expedition at 'Auja el-Hafir in southern Palestine. That simple, but not very solid, form of book was, therefore, long in use. If Luke's copy of Mark were of that style, the loss of four or more pages would have been easy. The apparent dislocations which spoil the connections in John's Gospel and the strange combination of three letters of Paul in II Corinthians are likewise more easily explained on the supposition that these books were put together from worn leaf books and papyrus sheets which had become disarranged.

The development of the codex seems almost providential. When Paul's letters were collected, toward the end of the first century, they could be put into one handy volume, whereas they would have demanded two cumbersome rolls. A little later the Gospels with the Book of Acts could appear together. Three handy volumes included the whole, even in manuscript form.

The simple, practical, nonliterary character of early Christianity is emphasized by what the recent discoveries have proved regarding their use of the codex. The Christians' religious books, both the Old Testament and the new writings which were in process of becoming sacred, were not for the leisurely reading of the well-to-do. Hard-working business people wanted as much as they could get into a book. They and the earnest Christian missionaries wished to be able to refer to this or that proof text quickly, without having to unroll many feet of papyrus. They were not dominated by any snobbish literary pretensions. Like the contents of the books, the form in which they appeared was a product of the vital moral and religious spirit which in some two centuries conquered the Roman Empire.

BIBLIOGRAPHY

McCown, C. C., "Codex and Roll in the New Testament," *Harvard Theological Review*, XXXIV (October, 1941), 219–50.

Hatch, W. H. P., *HTR*, XLV (1952), 79–85.

Madfeld, Georg, *Novum Testamentum*, I (1956), 153–55; *New Testament Studies*, III (1956), 79–81.

Roberts, Colin H., "The Codex," *Proceedings of the British Academy*, XL (1954), 171–204, with full references.

Sanders, Henry A., "Beginnings of the Modern Book," *Michigan Alumnus Review*, XLIV (February, 1938), 95–111.

The second, third, and fourth references I owe to Professor Jack Finegan; see also his article, "The Original Form of the Pauline Collection," *HTR*, XLIX (1956), 85–103. Professor Cross's statement regarding the absence of the codex at Qumran, I owe to the kind intervention of one of the editors of this volume.

16

EXPLORING THE MANUSCRIPTS OF SINAI AND JERUSALEM

KENNETH W. CLARK

For centuries there have remained unexplored in the Near East valuable deposits of ancient manuscripts. Occasional discoveries there have served only to emphasize the need for thorough investigations. For example, it was at Saint Catherine's monastery that Constantine Tischendorf discovered in 1859 a manuscript of the entire Bible in Greek. Written in the fourth century, Codex Sinaiticus has come to stand second only to Codex Vaticanus in age and importance, for these two sister codices are the chief sources of our New Testament text today. Again, it was in the same monastery thirty years later that Rendel Harris discovered in a Syriac manuscript the lost text of the second-century *Apologia* of Aristides, and this discovery led to its identification with the Greek original imbedded in a longer work already possessed. Another discovery was that of Archbishop Bryennios in 1873 in Constantinople when he recognized the texts of the Didache and II Clement in a Greek manuscript written in 1056 by Leo the Notary (now in the Greek Patriarchal Library in Jerusalem). Such discoveries have shown how urgent it has been to explore the great collections in the Near East.

In 1949–50 such an exploration was at last made possible. The plan was double-pronged, designed to explore two of the largest and the least accessible libraries. First, under the auspices of the American Foundation for the Study of Man in be-

half of the Library of Congress and in cooperation with the
University of Alexandria (Egypt), one expedition was dis-
patched to Saint Catherine's Monastery in the wilderness of
Sinai; second, under the auspices of the American Schools of
Oriental Research and the Library of Congress, another expe-
dition was sent to Jerusalem. Under appointment by the
Schools as Annual Professor in Jerusalem for 1949–50, the
writer served as General Editor in these expeditions.

I. SAINT CATHERINE'S MONASTERY IN SINAI

The Sinai expedition gathered a larger personnel and more
diversified specialists, and remained in the monastery longer,
than had been possible on any previous expedition. A long list
of expeditions is known, from the sixteenth century on, of Ital-
ians, French, English, Russians, Greeks, and Americans—first,
consular representatives; then, ecclesiastical representatives;
and last, scholars of the academic world. Each was a small
group and usually stayed only a brief period. The objective,
especially in earlier centuries, was to discover and acquire notable codices to carry away.

A different objective is reflected in the expedition of Kyrillos,
a librarian from Mount Athos, who in 1840 made the first
significant attempt at cataloguing when he listed indiscrimi-
nately about 1500 manuscripts and printed volumes. About
the same time the Archimandrite Porphyrios Ouspensky made
repeated visits to secure descriptions of numerous manuscripts selected from the Greek collection, though these were
never published until used by Beneshevitch. In 1870 Antonin
Kapoustine visited the monastery, and catalogued 1310 Greek
manuscripts, 500 Arabic, 38 Slavic, and some Syriac. He is reported to have taken with him a photographer, and this may
have been the first use of photography at the monastery. It
was in 1880 that Victor Gardthausen spent forty days alone
at the monastery and catalogued 1223 Greek manuscripts,
having been shown about 1000 and adding the rest from the
data of Antonin. Rendel Harris' second expedition in 1893 resulted in checklists of the Arabic and Syriac collections by Mrs.
Gibson and Mrs. Lewis, sisters from Cambridge. Caspar René

Gregory, whose world checklist of Greek New Testament manuscripts became official fifty years ago, was refused permission to explore the Sinai library. Vladimer N. Beneshevitch spent a few months at the monastery in 1907, 1908, and 1911 to accumulate a catalogue of 2151 Greek manuscripts, using much of Ouspensky's data, and carrying on where Gardthausen left off.

The expedition of 1949–50 had an objective different from that of any previous expedition. It was neither to search for special treasures, nor to acquire manuscripts for western libraries, nor to prepare library catalogues. The objective was to examine the entire library of manuscripts in all languages and to select the most important texts to reproduce on microfilm, in order that this selected portion might be made accessible to all scholars and be submitted to manifold researches. The plan was to assemble an adequate group of specialists to match the varied resources of the monastery collection, and to remain long enough to accomplish thorough results. It was to require about twenty co-laborers, and a seven-month operation, to explore the entire collection and to record the selected portion permanently on film.

Initial negotiations with Archbishop Porphyrios III and his Synod, and with the Egyptian Foreign Office, were conducted by Wendell Phillips, President of the American Foundation for the Study of Man. By December of 1949 the expedition was assembled in Cairo under the Field Director, William Terry. There were six Americans, a Belgian, and five Egyptians who formed the core of the staff, besides other Egyptian and Greek associates. The General Editor (from the American School in Jerusalem) and the Chief Photographer (from the Library of Congress) remained throughout the operation, while other members served for varying periods. At times the group was further enlarged by visitors.

An expedition of such size, duration, and objectives required extraordinary equipment and supplies. From America came four motor vehicles especially equipped for desert travel, two gasoline generators and heavy cable, a typewriter and other office equipment, and medical supplies. The Library of Congress sent three microfilm cameras with book boxes, a 4 x 5 viewing camera, more than 1000 rolls of microfilm, and other accessories. From Egypt were secured beds and bedding, dishes, cutlery, hardware, fuel for generators and stoves and lamps and the busy vehicles, and great quantities of food. With bases in Cairo and at Abu Rudeis, *en route* on the coast of Sinai, the principal establishment for the expedition was at the monastery. The monks assigned to us large rooms for work and living, convenient to the library. The expedition cook prepared all meals for our personnel.

The Sinai Library

In the sixth century Procopius, historian under Justinian, wrote that the emperor provided some books for the monks of Sinai. Since then, throughout the centuries, the monks have copied many manuscripts for themselves. The earliest scribal signature at Saint Catherine's is found in an uncial copy of the Psalter (Gr. 32) of the eighth century. The scribe was Michael the Priest, of Sinai, who wrote his note in Cufic; he claimed that "contact with this book will heal pain," and vowed that the despoiler "will have no share with Mother Mary." One of the most impressive books made at Sinai is a large Lectionary of the Gospels written about 1200 and beautifully rebound in votive silver-gilt in the sixteenth century (Gr. 209). A scribal colophon affirms: "God will save those who made this *Evangelion,* the one who bore the expense and those who wrote it—two monks of Sinai."

The most prominent Sinai scribe was the Archbishop Arsenius (1290–99) who copied at least five books and wrote both Greek and Arabic. A number of Sinai manuscripts are bilingual, mostly in Greek and Arabic, some in Greek and Turkish, ranging from A.D. 800–1350; and there is one Arabic-Coptic *Horologion* of the thirteenth century. These bilingual codices also suggest a Sinai origin, although they are unsigned. A century after the first printing press, Joasaph the Monk (Gr. 1552), Macarius the Monk (Gr. 92), and Nicephorus Nathaniel of Crete (Gr. 87, 124) were among those who copied books at Sinai. The printing press which first appeared in Germany about 1450 did not soon affect the making of books in the Near East, especially in the monasteries. In Palestine a press began operation in 1588, but printing was not effective in Asiatic Turkey until the eighteenth century; and even then ecclesiastical works were restricted. Furthermore, both habit and poverty would determine that books continue to be produced in the monasteries by hand.

Many other manuscripts in the Sinai library were brought in by new members of the order. Notes in the books themselves make it clear that many a monk brought a small library with him, and that many books were brought to be dedicated in the church. Some of these monks had produced their own books elsewhere and later brought them to Sinai. Special gifts of manuscripts were made by the Patriarch Joachim of Alexandria (fl. 1550), the Bishop of Cythere in 1602 (nine cases of books and many manuscripts), and the Patriarch Nektarios of Jerusalem (fl. 1660).

A number of Sinai manuscripts are copies of works originally composed by Sinai monks; for example, there are twenty copies of "The Ladder of Paradise" by John Climacus, who dwelt in the Sinai desert in the sixth century. Another author represented is the ascetic Saint Nilus (fl. 375), who had been an officer in the court of the Emperor Theodosius but who left wife and daughter in Constantinople and took his son to live on Sinai's peak. Other Sinai authors of the sixth and seventh centuries were Nicon, Kosmas Indicopleustes, John Moschos, Anastasios, and Daniel of Raithos. By about 1700 the numerous convents and hermit cells throughout the area were abandoned and the monks gathered into the great monastery, along with their books. It is stated by Beneshevitch that Archbishop Kosmas I (1702-7) was the first to put the library in order and to prepare a catalogue.

The book collection remained informal and even neglected for a long time. In 1674 the French consul at Cairo spent 1000 pounds to acquire some of the manuscripts, on instructions by Colbert. A French expedition in 1697 even included two merchants from Marseilles. Michael Eneman of Uppsala in 1712 reproached the monks for their negligence because the manuscripts were all piled along the wall "as I have never seen." When in 1715 the Jesuit scholar, Claude Sicard, reached Sinai the monks complained that manuscripts were lost whenever they opened the library. Nevertheless, he succeeded in acquiring some for the King of France. Sicard reported that the manuscripts had been moved often and were in general confusion, but in 1735 Archbishop Nicephorus built a new library and charged the Monk Isaiah with assembling and arranging all the books. A century later the Russian, A. Oumantz, described the library as "a small section lined with book shelves" in which the books were heaped in complete disorder. Tischendorf and Ouspensky about 1844 report that the books were shelved in alphabetical order, by contents. But M. Bonar declared in 1856 that he "saw books in utter confusion but that another room and better bookcase were being prepared." Gardthausen reports as late as 1880 that the manuscripts were collected in four different places in the monastery. The final move came about 1945 when a great structure along the south wall included a large and light, fireproof room where the manuscripts today stand in good order, in cleanliness and security.

Earlier explorers at Sinai returned with estimates that were sometimes glowing and sometimes completely deflating. The first to describe the library was Michael Eneman, eminent orientalist of the University of Uppsala. He reports finding in 1712 numerous Greek, Arabic, Coptic, and Syriac manuscripts, some in the library and others in a large double cupboard in the church, printed books and parchment manuscripts of all ages. Probably his "Coptic" manuscripts were Ethiopic. About the same time (1715) Claude Sicard revealed that despite their losses "their library is still very numerous, rich especially in Greek, Russian, Arabic, Syriac, Abyssinian, and others." These are exactly the chief languages found in 1950, if by "Russian" is meant Georgian and Slavonic, and by "Abyssinian" is meant Ethiopic. A Polish religious in 1729 made a catalogue of about 300 books, in print and manuscript. But in 1739, R. Pococke returned with the estimate that there is "no rare manuscript, but a few incunabula." Vitaliano Donati in 1761 claims to have seen the entire library and to have found a large quantity of very old manuscripts ("Greci, Arabi, Soriani, Caldei, Illirici, and Etiopi . . ."). Beneshevitch says that Donati was the first to mention Codex Sinaiticus when the latter reported: ". . . in ispecie una Biblia in membrane bellissime, assai grandi, sottili, e quadre scritta in carattere

rotondo e bellissime . . ." (". . . especially a Bible written in
round and beautiful letters on most beautiful parchment sheets
which are quite large, thin, and square. . . .") This is quoted
by Beneshevitch in *Texte und Forschungen zur Byzantinisch-
Neugriechischen Philologie*, No. 21 (1937), p. 21. In 1815,
W. Turner was told by the Sinai monks that they had only
three Greek biblical manuscripts, but W. J. Banks found 1500
manuscripts (1350 Greek) and 500 printed books. Between
1816 and 1838, Rifaud found the collection "poor in manuscripts," de Geramb estimated it "still considerable," J. L.
Burkhardt guessed at 1500 Greek manuscripts ("none worthy
of attention") and 700 Arabic, Robinson reported 1500 manuscripts, and Combes believed there were 3000. But John Wilson in 1843 thought Burkhardt had exaggerated, and even Tischendorf on his second visit of 1853 estimated the manuscripts
to number only 500 to 1000. Gardthausen in 1880 was shown
only 1000 Greek manuscripts and declared that only Antonin
Kapoustine knew of any more.

The reasons for all this confusion are several. First, the books
were kept until recently in several places in the monastery and
in Cairo. Second, the monks were not consistently cooperative
with all visitors. Third, many of the vistors made fleeting, and
often inexpert, exploration of the collection. Again, some
searched only for the sensational and counted all else insignificant. Perhaps most important, manuscripts and printed books
were as one to the monks. All alike were "books" and even
catalogues did not distinguish between them. Great age in a
manuscript copy was a detriment rather than an asset—a
legible text was the thing. The collection must have reached
its present size long ago, except for a few monastery record
books in Greek. The more extended catalogues of Kyrillos
(1840) and Antonin (1870) and Gardthausen (1880) and
Kondakov (1881) reported only a small part of the collection
which even then existed. A more adequate accounting was
made by Mesdames Lewis and Gibson (1894) and Beneshevitch (1914). The expedition of 1950 should be definitive in
this matter, for the entire library of 3,300 manuscripts—as distinguished from perhaps 10,000 printed books—in all languages, has now for the first time been explored book by book.

The Manuscripts

On January 23, 1950 we were first admitted to the library. We chose to examine first a dozen choice volumes kept in a special cupboard, only three of which had been described by Gardthausen. We began with a Lectionary of the Gospels (Gr. 207) completely encased in a silver-gilt box-cover, Russian art of the sixteenth century. On the front of this votive cover was depicted the Resurrection, and on the back the Crucifixion. The front panel showed the four Evangelists, and on the top panel appeared Virgin and Child with Moses and Saint Catherine. The text of this manuscript was written in the twelfth century, and it includes contemporary portraits of the Evangelists John and Luke. Another twelfth-century lectionary (Gr. 208) was equally impressive with a silver-gilt cover showing the Voivode John Michael and two others kneeling, and bearing the inscription of the Voivode John Alexander whose rule included Sinai. Another lectionary (Gr. 213), called the "Gospel of Mount Horeb," was first reported by Ouspensky in 1845 who noted the scribal colophon by Evstathios the Presbyter in A.D. 967.

The manuscript most prized by the monks, in this special group, is the Theodosius Lectionary called the "Golden Gospels" (Gr. 204). It is a noble book on fine parchment, in large golden uncials throughout, written about A.D. 1000. The 1704 Catalogue of the Archbishop Kosmas I may have referred to it, as "a very beautiful *Evangelion*." Hippolyte Vichensky saw it in 1709 in the Basilica of the Transfiguration, and at that time repeated the claim that the Emperor Justinian was the scribe. When Lord Prudhoe looked at it in 1827 he offered 250 pounds for it, but the sixty monks could not agree on how the money would be used and so declined the offer. It was not included in the 1840 Catalogue of Kyrillos, and was kept even from Tischendorf in 1844. Kondakov again tried to buy it in 1881, offering 1000 pounds from an English Lord. Today the monks tell that the Emperor Theodosius was the scribe who produced this book; however, in the library catalogue, it is attributed to the tenth century. It is probable that the monks refer either to Theodosius II (408–51) who assumed the epithet "Calligraphos," or to Theodosius III who retired to a monastery after A.D. 717.

We next examined a manuscript already famous (Gr. 1186) because it contains fifty-seven illustrations for the rare text of a well-known traveler, Kosmas Indicopleustes of the sixth century. The twelve books of this cosmographia, which opposed the earth's roundness, have been recovered from only a few manuscripts, and this copy was made in the twelfth century. His namesake, Archbishop Kosmas I, was the first to report this manuscript, in 1704. Ouspensky saw it in 1845, and may have extracted the four missing miniatures. The last item from the special cupboard was the small "Psalter of Cassia," written in the fourteenth century. This is a leather-bound book only 5 x 3 inches, in which 151 Psalms are written on only six paper folios in a microscopic but clear hand, and in this same century Archbishop Joseph wrote on the flyleaf that it "belongs to the Monastery of Mount Sinai." It was mentioned as early as 1709 by Vichensky, who reported the tradition that the Virgin Saint Epistimi had written it. The story is told that Epistimi and her husband, Galaktion, decided to withdraw from the world. From Emesa they traveled ten days to reach Mount Sinai, where they found separate dwellings. Galaktion joined ten hermits, while Epistimi with four virgins lived in a neighboring convent hid among the mountains. Both Galaktion and Epistimi were martyred, and the separate convent was later used to house slaves sent in by Justinian. The story does not tell how the name of Epistimi came to be connected with the charming little Psalter. Such were the manuscripts from the Treasury that made up our first day of work, and all of which were photographed completely.

The oldest Greek manuscript found at Saint Catherine's (Gr. 212) is a lectionary with readings from the Gospels and Pauline Epistles. It was written in the seventh century, and a still earlier Greek text (unidentified) lies beneath this. This old codex has lost its covers and become disarranged. Especially notable is a tenth-century copy of Eusebius' "Ecclesiastical History" which includes "The Martyrs of Palestine" (Gr. 1183). Most impressive is the Chrysostom collection of more than thirty manuscripts, of which the oldest is from the eighth century (Gr. 491) and one is the earliest dated Greek manuscript at Sinai, A.D. 893 (Gr. 375). Smyslajev wrote in 1865 that there were "four volumes of the works of Saint John Chrysostom, they say by his own hand or, according to the opinion of scholars, by a hand contemporary with the saint" (i.e. in the fourth century). A hope so great is not fulfilled at Sinai. But the patristic manuscripts are numerous and because of their miscellaneous character have yet to reveal their contents in detail. In this class of materials, hope of important discovery is high.

There are more than 500 manuscripts of biblical text at Saint Catherine's, in five languages (200, Old Testament; 300, New Testament). More than 300 of these are in Greek, of which 175 contain New Testament text which are now for the first time under study. One complete New Testament (Gr. 1342) of the thirteenth century contains a canon of twenty-nine books, as follows: Gospels, Paul, Acts, Catholics, III and IV Maccabees. Two other New Testaments begin with the Psalter, one of them concluding with the Gospels. Only three complete Testaments include the Apocalypse of John, the book for which the fewest witnesses exist today. In contrast, there are sixty-five copies of the Gospels and seventy-five lectionaries of the Gospels, ranging from the seventh century to the seventeenth. There are more than a hundred Psalters, several of which were copied in the eighth and ninth centuries. Such is the wealth of Greek biblical material, and all of this is now available.

The chief treasure at Sinai today is the Codex Syriacus (Syr. 30) discovered by Mrs. Lewis in 1892 on her first visit to the monastery. It is an old copy (A.D. 778) of the "Lives of Holy Women," but Mrs. Lewis detected underneath a Syriac text of the Gospels written about A.D. 400. Today this manuscript is one of two on which the Old Syriac version is based. Many of the Syriac manuscripts at Sinai are very ancient: e.g., a Four Gospels, and a fragment of the Acts and Epistles, of the sixth century; I Samuel, the Works of Dionysius the Areopagite, the Gospel of Luke, and Pauline Epistles, from the seventh century. There are complete New Testaments in the shorter Syrian canon, from the eighth and ninth centuries. The earliest dated Syriac manuscript at Sinai was written in A.D. 758 and contains the Works of Mar Isaiah (Syr. 38). The

Georgian manuscripts are amazingly early, for more than fifty were written before A.D. 1100, and the earliest is a Triodion dated in 852 (Geo. 5). One book of Homilies, found separated and listed as three (Geo. 32-57-33), was written in A.D. 864. Many of the bindings of the Georgian manuscripts appeared to be the original. At least one cover contained papyrus stiffening but permission to investigate further was not granted.

The second language in Sinai has long been Arabic. It was therefore no surprise to find that the Arabic collection is very large, including about a hundred biblical manuscripts. The two oldest contain the Acts and Epistles (Arab. 154 and 151), written in the eighth century and in A.D. 867. Other ninth-century copies contain the Old Testament, Gospels, Pauline Epistles, and the Wisdom of Ben Sirach. Perhaps the most interesting of the Arabic manuscripts is a palimpsest first noted by Mrs. Gibson in 1902 (Arab. 514). This Arabic miscellany of the early tenth century was written upon parchment from two books, one a sixth-century Syriac Peshitta text and the other a seventh-century Greek text. Other languages represented in the great Sinai library are Ethiopic, Latin, Armenian, Persian, Turkish, and Coptic.

At Work

The monks agreed to open the library for the expedition seven hours a day, six days a week. The Abbot, Father Joachim, was responsible for this fabulous collection and faithfully supervised every moment through seven months. He was assisted chiefly by the twenty-eight year old novice, Evstratios, an Alexandrian who entered the order in 1948 after serving as a mechanic in the Royal Air Force. The monks arose at three-thirty in response to the bells and simantron, and performed the liturgy in the Great Church from four until seven-thirty. We arose at six-thirty, in the winter chill at 5000 feet altitude and always in the shadow of mountains. Eight o'clock found us at the library door, prepared to select manuscripts for the morning's work. Five or six departments worked simultaneously and each one had to be supplied until noon when all manuscripts were again returned to the library. Two hours of intermission were consumed by lunch, walking in the sun to dispel the chill, and preparing for the afternoon's work. Again at two o'clock the scores of manuscripts were carried in large baskets along the fourth floor balcony to the work room sixty feet away. The three microfilming cameras had a daily capacity for twenty-five manuscripts and 300 firmans (see below). Often mutilated manuscripts had to be reconstructed or repaired before microfilming. Books bound in disorder required special instructions to the photographer. Separate parts were often identified and reunited, and "missing" manuscripts recovered. But in the course of seven months the entire library was examined and more than half was photographed. The basic criterion was to select all manuscripts before A.D. 1600, except that the limit was placed at A.D. 1400 for the abundant liturgical manuscripts. All biblical texts were selected, whatever the date. Commentaries and patristic texts were given high priority. A substantial representation of Byzantine musical types was obtained. The smaller language groups were microfilmed completely—Georgian, Slavonic and Ethiopic. About half of the larger collections was microfilmed—Greek, Arabic and Syriac. Scholars and institutions, in America and Europe and Egypt, submitted special requests for texts needed in their researches. These provided guidance to the editors who sought to fulfil every request and thus to serve researches already in process.

STATISTICS OF SINAI LIBRARY AND MANUSCRIPTS FILMED

	In Library	Filmed
Greek	2291	1087
Arabic	600	305
Syriac	257	159
Georgian	88	88
Slavonic	40	40
Ethiopic	6	6
Totals	3282	1687

Special Features

A notable discovery in 1950 was a large collection of firmans in Arabic and Turkish. These are official documents, issued by

Muslim rulers, for the protection of this Christian monastery through centuries of Muslim rule. The existence of this type of document was mentioned by Archbishop Nektarios in his history of Sinai in 1660, and again by Ouspensky in 1850. An ill-fated expedition in 1914 by Bernhard Moritz and Carl Schmidt, all of whose photographs were destroyed when war broke out, had found a hundred of these, the earliest of which was a decree in Fatimid times, A.D. 1130 (Firman 962). But in 1950, more and more of these were found until they numbered in all 1,742, beginning with a deed issued in 1040 (Firman 237). The entire collection is now on microfilm and forms a newly accessible historical resource.

Dated manuscripts at Sinai are numerous but they have not yet been employed in palaeographical studies. There are thirty-two examples up to A.D. 1200, none of which are included in the great Lake corpus. The oldest shows a hand of A.D. 893; four fall in the tenth century; thirteen, in the eleventh; and fourteen, in the twelfth. But because most Greek manuscripts extant were written between 1200 and 1600, the need for palaeographical studies in this period is urgent. The primary sources for this study are now abundantly supplemented, for Sinai has yielded about 160 examples well distributed over the four centuries. The 1950 expedition microfilmed all manuscripts dated before 1600 and, indeed, representative groups for the two centuries following. Many a Sinai manuscript is signed by the scribe who, with but few exceptions, becomes a new acquaintance among medieval scribes within our knowledge.

A surprising collection of secular, even non-Christian, materials was found in this monastic library. For example, classical works include Homer's Iliad, the plays of Sophocles and Euripides, the aphorisms of Hippocrates, and Aristotle on logic, politics, ethics and rhetoric. Represented are Clitophon the Rhetor, the sophists Theon and Libanius, Plutarch, Apollonius of Rhodes, Galen, Herodianus, and even the Sibylline Oracles (Gr. 1409) copied as late as the eighteenth century. A wide range of interest among the monks is reflected in manuscripts on philosophy, mathematics, astronomy, cosmography, geography, history, medicine, law, grammar, lexicography, rhetoric, and musical theory.

The art of Sinai is breath-taking. Hundreds of icons of all ages, treasures in gold and silver and precious gems, beautiful fabrics in ecclesiastical robes—all these are found outside the library. Within the library are fine examples of metal book-covers, some of which have been mentioned above. But primarily attention of the expedition was fixed upon the illuminations in the manuscripts, which start as early as the ninth century. Already well known are the famous Job (Gr. 3) whose text is enlivened with twenty-five illustrations, the Kosmas Indicopleustes (Gr. 1186) richly illuminated with fifty-seven paintings, and the twelfth-century copy of John of the Ladder (Gr. 418) with forty-three fascinating illustrations. Little known, however, was a complete New Testament preceded by the Psalter (Gr. 2123), which was found in the convent in Cairo. It bears a scribal date of 1242 and is adorned with thirty illuminations, which include portraits of Michael and John Paleologus and a sphere (!) representing the world. A most amazing picture gallery was discovered in a sixteenth-century Sacred History. There are 367 illustrations lavishly spread over 205 folios. The text is a metrical paraphrase of Genesis and Exodus, by Georgios Choumnos, and is preserved in only three or four other copies, one of which in the British Museum (Add. 40724) also bears a Sinai colophon. More than one hundred Sinai manuscripts contain miniatures, comprising a corpus of 1284 paintings, all of which have now been photographed with a 4 x 5 camera which the expedition took to Sinai especially for this purpose.

II. THE JERUSALEM GREEK PATRIARCHATE

The other prong in the 1949–50 plan of exploration was directed at Jerusalem, where one of the great manuscript libraries of the Near East is found in the Patriarchate of the Greek Orthodox Church, established in A.D. 451 by the Council of Chalcedon. This library is really a collection of libraries for they were gathered together only about seventy years ago. The nucleus was the collection of the Holy Sepulcher and to this was added the large and ancient library of Mar Saba, the sixth-century monastery in the Judean hills. Other smaller libraries were merged, from the convent of the Holy Cross (now within Israel), the Chapel of the Resurrection, and the Chapel of Abraham, besides a few other minor groups. Although Jerusalem is not as inaccessible as Sinai, this important library has been neglected almost as badly.

The expedition to Jerusalem was undertaken by the American Schools of Oriental Research, and the Jerusalem personnel was different from that for Sinai except for three members of the Jerusalem School and the Library of Congress photographer. The writer opened negotiations with the Patriarchate soon after arrival in Jerusalem in August, 1949. His Beatitude, the Patriarch Timotheus II, and the Synod granted permission for work in the library until Christmas, when we expected to leave for Sinai. In the following spring, this permission was extended to make possible a complete exploration of the entire library which was three-fourths as large as the Sinai library. It so happened that the Jerusalem expedition assembled first, early in November, 1949. The Library of Congress photographer brought cameras and film by plane, and a generator also was received from the United States. In Jerusalem, expedition headquarters were established in the American School, from which daily trips to the Patriarchate were made. The librarian, Father Aristovulos, received us daily, at eight each morning, and by his friendly and capable assistance enabled us to complete a systematic exploration. (This priest has now become the Archbishop of Kyriakoupolis, or resident Archbishop in Amman, capital of Jordan.)

The Manuscripts

It was November 14, 1949, when we began to work through the hoard of 2,400 manuscripts, in eleven languages, whose texts ranged from the fifth century to the eighteenth. The oldest text found was a Greek fragment of the Wisdom of Ben Sirach, which had earlier been identified in the underwriting of palimpsest folios used for repair in the twelfth century. The later writing of this codex (Taphou 2) is a ninth-century copy of the Septuagint, which impressed Lord Curzon on his pilgrimage to Mar Saba in 1833. Another Greek palimpsest (Stavrou 36) contains an eighth-century text of Chrysostom on Job under a twelfth-century text of Basil of Coes. Still another (Taphou 36) has a tenth-century text of Euripides under a twelfth-century text of the Old Testament prophets. There were found a dozen manuscripts of the works of John of Damascus, himself a monk at Mar Saba in the eighth century. Chrysostom's influence was reflected in no less than sixty-five copies of his works, in Greek, Georgian, Arabic, and even Ethiopic. Half of these Chrysostom manuscripts had belonged to Mar Saba, including four copies from the ninth century. One of the most notable manuscripts now in Jerusalem is a copy containing the "Apostolic Fathers" (Taphou 54). This was written in 1056 by Leo the Notary, and has now become an important source for the Greek text of I Clement, II Clement, Epistle of Barnabas, the Didache, and the Ignatian epistles both genuine and spurious. This manuscript was formerly in the Metochion of the Holy Sepulcher in Constantinople where Bryennios found it in 1873.

The Jerusalem library possesses a wealth of biblical texts, about 270 in all languages (80, Old Testament; 190, New Testament). There were found Gospels and Psalters in Greek, Arabic, Georgian, Syriac, Slavonic, and Ethiopic. Only four copies of the Apocalypse of John were found, all in Greek. But of the Gospels, including lectionaries, there were 140 copies in all languages, about 90 of which are Greek. Gregory had listed these New Testament Greek manuscripts by 1909, but they have now become accessible to textual critics. The Jerusalem library is not as rich in classical authors as is Sinai, but nevertheless there are manuscripts of Homer, Euripides, Plato, Aristotle, Hippocrates, and the later Eutropius whose history is contained in the only Latin manuscript in the library (Taphou 27). Special interest in Aristotle is evidenced by numerous texts of late date. Liturgical manuscripts, and especially books of music, are less abundant than in Sinai. Next to the Greek, the most impressive collection in the Greek Patriarchal library is the Georgian. It was found to consist of 160 manuscripts, many of them as early as the eleventh century and three were explicitly dated in that century.

This library has already made a significant contribution to Greek palaeographical studies, for the Lake corpus reproduces folios from all its dated manuscripts up to A.D. 1200, fifteen in number, the earliest of which was written about A.D. 900. But for the next four centuries, in which palaeographical materials are greatly needed, the Greek Patriarchal library contains more than fifty examples of dated manuscripts. Altogether, the expedition photographed about 150 dated Greek manuscripts in Jerusalem. Numerous scribal signatures in these manuscripts will add further to our knowledge of medieval scribes.

In the Treasury was found a complete New Testament in Greek, which has not hitherto been noted. It was written in the eleventh century and contains miniatures of the evangelists. Its cover is of gold, with green and blue enamel representations of the Crucifixion and Resurrection, and Russian inscriptions. There were also three regal copies of the Gospel lectionary, sixteen inches tall, with covers of gold and evangelist portraits. The metal covers are Russian work of about A.D. 1600. One of these, the "Golden Gospels," bears the signature of the Patriarch Theophanes who brought it to the Holy Sepulcher in 1605. Another one, which contains several pages of gold writing, was a gift to the Voivode of Moldavia by Gabriel in 1670 and was later presented in the Holy Sepulcher as a votive offering. The other copy was a gift from the Voivode of Bessarabia whose portrait appears in the volume. These along with other Gospels in Georgian and Slavonic, previously unrecorded, were brought out from the Treasury and photographed. One of the finest manuscripts, a Lectionary of the Gospels, was brought from the Convent of the Virgin where it continues in use. It was written in 1061 by a certain John "by great sweat and toil." In the thirteenth century this codex belonged to the Monastery of Saint Gerasimos "beside the Jordan River in the Jericho Plain." A century later it was placed in the Jerusalem convent in memory of the nun Euphrosyne of Trebizond, who possessed it until her death. In 1615 it was adorned in its present gold covers by a Jerusalem artisan.

The miniatured manuscripts are remarkable, and several have previously been much studied. However, complete photography of these, as well as of others unknown, was a desideratum. About 750 paintings were reproduced, drawn from about fifty codices. There was the wonderful gallery of Job illustrations in Taphou 5, of the thirteenth century; the

eleventh-century Gregory Nazianzen (Taphou 14); the thirteenth-century copy of Barlaam and Joasaph (Stavrou 42).
An early series of miniatures (A.D. 1053) illustrates the Psalter
(Taphou 53). From about A.D. 1600 come two important
series of Gospel illustrations (Anastaseos 1 and 5). Another
series was found in a Georgian Four Gospels out of the Treasury. Although few in number, there are some miniatures to
illustrate the art of Arabic, Syriac, Slavonic, and Ethiopic
books.

III. THE ARMENIAN PATRIARCHAL LIBRARY

One week was allotted for work in the Armenian Patriarchal
library in Jerusalem, in December of 1949. In the process of
our negotiations His Beatitude, the Patriarch Guregh II, was
stricken with a fatal illness. The graciousness of the Patriarch
was reflected in his successor, His Grace, the Locum Tenens,
Archbishop Eghishe Derderian, and the Synod, who granted
the desired permission. Most helpful cooperation was given by
the librarian, Bishop Norayr Bogharian. The great library of
4,000 manuscripts is most appropriately housed in the lovely,
ancient Chapel of Saint Theodore and there we worked in the
midst of a wealth of material. The primary objective, however,
was to select a few manuscripts of particular value for iconog-
raphy and in this we were guided by an initial list prepared
by Dr. Sirarpie Der Nersessian of Dumbarton Oaks. Thirty-
two manuscripts were microfilmed completely and from
twenty-two of these a wealth of 432 miniatures was secured
on film. This included four large eleventh-century copies of
the Four Gospels in uncial letters, one of which was signed
by the scribe Stephanos in A.D. 1064 (MS 1924). There were
also four copies of the Bible, the oldest of which was written
in 1269 at Erznka (Erzinjan) by three scribes—Moses, Mar-
gare, and the Monk Jacob (MS 1925). There was a New Testament with the Psalter written in 1323 by Grigor at Sis, an
illustrated Medical Treatise copied in 1294 and two large Mis-
sals of the fourteenth century.

In the Special Treasury were found eight copies of the Four
Gospels, some of them in beautiful covers of silver or gold put

on in the early eighteenth century when Gregory the Chain-bearer was Patriarch. Two of these are great tomes that go back to the eleventh-century rule of King Gagek, and one was the king's personal copy (MS 2556). It stands twenty inches tall in its heavy metal covers, contrasting with a tiny gold-covered copy of A.D. 1612 which stands little more than four inches high (MS 2625). Three other royal copies belong to the thirteenth century: the Gospels of Leo and Keran (A.D. 1262), the Gospels of Prince Vassak, and the splendorous Gospels of Queen Keran (A.D. 1272). This last contains about 125 miniatures on lovely white parchment and includes a picture of the royal family with its five children. The solid gold box-cover was put on in 1727 for the Patriarch Gregory who signed a note to this effect (179r.). Another one of the Treasury codices is known as the "Miracle Gospels" and many cures are associated with it (MS 2649). Written in 1332, it contains a long series of gospel illustrations. One royal manuscript which we requested could not be located at that time—the Gospel of King Hethum II (A.D. 1267). In one short week, concluding on Christmas Eve, we became increasingly aware of the importance of this Armenian collection, the second largest in the world.

STATISTICS OF JERUSALEM LIBRARIES AND MANUSCRIPTS FILMED

	In Library	Filmed
Greek	1866	692
Arabic	234	106
Georgian	160	130
Syriac	50	26
Slavonic	23	23
Ethiopic	21	21
Greek Patriarchate	2354	998
Arm. Patriarchate	4000	32

Scholars and Their Research

When it became known in 1949 that an expedition would go to Sinai and Jerusalem many scholars and institutions submitted special requests for materials. Most extensive were the lists of Greek, Arabic, and Syriac manuscripts received from the *Corpus Scriptorum Christianorum Orientalium* in Louvain. This vigorous research institution acted as a clearing house for several scholars. For example, its secretary, Professor Draguet, required four manuscripts at Sinai which contain the Lausiac history of Palladios, and also two patristic texts dated in A.D. 1004 and about 1300. Professor Hespel requested a Canonica written about 1300. Professor Schmid of Bonn University needed a fourteenth-century copy of the Apocalypse. From the Greek Patriarchate in Jerusalem, Professor Draguet desired four Patristica, from the tenth century on. In addition the CSCO in Louvain cited sixty-four Greek manuscripts, seventy-three Arabic manuscripts and twenty-seven Syriac manuscripts needed for researches.

A list of fifty-three Greek manuscripts was submitted by Marcel Richard of the National Center for Scientific Research in Paris, acting for eight French scholars. From Director J. Hoock of the Byzantine Institute in Scheyern, Austria, came a list of thirty-seven Greek manuscripts desired for research. Other requests came from the Bollandist Society of Brussels, and from additional individual scholars—Abbot René Laurentin of Paris; Dom Julian Leroy of Tarn, France; Noel Charlier in Rome; Cardinal Mercati; and Cyprian Rice of the Dominican convent in Cairo. The texts requested by all these scholars range widely in contents and it is not possible as yet to report on their respective projects. However, these requests were fulfilled by the expedition as fully as possible and thus we were directed to valuable selections. They further illustrate the immediate uses to which the microfilmed text is being put and emphasize the widespread researches already active to which the expedition has contributed.

In America, numerous important research projects sought assistance. At Harvard University, Professor Jaeger and his associates had long pursued an intensive study of Gregory of Nyssa and for this manuscripts in Jerusalem and Sinai were copied. The late Professor Blake had also requested Georgian texts of the New Testament. Dr. Sirarpie Der Nersessian at Dumbarton Oaks, and Professors Weitzmann and Friend at Princeton were among those who desired miniatures for iconographic studies. Still other materials contributed to the studies of individual scholars in musicology, canon law, and the Church Fathers.

American scholars who served the expedition abroad included, besides myself as General Editor, C. Umhau Wolf—then of the Chicago Lutheran Seminary in Maywood, Illinois, and now minister in Toledo; Howard Kee of Drew University; and Lucetta Mowry of Wellesley College. In Sinai, the chief associates were Aziz Suryal Atiyah of the University in Alexandria, and Gerard Garitte of Louvain University; and in Jerusalem, D. C. Baramki of the American University of Beirut. Most of these members of the expedition have since undertaken further researches upon selected texts. The usefulness of the film collection, now in the Library of Congress, has already been fully demonstrated and active research has quickly expanded. Checklists of the 2,717 manuscripts and 1,742 firmans have recently been released by the Library of Congress: the one for Sinai, in September, 1952; and the one for Jerusalem, in March, 1953. The University of Manchester in England has acquired a duplicate film of the entire collection of 2,685 manuscripts copied. The Sinai portion can be consulted also in Louvain, Belgium, in the *Corpus Scriptorum Christianorum Orientalium;* and also in the University of Alexandria, Egypt.

The most extensive research project behind our expedition to the Near East was the International Greek New Testament. Indeed, this organization supplied the first and greatest impetus because of its need for more witnesses to the New Testament text. The project was designed to publish the Greek New Testament text in eight volumes, citing the various readings in hundreds of manuscript witnesses, many of which have not heretofore been studied. Such a project required quantities of unexplored materials and such materials lay at hand in Sinai and Jerusalem. It is estimated that there are about 4,500 manuscript copies of Greek text of the New Testament known today though few of these are complete testaments. Yet the text of the Gospels is contained in about 2,000 extant manuscripts while the text of Paul is preserved in about 700 manuscripts. Because of these many witnesses to the text it is often stated that the New Testament is favored beyond any other ancient writing for the preservation of its true text. It is a fact, however, that few of the known manuscripts have actually been studied. Indeed, most of them have been merely numbers in a library, and this is especially true of the notable but isolated collections at Mount Athos, Jerusalem, and Saint Catherine's Monastery on Mount Sinai. Like a promising "tell" which the archaeologist hopes some day to excavate, these great eastern libraries have kept their secret too long, and researches upon the Greek text of the New Testament have hitherto received almost no assistance from them. For this reason, among others, the expedition of 1949–50 assigned to New Testament manuscripts the highest priority. As a result, from Sinai and Jerusalem have come about three hundred witnesses to yield their testimony on the Greek text, while others bear witness to the versions. Together they make possible the broadest survey of the New Testament text ever yet undertaken.

Many have asked about new discoveries. It is inevitable that some discoveries should be made in so extended and thorough a search, in such venerable and massive collections. Certain new manuscripts have been cited above, of modest but unmistakable importance. To examine minutely these vast collections of thousands of manuscripts in a matter of months was obviously impossible. It seemed the wiser plan to be inclusive rather than meticulous. Therefore, the emphasis of the expedition was to secure on transportable film a large portion, and the most important sections, of the great collections. Consequently, there stand today in orderly array in the Library of Congress about 2,700 ancient "volumes" which previously were inaccessible for examination. We do not yet know fully all that they contain, nor are we yet aware of the full significance of particular texts. Assuredly "discoveries" are yet to be made, but it is now possible for many to participate in the search. Like Mohammed's mountain, the great libraries of Sinai and Jerusalem have been brought to the scholar and have created a new and challenging horizon.

17

THE GEOGRAPHY OF
EZEKIEL'S RIVER OF LIFE

WILLIAM R. FARMER

One of the most beautiful symbolic pictures in the Bible is that in Ezekiel 47:1–12. In the prophet's vision of the new age Palestinian geography is radically altered. Even the wilderness of Judah between Jerusalem and the Dead Sea will become a paradise because a great river will flow from beneath the temple through the wilderness to the Sea.

The terms "water," "sea," "river," and the like, are frequently used in the Bible in a rich context, so that they carry a wealth of symbolic meaning. In most instances, the reference is to the waters of chaos, the salt-water deep which was believed to surround the universe. These waters were controlled at creation, but they remain, it was thought, as a continual threat so that our world lives in continual danger of reversion to the primeval, formless void. Professor Herbert G. May has recently marshalled a rich body of evidence around this point.[1] With regard to the river in Ezekiel 47, Professor May reasons that, since it was not fed by tributaries, it must have been the cosmic deep which was the source of this river, the subterranean ocean from which all fertility was derived.

We should be clear that the ancient peoples of Mesopotamia, Syria and Palestine distinguished two deeps. The one was the source of the salt water oceans and the enemy of world

[1] "Some Cosmic Connotations of *Mayim Rabbim*," JBL, LXXIV (1955), 9–21.

order; the other was the fresh water ocean beneath the earth which is the source of our sweet water streams and springs, and, therefore, the source of life. In Gen. 2:10 a flood (see R.S.V.) issues from the underground fresh water deep in Paradise and is the source of the world's rivers.[2] To this river the Psalmist makes figurative reference when he describes God's people as drinking from "the river of thy delights," for with God alone is the "spring of life" (Ps. 36:8–9). In Ezek. 31 the Egyptian Pharaoh who is about to be brought low has achieved his great height, like a cedar of Lebanon, because the fresh water of the deep nourished him and made him grow.

Ezekiel's river of life (in Chap. 47) which flows from the temple is not a mere "cosmic sluicegate," however, through which waters of fertility are channeled to the earth's surface. It is rather a focal point of cosmic salvation. To be sure, the water is to flow down into the wilderness of Judah to make the desert bloom. Yet more than this is to happen: the river is also to flow into the Dead Sea where a great miracle of healing takes place. The sick waters of the sea, burdened with brine, are to be healed, to be made fresh and capable of sustaining life. Where the river goes, everything will live (Ezek. 47:9). The waters of the sea will swarm with every kind of fish, and the banks of the river will be lined with every kind of tree. Yet more than luxuriant fertility is involved. The fruit of the trees will be fresh every month and the leaves of the trees will be for healing (verse 12). With such symbolism the temple is pictured as the focal point of cosmic salvation, the source of the waters which heal. The marvelous work and presence of God is not merely the source of a more abundant life (fertility), but it is the source of new life (healing). At Ezekiel's temple the lame shall be made to walk and the brokenness of national life shall be made whole.

It is important for the biblical topographer to note that although Ezekiel is caught up in his vision he is by no means out of touch with the real world of his own day. The water which flows from beneath the temple runs in an eastward direction down into the Arabah and then empties into the Dead Sea. All these topographical details are verifiable. This water

[2] See now E. A. Speiser, "'Ed in the Story of Creation," *BASOR*, No. 140 (Dec. 1955), pp. 9–11.

has a natural channel in the Kedron valley which as it descends through the Arabah takes the name *Wadi en-Nar*. As it empties into the sea this water fans out in all directions and its healing effect is evident up and down the coast. The sea which now has no fish will have in that day fishermen standing on its shores "from En-gedi to En-eglaim" (Ezek. 47:10).

No one has ever doubted that En-gedi and En-eglaim were real places which Ezekiel knew in his own day. All modern topographers agree in identifying En-gedi with *'Ain Jidi*. Linguistically, this identification is perfectly clear. And topographically, as the only settled oasis south of the mouth of the *Wadi en-Nar*, *'Ain Jidi* satisfies the picture Ezekiel is trying to create. The healing effect of the living water from the temple will be felt not only at the mouth of the *Wadi en-Nar* but all the way down to *'Ain Jidi*.

The case of En-eglaim, however, is quite another matter. Some have suggested that it be identified with *'Ain Hajlah*, while others have suggested *'Ain Feshkhah*. Most authorities, however, regard the matter as unsettled.

Some have claimed that linguistically the evidence is somewhat in favor of *'Ain Hajlah*. At least T. K. Cheyne held that it was hardly too bold to amend the text and read for Eglaim, Hoglah. Yet there are serious topographical objections to this identification. We have seen that the topographical features in this vision of Ezekiel are verifiable to a remarkable degree. Water flowing from the temple does have to flow in an eastwardly direction; it does have to run down through the Arabah; and it does have to empty into the (Dead) Sea. En-gedi is a known place on the west shore of that sea south of the point of influx. Ezekiel's image demands a corresponding place on the west shore of the sea to the north of the point of influx. That point of influx is, as we have seen, the mouth of the *Wadi en-Nar*. There is only one such place on the shore of the Dead Sea between the mouth of the *Wadi en-Nar* and the mouth of the Jordan. That is *'Ain Feshkhah*.

According to Ezekiel's vision fishermen are to stand beside the sea from En-gedi to En-eglaim. This they simply cannot do if En-eglaim be identified with *'Ain Hajlah*. *'Ain Hajlah* is high and dry over three and one half miles from the shore of the Dead Sea and over two miles from the banks of the river

Jordan. On the other hand, if En-eglaim be identified with *'Ain Feshkhah,* this topographical feature of Ezekiel's vision becomes perfectly intelligible. *'Ain Feshkhah* is on the shore of the Dead Sea, and lies north of the *Wadi en-Nar.* Fishermen would be able to stand beside the sea from *'Ain Jidi* to *'Ain Feshkhah.* *'Ain Feshkhah* and *'Ain Jidi* are the two major oases on the west shore of the Dead Sea and as such they constitute the natural points of reference for Ezekiel's vision.

These topographical considerations would seem to weigh the balance heavily in favor of identifying En-eglaim with *'Ain Feshkhah.* However, the matter is further complicated by a subsidiary topographical factor. In order to perfect the picture he is trying to create in this passage, Ezekiel needs not merely an *oasis* on the northwest shore of the Dead Sea, but a *settled* oasis well known to his readers. *'Ain Jidi* was settled and well known in the pre-Exilic period, but was *'Ain Feshkhah?* Until recent times we have known of no evidence to indicate that there was any pre-Exilic settlement in the *'Ain Feshkhah* area. Therefore, because *'Ain Hajlah* had evidences of an Iron Age settlement, which is usually identified with the biblical Beth-hoglah (Josh. 15:6; 18:19, 21), it has seemed that the requirement that Ezekiel's En-eglaim be identified with a site well known in his day was most safely met by identifying it with *'Ain Hajlah,* in spite of the topographical difficulties this identification presents. At any rate in the expert judgment of Father Abel, *'Ain Hajlah* was a more probable identification than *'Ain Feshkhah.*

Significantly enough, however, since the death of Abel, new evidence has been brought into view by the excavations under the direction of Father de Vaux at Qumran. We now know that beneath the ruins of the Qumran community lie the foundation walls of an Iron Age settlement in the *'Ain Feshkhah* area.[3] Our problem is, therefore, finally resolved into

[3] *Revue biblique,* April, 1954. It has long been known that only two settlements on the west shore of the Dead Sea are mentioned in biblical literature. They are En-gedi and *'Ir-ham-Melah,* City of the (Sea of) Salt. *'Ir-ham-Melah* is mentioned in Joshua 15:62. If the town is to be identified with the Iron Age settlement at Qumran, then it seems all the more likely that Ezekiel would have used these geographical points to suggest the magnitude of his miracle of healing. If one asks why the seer did not say "from En-gedi to *'Ir-ham-*

the question of what weight is to be given to the linguistic advantage of 'Ain Hajlah, and what weight is to be given to topographical advantage of 'Ain Feshkhah. Since the linguistic evidence is very conjectural, while the topographical evidence is quite clear, it would seem that the balance of evidence is finally weighed in favor of identifying Ezekiel's En-eglaim with modern 'Ain Feshkhah.

Ezekiel's picture would then be understood as follows: the healing waters from the temple would freshen the sea all the way from 'Ain Jidi on the south to 'Ain Feshkhah on the north.[4]

This picture fits perfectly what Ezekiel says in verse eleven. "But its swamps and marshes will not be healed, they are to be left for salt." These marshes from which salt is recovered lie on the north shore of the Dead Sea between 'Ain Feshkhah and the mouth of the Jordan.[5] If we identify En-eglaim with 'Ain Feshkhah, what Ezekiel seems to be saying is this: The healing waters from the temple shall flow forth into the Salt Sea and shall freshen its waters from 'Ain Jidi to 'Ain Feshkhah, but they shall not touch the marshes which supply God's people with salt!

Finally, this passage in Ezekiel may very well have influenced the "Children of Light" of the Dead Sea Scrolls in their decision to establish their community center at Qumran. We know from the Manual of Discipline (8:14) that the injunction of the prophet Isaiah to prepare the way of the Lord in the

---

Melah," instead of "En-gedi to En-eglaim," the answer could be found in the fact that En-gedi ("fountain of a kid") finds its more natural parallel in En-eglaim ("fountain of two calves"). One other thing is worth pointing out; the springs of 'Ain Feshkhah could have first suggested to Ezekiel his image of the river of life healing the stagnant waters of the Dead Sea. These numerous springs pour forth a considerable quantity of fresh water into the sea which sometimes dilutes the water sufficiently to enable fish to swim out a yard or more from the shore. This unusual sight has been observed and verified in modern times, but there is no reason to doubt that the same phenomenon was occurring in Ezekiel's day. (See Quarterly Statement, Pal. Exploration Fund [1902], pp. 406–7.)

[4] Not that the waters of the sea would be freshened only up to these extreme points, but rather that fishermen standing at these widely separated places would still be within the range of the miraculous healing effect.

[5] See Quart. Statement, P. E. F. (1904), pp. 91–92.

wilderness was taken very seriously by them. But Isaiah does not specify *where* in the wilderness they should go. Why did the "Children of Light" settle at Qumran?

Among other very important considerations,[6] could there have been the understandable desire to be as close as possible to the actual scene of a certain and unmistakable sign of the Lord God's coming? The Covenanters of Qumran constituted a tightly organized religious order, a "standing army" for God, ready to go into action at a moment's notice. All that was needed was an unmistakable sign. Did not Ezekiel's vision promise them precisely this? Would not these bitter waters one day turn sweet? That would be the day of the Lord God's coming! On that day the priests would blow their trumpets and men and angels would march forward shoulder to shoulder to do battle against the "Children of Darkness" and the hosts of Belial!

[6] As for the economic, commercial, political, and religious considerations which marked out the Qumran site as an ideal location for an Essene-like community, these have received little attention from scholars so far. I have made a beginning at this study in "The Economic Basis of the Qumran Community," *Theologische Zeitschrift* (August–September, 1955).

18

LEVIATHAN AND
THE BEAST IN REVELATION

HOWARD WALLACE

One of the perplexing problems of New Testament study has been the source and interpretation of the beast in the Book of Revelation. Through the centuries hundreds of names have been advanced as the true interpretation of 666, the number of the beast. However, it is not within the scope of this article to discuss the problems of interpretation, but rather to note possible sources for the figure and symbol of the beast.

The dragon theme may be classed as almost universal in mythology. As early as 1675 Père Marquette rounded a bend on a river near what is now Alton, Illinois, and suddenly saw before him, painted and carved into the rocky bluff, the huge picture of a strange monster. He later related in his diary that this creature had the face of a man, the horns of a deer, the beard of a tiger, and the tail of a fish so long that it passed around the body and over the head, and between the legs. He had stumbled across the famed Piasa Rock of the Illinois Indian tribe, which stood for almost a century-and-a-half after Marquette's discovery. The early explorer explained, "The name Piasa is Indian and signifies, in the Illini, the bird which devours men."[1]

The Pueblo Indians of the Southwest, the Mayas and Aztecs of ancient Mexico, and the Kwakiutl of British Columbia all have similar dragon-like monsters in their mythology. The

[1] Smith, G. Elliot, *The Evolution of the Dragon*, p. 93.

ancient Egyptians believed that there was an eternal struggle between Re, the Sun-god, and Apophis, the dragon or serpent which tried daily to overcome it. The *Enuma Elish*, a Babylonian creation epic, describes the tremendous conflict between Marduk and Tiamat. Marduk represented the forces of order, and Tiamat was the personification of watery chaos.

This Babylonian Creation story, many times referred to as the *Babylonian Genesis*, offers interesting parallels to the story of the creation as recorded in Genesis. However, Heidel carefully points out that the Hebrew word, *tĕhôm* 'deep,' is the general designation for watery chaos, while Tiamat in the Babylonian myth is but the personification of the female part of watery chaos. Apsu represents the male part. In the Babylonian myth Marduk, the chosen representative of the gods, slays Tiamat and forms the heavens from her body. In the first chapter of Genesis it is obvious that *tĕhôm* is in no way personified.

It is still uncertain whether or not Tiamat was a dragon-like monster. Heidel strongly objects to such a designation, and maintains that the evidence for it is too flimsy.[2] At the same time, numerous similarities between Tiamat and the monsters of the Old Testament support the possibility of some connection. Be that as it may, there is no question that the most famous monster of western civilization is the biblical Leviathan, whose immediate background is to be sought, not in Babylonian, but in Canaanite mythology.

The Ras Shamrah texts, found in Syria at the ancient site of Ugarit nearly twenty years ago, record Canaanite myths of the period from 1700 to 1400 B.C. A section of one text tells of the fight of Anath and the dragon. At one point Anath shouts:

> I have destroyed the Sea-Dragon, beloved of El,
> I have slain River of El, the Chief;
> I muzzled Tannin, I muzzled him (?).
> I have destroyed the winding serpent,
> Shalyat of the seven heads;
> I have destroyed the underworld dragon, beloved of El.[3]

[2] Heidel, Alexander, *The Babylonian Genesis*, pp. 72–75.
[3] Albright, W. F., "Anath and the Dragon," *BASOR*, No. 84 (Dec., 1941), p. 16.

In another of the texts ("Baal and the Waters"), we learn of the seven-headed Lotan, the very name from which the word "Leviathan" in the Old Testament is derived. A comparison of the vocabulary of Isaiah 27:1 and three lines from the Ugaritic epic, "The Death of Baal," shows the direct borrowing of the Hebrew from the Canaanite. Two words which describe Lotan and Leviathan are identical in the two languages. They are *brḥ*, usually translated 'swift' or 'gliding,' and '*qltn*, usually translated 'crooked' or 'tortuous.'

A cylinder seal found in Tell Asmar in Mesopotamia shows a seven-headed dragon being subdued by two deities. This is the type of monster which raged against the prevailing gods in Canaanite mythology, the Leviathan to which the Old Testament alludes.

Thus the Old Testament Leviathan exists as part of a widely spread dragon theme. However, the treatment of this mythological monster in the writings of Israel and in subsequent Apocryphal and rabbinical literature gives it a unique place. It is the purpose of this article to show that the Leviathan concept underlies the usage of the Beast in Revelation.

The longest passage concerning Leviathan in the Old Testament is the forty-first chapter of Job. These verses are part of the speech of Yahweh from the whirlwind in which he numbers his creative acts, indicates his majesty and strength, and points out his power and control over the great creatures Behemoth and Leviathan. When He is finished, Job is completely humbled and admits his wrong attitude. The chapter opens with God's questioning of Job:

> Canst thou draw out leviathan with a fishhook?
> Or press down his tongue with a cord?
> Canst thou put a rope into his nose?
> Or pierce his jaw through with a hook?

The bewilderment of early commentators is noticed in the comparison of Leviathan with a crocodile, a whale, a large fish, and a dragon. While the author of Job may have included some of the characteristics of the crocodile in his description of Leviathan, certainly those characteristics are incidental to what he was trying to picture. We know now that Leviathan is a seven-headed serpent connected with water. This knowledge has come from the background material furnished to us by the Ras Shamrah texts.

Summing up what we learn of Leviathan in Job 41: (1) Verses 1-11 indicate that he is a mighty creature which no man can harness. He is under the eternal control of Yahweh. (2) Verses 12-32 are a description of the monster; his very form strikes terror into men; he is covered with scales, strong and impregnable; he breathes fire; no weapon made by man can harm him; the sea foams as he swims through it. (3) In verses 33-34 we find that he is king of all the sons of pride.

A second passage concerning Leviathan is found in Job 3:8.

> Let them curse it that curse the day,
> Who are ready to rouse up leviathan.

Cheyne, Schmidt, and Gunkel change yôm 'day,' to yām 'sea,' probably with justice. Thus, "Let them curse it that curse the sea; who are ready to rouse up Leviathan." The sea, as in many strains of older mythology, is here regarded as the primeval enemy of God, and identified with Leviathan by the poetic parallelism. When tied in with the next passage, it indicates that Leviathan is conceived as having fought with and been conquered by God.

A third passage, which indicates that Leviathan has more than one head, is Psalm 74:14. Verses 12-15 read:

Yet God is my king of old,
Working salvation in the midst of the earth.
Thou didst divide the sea by thy strength;
Thou brakest the heads of the sea-monsters in the waters.
Thou brakest the heads of leviathan in pieces;
Thou gavest him to be food to the people inhabiting the wilderness.
Thou didst cleave the fountain and the flood;
Thou driest up mighty rivers.

Although there is a definite borrowing here from Canaanite mythology, and perhaps some relationship to Babylonian mythology, the Israelites did not borrow any fundamental ideas of God from these two sources. They took subsidiary ones and fitted them into their scheme of monotheism. John Patton points out that although the authors and readers of the Psalms

remembered traditional myths of the battles of gods with
monsters, their names were forgotten. The important id
that God formed these monsters and was strong enoug
destroy them.[4] In the Ras Shamrah texts, the seven-he
dragon, the creature Lotan (Leviathan), was vanquishe
Baal with the aid of trusty allies.

A fourth Leviathan passage is Psalm 104:26. Its readi
widely disputed:

> There go the ships;
> There is leviathan, whom thou hast formed to play there

Oesterley changes "ships" to *Tannînîm* 'sea-monsters.'
parallelism is more understandable. The passage, howev
not of great significance.

The last, and perhaps crucial, Leviathan passage in the
Testament is Isaiah 27:1. The writer is speaking of the
when Israel will be delivered from all her enemies. She
be redeemed by Yahweh. The forces of evil are personifi
the serpent, Leviathan.

> In that day, Yahweh with his hard and great and stro
> sword will punish leviathan the swift serpent, and lev
> than the crooked serpent, and he will slay the mons
> that is in the sea.

In this section of Isaiah, usually dated in the post-Exili
riod, the conception of Leviathan has undergone a re
process. Here he represents the terrible force of evil i
world. The symbol of triumph in the Day of the Lord i
destruction of this monster. Hence, the writer of this
falls back on old mythological ideas to express the ele
conception that Yahweh is a righteous God and ultimatel
triumph over all.

It must be noted that several Old Testament words are
cally related to Leviathan. One is *tĕhôm*, a word desig
primeval chaos. While it is not personified, it is mention
Job 41:31, 32 as being the dwelling place of Leviathan.
also Job 28:14; Prov. 3:20; 8:24; Ps. 42:7; 71:20.) *Yām*
is more than a mere body of water in many passages; it

---

[4] *Canaanite Parallels to the Book of Psalms*, p. 27.

active force, probably reflecting the old myth of the struggle between order and chaos. One of the most interesting of these passages is Job 7:12:

> Am I a sea, or a sea-monster,
> That thou settest a watch over me?

In Ugaritic epics, Baal fights against Zebul-Yam, Prince Sea. The waters or sea rebel against the ruling power in Canaanite mythology, and therefore must be watched by the chief god. Leviathan dwells in the sea. *Rahab*, a sea-monster, can be equated with Leviathan in a number of passages (Job 9:13; 26:12; Isa. 51:9; Ps. 89:10). *Tannin* can mean a similar sea-monster (as in Ps. 74:13), though having other translations.[5]

In apocryphal and rabbinic writings, all these names, with the exception of Leviathan, drop out of use. Enoch 60:7-9 states, "On that day (the Day of Judgment) two monsters will be produced, a female monster named Leviathan to dwell in the depths of the ocean over the fountains of the waters; but the male is called Behemoth who occupies with his breast a waste wilderness named Dendain on the east of the garden where the elect and righteous dwell." This passage reflects the description of Behemoth in Job, chap. 40, and Leviathan in Job, chap. 41.

According to II Esdras 6:49-53, God created on the fifth day two great monsters, Leviathan and Behemoth. He assigned the watery portions to Leviathan and the dry to Behemoth. At a specified time in the future, these monsters will be eaten. A similar theme is found in the Syriac Apocalypse of Baruch 29:4. Order will prevail on Judgment Day, and there are two hints of a messianic feast at which time the flesh of the two monsters will be eaten by the righteous and elect. This event, then, is a peculiarly apt symbol for the complete triumph of God and the righteous over the evil forces of the universe.

---

[5] Heidel maintains that these terms are figures of speech applied to the powerful enemy nations of Israel (*Babylonian Genesis*, p. 92). Though these names of monsters may, in some instances, be used for this purpose, the fact that they are used indicates a mythological strain. The writer is not at all convinced that this usage is as widespread in the Old Testament as Heidel claims.

Early rabbinical sayings which have been attributed to Rabbi Johanan ben Zakkai and Rabbi Joshua ben Hananiah, of the late first century A.D., emphasize the place of Leviathan and Behemoth. Admittedly, many later Jewish rabbis wrote in the names of the early ones, which makes it difficult to establish the source of such sayings. However, it is safe to assume that at a very early date in the Christian era, Christians were familiar with the symbols of Leviathan and Behemoth as used by the Jews. In later Jewish gnosticism Leviathan and Behemoth form two of the seven circles or stations which the soul had to pass in order to be purged and obtain bliss.

What, then, is the situation in the Christian community toward the end of the reign of Domitian in A.D. 96? Violent persecution had broken out, and the author of the Book of Revelation, wishing to express his faith in the ultimate triumph of God over evil, needed a symbol to express it. What apocalyptic material did he have from which to draw? Daniel, of course, and Ezekiel, and also the theme of Leviathan, which, through the Old Testament and Apocryphal writings and rabbinical tradition, had come into that period as a symbol of evil.

We are not concerned in this article with what the beast of the Book of Revelation symbolizes in the way of earthly kingdoms or personalities. Rather, we are pointing out that the underlying mythological basis for this creature comes from the Leviathan theme.

Revelation 11:7 reads:

> And when they have finished their testimony, the beast that ascends from the bottomless pit will make war upon them and conquer them and kill them.

Thērion is the Greek word which is translated 'beast.' It will come forth from the *abyssos*, 'bottomless pit.'

In Rev. 12:3, the "great red dragon, with seven heads, and ten horns, and seven diadems upon his head" is mentioned. *Drakōn* 'dragon,' is the usual Septuagint rendering of Leviathan. Only once is Leviathan translated *ketos*, 'sea-monster' (Job 3:8). From Rev. 13:1 on, the beast and the dragon are used interchangeably, as are Leviathan and Rahab and Tannin. It may also be noted that *abyssos* is the Septuagint rendering of *tĕhôm*, the watery deep. However, by New Testament times, it had become a bottomless pit full of fire and smoke.

In the description of the war in heaven between the dragon and Michael and his angels (Rev. 12:7–12), verse 9 is especially interesting.

> And the great dragon was thrown down, that ancient serpent who is called the Devil and Satan, the deceiver of the whole world—he was thrown down to earth, and his angels were thrown down with him.

The war in heaven is an echo of the war in which Tiamat and her hordes were defeated by Marduk and the gods in the Babylonian Creation Story, and in which Baal of Canaanite lore fought against the rebellious waters. Yahweh destroyed Leviathan in the dim past. Since the Leviathan theme was close at hand for the author of Revelation, we can assume he used it along with other sources. The primeval struggle between Yahweh and the powers of chaos is transformed in the Christian context into a struggle between God and Satan. Though the heathen powers, and Rome especially, rage as they will, God will triumph over them in the end.

In Chapter 13, two beasts appear.

> And I saw a beast rising out of the sea, with ten horns, and seven heads, with ten diadems upon its horns and a blasphemous name upon its heads.

This beast which comes out of the sea in the first verse is an exact description of the great red dragon of chap. 12:3. Both descriptions seem to be based on Dan. 7:2 ff., and upon the idea that Leviathan has seven heads.

Verse 11 reads:

> Then I saw another beast which rose out of the earth;
> It had two horns like a lamb and spoke like a dragon.

The beast from the earth and the beast from the sea appear very much like Behemoth and Leviathan in Job, chaps. 40, 41. II Esdras 6:49–53 indicates that Behemoth and Leviathan will both occupy portions of the world until Judgment Day. Leviathan, as has been stated, was specifically assigned the

watery portions, and Behemoth the dry portions. Sinc
of these beasts play such an important part in Jewish
lyptic writings, the author of the Book of Revelation
turn to them in attempting to paint the vivid picture
coming of the last days.

The last part of chapter 19 and the first part of chaj
picture the overthrow of the beast and his armies. "The c
that ancient serpent who is the Devil and Satan" in Rev
is bound and thrown into the bottomless pit. The *abyss*
its relation to *těhôm* is again indicative of the whole Le
strain, in which Leviathan is the representation of the
forces of chaos, later to become the representation of

"Then I saw a new heaven and a new earth; for tl
heaven and the first earth had passed away, and the s
no more" (Rev. 21:1). The turbulent waters, the sea,
had been in rebellion against the gods in Babylonian
ogy, against Baal in Canaanite literature, and against Y
in the Old Testament, the sea was gone! This is a
symbol of the complete abolition of evil in the world.

In summary: Leviathan is part of a dragon theme in r
ogy which is found in several ancient religions. While
yet clear how close the relationship of the Babylonian
is to the biblical Leviathan, the close kinship of Levia
North-Canaanite literature, as evidenced in the Ras Sl
texts, is unmistakable. Leviathan is myth; but when it b
refined by Hebrew monotheism, it expresses truth in a
way. Leviathan is under the direct control of Yahweh,
Isaiah 27:1 and subsequent apocryphal and rabbinic
ings blossoms out into a magnificent and terrible syr
evil and disorder. Leviathan is the source for the usag
beast, *thērion*, and the dragon, *drakōn*, in the Revela
John. In this apocalypse the conflict between good a
is pictured in intense form, and the figures of the
beast and the red dragon go down to defeat in the cata
battle which results in a new heaven and a new eartl

19

THE GNOSTIC LIBRARY OF CHENOBOSKION[1]

VICTOR ROLAND GOLD

One of the most interesting and most familiar of the early sects of Christendom was that represented by Gnosticism and its various subdivisions. Although well known by name, our information regarding them has come almost exclusively from the writings of the early Church Fathers. Among these are Irenaeus (d. about 202; especially in his *Adversus Haereses* I), Tertullian (d. about 222), Hippolytus (d. about 235; especially in his *Refutatio*), Origen (d. 253), Cyril of Jerusalem (d. 386), Epiphanius (d. about 404; especially in his *Panarion*) and Augustine (d. 430). To this group should be added the Neoplatonist, Plotinus (d. 270). The information provided by the Church Fathers and Plotinus was sufficient to give us a general impression of the distinctive doctrines and attitudes of the Gnostics, but it was at best of limited value because of its brevity and its unsympathetic attitude toward the heretical group.

To this patristic material are to be added three codices containing original Gnostic works. These are the fourth century Codex Askewianus, the fifth century Codex Berolinensis, and

[1] The writer wishes to take this opportunity to express his gratitude to Professor W. F. Albright of the Johns Hopkins University for his many invaluable suggestions and generous assistance given during the preparation of this paper.

the Codex Brucianus, from the fifth or sixth century.[2] Two papyrus fragments, one from the fourth century, in the British Museum, and the other, Rylands Papyrus 463, from the third century, until recently, completed the list of primary and secondary sources for our knowledge of Gnosticism.[3]

Our lack of extensive original Gnostic material which could provide us with information concerning the origins of Christian Gnosticism, its relationship with the early Christian churches, systematic treatment of its teachings and its position in the development and content of certain sections of the New Testament canon has been felt acutely because of the attribution, in some circles, of Pauline and Johannine materials to Gnostic influences. Although the discovery in 1947 and subsequent publication of the now famous Dead Sea Scrolls have contributed much to show that this New Testament material was not so influenced,[4] the recovery of original Gnostic materials would aid materially in revaluing the evidence, if any, which has been adduced to indicate Gnostic influences on the New Testament material in question.

A step in this direction was accomplished in 1930 when a

[2] The Codex Askewianus, written on parchment, was purchased by an Englishman, Askew, in the second third of the eighteenth century and was first publicized in 1778. It is now in the British Museum. It contains the treatise *Pistis Sophia* and a treatise on penitence.

The Codex Brucianus, written on papyrus, was purchased by a Scotsman, James Bruce, in the region of Thebes about 1769. It became the property of Bodleian Library, Oxford, in 1848. It contains the two *Books of Yeu* and a work without a title. The latter was published by Charlotte Baynes in 1935, *A Coptic Treatise contained in the Codex Brucianus* (Cambridge).

The Codex Berolinensis, also on papyrus, was secured by Dr. C. Reinhardt from an antiquities dealer in Akhmim in 1895 and is now in the collection of the Egyptian Museum in Berlin. In addition to some non-Gnostic material, it contains the Gnostic *Apocryphon of John,* the *Wisdom of Jesus,* and a part of the *Gospel of Mary.*

[3] The Mandaean literature, first published by M. Lidzbarski (1905–25), furnished additional information concerning Gnosticism. The Mandaean system arose in southern Iraq in the fifth century A.D. and draws from Manichaean teachings, among others.

[4] For example, the dualism of light and darkness is reflected in the "War between the Children of Light and the Children of Darkness."

cache of Manichaean manuscripts was found in a wooden
chest in the cellar of a ruined house in the Egyptian village
of Medinet Madi, ancient Terenouthis, in the southern Fayyum. These documents of Manichaeism, a syncretistic sect
which borrowed from Zoroastrianism, Judaism, and heterodox
forms of Christianity, especially Gnosticism, provided some
light on the Gnostics, but for Gnosticism, it was still secondary
material.

The Discovery at Chenoboskion[5]

However, sometime in 1946, some peasants accidentally discovered an entire library of Gnostic writings. The place of
discovery was about thirty-two miles north of Luxor, in the
region of Nag Hammadi, near el-Qasr es-Sayyad (ancient
Sheneset-Chenoboskion), at the foot of a steep mountain,
Gebel et-Tarif, on the east bank of the Nile. It was in this
vicinity that St. Pachomius began his monastic community
early in the fourth century A.D. The exact location of the manuscript deposit is still unknown; the region is honeycombed
with caves and tombs. It has been determined, however, that,
as in the case of the Dead Sea Scrolls, they were preserved in
jars, perhaps in only one very large jar.

When word of the discovery was first received, it was accompanied, as is to be expected under such circumstances, by
unsubstantiated rumors. For example, it was said that some
of the peasants, unaware of the retail value of the manuscripts,

[5] The material for this paper is drawn from the following preliminary reports: "Le papyrus gnostique du Musée Copte" by Togo
Mina (*Vigiliae Christianae* II [1948], 129–36); "Trois livres
gnostiques inédits" by Jean Doresse (*ibid.*, 137–60); "Nouveaux
textes gnostiques coptes découverts en Haute-Egypte" by Jean
Doresse and Togo Mina (*VC* III [1949], 129–41); "Une biblio-
thèque gnostique copte" by Jean Doresse (*La Nouvelle Clio* I
[1949], 59–70); "Die Gnosis in Ägypten" by Walter C. Till (*La
Parola del Passato*, fasc. 12 [1949], 230–49); "Les nouveaux
écrits gnostiques découverts en Haute-Egypte" by H.-C. Puech
(*Coptic Studies in Honor of Walter Ewing Crum* [Boston: The
Byzantine Institute, Inc., 1950], pp. 91–154). "Les Apocalypses de
Zoroastre, de Zostrien, de Nicothée . . ." by Jean Doresse (*ibid.*,
pp. 255–64); "The Apocryphon of John" by Walter C. Till (*Journal
of Ecclesiastical History* III [1952], 14–22).

used some of them as fuel—a story circulated also when the
Origen manuscripts were found at Tura, near Cairo. The discovery of ancient materials in Egypt is sufficiently common
so that it is almost certain that the discoverers of the library
attached some monetary value to the find simply on the basis
of its antique appearance. As nearly as can be determined, the
lot of manuscripts was divided up and eventually appeared,
by diverse routes, in Cairo. One incomplete codex is in the
hands of a dealer; another, complete, was purchased by Togo
Mina for the Coptic Museum in Cairo, while the remainder,
nine more or less complete volumes plus remains of two other
collections, eventually fell into the hands of a collector, making a grand total of thirteen codices! The last group was later
brought to the Coptic Museum, and negotiations are under
way to acquire them permanently for the Museum collection.
The Egyptian government has forbidden the exportation of the
manuscripts and has committed them to the hands of a com-
mittee for study and eventual publication. So far as is known
to the present writer, this situation still holds.

Leather-Bound Codices in Coptic

The state of preservation of this invaluable library is most
remarkable. Except for some abrasions on the covers and the
loss of a few fragments of papyrus, probably through modern
handling, nine of the codices are complete with leather covers,
which seem to resemble modern portfolios rather than regular
bookbindings. Some of the covers have been decorated, one of
them with what appears to be a *crux ansata* (handled cross).
In view of the extremely brittle nature of the papyrus, the
present state of the codices is even more astonishing, especially
when one recalls the vicissitudes of marketing to which at
least nine of them were exposed. Out of about a thousand
pages of manuscript, 794 are intact!

Another interesting feature of this collection is the fact that
all of them are in Coptic; they are virtually the oldest Coptic
manuscripts yet found. Most of them are in the dialect called
Sahidic, though an earlier form of the dialect than previously
known. The remainder are in an early Coptic dialect which
has since disappeared. The hand naturally varies in style, etc.,

since a number of scribes are represented in the collection, but on the whole it is excellent. On the basis of language and palaeography, the scholars who have been able to refer directly to the manuscripts agree in dating them between the middle of the third and the end of the first half of the fourth century A.D. The oldest extensive manuscript of the Greek Bible, including the New Testament, is the Codex Vaticanus, dating from the fourth century A.D., about the same time as the completion of the collection at Chenoboskion. Thus, at about the same time that an orthodox scribe was completing our oldest copy of the Greek Bible in Alexandria in Lower Egypt, a heterodox community at Chenoboskion in Upper Egypt was completing its collection of the oldest Gnostic manuscripts yet discovered.

In spite of the fact that all of our manuscripts are written in Coptic, it is agreed that most, if not all, of them rest on Greek originals. J. Doresse thought that the *Wisdom of Jesus,* based upon the *Epistle of Eugnostos,* was composed in Coptic. However, H.-C. Puech has discovered in Oxyrynchos papyrus No. 1080 (third or beginning of fourth century A.D.) what he considers to be a copy of the Greek original of the *Wisdom of Jesus.* Thus it appears likely that we have no original Coptic work represented in this collection.

The variety of material contained in the collection is also of considerable interest. It consists of discussions of cosmogony (world origins), treatises of a dogmatic nature, dialogues, prayers, "gospels," "epistles," and apocalypses. Some of the material is said to have been confided by Jesus to one or more of his disciples either during his earthly career or after his resurrection. In other instances they are prophetic visions or simply learned discussions by one of the teachers of the sect. All of them, regardless of alleged origin or content, transmit material not intended for general information but only for the initiated. Possession of this information purports to make the individual able to overcome his earthly nature, to free himself from its bondage and to acquire salvation.

Gnostic Apocalyptic Literature

In our newly discovered literature, this *Gnosis* (Knowledge) is presented in a variety of ways, but always in an esoteric manner. First of all, we may note the three great apocalypses, which seem to be those which, according to the pagan writer, Porphyry, were combated by the Neoplatonist Plotinus: *Allogenes Supreme*, *The Apocalypse of Messos*, and the *Apocalypse of Zostrianus*.[6]

Epiphanius tells us that the Archontics, a Gnostic sect related to the Ophites, called Seth *Allogenes*, 'the Stranger,' while Sethians (also an Ophite sect), Barbelognostics,[7] and Archontics designated the seven sons of Seth as *Allogeneis*, 'the Strangers.' In the first instance, we have a transcendent God as a stranger to this world while in the second case we have hypercelestial entities such as Eternal Life or individuals of the Kingdom of Light such as Man, Adam, or the Savior— just as one finds among the Syriac-speaking Marcionites and Mandeans in the synonymous term, *nukraya* ('the strangers').

---

[6] The classification of the treatises follows that of Doresse in *La Nouvelle Clio* (cf. note 5). The primary division is based on difference in dialect: 1. Sahidic; 2. the previously unknown Coptic dialect, first thought to be Sub-akhmimic, but now recognized as an extinct Coptic dialect or subdialect. The secondary division is based on content.

[7] The Ophites (Greek *ophis* = snake) or Naassenes (Hebrew *naḥaš* = snake) are so-called because of the importance the serpent played in this Gnostic system. It is an early Gnostic sect with many subdivisions and is described by Hippolytus, Irenaeus, Origen, and Epiphanius. The serpent played the role of the divine entity placed by God in Paradise in the *Apocryphon of John* (q.v.). In some groups the serpent is identified with Sophia ('Wisdom'), who is a divine spark which fell on the waters when Christ and his mother (female Holy Spirit) flew upward toward heaven. The Barbelognostics resembled the Ophites in many ways but their particular emphasis was placed upon the female being Barbelo (cf. the *Apocryphon of John*). The Barbelognostics are another major group of Gnostic sects though smaller than the Ophite group. For a good discussion of Gnosticism even though it does not include the materials from Chenoboskion, cf. Hans Leisegang, *Die Gnosis*, 3rd edition (also available in a French translation *La Gnose*, based on the 3rd German edition, Paris: Payot, 1951).

One finds similar ideas among the Valentinians[8] and in the author of the *Apocryphon of John*. Seth stands apart, separate, and distinct from the remainder of the inhabitants of the world who are divided between the Material and the Psychic. His group consists of the Spiritual Ones. The Sethians explain this by having Seth brought into the world by a "superior power," called Mother or Woman, while Cain and Abel were begotten by the angelic creators of the world. The Archontics, and later the Manichaeans, traced Cain and Abel to a union of the devil (in the *Apocryphon of John*—Yaldabaoth) and Eve while the father of Seth was Adam—thus Cain is the principle of the Material Race, Abel the Psychic, and Seth the Spiritual. Regardless of the variations, Seth, the third son of Adam,[9] represented a being apart from the others and so his followers were likewise apart—strangers. That this conception forms the background of Paul's idea of Christians as pilgrims and strangers here on earth is obviously most unlikely.

Whether this apocalypse is a revelation of Seth himself or simply under his patronage remains to be seen. It seems probable that our treatise is a Gnostic-Sethian document, composed in the early third century A.D., or a bit later. It appears to have been read in Rome by Plotinus; it enjoyed a place of authority in Egypt in the fourth century, as noted by Epiphanius; and occupied an honorable place along with the *Apocryphon of John* among the esoteric works of the seventh–eighth century sect, the Audians ('odaye), cited by the Syriac author, Theodore bar Konai.

With the *Apocalypse of Allogenes*, Porphyry mentions in his biography of Plotinus four additional apocalypses, those of Zoroaster, Zostrianus, Nikotheos, and Messos. The significance of the title of the last named had been a source of some dis-

---

[8] The Valentinians are an early Gnostic sect founded by Valentinus who was born in Lower Egypt, according to Epiphanius, educated in Alexandria, and lived in Rome from about A.D. 135–60. Through him, Gnosticism was transformed into the heterodox sect which was able to compete seriously with Christianity and evoked such bitter criticism from the Church Fathers.

[9] Prof. Albright has pointed out that not only was Seth the third son of Adam but also the Egyptian god who was the adversary of Osiris and was identified nearly 4,000 years ago with Canaanite Baal. Later Seth became a sort of Egyptian Satan.

cussion. Since the name of Messos was most unusual, some amended it to read Moses; others interpreted it to refer to a mediator or to some central place in mystic Gnostic topography. Although without a title, the manuscript in question contains references in its text to Messos. So the solution is simply that Messos is the name of a man, perhaps a Gnostic prophet or seer.

Whether or not the *Apocalypse of Zoroaster* is a part of the *Apocalypse of Zostrianus* is still a matter of discussion, but we can now be sure of having at least three of the five Gnostic apocalypses mentioned by Porphyry—and the two remaining (Zoroaster and Nikotheos) may yet be recovered when all the new texts have been studied carefully. The composition of all three antedates A.D. 240 and come from the same Sethian circle.

In addition to these, there is a group of apocalypses more or less directly attributed to the Great Seth. Among these may be noted two copies of the *Book of the Great Invisible Spirit* or the *Gospel of the Egyptians,* composed by the Great Seth and written down by the learned Eugnostos, also called Goggessos (cf. below). Another important revelation is the *Paraphrase of Seem* or the *Second Treatise of the Great Seth.* This work is the *Paraphrasis Seth* mentioned by Hippolytus and may be among those to which Epiphanius refers in the large collection of works used by the Gnostics and attributed to Seth. Finally, it may be noted that among the Manichaeans, Sem, who was considered to be the same as Seth or Sethel, was counted as one of the "prophets of the nations" in the list of celestial envoys in the course of history from Adam to Mani.

In this same category is the *Revelation of Adam to his Son Seth,* which, in general terms, describes the coming of different saviors. It is possibly one of the *Apocalypses of Adam* mentioned by Epiphanius in his *Panarion;* reminiscences are probably to be found in the Manichaean *Book of Mysteries* and in later Syriac and Armenian Gnostic works also attributed to Adam.

Another book mentioned by Epiphanius is that of *Noria,* called the *Hypostasis of the Archons* in the newly discovered Gnostic documents. In this book, Noria is the faithless wife of Noah; she succeeds in burning the ark three times but eventually the patient Noah completes its construction and escapes the Deluge, brought on by the Demiurge and his entourage of archons. Variations on the theme are to be found in the account of Theodoret where Noria is the wife of Adam, in that of Pseudo-Tertullian and Pseudo-Jerome in which the celestial mother, Barbelo (cf. below), sends the Flood, and others. In Mandaean writings she appears as the wife of Noah, though on other occasions she is the wife of the scribe Dinanukht. It is possible that the *Hypostasis of the Archons* represents an earlier account on which the other versions of the story of Noria are based or to which they are at least related.

Although the *Apocalypse of Dositheus* immediately calls to mind the Samaritan messiah, Dositheus, preliminary observations seem to preclude the possibility of associating the two. In the outline of the origin of Gnosticism according to some early ecclesiastical authors, the Samaritan Dositheus was the teacher of Simon the Magician[10] with subsequent Gnostic sects simply the heirs of their doctrine. Our *Apocalypse of Dositheus,* apparently unrelated to the Samaritan sect, may simply have appropriated the name of an early Gnostic "father" to give it claim to authority. It is likewise doubtful that it belongs to the books of Dositheus mentioned by Origen. However, it is possible that there is no relation with the Dositheus of history and tradition but with someone entirely unrelated. The treatise also bears the sub-title, *The Three Steles of Seth,* from which one might infer that the material contained in the document was originally engraved on stone and hidden in an inaccessible place until the proper time for its recovery and interpretation for the initiated. Dositheus may therefore have been the discoverer and/or interpreter of this revelation from the Great Seth.

The nature of its contents places the *Apocryphon* or *Secret Book of John* in the category of apocalypses. The three editions of the *Apocryphon* found in the Library of Chenoboskion to-

---

[10] Simon Magus is the Samaritan sorcerer whom Philip baptized (Acts 8:5–24). His conversion seems to have been short-lived for, although we hear nothing about his defection in Acts, the Church Fathers preserve a tradition that he was the founder of the Gnostic movement, some of whose teachings later appear in the Valentinian system.

gether with the copy which forms a part of the Codex Berolinensis should provide a critical edition of this work which
was used about A.D. 180–85 by Irenaeus as a basis for his
criticism of the Barbelognostics (*Adversus Haereses* 1. 29),
making it an important early document of Gnosticism, though
our present copies are of a later date.

Although the work entitled *Pistis Sophia* has been familiar
since the publication of the three books of *Pistis Sophia* contained in the Codex Askewianus by Schwartze and Petermann
in 1851, the source of the title has remained enigmatic. Among
the treatises discovered at Nag Hammadi is a rather long apocalyptic work, without title, which seems to have served as a
source for sections of the *Pistis Sophia*. Apparently used by
the Ophite sect, its composition antedates A.D. 250. In the
Letter of Eugnostos, the name Sophia Pangeneteira appears
as the feminine component of a bisexual creature whose masculine name is Soter (Savior), Creator of all things. Sophia
Pangeneteira is also called "Pistis." This bisexual creature,
Soter and Pistis Sophia, produces six bisexual spirits. The name
of the sixth one is Archigenetor (masc.) and Pistis Sophia
(fem.). The *Wisdom of Jesus*, based on the *Epistle*, mentions
Pistis Sophia or Sophia Pangeneteira as one of the aeons. Thus
it appears that Pistis Sophia is drawn from the Gnosticism
represented by the newly recovered library, and a century-old
question can be answered.

In addition to two apocalyptic works without titles, there
is the final part of a treatise called the *Triple Discourse of the
Triple Protennoia*, qualified by the sub-title, *Sacred Book written by the Father* (i.e., by the Great Seth). This group of
Gnostic apocalypses is completed by another apocalypse without a title but is attributed to the Great Seth and ends with a
theme common to these documents, "As for these revelations,
do not disclose them to anyone who is in the flesh, but impart
them only to the brethren who belong to the generation of
life."

Gnostic Commentaries or Abstract Treatises

There is a small group of commentaries or abstract treatises
of the same Sethian nature as the apocalypses just noted. The

most important of these is the Sethian cosmogony, *The Epistle of Eugnostos the Blessed*, of which there are two editions.

Although it has been impossible to study the text, it is possible that the *Exegesis concerning the Soul* contains a discussion of the soul and its many attributes which, according to Hippolytus, was a favored theme of the Naassenes.[11] Completing this group of works are three treatises of a cosmogonic nature but without titles.

New Hermetic Writings

Completely unexpected and most surprising is the existence of five Hermetic works in the collection of manuscripts from Chenoboskion, four of which were not even known to have existed. Included in this group are the *Authentic Discourse of Hermes to Thoth, Meditation on the Supreme Power* (a prophecy filled with biblical and Christian allusions), a Hermetic epistle without a title, a treatise of Hermes to his disciple, but without a title, and finally *Asclepius*, chapters 7 and 11, which were previously known from a Latin translation by Pseudo-Apuleius, although the tone of the Coptic work is more sober than the Latin translation had indicated. Hermes was the name given by the Greeks to the Egyptian god of wisdom, Thoth. Our previous literature on the subject had been limited to that attributed to Hermes Trismegistos (Thrice-greatest Hermes), such as that contained in the eighteen treatises of the *Corpus Hermeticum* (of which *Poimandres* is the best known), and in quotations in Stobaios and Latin and Arabic authors. Now we are able not only to supplement this literature, but also to see that its connection with heterodox Christianity was more direct than had been previously supposed by most scholars. That this collection of Hermetic works was not simply a result of accidental inclusion in the cache or an acquisition of miscellaneous esoteric works as a matter of interest but not for regular use is indicated by the fact that in the same codex, written in the same dialect and by the same hand, is a strictly Gnostic work, *The Acts of Peter and the Twelve Apostles*. Furthermore, this particular codex seems to

[11] Cf. note 7.

have been used more than any of the rest and some of the pages are even marked with signets made of bird feathers.

Christian and pagan Gnosticism had much in common: doctrines, expressions, imagery, and general background. Comparison had been made between the Valentinian system and *Poimandres*. In addition, it had been noted that the Manichaeans, spiritual heirs of Gnosticism, not only possessed at least two, if not five, of the writings also held by the sectaries of Nag Hammadi, but they also granted an honorable place to Hermes Trismegistos, whom they ranked beside Plato and Jesus as "Heralds of the Good God" and "Preachers of the Truth." Moreover, some scholars have detected Hermetic affinities in the Gnosticism combated by Plotinus in Rome between 263 and 267. Although our evidence at this point is still quite tenuous, further study of these newly discovered Hermetic documents should shed much new light on the relationship of Christian Gnosticism and Hermeticism as well as augment our knowledge of Hermeticism itself.

Pseudo-Christian Apocrypha

The fourth group of writings, consisting of pseudo-Christian apocrypha, contains the *Wisdom of Jesus*, which is based upon the *Epistle of Eugnostos*. It is in the form of a dialogue between the resurrected Lord, his twelve disciples, and seven holy women. Questions are asked of the Lord concerning cosmogony and the salvation of man. In addition there is a short appendix in which Mary Magdalene inquires, among other things, concerning the origin and function of the Lord's disciples. What follows reminds one of the story of Sophia and the origin of evil in the *Apocryphon of John* (cf. below). Not as well preserved is the *Dialogue of the Savior*, a cosmogonic treatise in the form of a dialogue between Jesus and his disciples.

The *Gospel according to Thomas* begins with the words, "These are the secret words which Jesus spoke and which Didymus Jude Thomas has written." This is followed in the same codex by the *Gospel according to Philip* and, after a few intervening treatises, by the *Book of Thomas*, which begins, "Secret words spoken by the Savior to Jude and Thomas and recorded by Matthias." In *Pistis Sophia*, Jesus confides his words and deeds to Philip, Thomas, and Matthew (or Matthias, according to Zahn)—three witnesses to establish the authenticity of the material (cf. Deut. 19:15; Matt. 18:16). In the *Wisdom of Jesus*, Philip, Thomas and Matthew, together with Bartholomew and Mariamme, speak with Jesus. Hippolytus cites the use of a *Gospel according to Thomas* among the Naassenes and other Gnostics; Origen mentions a similar work and later it appears among the Manichaeans. A detailed study of this Gnostic work may also provide an answer to the question regarding the relation, if any, of the legendary account of the infancy of Jesus, of which Thomas is also supposed to be the author, to the Gnostic *Gospel according to Thomas*.

It is quite possible that the *Gospel according to Philip* is the one to which Epiphanius refers in his *Panarion* and which was later adopted by the Manichaeans. According to the opening words of the *Book of Thomas* it is quite likely that we have a *Gospel according to Matthias*, the existence of which is noted in Origen and Eusebius, along with a *Gospel according to Thomas* in a list of heterodox works, and both gospels were on a proscribed list published by the Byzantine Church in the seventh century. The *Gospel according to Matthias* may be the same as the *Traditions of Matthias* mentioned by Clement of Alexandria as belonging to the Nicolaitans[12] and the Basilidians.[13] Its existence seems to be indicated by Hippoly-

---

[12] The Nicolaitans seem to have had a Gnostic system bearing many similarities to that of the Barbelognostics. It is possible that they are the Nicolaitans referred to in Revelation 2:6, 15. Irenaeus says that Nicolas, their founder, was Nicolas of Antioch, one of the first seven deacons of the Church in Jerusalem (Acts 6:5).

[13] With Simon Magus and Valentinus, the heresiarch Basilides taught a docetic doctrine of Christ. According to Irenaeus, Hippolytus, and Epiphanius, Basilides was a student of Simon Magus. Though there are some variations, the description of the Gnostic system of Basilides and that of Valentinus, a younger contemporary of Basilides in Alexandria, had many similarities. The patristic view of Gnostic origins—Simon Magus-Basilides (and Saturninus of Menander)-Valentinus-subsequent Gnostic sects—is being treated with much less skepticism by current writers on the subject than it was some years ago.

tus as well. Thus we have apparently recovered at least three
of the major early Gnostic gospels.

The *Apocalypse of Peter* has nothing in common with the
Apocalypse of Peter which was current in the Church toward
the end of the second century and for a short time enjoyed a
degree of canonicity. The *Apocalypse* in the writings from
Nag Hammadi is definitely Gnostic in content and much
shorter than the Christian *Apocalypse,* a complete copy of
which exists in Ethiopic, along with fragments in Greek and
Arabic. The *Teachings of Silvanus* (= Silas) is an apocryphon
attributed to the companion of St. Peter and St. Paul.

The contents of the *Epistle of Peter to Philip* are still unknown while the *Acts of Peter and the Twelve Apostles* seem
to have no connection with the *Acts of Peter* known in non-
Gnostic circles or with the Ebionite *Acts of the Apostles* or
the Manichaean *Acts of the Twelve Apostles*. A final treatise
claiming the authority of the Apostle Peter is the *Prayer of the
Apostle Peter*. It is quite possible that this work deals with
the strange story of the daughter of Peter whom he first healed,
though she later became paralyzed again, as a result of the
prayer of her father. The story is found in the *Acts of Peter*
contained in the Codex Berolinensis and was also known
among the Manichaeans.

The *Apocalypse of Paul* is not the *Apocalypsis, Revelatio*
or *Visio Pauli,* or *Apocalypse of Paul the Apostle* known from
Greek, Latin, Syriac, Coptic, Armenian, and Old Slavonic versions, nor, in spite of some opinions to the contrary, does there
seem to be any Gnostic background in the Christian apocalypse. It is more likely that there is a connection between our
Gnostic writing and the *Ascension of Paul* which Epiphanius
and others cite as being used among some Gnostic sects. This
apocalypse, as the Christian, is based on II Cor. 12:2-4, with
special attention being given to revealing the words which
Paul chose not to relate to his readers. Other Gnostic sects
possessed ascensions of Elijah and Isaiah, who returned to
earth after having been taken up to heaven. Whether our
Apocalypse of Paul is identical with the *Ascension of Paul* or
is simply one of a group of writings claiming the authority of
Paul current in Gnostic circles is yet to be determined.

There are three editions of the *Apocalypse of James*, two

in one codex and a third in a codex written in the hitherto unknown Coptic dialect, each apparently different from the other. It is impossible to compare this *Apocalypse* with the previously published Coptic *Book of James*. One is more inclined to recall the account of Hippolytus in which he says that among the Naassenes there was a teaching concerning the primordial man, the bisexual Adamas, triple principle of the universe, which was said to have been given to Mariamme (= Mary Magdalene)[14] by James, the brother of the Lord. It is possible that one or more of the *Apocalypses of James* in the new Gnostic library will contain this revelation to which Hippolytus refers.

The last of this group of pseudo-Christian apocrypha is a treatise without a title which deals in particular with the baptism of Christ and the person of John the Baptist.

Texts in the New Dialect

The final category of manuscripts is that written in the previously unknown Coptic dialect. In addition to the *Apocalypse of James* and the *Prayer of the Apostle Peter*, which have already been mentioned, are the following: *The Interpretation of Gnosticism* (contents still unknown), *Discourse by Reginos concerning the Resurrection* (contents still unknown), and the *Gospel of Truth*, quite possibly the Valentinian work mentioned by Irenaeus. Finally, there are some fragments of a treatise dealing with the nature of the universe and of a work which dealt with various subjects, among them questions concerning morals and the influence which demons exerted upon the soul.

The Apocryphon of John

Thus there are a total of at least 48 treatises in the Gnostic Library of Chenoboskion, of which at least 44 are different.

[14]Mary Magdalene played an important role in Gnostic literature. In the Codex Berolinensis, one of the treatises is a *Gospel according to Mary* (cf. the article by Walter C. Till, "Euangelion kata Mariam" in *La Parola del Passato*, II [1946], 260–67). The popularity of Mary Magdalene continued among the Manichaeans as illustrated by the Manichaean writings discovered in the Fayyum.

The information given reflects the present state of our knowledge concerning this new material except for a very few which have been studied in detail, all of which are contained in the codex acquired in 1946 by the Coptic Museum. An excellent summary of the first of these, the *Apocryphon of John,* based on the text contained in the Codex Berolinensis, is given by Walter C. Till. This text, which undoubtedly compares favorably with the three editions contained in the new manuscript, presents Gnostic doctrines in the most systematic manner of all the original Gnostic works which we possess.

The revelation contained in the *Apocryphon* is given by the Savior to St. John on the Mt. of Olives with the warning that it is to be revealed only to those who are worthy of it and in a position to understand it. God, the highest being in the world of light, is completely different from anything in the world in which we live. On the other hand, we and everything about us—our thoughts, minds, etc.—are completely bound to this material world so that it is impossible for us to understand God or conceive of him in any way. The Savior concludes his statement concerning God by saying, "What shall I tell thee about the Inconceivable One that thou art able to understand? Who might ever apprehend him by means of spoken words?"

Then follows a description of how the other divine beings came into existence. First, God looked at his image reflected in pure water of light with the result that the female being, Barbelo, the image of the Invisible One, came into existence. At her request, God created four divine beings, including Foreknowledge and Eternal Life. By meditating intensely on God, Barbelo brought forth a divine spark. God was so pleased with the new light, the first son, that he anointed him with his kindness (*chrestos*); hence, a double explanation of "Christ." Christ, in his turn and with God's permission, brought into existence three additional divine beings, including Nous and Logos, after which God made Christ god of all the universe and gave him all power.

Then God created the Four Great Lights, each of which has three aeons (divine beings). Later, the first Great Light becomes the residence of the first man, Adam; the second that of Adam's *first* son, Seth; the third that of Seth's offspring

(= the Gnostics who have become perfect); and the fourth that of those souls who accept Gnosticism after some hesitation.

Sophia, 'Wisdom,' the third aeon of the fourth Great Light, Heleleth, since she was the last divine being to be created, seems to have been farthest from God and therefore most likely to do something contrary to his law. Without his consent, she brought forth an illegitimate son who was a thoroughly bad creature, both in appearance and conduct, and so evil came into existence. His name is Yaldabaoth;[15] sometimes he is also called the first Archon. Since she was ashamed of this creature, Sophia hid him behind a cloud of light so that he could not be seen by any of the other divine beings.

Unaware of the existence of the world of Light, Yaldabaoth used his divine power of creating to create a world of his own, which is the material world in which we live. He created the firmament and an entourage of 360 angels. He installed seven kings of the sky which are the planets who rule the seven days of the week. Each of these has a name, a "face" (= description), a special power, and later each performs a special function in the creation of man. Yaldabaoth also set up five kings over the "chaos of the underworld."

In all of his creating, Yaldabaoth is careful not to give any of his creatures the divine power which he had inherited, so that he would remain superior and rule over them. Since he was ignorant of the other divine beings, except his mother, he considered himself the only God and tells his creatures, "I am a jealous god" and "there is no other god beside me" (cf. Deut. 5:9; Ex. 20:3); thus Yaldabaoth is the God of the Old Testament with the result that everything in the Old Testament, though true, is biased so that it must be corrected and interpreted in the Gnostic manner.

Sophia, Yaldabaoth's mother, suffers pangs of conscience because of her evil deed and is unable to return to the world of Light as long as her fault remains. The divine spark which

---

[15] Prof. Albright has called the attention of the writer to the fact that Yaldabaoth has long been explained as Aramaic "Child of the Primordial Chaos." He suggests that it would be perhaps better to treat it as Phoenician *Yald(a)bahot, which has the advantage of fitting with Achamoth, etc., now recognized as of Phoenician origin.

had entered into the monster Yaldabaoth had to be returned.

So God showed the seven planet kings his image in water. They were so impressed that they resolved, "Let us make a man in the image of God" (cf. Genesis 1:26). So they made man, each contributing his special skill and function, but the completed work was still imperfect: it could not move. God's next move was to send Christ and the Four Great Lights, disguised as Yaldabaoth's angels, to Yaldabaoth with the advice that he blow into the new creature's face the divine power which he had inherited from his mother, Sophia. He did and in that instant, Adam became superior to Yaldabaoth himself.

Yaldabaoth realized immediately what had happened but it was too late; and from that time on there has been a struggle between him and the Kingdom of Light to keep the divine spark in man from returning to the world of Light.

As their first move, the material powers made a body for Adam, composed of the four elements, earth, water, fire and air, which binds him to the material. Then Yaldabaoth created Paradise and put Adam into it, the intention being that everything should be so pleasant that Adam would not leave this world for the world of Light. To keep man from knowing the truth, Yaldabaoth caused a deep sleep to come over Adam during which time he created a woman—the name "Eve" does not occur in the account.

However, God was not idle. He placed in Paradise the tree of the knowledge of good and evil, which was really a divine entity to assist man in his struggle against Yaldabaoth and teach man his real place in the world of Light. To prevent man from learning this, Yaldabaoth forbade him to eat of the tree. So Christ, not the serpent, encouraged man to eat of the tree. The serpent, an agent of Yaldabaoth, implanted the sexual desire in man since by man's begetting children, there is an increase in the number of divine sparks which can potentially come into Yaldabaoth's power.

Since man had eaten of the tree, Paradise had lost its purpose, so man was expelled by Yaldabaoth. Overcome with passion, Yaldabaoth begets two sons by Adam's virginal wife: Cain and Abel, in human terms, or the unjust Yave (Yahweh) and just Eloim (Elohim) in Gnostic terms. The former was placed over water and earth, while the latter ruled over fire and air. Adam's first son by his wife was Seth.

When it became obvious to Yaldabaoth that he could not regain the divine breath he had blown into Adam, he "repented" and decided to destroy mankind by a great flood. The same entity that God had placed in Paradise informed Noah of Yaldabaoth's plan. Noah and his companions covered themselves with a cloud of light (= the ark) and escaped the great darkness (= the flood). Failing in this attempt, Yaldabaoth sent some of his angels to have children by human wives (cf. Gen. 6:2) in order to counterbalance the influence of the divine spark in man and thus lead man astray.

This struggle for the divine spark in man continues. In order to be freed from the power of Yaldabaoth, a knowledge of truth is absolutely necessary; man receives this from Gnostic doctrine. When man understands the truth and longs for the divine world of Light, moral rules become unnecessary since morality comes as a matter of course. He remains bound to the material body until he is found worthy. Then he is taken up to the eternal world of Light. Any suffering in the meantime is of no consequence and can do him no harm.

Since the divine power is in every man, it is possible for everyone to be saved from Yaldabaoth's power. If the opposing power is stronger than the divine spirit in a given individual, his soul returns after his death in a new human body and will eventually be saved. A soul is eternally lost only if it had the right knowledge and abandoned it—this is the sin against the Holy Ghost. Knowledge of the truth was brought by Christ, the Savior. Since not everyone is ready to receive the Gnostic doctrine of redemption, it is to be given only to men whose way of life and ability to understand make them worthy to receive it.

The Gospel of the Egyptians

Variation on the theme is provided by the *Sacred Book of the Great Invisible Spirit* or the *Gospel of the Egyptians*. With no introduction, matters of cosmogony and anthropology are revealed. From the Ineffable Father proceed three powers: Father, Mother, and Son, plus an aeon (divine being) called

Doxomedon. Three groups of divine beings of four couples each proceed from three great powers, after which follows the creation of other entities: the Seven Voices and the Three Male Children. After a lacuna of a few pages, the first man, Adamas, appears. We are told that Adamas and the divine Logos, one of the divine beings proceeding from the Great Power, the Father, unite to produce the Logos in Man. Then Adamas asks that he become the father of an incorruptible generation.

After this a power comes forth from the great Light, creating four great Lights as well as Seth, son of Adamas. This last creation is a notable departure from the cosmogony of the *Apocryphon of John*, in which Seth is the son of Adam and his wife. From each of the great Lights proceed four aeons (cf. three in the *Apocryphon*) and to each of the great Lights is added a "spouse" producing a total of five sets of four couples. The creation of sets of four couples (usually single creations having bisexual natures and both masculine and feminine names, and thus capable of autogenesis) is a recurrent motif in this treatise.

Then the incorruptible generation, the "Seed of the Great Seth," is called forth. The universe is shaken; in the four great Lights, the incorruptible spiritual Church multiplies and with one voice blesses the Father, Mother, and Son. An "Amen" concludes the benediction and the first section of the book.

In the second section, which one might call eschatological, appears the great Plesithea, mother of angels. From her comes the fruit of Sodom and Gomorrah. The Great Seth takes her seed from her and puts her in the fourth aeon of the third great Light. After about 5,000 years, Heleleth, the fourth Great Light, cries out, "There is but one power over chaos and hell." A cloud appears—and a large part of our text is missing. However, it seems that Sakla (= Yaldabaoth) is created by Sophia. He creates a dozen aeons (cf. the seven planet kings and five kings of the underworld in the *Apocryphon of John*) after which he declares, "I am God and there is none beside me." After this follows the creation of man and woman and the introduction of the seed of eternal life which is found in great incorruptible generation through the intervention of the Great Seth and the angel Hormos in some rather obscure fashion.

The Deluge is a figure for the end of the world and is intended by Sakla to destroy the incorruptible generation. But the Great Seth intervenes again and with the permission of the higher powers he diverts the deluge, the great conflagration and the judgment of the archons in order to save those who have strayed by a reconciliation of the world and a baptism of regeneration. Then follow several pages enumerating the powers present at this baptism, among them Jesus, followed by a series of prayers and entreaties mixed with cabalistic formulae. The latter apparently constitute the formulae of the sacrament and are expressed in the first person: "I have taken form in the cycle of the richness of light . . . I shall live before thee in the peace of the saints which is eternal. Amen. Amen."

The treatise is concluded with an attribution to the Great Seth. Both of its titles are given, along with the name of the writer, "The beloved Eugnostos, according to the spirit; in the flesh my name is Goggessos."

The *Epistle of Eugnostos*, and the *Wisdom of Jesus* which is based on the *Epistle*, present discussions of cosmogony and the like similar to those already described in the *Apocryphon of John* and the *Gospel of the Egyptians*, but with distinctive variations.

The Significance of the Discovery

In addition to the philological, palaeographic, and literary significance of these manuscripts, their significance for the history of Hermeticism and especially of Gnosticism is even more important. We have already indicated the extraordinary value of the newly recovered Hermetic texts and have noted the extreme paucity of original Gnostic documents. Almost overnight, our original materials, consisting of three codices containing about seven different writings, have been augmented by the addition of 13 codices containing at least 44 different writings! Of all the writings mentioned in patristic sources and attributed to the various Gnostic sects, not many are missing, and some of these may be discovered when it has been possible to study all the texts in detail. Indeed, seventeen centuries later, we are in a more advantageous position than the

earliest Christian writers on Gnosticism, since they were denied access to many of the Gnostic writings and were ac-
quainted with them sometimes only by name or, at best, by
not always unprejudiced reports, or summaries. However, the
picture of Gnosticism which they have drawn is shown by the
new treatises to be remarkably accurate. The works cited by
the Fathers and attributed to the various Gnostic sects are
not always assigned to the same groups by all the writers; in
our new collection we find, side by side, works said to be possessed by one group or another. Thus the apparent lack of
harmony is easily understood. The line of demarcation between the various Gnostic sects may have been little clearer
than that between some modern Christian denominations. The
presence of writings variously ascribed to different Gnostic
sects seems to indicate the existence of a common body of
writings which were handed down from one group to another.
Some of them, such as the *Apocryphon of John,* cited by
Irenaeus as early as A.D. 180 (and it may easily antedate this
by some decades) in his attacks against the Barbelognostics,
were important documents to the sectaries of Nag Hammadi,
who seem to be chiefly Sethian, and eventually found their
way to Mesopotamia where they appear among the Audians
at the beginning of the seventh century. Although the establishment of monasticism in the Nile Valley seems to have resulted in the decline of the sect to which our manuscripts belonged, Gnosticism seems to have continued there, but in a
milder form. John, Bishop of Parallos, at the beginning of the
seventh century, refuted a number of books which are strongly
reminiscent of our Gnostic works. Gnosticism also seems to
have infiltrated into some of the monasteries in the guise of
Christian apocrypha. According to patristic sources, the Sethian group was at its strongest during the third and fourth centuries A.D., which is precisely the period from which our
manuscripts come, the majority of which are Sethian!

Not only are the new manuscripts of extraordinary importance for the history of Gnosticism, but they also provide for
the first time a solid basis for the reconstruction of the Gnostic
system based not upon inferences from biased (though relatively accurate) and limited secondary sources and a few authentic documents, but upon a whole library of original docu-

ments. It is possible that some of our manuscripts present Gnosticism in a very primitive form. It is already known that the *Gospel of the Egyptians* and the *Epistle of Eugnostos* represent a system inferior to that represented by the *Apocryphon of John* in organization and content, and yet they are directly related to it. We have theological, cosmogonic, and eschatological revelations of Gnostic prophets, ethical and philosophical discourses of its teachers, and authentic information about its liturgies and other rites. We are therefore in an infinitely better position to determine the relation of Christian Gnosticism to Jewish and pagan Gnosticism and to the New Testament and early Church, as well as its background in Greek and oriental philosophy and mythology. Although we are able at the moment to indicate only in general terms the significance of the new manuscript discovery, since we are still awaiting publication, preliminary indications are that the relationship between Gnosticism and the New Testament and early Christianity are later and more superficial than had been previously thought, at least in some circles. We will also be able to determine more adequately the relationship of Gnosticism with the development of Manichaeism and subsequent heterodox sects.

Thus the implications and opportunities for research provided by the newly discovered Gnostic manuscripts are enormous. The recovery of the Gnostic Library of Chenoboskion is one of the largest and most important manuscript discoveries ever made in Egypt.

ADDENDUM

Since 1952 there has been an increasing number of books and articles containing surveys, translations, and interpretations of the Gnostic manuscripts from Chenoboskion. Among the pioneers was W. C. Till, who used one of the versions of the *Apocryphon of John* for his critical edition of the Berlin Codex to be compared with the *Apocryphon* contained in that codex.[1] This text of the *Apocryphon of John* is now available

---

[1] Till, Walter C., *Die Gnostischen Schriften des koptischen Papyrus Berolinensis 8502* (Berlin, Akademie Verlag. 1955); see above.

for all scholars in the publication of the first volume of *Coptic Gnostic Papyri in the Coptic Museum at Old Cairo* by Pahor Labib (Cairo: Government Press. 1956). Also included in this volume of plates is the missing part of the *Letter to Rheginos on the Resurrection* found in the Jung Codex together with the *Gospel of Thomas*, the *Gospel of Philip*, and the *Hypostasis of the Archons*.

In 1952, through the good offices of the Swiss psychologist, C. J. Jung, and the Bollingen Foundation, Gilles Quispel bought one of the codices which had come into the hands of a Belgian antiquities dealer, Albert Eid. It is now in the Jung Institute in Zurich. A description of the Jung Codex (as it is now called) was published in 1955; the following year the text and translation of the most important of the works contained in the codex, the *Gospel of Truth*, was published.[2] Other works in the Jung Codex are the *Epistle of James*, the *Discourse* (or *Letter*) *to Rheginos concerning* (or *on*) *the Resurrection*, a *Treatise on the Three Natures* (spiritual, psychical, material), and the *Prayer of the Apostle Peter* (see above, p. 313).

"The Gospel of Truth is joy for those who have received the grace from the Father of Truth to know Him through the power of the Word (*logos*, Jesus) who has come from the Pleroma, who was in the Thought and the Understanding (*nous*) of the Father, and who is the one called Redeemer for that is the designation of the work which He should accomplish for the redemption of those who did not know the Father, so that the term 'Gospel' is the expression of the hope which its finding means for those who seek Him (the Father)."[3] Thus the *Gospel of Truth* is really not a Gospel in the

[2] Puech, H.-C., Quispel, G., van Unnik, W. C.; F. L. Cross, ed. and trans., *The Jung Codex: A Newly Recovered Gnostic Papyrus* (London: Mowbray and Co., 1955); Malinine, M., Puech, H.-C., Quispel, G., eds., *Evangelium Veritatis* [The Gospel of Truth] (Zurich, Rascher Verlag. 1956); Filson, Floyd V., "The Gnostic 'Gospel of Truth,'" *BA* 20 (1957), pp. 76–78. Some of the leaves are missing in the Jung Codex but were found in Cairo, were published by Labib, and are included by Walter C. Till in "Das Evangelium der Wahrheit," *Zeitschrift für die neutestamentliche Wissenschaft* 50 (1959), pp. 165–85; and Kendrick Grobel, *The Gospel of Truth* (Nashville, Tenn., Abingdon Press. 1960).

[3] Translation of Till, "Das Evangelium," *op. cit.*, p. 169.

usual Christian sense, but rather a homiletical and meditative discussion of the Gnostic way of salvation based on Christian (Gospels, Pauline letters, Hebrews, the Apocalypse), Jewish and other sources. The work thus contributes to our knowledge of the development of the New Testament canon, for the *Gospel of Truth* originated in Valentinian circles, perhaps written by Valentinus himself, possibly between A.D. 140 and 150. Though Jesus as Redeemer from sin (indeed, sin itself) plays practically no role in the Gospel, it lacks much of the paraphernalia of later Gnosticism. Its content and emphases frequently seem to be almost Christian, which would explain the strong denunciation of it by Irenaeus in his *Against Heresies* about A.D. 185, as well as by other Church Fathers.

Rather than a "Gospel" which presented the words and deeds of Jesus in their historical context in dynamic form, this somewhat unsystematic work dispassionately presents a "Gnosis" (Knowledge) which consists of that which Jesus has revealed. The basis of all existence is "the Father" or "the Father of Truth." All has proceeded from him but, because of the separation from the Father, Knowledge of the Father has been forgotten. The result is Fear and Terror. To remove this ignorance, the Father sends the Son to bring Knowledge to Man for he "who has knowledge, knows" who he is, whence he has come, and whither he is going. It is as though he has awakened from a nightmare into the world of reality. Fear and Terror now disappear. Toward the end of the Gospel is a discussion of the name of the Father which he conferred on the Son. The Gospel concludes with a description of the felicity enjoyed by those who rest eternally secure in the full knowledge of God the Father with Whom they are inseparably united, "He in them, and they in Him." This Gospel presents a Christianity which is the revelation of God and of the nature of man, given by Jesus, who is "the transition from nothingness to the All."

The *Epistle of James*, the brother of Jesus, contains those things revealed by Jesus to James and Peter before his Ascension. This Valentinian composition may be based on the Christian tradition noted by Clement of Alexandria which reported that James, Peter, and John had received a secret Gnosis. At the end, Jesus ascends into Heaven in a chariot of Pneuma (Spirit). As Peter and James kneel to give thanks, they raise their hearts to Heaven where they hear sounds of war, trumpet and confusion. Then they lift up their *Nous* (Understanding) and ascend still higher where they hear angelic songs and heavenly music. But when they attempt to continue the ascent by raising up their *Pneuma* (Spirit) in order to come to God himself, they are barred. James then sends out the Twelve and he returns to Jerusalem.[4]

The *Letter to Rheginos on the Resurrection*, possibly written by Valentinus, is exceedingly important for it tells us that at this early date the Gnostic conception of the resurrection was *somewhat* similar to St. Paul's description of it. In our lives we suffer and die and rise with Christ. "But as we have come to manifestation in the world while we have put on the Christ, we are rays of the Christ and we are borne by him until we sink down. That is our death in this life. We are drawn up to heaven as rays by the sun, with nothing to hinder us. That is the spiritual resurrection which 'devours' the psychical and fleshly resurrection."[5] Though the resurrection is here understood in a purely spiritual sense, one does not find the Hellenistic idea of the natural immortality of the soul.[6] In this instance these Gnostics were closer to the biblical concept than are many modern Christians.

The *Treatise on the Three Natures* (called *Interpretation of Gnosticism* on p. 313), possibly written by the important Valentinian gnostic, Heracleon, begins with a description of God's indefinableness and indescribability. ". . . But Himself, in His essence and subsistence and being, no mind can understand Him, no word can express Him, no eye can see Him, nobody can touch Him by reason of His unfathomable greatness and incomprehensible depth and immeasurable height

---

[4] Quispel, *The Jung Codex, op. cit.*, pp. 45–47.

[5] Translation by Quispel, *ibid.*, p. 55. Quispel notes that the *Letter* is incomplete; presumably the sheets published by Labib (see above) complete it.

[6] The description of the faithful as rays of the sun drawn back at the hour of death to their source, the fountain of light, is one of the ways some Hellenistic and pagan Gnostic writers describe life after death. The Christian Gnostics have here adapted this in an interesting way.

and inaccessible will."[7] The *Treatise* continues with an insistent emphasis on God as a real Being who is conscious and who wills.

The work contains two interesting and surprising positions. The first is the assertion that the *Ecclesia* (Church) is eternal. Second, after an allegorical discussion of the Creation and Fall, there is a description of the course of history in which the Greek phase is treated as the material and the least valuable. In the author's opinion, Greek philosophy had nothing really useful to contribute. This new *Treatise* will require a modification of the frequent association of Greek philosophy with Christian Gnosticism. The Jewish or psychic phase is not internally contradictory (as was the Greek) and prepared for the coming of Christ. With the Redeemer who frees from slavery comes the Christian or pneumatic phase in which he reveals in detail the destiny of all three groups.

This significant *Treatise* outlines a Gnostic theology from the origins of the world and of man, through the intervening vicissitudes to final restoration and life. By comparing the *Gospel of Truth* and the *Treatise on the Three Natures* with canonical, Jewish apocalyptic and Qumrân materials, Quispel concludes that Gnosis is pre-Christian in its origins which go back to Jewish-Near Eastern occultism and Oriental mysticism.[8]

The *Hypostasis of the Archons* begins with a Gnostic interpretation of the Creation, Fall, and Flood narratives.[9] Phrased as an answer to the question of an inquirer, it is told in the third person. Samael, the name of a devil in late noncanonical Jewish literature, was thrown out of heaven for arrogating divinity to himself. Within his domain, though with the approving will of the Father of All, of which Samael was now ignorant, the Archons create man with a body like theirs

---

[7] Translation by Quispel, *The Jung Codex, op. cit.,* p. 57.

[8] Quispel, *ibid.,* p. 78. For other discussions of Gnostic origins, see R. M. Grant, *Gnosticism and Early Christianity* (New York, Columbia University Press, 1959) and R. McL. Wilson, *The Gnostic Problem* (London, Mowbray and Co. 1958).

[9] Schenke, H.-M., "Das Wesen der Archonten," *Theol. Lit.* 83 (1958), cols. 661–70.

but in the image of God which they had seen reflected in the water. Breath was blown into man so that he becomes alive but because of the weakness of his creators he was unable to move until the Spirit came out of the ground on which he had been lying and raised him up; thus every man is now a living soul. Like the archons man was androgynous—until woman was made of his rib. The story continues to the Flood episode when Noria, the wife of Seth,[10] attempted to board the Ark. Forbidden by Noah, she burned it. The chief of the Archons approached her with the demand that she serve them as did her mother Eve. When he pressed his demand, she cried to heaven for help which came in the form of the angel Heleleth.

The second half of the *Hypostasis* is a first-person revelation by Heleleth which describes the events in heaven preceding the expulsion of Samael (= Saklas = Yaldabaoth; see the *Apocryphon of John*). Pistis Sophia wished to bring into being a work without her mate's assistance. This took the form of the Heavens which served as a curtain between that which was above, the Kingdom of Light, and the Aeons beneath. A shadow formed beneath this curtain and became Material, and a separate domain. As a sort of miscarriage, out of the Material emerged an androgynous lion-like creature, who, when he surveyed the seemingly endless expanse of the Material, said, "I am God, and there is none other besides me." That creature was Samael. He was ruler of the demonic Demi-urges. He envied his son, Sebaoth, and so Envy came into existence; the child of Envy was Death. His repentant son, Sebaoth, was elevated by Sophia and her daughter Zoe to kingship of an intermediate kingdom in the seventh heaven, just beneath the "curtain" separating the Kingdom of Light from the Aeons. The revelation concludes with the Father of All promising the coming of the Spirit of Truth who would teach all Knowledge and anoint the saved with the unction of eternal life. The children of Light will then sing, "Righteous is the truth of the Father and the Son is over all and through all to all Eternity."

[10] Therefore this is not the same book as that mentioned by Epiphanius in which Noria is the wife of Noah.

The Valentinian *Gospel of Philip*[11] emphasizes primarily the Creation story with special attention to Eve's creation from Adam's rib; this meant separation from Adam and separation means death. A second interest of the writer is in the combination of baptism with anointing and the rise of a separate rite of confirmation. The third emphasis is concerned with sacred marriage. In addition *Philip* considers such other subjects as the fate and salvation of the Soul in the world; the various kinds and meanings of the names used for the Son (cf. the *Gospel of Truth* for similar interest in names); baptism by fire and by water; the eucharist with wine and water; the meaning of the concepts "Truth," "Knowledge," and "Love"; and many others. In the course of the discussion of this Gnostic theology many sayings of Jesus are quoted. Most of these are drawn from the New Testament; some are similar to those found in the *Gospel of Thomas* (see below); others are peculiar to Philip. Persons and episodes known from the canonical Gospels also figure in *Philip*. In both form and content there are many analogies between the *Gospel of Philip*, the *Gospel of Truth*, and the *Gospel according to Mary* (in the Berlin Codex).

Because of its claim concerning the sayings of Jesus the *Gospel of Thomas* has aroused more popular interest than the other Gnostic materials published to date.[12] The Naassene[13] *Gospel of Thomas* consists of a series of 114 Logia (Sayings) of Jesus, the largest collection of sayings of Jesus or attributed to him which, aside from those of the New Testament tradition, has yet to come to light. Of great significance to New Testament students and church historians was the identification by H.-C. Puech of the famous Oxyrhynchus Papyri 1, 654 and 655, which also contain sayings attributed to Jesus (but in Greek),

[11] See above, p. 310. For the most convenient summary, see R. M. Grant, "Two Gnostic Gospels," *Journal of Biblical Literature* 79 (1960), pp. 1–12.

[12] See above, p. 310. For a useful discussion of the whole problem of "Gospels," presentation of materials known before the Chenoboskion discovery, and translation and commentary on the *Gospel of Thomas*, see R. M. Grant, D. N. Freedman, Wm. R. Schoedel, *The Secret Sayings of Jesus* (Garden City, N.Y., Doubleday & Company, Inc., 1960).

[13] See above, p. 304, n. 7.

with the *Gospel of Thomas*. Thus these papyri are part of a Greek version of the *Gospel of Thomas* from the end of the third century, about the time Origen was condemning the Gospel.[14] Comparison with Manichaean writings shows that Mani also knew the *Gospel of Thomas*, another testimony to the importance of the document, this time in an area different from that with which we have been concerned.[15]

"These are the secret words which Jesus the Living [i.e., the risen Lord] spoke and (which) Didymus Judas Thomas wrote. And He said: He who will find the interpretation of these words will not taste death" (cf. Jn. 8:51 f.) is the beginning of this remarkable collection of sayings. Some of them are almost direct quotations, for example Logion 42: "Jesus said, He who has something in his hand, to him it will be given; and he who has nothing from him even the little he has will be taken away" (cf. Mk. 4:25; Lk. 8:18). With most early Christians *Thomas* rejected the need of circumcision (Logion 54), "His disciples said to him: Is circumcision profitable or not? He said to them: If it were profitable, their father would have begotten them circumcised from their mother. But the true circumcision in the Spirit has found complete usefulness" (cf. Phil. 3:3). An allusion to an early anti-Christian calumny is seen in Logion 102, "Jesus said: He who will know the Father and the Mother [i.e., the Holy Spirit] will be called the 'son of a prostitute' [i.e., Mary]."[16] Other Logia are sayings found in the Church Fathers but not in the canonical New Testament.

The recurrent use of the phrase "Jesus said" or something similar does not make this *Gospel* Christian (something many modern Christians in their defense of the New Testament might remember). Here Jesus does nothing but announce Gnostic doctrine. He is removed from the context of history and reveals Gnostic secrets. In contrast to the biblical view he

---

[14] For a detailed comparison, see J. A. Fitzmeyer, S.J., "The Oxyrhyncus *Logoi* of Jesus and the Coptic Gospel according to Thomas," *Theol. Stud.* 20 (1959), pp. 505–60.

[15] See H.-C. Puech in E. Hennecke and W. Schneemelcher, *Neutestamentliche Apokryphen in Deutsche Übersetzung*, 3rd ed. (Tübingen, J. C. B. Mohr [Paul Siebeck], 1959), pp. 199–223.

[16] Translations by Schoedel, in Grant, Freedman, Schoedel, *op. cit.*, ad loc.

rejects the world and all involved in it (family, marriage, etc.) as well as conventional religious expression (fasting, prayer, etc.). The all-important concern is that man *knows*.

Space precludes further discussion of other Gnostic gospels such as the *Wisdom of Jesus Christ, Dialogue of the Savior* and the *Book of Thomas to an Athlete*.[17] However, it is hoped that this brief survey may serve to indicate the growth in our knowledge of Gnosticism itself and in our understanding of the reasons for its challenge to the Christian Church of the second to fifth centuries A.D. which the study of these documents, though only in its preliminary stages, has already provided. As a result, for example, we are now better able to detect certain tendencies toward a "neo-Gnosticism" found in some current interpretations of Christian teaching and practice.

It is of interest to note how Valentinian Gnosticism, which was frequently so subtly distinct and deceptively similar to Christianity, differentiated into various systems and became increasingly flagrantly dissimilar from Christianity and therefore less dangerous. The presence of copies of this earlier material among the Chenoboskion Gnostics, who seem to be mostly Sethians, suggests that we may well have a deliberate collection of "Gnostica" here. The use of and dependence upon early Christian materials, canonical and patristic, provides new materials for the study and understanding of the development of the New Testament and of the early Christian Church.

The riches of this treasure-trove are now being tapped. The rapidly growing bibliography and the rising popular interest in these materials suggest that the day may be in sight when the term, "the Gnostic scrolls" (or something similar) will be as familiar as "the Dead Sea Scrolls."

[17] For a preliminary survey of these and others, see H.-C. Puech in Hennecke and Schneemelcher, *op. cit.*, pp. 158–271.

20

NEW RADIOCARBON METHOD FOR DATING THE PAST[1]

DONALD COLLIER

The commonest and usually the first question asked by visitors to archaeological digs and museums is "How old is it?" This general curiosity about the age of things made by man in the past is shared by archaeologists, for it is impossible to reconstruct the history of ancient civilizations without chronology. In the absence of written records, like those left by the ancient Egyptians and Mayas, archaeologists have had to depend on indirect methods for determining time sequences in the past. The single exception is that of the American Southwest where, thanks to the tree-ring method of dating, it has been possible to trace with great accuracy the history of Indian cultures during the past 2,000 years. The indirect methods, such as stratigraphy, typological cross-dating, and correlation of human remains and artifacts with geological events and climatic changes, are laborious and inaccurate and do not yield dates in years but only relative sequences.

The new method of radiocarbon dating, developed by Dr. Willard F. Libby at the Institute for Nuclear Studies of the University of Chicago, promises to revolutionize dating problems in archaeology. This method determines the age of things that lived during the past 20,000 years by measuring the amount of carbon 14 they contain.

[1] Reprinted by permission from the *Chicago Natural History Museum Bulletin*, XXII: 1 (Jan. 1951).

Carbon 14 is an unstable (radioactive) heavy form of carbon with an atomic weight of 14. Normal, stable carbon has an atomic weight of 12. The half-life of carbon 14 is about 5,500 years. This means that an ounce of carbon 14 is reduced by decay to half an ounce in 5,500 years, that half the remainder decays during the next 5,500 years, leaving a quarter of an ounce, and so on.

Carbon 14 is constantly being formed in the earth's upper atmosphere as the result of the bombardment of nitrogen-14 atoms by cosmic rays (neutrons). The carbon-14 atoms thus created combine with oxygen to form carbon dioxide, which becomes mixed in the earth's atmosphere with the vastly greater proportion of carbon dioxide containing ordinary carbon atoms. The carbon 14 then enters all living things, which, through the life process, are in exchange with the atmosphere. This exchange is carried out through photosynthesis in plants. Dr. Libby has shown experimentally that all living matter contains a constant proportion of carbon 14, which is about one trillionth of a gram of carbon 14 to each gram of carbon 12. This constant proportion results from the equilibrium between the rate of formation of carbon 14 and the rate of disintegration of the carbon 14 contained in the atmosphere, in the ocean, and in all living things.

When a plant or an animal dies, it ceases to be in exchange with the atmosphere and hence there is no further intake of carbon 14. But the carbon 14 contained at death goes on disintegrating at a constant rate, so that the amount of carbon 14 remaining is proportional to the time elapsed since death. Given the carbon-14 content of contemporary living matter and the disintegration rate of carbon 14 (the half-life), it is possible to calculate the age of an ancient organic sample from the amount of carbon 14 it contains.

Samples Are Burned

The laboratory procedure consists of burning the sample to be dated, reducing it to pure carbon, and measuring its radioactivity (rate of atomic disintegration) in a specially constructed, extremely sensitive radiation counter (a form of Geiger counter). The measurement is expressed in terms of the number of carbon-14 disintegrations per minute per gram of carbon. This value is 15.3 for contemporary living samples, 7.65 for samples 5,568 years old, and 3.83 for samples 11,136 years old. Very old samples contain such a small amount of carbon 14 that the error in counting becomes very large, so that the effective range of the method with present techniques is something less than 20,000 years. But there exists a method for enriching or concentrating the carbon 14 in a sample that may make it possible to obtain useful dates back to 30,000 years. At present the year error in dating samples ranges from 5 to 10 per cent.

Although carbon 14 is present in all organic matter, certain kinds of material have been found to be most useful for dating. These are plant material and wood, charcoal, shell, antler, burned bone, dung, and peat. Unburned bone appears to be unreliable because it is more easily altered chemically than these other materials and hence may lose or gain carbon-14 atoms by exchange during the time between death of the animal and the present.

This method has the disadvantage that the sample to be dated must be destroyed by burning. However, in most cases this is not serious because the size of the sample needed is relatively small. The minimum amount of pure carbon necessary for a single counting run (the amount of carbon placed in the Geiger counter) is 8 grams (about a third of an ounce). Since the carbon content of different organic materials varies, the size of the sample needed to yield this much pure carbon also varies. In general, it is necessary to have about 2 ounces of plant material or wood, 1 to 3 ounces of charcoal, 4 ounces of shell, 5 to 10 ounces of dung or peat, and one to several pounds of antler or burned bone. For the greater accuracy obtained by making two independent counting runs these quantities would need to be doubled.

History of Process

A brief review of the history of the development of radiocarbon dating will help to make clear the nature of the method. In 1934 shortly after the discovery of artificial radioactivity, Dr. A. V. Grosse predicted the possible existence of radioactive elements produced by cosmic rays. In 1946 Dr. Libby predicted that natural or "cosmic" carbon 14 would be found in living matter. The following year he and Grosse checked this hypothesis by testing methane gas derived from sewage (an organic product) and found carbon 14 to be present in the expected amount.

The next step was to test the assumption that carbon 14 was present in the same concentration in all living matter. This research, called by Dr. Libby a "world-wide assay of natural radiocarbon," consisted of measuring the carbon-14 content of contemporary living material from various parts of the world, various latitudes, altitudes, and geographical situations. This Museum contributed to this part of the research by furnishing from the botanical and anthropological collections wood samples from the Pacific Ocean, South America, Europe, Africa, and the Near East. These measurements, made by Dr. E. C. Anderson, confirmed the assumption and established the value for the carbon-14 content of present-day living matter.

Egyptian Boat Plank Used

The next phase, carried out by Dr. J. R. Arnold and Dr. Libby, consisted of testing the dating method by measuring some ancient samples of relatively accurately known age. These were wood from Egypt and Syria, a sample of wood dated by tree-rings, and a piece of old redwood. They ranged in known age from 1,300 to 4,600 years. One of the Egyptian samples, which was supplied by this Museum, was a piece of deck plank from the mortuary boat of King Sesostris III, who died about 1849 B.C. The dates obtained on this and the other samples agreed with the known ages within the calculated error of the method.

The final phase of this research has consisted of further checking of the method by dating selected archaeological and geological samples of unknown age. An effort was made to obtain from various parts of the world samples whose relative age had been established by the usual archaeological and geological methods. In some instances it was possible to secure several samples coming from different layers of a single stratified deposit. These stratified series were particularly valuable in testing the consistency of the carbon-14 dates obtained. By 1951 more than 150 samples of unknown age from North and South America, Europe, and the Near East had been dated. These range in age from a few centuries to more than 20,000 years, and relate to the problems of dating early man in North and South America; the Archaic Indian cultures of the eastern United States; the early cultures of the Southwest, Mexico, and Peru; the Late Paleolithic, Mesolithic, and Neolithic periods in Europe and the Near East; and the last glaciation in North America and Europe.

Test Museum Specimens

Among these samples were several furnished by this Museum. Two were portions of wooden implements from the Early Nazca culture on the south coast of Peru, excavated by a Museum expedition in 1926. Dr. Libby's results show them to be about 2,000 years old, which is consistent with other carbon-14 dates obtained from Peruvian samples. Two other samples were charcoal from hearths belonging to the Chiricahua stage of the Cochise culture in western New Mexico. These hearths were discovered by the Museum's 1950 Southwest Archaeological Expedition. The carbon-14 date indicates that these hearths were in use about 2500 B.C. This date is consistent with one obtained from a site of the Chiricahua stage in Arizona. Samples of charcoal, bark, and wood from the Hopewell culture of Ohio were also given to Dr. Libby. These turned out to be considerably older than archaeologists had believed.

Full assessment of the results of the final phase of Dr. Libby's research on radiocarbon dating has not been made. But the general consistency of the results, including the dates on samples from periods older than 5,000 years, for which there are no absolute dates for checking, leaves little room for doubt that the method is sound and that dates accurate within the experimental error of the method can be obtained. Radiocarbon dating is destined to have a very important role in archaeology, both in increasing the accuracy of its findings and in reducing the amount of time and effort devoted to problems of dating. This will mean that, in the future, archaeologists can move on with greater facility to the syntheses and generalizations that are the ultimate aim of their work.

The method will be extremely useful also in the aspects of geology, paleontology, and paleobotany dealing with events and processes that occurred during the past 30,000 years. Dr. Libby has already obtained dates relating to the time of the last glaciation in North America and Europe. These dates indicate that the last glaciation was considerably more recent than accepted geological estimates. It will be possible with additional work to date the retreat of the glaciers quite accurately, and this information will have a crucial bearing on time estimates for the whole Pleistocene period, which is variously estimated to have lasted from 400,000 to 1,000,000 years. Radiocarbon dating will also give more reliable information on the time required for the formation of new species among plants and animals. In these and many other ways carbon-14 dating promises to be an extremely important scientific tool.

ADDENDUM

During the past nine years continuous and rapid development has occurred in the field of radiocarbon dating. In 1959 there were 36 radiocarbon laboratories in operation in the following countries: Australia, Canada (3), Denmark, England (3), Finland, France, West Germany, Italy (2), Japan, Netherlands, New Zealand, Norway, Poland, Sweden (3), Switzerland, and the United States (14). The names and addresses of these laboratories are listed by Flint and Deevey (1959, pp. 215–18). Well over 3000 archaeological, geological, and palaeontological samples from all parts of the world have been dated. The majority of these dates have been published from time to time in the journal *Science* and in the Radiocarbon Supplement of the American Journal of Science (Flint and Deevey, 1959). This publication also contains a bibliography covering published lists of dates and articles on method and interpretation (pp. 199–214). Many improvements in the laboratory techniques have been made. The most important innovation has been the shift from dry-carbon counting to the use of a gas counter in which the carbon sample is measured in the form of carbon dioxide, methane, or acetylene. This new method of measurement is more sensitive and eliminates the danger of contamination of samples by radioactivity in the atmosphere during processing in the laboratory. It is now possible to get usable dates from samples up to 40,000 years old. Optimum results can now be obtained with smaller samples than formerly (40 gm. of charcoal, 50 gm. of wood, 100 gm. of peat or charred bone, 180 gm. of shell), and very small samples will suffice, if necessary, to obtain dates (1 gm. of charcoal or wood, 2 gm. of peat or charred bone, 8 gm. of shell).

Although a few radiocarbon dates have been completely out of line with stratigraphic, historical, or other reliable chronological evidence, the over-all validity of the carbon-14 method has been amply demonstrated. Some of the wrong dates have proved to be due to laboratory contamination or misinterpretation of their archaeological or geological contexts; a few were evidently due to contamination or alteration of the samples in the ground. Considerable research on the problem of sample reliability has been done and this line of investigation is being continued. The present indication is that the not very frequent circumstances that lead to seriously erroneous dates can be guarded against in the future.

It is impossible to summarize briefly the great range and number of existing radiocarbon dates, but a few of the most important results may be mentioned. Most geologists now accept the carbon-14 dates indicating that the last major glacial advance in North America (Valders advance) took place about 11,000 years ago, in contrast to the former estimate of 25,000 years; the Two Creeks interstadial (Cary-Valders interval) has been shown to be of the same age as the Alleröd horizon in western and northern Europe, giving the first transatlantic glacial correlation. The Hopewell culture of Ohio and Illinois flourished from 500 B.C. to A.D. 200 (previous guess dates, A.D. 500–900). The Pre-Classic or Formative epoch of Mexico and Peru dates about 1500–200 B.C., 500 to 1000 years earlier than previous estimates. Man had reached the southern tip of South America before 6500 B.C. The paintings in Lascaux Cave in France were made about 15,000 years ago (previous estimates, 20,000–30,000). Incipient cultivation first appeared on the hilly flanks north of the Fertile Crescent in Kurdistan about 8900 B.C. (Zawi Chemi site). Settled village agriculture was established in the same region by about 6500 B.C. (Jarmo phase), and a second agricultural stage (Matarrah-Hassuna phase) dates from about 5750 B.C. Farming based on irrigation canals along the Tigris and Euphrates in southern Mesopotamia was established by 4000 B.C. (beginning of Ubaid phase), and urban civilization developed there about 3500 B.C.

BIBLIOGRAPHY

Braidwood, Robert J., "Near Eastern Prehistory," *Science*, Vol. 127, No. 3312, pp. 1419–30, (1958). Lancaster.

Broecker, W. S., and Kulp, J. L., "The Radiocarbon Method of Age Determination," *American Antiquity*, XXII, i (1956), pp. 1–11.

Flint, Richard Foster, and Deevey, Edward S., Jr., *American Journal of Science, Radiocarbon Supplement*, Vol. 1, 1959. New Haven.

Johnson, Frederick (compiler), *Radiocarbon Dating*. ("Society for American Archaeology, Memoir, No. 8.") Salt Lake City, University of Utah Press, 1951.

Libby, Willard F., *Radiocarbon Dating*. 2nd ed. Chicago, University of Chicago Press, 1955.

DATE OF CLOTH FROM QUMRAN, CAVE 1

O. R. SELLERS

Along with the pieces of manuscript and pottery which were found early in 1949 by Mr. G. Lankester Harding and Father

R. de Vaux in their excavation of Cave 1 at Qumran in which the first group of Dead Sea Scrolls were found, there was a quantity of linen cloth (*BASOR*, No. 118 [Apr., 1950], pp. 9–10). From the bedouin who brought to him the Dead Sea Scrolls, the Syrian Metropolitan, Mar Athanasius Yeshue Samuel, had secured similar cloth, in which the scrolls were reported to have been wrapped. A piece of cloth from the cave and a piece of the Metropolitan's cloth were on display in a recent exhibition of the scrolls at the Oriental Institute, University of Chicago.

The possibility of dating the cloth came with the development of the carbon-14 process at the Institute for Nuclear Studies of the University of Chicago. So it was suggested to Mr. Harding that he send over enough of the cloth to be measured. He readily agreed and the cloth was brought to America by Professor J. L. Kelso when he returned from Jordan after his year as director of the American School of Oriental Research in Jerusalem. Through Professor Carl Kraeling the cloth was turned over to Professor W. F. Libby of the Institute for Nuclear Studies.

On January 9, 1951 Professor Libby reported to Professor Kraeling: "We have completed a measurement on the linen wrappings from the Dead Sea Scrolls which you furnished us on November 14, 1950. . . . The date obtained is 1917, plus or minus 200 years, or A.D. 33, plus or minus 200."

Thus the cloth by the carbon-14 process is dated between 167 B.C. and A.D. 233. So epigraphy, archaeology, and nuclear physics now combine to support the genuineness and antiquity of the material found in the cave.

SOME RADIOCARBON DATES

G. ERNEST WRIGHT

In September, 1950 Professors J. R. Arnold and W. F. Libby of the Institute for Nuclear Studies of the University of Chicago published a number of dates which they had obtained during the first eighteen months of their work with ancient organic material by testing the amount of carbon 14, according to the process described above by Mr. Donald Collier. Certain of the results may be of interest.

In the spring of 1948 Professor Robert J. Braidwood conducted the first campaign of excavation at the site of Jarmo in northern Iraq. In a stratified area he found the first introduction of pottery immediately following pre-ceramic levels. This is the first time in the Near East that a cultural horizon has been found at the inception of village culture comparable to that at earliest Jericho in Palestine. Some land snail shells from the pre-ceramic levels were tested and found to be 6707 years old, with a margin of error computed at 320 years; that is, they are to be dated somewhere between 5077 and 4437 B.C. This gives us an approximate but reliable date for the first village culture and for the introduction of pottery. Heretofore, our dating for such early material has been largely guess-work.

When was the last glacial age? Several samples of wood and peat were tested which were recovered from the Two Creeks Forest Bed in Manitowoc Co., Wisconsin. Here a spruce forest is thought to have been buried by the last advancing ice sheet in this region. The average date of the samples came out at 9454 B.C., the margin of error being considered 350 years either way.

A confirmation of the general reliability of this method of dating came from three samples found in Egypt. One was a slab of wood from a beam in the tomb of a Vizier, named Hemaka, who lived during the First Dynasty. This Dynasty is generally dated today somewhere between 3100 and 2800 B.C. Two counting runs were made on the sample; the average date obtained was 2933 B.C. with a margin of error computed at 200 years. Among the earliest village cultures in Egypt are the remains excavated in the Faiyum. The date of a sample of wheat and barley grain from Faiyum A averaged about 4145 B.C. with a margin of error of 250 years. Excavations at el-Omari near Cairo have unearthed a culture which would appear to belong somewhere between the two mentioned above, judging from a typological comparison of the material. The testing of some charcoal from this site produced a date *ca.* 3306 B.C. with margin of error computed at 230 years. These three dates from early Egypt come out very nicely, since the material tested was from archaeological contexts which can be arranged in a sequence, the latest of which is in the First Dynasty.

A chapel was unearthed at Tell Tainat (ancient Hattina) in northern Syria by the Oriental Institute in 1936. It has been dated to the eighth and seventh centuries B.C. Wood from the floor of a central room in the palace with which the chapel was associated was tested by three different counting runs. The first run produced a date at 746 B.C. with margin of error of 270 years; the second came to 698 B.C. with the same margin of error; the third to 289 B.C. with the same computed possibility of error. In other words, the first two runs produced dates which are certainly correct with the margin of error allowed. The date which came from the third run is strangely disconcerting, and seems difficult to believe even when the range of error is taken into account.

From the above sample dates it is clear that the carbon 14 contribution to the problem of dating archaeological material is certain to be very great, especially in the earlier periods. At the moment, however, the margin of error which must be allowed is too great to be completely satisfactory for the historical periods, since it is often possible by various other means to fix the date more definitely. On the other hand, issues under sharp debate, such as that over the date of the Dead Sea Scrolls, can receive considerable help from the process. The date of the linen found in the cave, as determined by Professor Libby, certainly indicates that a medieval date for the cave material is out of the question, even though a more precise date than the process is able to give must be determined by other means.

ADDENDUM

Since the above was written (in 1951), so many radiocarbon dates have been published that it has been difficult to keep up with them. For the Near East a pattern has emerged which permits a far more precise chronology than one would have dared to hope for two decades ago. As Mr. Collier has indicated above, the end of the Paleolithic or Old Stone Age must be lowered to the period between about 12,000 and 10,000 B.C. The end of the last ice age may be placed roughly around 8000 B.C., that being the period also when the first sickle blades appear in the Mt. Carmel caves in Palestine. That is, what has been called the Mesolithic Age is now reduced to a comparatively brief transitional period around the end of the ice age when incipient agriculture was begun. Whether this meant anything more than reaping wild wheat, and *perhaps* the domestication of the dog and certain other animals, is at this point unknown.

The period that has been called Neolithic now emerges as the time immediately following the last glaciation when man left "savagery" behind in the Near East, emerged from his caves, began building structures on the terraces in front of them, and in slowly increasing numbers established the first villages. The greatest monuments of the age are probably the dolmens in Palestine and the eight-acre village of Jericho with its tremendous fortifications. When the carbon 14 dates for the earliest Jericho village were published they could scarcely be believed, for they indicated that the first great wall and the round-house period ("hog-backed brick" phase) was to be dated in the early seventh millennium B.C., while the second main phase (rectangular houses with polished floors and walls) was flourishing in the latter part of the same millennium. Then new dates from Jarmo in Iraq, a small, unfortified village in Kurdistan, appeared, indicating that this site also was flourishing in the same millennium. Thus we are not far wrong if we date the Neolithic *ca.* 7000–4500 B.C. and see it as the first period of efficient agriculture. The first part of it in the seventh millennium, as indicated by Jericho and Jarmo, was before the invention of pottery. Pottery vessels first made their appearance in the second Neolithic phase during the sixth millennium at Jericho and at Matarrah, Hassuna, and Jarmo in Iraq.

The first appearance of copper, and hence the beginning of the Chalcolithic Age, is in the Halaf painted-pottery culture of northern Iraq from the second half of the fifth millennium, though the contemporary Faiyum culture in Egypt probably had no knowledge of the new developments. In Iraq the main part of the Chalcolithic period is taken up by the Obeid painted-pottery culture (*ca.* 4000–3300 B.C.), when the first great temples were built, and irrigation and farming were extended into southern Iraq. Our knowledge of what went on in Palestine during this age is very scant. Only the Ghassulian culture from the end of the period is well known, particularly from the Jordan Valley and the Beer-sheba area. From the latter a carbon 14 date of *ca.* 3350 B.C. fixes the general period, while another date of *ca.* 3250 B.C. from Tomb A94 at Jericho indicates the beginning of the Palestinian Early Bronze I (in the writer's terminology). The Early Bronze Age marks the beginning of "civilization," when urbanization proceeds rapidly, the city-state system first becomes the basic political pattern of the country, while the unification of Egypt in the First Dynasty takes place (*ca.* the twenty-ninth century, which introduces Early Bronze II in Palestine).